PLACE IN RETURN BOX to remove this checkout from your record.
TO AVOID FINES return on or before date due.

DATE DUE	DATE DUE	DATE DUE
_____	_____	_____
_____	_____	_____
_____	_____	_____
_____	_____	_____
_____	_____	_____
_____	_____	_____
_____	_____	_____

MSU Is An Affirmative Action/Equal Opportunity Institution

c:\circ\datedue.pm3-p.1

Macroeconomic Considerations in the Choice of an Agricultural Policy

A Study into Sectoral Independence with Reference to India

SERVAAS STORM

Avebury

Aldershot · Brookfield USA · Hong Kong · Singapore · Sydney

Published by
Avebury
Ashgate Publishing Limited
Gower House
Croft Road
Aldershot
Hants GU11 3HR
England

Ashgate Publishing Company
Old Post Road
Brookfield
Vermont 05036
USA

British Library Cataloguing in Publication Data

Storm, Servaas
  Macroeconomic Considerations in the
  Choice of an Agricultural Policy: Study
  in Sectoral Independence with reference
  to India
  338.10954

ISBN 1 85628 616 9

Printed and Bound in Great Britain by
Athenaeum Press Ltd, Newcastle upon Tyne.

Chapter 5   *Numerical Specification of the Model –
Estimation and Calibration*

Figures

Tables

APC	Agricultural Prices Commission (see CACP)
ASI	Annual Survey of Industries
BE	Budget estimate
CACP	Commission of Agricultural Costs and Prices
CES	Constant elasticity of substitution
CGE	Computable general equilibrium
CPI	Consumer price index
CSO	Central Statistical Organisation
DGCI&S	Directorate General of Commercial Intelligence and Statistics
EAC	Economic Advisory Council
FAI	Fertiliser Association of India
FCI	Food Corporation of India
GDP	Gross domestic product
HYV	High yielding variety
IMF	International Monetary Fund
LES	Linear expenditure system
NAS	National Accounts Statistics
NCAER	National Council of Applied Economic Research
NSS	National Sample Survey
PDS	Public Distribution System
RBI	Reserve Bank of India
RE	Revised estimate
RPS	Retention Price Scheme (for fertilisers)
SAM	Social accounting matrix

Crore	Ten million (10^7)
Lakh	Hundred thousand (10^5)
Milliard	Thousand million (10^9)

INTRODUCTION AND OVERVIEW

1.1   *Scope and Objective of this Study*

The impact which macro–economic policies may have on the nature and range of agricultural policy options is well–documented. It is often found, for instance, that indirect discrimination against agriculture *via* overvalued exchange rates and industrial protection has a more important bearing on agricultural production than commodity–specific direct agricultural policy interventions (Krueger *et al.*, 1988). Less known, however, is the impact which agricultural policy–making may have on the other sectors in the economy and the country's macro–economic balance. Sometimes, agriculture's importance is even such that policies which concentrate on macro–economic variables such as the budget deficit and the level of interest rates, while neglecting measures to strengthen agricultural production, prove inadequate and self–defeating (Killick, 1985).

This study considers the ways in which in India agricultural policies impinge on the rest of the economy and considers implications for the design of economic policy. Its theme is that, in large low–income economies having a large agricultural sector such as the Indian, an unsatisfactory rate of agricultural growth may act as a major constraint by limiting the possibilities of non–inflationary industrial expansion in a variety of ways. Shortfalls in food availability may lead to price rises which erode investible surpluses; the slow growth in agricultural inputs used in manufacturing can limit the growth rate of certain key sectors; and most important, the slow rise in agricultural productivity can lead to a deficiency in (domestic) demand for industrial products. It is in these circumstances that the formulation of agricultural policy acquires an economy–wide importance and that one is likely to require a general equilibrium framework, such as the one developed in this study, to satisfactorily analyse the direct and indirect effects of agricultural policy changes.

This chapter serves the purpose of an introduction and an overview, giving an outline of the various chapters and the interconnections between them. It is organised as follows. Section 1.2 discusses the background of the research and identifies the main questions which are addressed. Section 1.3. deals with a number of theoretical considerations which guided the model specification. The reasons to choose India as the economy under consideration are given in 1.4. Section 1.5 addresses important methodological issues related to any economic modelling project. Section 1.6 reports on the accuracy and reliability of the model's data base. Section 1.7 deals with the agricultural policy instruments, the economy–wide effects of which are to be assessed. Finally, in Section 1.8, I summarise some of the major (policy) conclusions, before turning to the details of the research in the next chapters.

1.2   *Research: Background and Questions*

The present study was motivated by two, seemingly unrelated, observations. Firstly, I found that, in most macro–economic analyses of low–income economies, the relative price insensitivity of both food supply and food demand is not taken into account. Secondly, I found that most of the literature on the effects of agricultural policy–making is based on a partial equilibrium approach, neglecting the economy–wide impact of agricultural policy changes. Both observations require further elaboration.

The first observation is related to the re–evaluation of the long–term role of agriculture in economic development which arose from the examination of the actual experience of low–income countries and its observed variance with previous theoretical constructs (Singh and Tabatabai, 1992). In the light of this experience, economists became sceptical of the validity of the Lewis–type growth models in which the agricultural sector plays a basically passive and accomodating role to the requirements of the 'modern', industrial sector (Lipton, 1977). Instead, agriculture came to be seen as a 'dynamic' sector, the potential of which was suppressed by an alleged 'urban bias' in policy–making. To eliminate this 'urban bias', measures were advocated to increase the relative prices and profitability of agricultural goods through for example currency devaluations, reduced export taxes and lower input prices (by reducing or eliminating domestic industrial protection). Frequently, these measures were implemented as part of so–called structural adjustment

2

programmes, based on the principle of 'getting the prices right' advocated by many neoclassically oriented economists (*e.g.* Timmer, 1986). In general, the supply response of agriculture and the price elasticity of demand for food (which are both known to be low in low–income economies) were not included in the analysis of the effects of dismantling indirect discrimination, although these factors can be expected to determine to a crucial degree the success or failure of these structural adjustment programmes.[1]

Hence, while there are strong reasons to believe that, in many low–income economies, agricultural performance has a considerable impact on non–agricultural growth, the government budget and the balance of payments (Killick, 1985), its economy–wide effects are virtually ignored in the large literature on macro–economic policy–issues facing these economies. For example, it is clear from reading Arida and Taylor's (1988) comprehensive survey that the recent literature on short–run macro–economic policy issues facing low–income economies generally fails to appreciate agriculture's importance for macro–economic policy. The failure to deal with the economy–wide implications of agricultural change is also recognised in a recent survey of the literature dealing with matters of agricultural policy. According to its author 'the link from macro–policy to agriculture is quite strong. In the other direction, the general equilibrium consequences of agricultural adjustments to shifts in these policies are not yet understood in other than the roughest theoretical and empirical way' (Timmer, 1988:318). This is not to deny that there are major exceptions to the general tendency to neglect agriculture's economy–wide importance. Kalecki (1955) is an early exception, noting that, in a situation of shortage of foreign exchange, the supply inelasticity of the agricultural sector is a critical factor constraining the rate of non–inflationary economic growth. Sen (1981) provides an important restatement of Kalecki's argument in an open–economy frame- work. Further notable exceptions include Taylor (1979) and Chichilnisky and Taylor (1980), who showed that, with relative price insensitivity of both food demand and food supply, macro–economic policy changes, including a currency devaluation and an increase in fiscal spending, may not yield the expected results.

The second observation is related to the partial equilibrium framework within which the effects of agricultural policy–making are generally

---

[1] For example, in their design of a conceptual framework for the analysis of the effects of so-called growth–oriented adjustment programmes, based on the monetary approach to the balance of payments and an open–economy neo-classical growth model, Khan and Montiel (1989) do not incorporate the above–mentioned characteristics of agricultural demand and supply. The main objection to this approach is that it assumes away critical characteristics of a low–income economy's structure which may have a considerable impact on its response to changes in macro–economic policy.

3

analysed.[2] Representative examples of the partial equilibrium approach, which is also known as the 'Marshallian approach' after Alfred Marshall who used it as method of analysis in his *Principles of Economics*, include Scandizzo and Bruce (1980) who develop partial equilibrium methodologies for measuring the effects of agricultural price intervention, and Timmer (1986), who examines the scope and limitations to agricultural price policy in a partial equilibrium framework. The partial equilibrium approach is justified by the *ceteris paribus* assumption that prices and quantities in the rest of the economy are constant and remain unaffected by adjustments in the agricultural sector. Each market in the partial equilibrium methodology is thus regarded independently of the others and neither changes in macro–economic policies affecting the agricultural sector nor the effects of changes in agricultural policies on the rest of the economy are taken into account. It is the *ceteris paribus* assumption that I find wanting, because in many low–income countries, the effects of agricultural policies can be expected to spill over into production and income of other sectors in the economy, affecting the distribution of income, the government's budgetary position and the country's balance of payments position.

This may happen because, in many low–income economies, agriculture is an important sector not only on account of its large share in national income or employment, but also because food is still a major wage good and makes up a significant share of consumers' budgets. Further, at low levels of income, consumer demand for food is characterised by a relatively high income (or expenditure) elasticity and a relatively low price elasticity (Lluch *et al.*, 1977). Consequently, food price changes may have substantial real income effects and lead to large reallocations of budget expenditures, which spill over into demand changes for commodities from other sectors and considerably affect aggregate demand and the utilisation of non–agricultural production capacity. Moreover, given the relative price inelasticity of agricultural supply (Binswanger, 1991), even marginal increases in food demand may lead to significant increases in food prices, often leading to general inflationary pressure. Hence, macro–economic variables such as the real industrial wage rate and the real exchange rate depend, to a considerable extent, on agricultural prices. In these circumstances, any policy analysis based on a partial equilibrium approach can be misleading since it ignores important spill–over and/or feedback effects. The limitations of the partial equilibrium approach can be overcome by adopting a general equilibrium approach, which takes account of the fact that markets of all commodities and all productive factors are interrelated and that the outcome of a particular policy change for any one agricultural good or service ultimately depends on its effects on

---

[2] A notable exception is the agricultural policy model developed by Narayana *et al.* (1991), major features of which are discussed in Chapter 8.

all other product and factor markets.

In view of the above, the purpose of my study is to assess whether and, if so, to what extent, in India, the rest of the economy is affected by the performance of the agricultural sectors. This question in turn gives rise to a number of important issues. First, which are the major interrelationships between agriculture and the rest of the economy? Second, in case the ties between agricultural performance and industrial growth prove to be quite tight, is there a proper balance between agricultural and non–agricultural policies, stimulating both agricultural performance and industrial growth? To answer these questions, a multisector model of a computable general equilibrium type was constructed incorporating the main agricultural–non–agricultural linkages in the Indian economy (see Section 1.5 for a discussion of the model). The model is used to assess the short–term as well as medium–term effects of changes in agricultural policy on sectoral growth rates, the rate of inflation, the public budget deficit, the country's balance of payments position, and the factorial distribution of incomes. The agricultural policy instruments included in the analysis are procurement prices and quantities for foodgrains, a fertiliser subsidy, food subsidisation, and public investment in irrigation (see Section 1.7, below).

1.3   *Theoretical Aspects*

There is no escape from the fact that every economist must employ a body of theory when addressing particular empirical issues (Lawson, 1987). Empiricist inclined accounts which claim the primacy and objectivity of collected data as though these represent uninterpreted facts, uncontaminated by judgement and theory, and as though knowledge arises from them *via* inductive inference, are untenable. The choice of the research question itself is a matter of the researcher's preference, and point of view. To quote: 'The choice of premisses, the interpretation of observations, even the choice of questions to be addressed all provide scope for disagreements which evade settlement on the grounds of logic alone, even though they are transmitted or justified by reasoned argument.' (Dow, 1985:31). In the choice between different theoretical specifications, empirical observations are not necessarily decisive. If they were, economic thinking would not display such a variety of ideas as it presently does and has always done. Hence, the first task in the research, the result of which is documented in Chapter 2, was to compare and classify the theoretical approaches to agriculture–industry relationships in terms of the questions asked, their premises, and policy conclusions, with the aim to facilitate the choice between them. This classification of theories is an important step in the construction of the general equilibrium model, because it helps in making up one's mind about the model's most appropriate specification – the model specification being important, because the simulation results are sensitive to it (Taylor and Lysy, 1977).

Theoretical analyses of the interrelationships between the agricultural and the non–agricultural (industrial) sector have a long history in economics, with contributions from the Physiocrats during the 17th century, from the early political economists including Ricardo, Malthus and Marx during the 19th century, and from such diverse 20th century economists as Preobrazhensky, Lewis, Jorgenson, Kalecki, and Kaldor. While the ultimate aim of all is to draw policy conclusions, the contributions to the analysis of agriculture–industry relationships differ considerably in premises and method, and, consequently, in policy recommendations. In Chapter 2, I classify the various contributions to the literature into three categories, *viz.* the classical, neoclassical, and post–Keynesian approaches. In Figure 1.1, I have tried to summarise the classification adopted in Chapter 2 in a concise manner, classifying the three theoretical approaches according to only two citeria, *i.c.* whether they assume Say's law to hold or not, and whether they assume that there exist fundamental asymmetries in production conditions between agriculture and industry.

With respect to the first criterion, both the classical and the neoclassical approach are similar in their adherence to Say's law. In their explanation of Say's law, if there is an excess supply of a factor or a commodity, the price of the factor or commodity will fall. The factor or commodity will thus be cheaper relative to other factors or other commodities and, hence, will be substituted for the factors or commodities that are relatively more expensive. Though it is not always clearly acknowledged, this mechanism implies the assumption of *perfect substitution* of all factors and all commodities as well as certain income elasticity assumptions. Say's law is most easily supported by assuming income and substitution elasticities equal to one with constant returns to scale. What is implied by Say's law is that there is always a set of relative prices (including a rate of interest) which eliminates excess supply or demand, generating the full employment of all factors of production.[3] Post–Keynesians, on the other hand, reject the validity of Say's law, stressing the possibility of a less than full–employment level of aggregate demand. Following Keynes (1936), they stress the importance of uncertainty and individual expectations, particularly in relation to investment decisions. Thus, when the expectations of individual investors are depressed, investment demand will be low, resulting in a less than full–employment level of income. A sharp decline in the rate of interest

---

[3] As was noted by Sen (1963:55), it is assumed in the neoclassical approach that full employment savings and investment can always be brought into equality at a rate of interest at or above the minimum interest rate at which the liquidity preference becomes perfectly elastic – a problem that worried Keynes.

Figure 1.1
Cross-Classification of Theories

		M A C R O	
		Say's law holds	*Say's law is rejected*
M **I** **C** **R** **O**	*Structural Asymmetries between Agriculture and Industry*	*Classical Theory*	*Post – Keynesian Theory*
	No Structural Asymmetries between Agriculture and Industry	*Neo – Classical Theory*	

will not persuade them to step up their investments, as it is held that the impact on investment of the rate of interest is only secondary to the impact of expectations (Kahn, 1972:90).

With respect to the latter criterion, only neoclassical economists, often implicitly, assume that there is no basic distinction in terms of production conditions and producers' behaviour between the two sectors. Similar to other agents in the economy farmers are believed to be constantly striving for maximum profits on the basis of prices which are formed in perfectly competitive markets, constrained by their initial resource endowments and by consumers' preferences. In some of the neoclassical models, it is assumed that both sectors are working under similar technology, *i.c.* constant returns to scale (Kelley *et al.*, 1972), only allowing for agriculture–non–agriculture differences in the parameters of consumer demand. Classical and post–Keynesian approaches, on the other hand, emphasize structural asymmetries between agricultural and non–agricultural production. The critical assumption underlying the classical approach is that, in contrast to industrial

7

production, agricultural production is characterised by the existence of 'surplus labour'. Agriculture is regarded as being largely non–commercialised, producing no or only a limited marketable surplus, and consisting mainly of subsistence farmers.[4] The crucial assumption of the post–Keynesian approach is that agricultural and industrial sectors respond differently to a situation of excess demand. Prices adjust to clear agricultural markets, while in the industrial sectors supply–demand balance is brought about by output adjustments. Two issues underlie the response associated with each sector: supply conditions and market structure. Taking supply conditions first, since agricultural production processes are both seasonal and weather dependent, current market supply (apart from changes in stocks) is determined by the most recent crop. Given agriculture's relatively low short–run supply response, prices adjust to remove excess demand. Industrial production is assumed to operate under conditions of excess capacity and to vary with the level of demand (at an unchanged price). Market structure reinforces these sectoral adjustment patterns. Because most private agricultural enterprises are relatively small and family–owned and –operated[5] and, hence, have only limited market power as producers in the agricultural commodity markets, agricultural prices are determined by demand and supply. Market structure in non–agriculture, on the other hand, is considered to be oligopolistic, with industrial prices being 'administered', *i.e.* fixed by the producers by adding a mark–up to variable costs.

Following the classification into and comparison of the classical, neoclassical and post–Keynesian approaches in Chapter 2, the next step in the research was to make an argued choice between them. To this end, I proceeded by collecting 'stylised facts', representing the structure of the economy under consideration and its working during a particular period.[6] These stylised facts were derived from empirical observations as well as from earlier analyses of the Indian growth process discussed in Chapter 3. However, before proceeding to the discussion of the major stylised facts included in the model in Section 1.5, I want to comment on the choice of India as the economy under consideration.

---

[4] Fei and Ranis (1964) differentiate between subsistence farmers and capitalist farmers (the class of landowners) and accord the principal role in their description of agricultural transformation to the latter. See Section 2.2.4 (below).

[5] Farmers with large numbers of non–family workers are found only in centrally planned economies with a collectivised agriculture or in some tropical economies having a plantation agriculture.

[6] The notion of 'stylised facts' is based on the view that economic behaviour cannot entirely be deduced from general principles. See Kaldor (1985) on the use of stylized facts in theory building and Lawson (1989) for a comment.

1.4 *Empirical Relevance: The Case of India*

The choice of the Indian economy seems entirely fitting in view of the importance of its agricultural sector. India is primarily a land of a tropical monsoon climate and, with less than half of its cropping area being irrigated, the level of agricultural output may strongly fluctuate depending on whether the monsoon has been good or bad. During the period 1965–1980, agriculture's sensitivity to adverse weather conditions resulted in sometimes massive harvest failures which, through their adverse implications for wage–good availability, gave rise to major macro–economic stabilisation problems. In drought years, the immediate policy concern was to keep inflationary pressures within controllable limits *via* strong demand management, curbing public expenditure with the burden falling on public investment. Due to this decline in public investment, in most instances, a drought year was followed by a short recessionary period in which growth rates were significantly below trend levels and inflation rates were high. Hence, it will become clear from reading Chapter 3 why Indian economic growth during the period 1965–1980 was generally interpreted, most notably by Bagchi (1970), Chakravarty (1974), and Raj (1976), as being critically dependent on the performance of the agricultural sector. More recently, Sen (1981) argued that slow agricultural growth effectively constrained overall economic growth in India during this period – an argument which can also be found in a slightly modified form in Balakrishnan (1991).

However, in the early 1980s, when the growth rates of industrial production began to improve and the growth rate of real GDP was stepped up to a level of about five per cent per annum, the earlier 'consensus' view of agriculture as the major constraint on non–agricultural expansion was rejected, most notably by Ahluwalia (1985), in favour of an alternative explanation of the slow growth during 1965–80, which stressed the negative impact of governmental regulation of both industrial investment and foreign trade. At the time of the formulation of the Seventh Plan, with India being over the threshold of self–sufficiency[7] in cereals and with huge public stocks of foodgrains which were accumulated mainly on the basis of domestic procurement, it was generally felt that the danger of acute agriculture–induced inflation had been substantially reduced. In view of these major achievements on the agricultural front, agriculture was no longer seen as a constraint on economic growth and, hence, could be subjected to 'benign neglect' – a phrase borrowed from Singh and Tabatabai (1992). Accordingly, emphasis in policy shifted to the non–agricultural sectors, because, as was

---

[7] Self–sufficiency in cereals is defined as the matching of domestic supply with domestic demand based on the current level of income and its distribution.

argued by the Planning Commission (1984:2), 'as the agricultural constraint is loosened in the Seventh Plan, it should be possible to plan for higher rates of industrial growth.' Drawing on the South Korean example,[8] liberalisation of international trade and exchange was by many considered to yield great benefits in terms of more 'efficient' and faster growth of industry and overall GDP, based on the demands generated by the growing middle class as well as by an increase in exports. Hence, the emphasis of the Seventh Plan strategy was on increasing efficiency and competition in manufacturing, and on the modernisation and upgradation of industrial technology.

It is against the background of these major directional changes in policy–making that the question of agriculture's role in India's longer–term development strategy arises. More specifically, one can ask whether the agricultural sectors will be able to accomodate to the requirements of an industrialisation–led investment strategy or what would be the impact on manufacturing and services if the government were to adopt an alternative, 'agriculture–first' strategy. To appreciate the factors underlying the policy changes, it is necessary to have some understanding of the Indian development strategy as it has evolved over time, and of the changes it has brought about in the economy's structure. To this end, Chapter 3 reviews the evolution of India's strategy of planned development and tries to relate it to the economy's growth performance. This chapter is, however, not intended to provide a comprehensive assessment of post–Independence Indian economic planning and performance, for which the reader is best referred to Chakravarty (1987). The survey of the literature and the appraisal of empirical data, included in Chapter 3, suggest that, despite a very remarkable growth of agricultural output since 1965–66, it would be wrong to underestimate the various problems faced by this sector. There are at least three reasons to caution about over–optimistic conclusions regarding the economy's resilience in the face of severe weather stress, *i.c.* (*a*) the New Agricultural Strategy has not increased the stability of agricultural growth in any significant manner (Rao *et al.*, 1988), whereas at the same time, capacity creation in crucial infrastructural sectors including power and irrigation slowed down due to the declining trend of public investment (EAC, 1989); this may have increased the inflationary potential; (*b*) the increase in (intermediate input) costs of agricultural production during the period 1965–1990 was not matched by a corresponding rise in agricultural productivity, which led to higher

---

[8] As was pointed out, *inter alia*, by Chakravarty (1987a), it is a mistake to associate South Korea's high growth with a laissez–faire economic policy. A closer look reveals that South Korea's fast export growth rested upon substantial public intervention in a controlled economy. In fact, following a period of import substitution supported by substantial foreign capital inflows, exports were stimulated by direct and indirect intervention including subsidised credit, producers' subsidies, devaluation, wage repression, and supportive public investment.

agricultural prices and contributed to overall inflation; and (c) the relatively low level of average per capita food consumption indicates that there exists a large latent excess demand for food, not yet backed up by purchasing power; in other words, only given the existing (unequal) distribution of purchasing power, domestic food supply is able to meet food demand, making the economy only marginally self–sufficient in food.

1.5   *Methodological Issues*

The questions posed in Section 1.2 are studied with the help of a formal model (of the so–called computable general equilibrium type) described in Chapter 4. Any formal economic modelling undoubtedly demands care, since the type of model chosen, its specification, and the parameter values relied upon should all correspond to the characteristics of the economy under study, the types of questions asked and the reliability of the data available. The present model was specified by comparing the critical assumptions of possible theoretical specifications which were summarised in Chapter 2, to the stylised facts on the Indian economy, obtained from Chapter 3, and incorporating those assumptions in the model which seemed in accordance with empirical evidence. The model thus obtained has four distinguishing features.

First, it reflects the structural asymmetries between agriculture and non–agriculture, characteristic of the Indian economy. The agricultural sector to some extent exhibits neoclassical features, especially with regard to the formation of prices, which fluctuate in response to supply as well as demand conditions. However, government intervention in the markets for foodgrains, through an incentive–price based minimum support scheme, significantly affects the behaviour of foodgrain prices. The industrial sector on the other hand, which is characterised by oligopolistic competition and capacity underutilization, displays Keynesian/Kaleckian features of price setting and demand determinedness of production. The above specification is in accordance with the comment in Chakravarty (1979:1237), that '... there are important departures from the assumption of perfect competition in the product markets, including even agriculture, after price support operations were accepted as a part of the rules of the game since the late sixties.'

Second, in the model, the *ex – post* equality between investments and savings is brought about by changes in both the level and distribution of incomes. This particular specification reflects the following three empirical observations. First, it is found that the bulk of the savings originates in the household sector, while most of the investment is done by the government and the private corporate sector. This inter–sectoral mismatch between the increase in savings and the increase in investment demand which, according to Chakravarty (1987:83), formed the crux of plan financing in the context of the

11

Seventh Plan, renders untenable the classical assumption that savers are necessarily the same as investors – a conclusion which is also drawn by Chakravarty (1979; 1984) and Rakshit (1989). Second, there is historical evidence (discussed in Chapter 3) as to suggest that private investment demand in India does not respond regularly and predictably to changes in the real rate of interest. Specifically, it can be argued that, during 1967–74, lack of sufficient investors' confidence led to low private investment demand, even though real interest rates were low and sometimes even negative. This interest inelasticity of private investment demand is confirmed by the results of econometric studies including Bhattacharya (1984) and Pandit (1985). These findings render untenable the neoclassical approach in which it is (often implicitly) assumed that the rate of interest is able to balance investment demand and savings supply.[9] Finally, there is evidence in support of the post–Keynesian specification, which is brought forward by Chakravarty (1979) and Kumar (1990) and discussed in Chapter 3, that at least part of the increase in savings during the post–green revolution period was financed through income–distributional changes, leading to reductions in the consumption of the lower–income (and lower–saving) groups, particularly agricultural labourers, small farmers and ununionised labour.

Third, imports and exports of cereals are exogenous in the model, reflecting the fact that international grain trade is a monopoly of the central government, which – acting through the Food Corporation of India – decides which foodgrains are to be imported and at what time and from which country (Tyagi, 1990:36). It ought to be appreciated that there are two reasons why the scope for regulating the domestic availability of foodgrains through international trade is limited. First, the amount of foodgrains traded internationally constitutes only a small part of the total domestic demand for foodgrains,[10] which implies that a percentage–wise small foodgrain shortage in India would require the country to import the larger part of total world trade. In practice, this might prove difficult to realise and, even if it were possible, it might lead to a considerable drain on the country's foreign exchange reserves, because even a signal for foodgrain imports (or, for that matter, exports) by India is bound to lead to a tremendous increase (or decrease) in world prices. Second, given the volatile nature of the world

---

[9] One may further note that, in India, interest rates are policy–determined and, hence, not able to balance investments and savings. In fact, interest rates on public debt are fixed by the government, while interest rates on private debentures and dividends on preference shares are subject to a publicly stipulated ceiling.

[10] For example, the total world trade in rice is only 10 to 15 million tonnes per annum, while domestic rice consumption in India amounts to about 65 million tonnes per year. See Bhalla (1991).

market prices of wheat and rice,[11] it is possible that, in a year when India wants to export wheat or rice, the world market prices will be lower than the domestic prices (neglecting the possibility that the increase in Indian exports will depress world market prices). This would require that the exports of wheat or rice be subsidised. However, if the government adopts this policy, it would come under attack for subsidising consumers in *other* countries rather than subsidising consumers at home (Tyagi, 1990a:82). In sum, the world market does not provide a stable outlet for domestic overproduction nor a guaranteed source which can be tapped to meet domestic excess demand. It is for these reasons that, in what follows, any possibility of regulating the domestic availability of foodgrains through foreign trade is not taken into account.

Finally, the model constructed is that of a mixed economy, *i.e.* an economy in which public and private sectors co–exist in most spheres of economic activity. Direct state control is limited to only a part of the economy, in which the larger part of public industrial investment is concentrated. Particularly in agriculture, public investment exhibits significant positive externalities, which considerably enhances government's impact on the economy. State influence on the private sector is exercised mainly through indirect policy instruments including taxes, subsidies, and minimum support prices, that affect private decision making. The outcome of a change in one or more of these policy instruments is largely determined by the interplay of the reactions of private decision makers. The model tries to capture these behavioural responses of private agents (*e.g.* farmers, industrialists, trade unions, *etc.*) to public policy choices with respect to the agricultural sector, and the feedback effects of these responses, mostly through their effect on public revenues and expenditures. Such, as well as other, features of the Indian economy which are described in Chapter 3, are reflected in the model, and all that is described in Chapter 4.

The model belongs to the tradition of computable general equilibrium models and builds on the static model developed for India by Lance Taylor, Hiren Sarkar and Jørn Rattsø (1984) and its dynamic version, developed by Jørn Rattsø (1989). The overall model consists of a static, within–period adjustment model linked to a 'dynamic', intertemporal adjustment model. Within each period, the degree of adjustment is constrained by non–shiftable sectoral capital stocks, by a given amount of cultivated area with a given

---

[11] That the world market prices for foodgrains are highly volatile is shown by their coefficients of variation. The coefficient of variation for the world market prices of wheat and rice during 1968 to 1978 were estimated to be 36.8 per cent and 28.9 per cent respectively, while the coefficient of variation for the domestic prices of wheat and rice during the same period was only of the order of 8 per cent. Moreover, the trend growth of the world market prices for foodgrains has been negative during the 1980s and is expected to remain negative, because global food production is expected to increase rapidly in the coming decade. See Tyagi (1990:176).

13

irrigation coverage, and a fixed allocation of area across crops, by imperfectly indexed nominal wage rates in non–agriculture, and by given constraints on exports and imports of final goods. Between periods, some flexibility for adjustment is provided by capital accumulation, changes in nominal non–agricultural wage rates, increases in cultivated area, changes in irrigated area due to agricultural investment, and a re–allocation of area across crops. Not surprisingly, the focus on agriculture–industry relationships has conditioned the model's sectoral disaggregation. The production side of the model is disaggregated into nine producing sectors, five of which are agricultural. Within agriculture, a distinction is made between the crop sectors and other agriculture, including sectors as diverse as milk and milk products, animal services, fishing, forestry and logging, and other livestock products. Within crop agriculture, the model differentiates between foodgrain production and commercial crop production, which mainly includes plantation crops such as tea, coffee, rubber, jute and cotton. Finally, within foodgrains, the model distinguishes between rice, wheat, and other food crops, the latter including the so–called coarse cereals, pulses and gram. Within non–agriculture, an obvious distinction is made between services and manufacturing. Because of its importance as an intermediate input in agricultural production, the fertilisers sector was separated from the other manufacturing sectors. Similarly, a consumer goods sector was distinguished, because of its known strong backward linkage with agriculture which operates mainly through agro–based industries producing sugar, tobacco, textiles, leather, and beverages. The remaining part of manufacturing consists of basic, intermediate and capital goods production and is important in providing investment goods required for agricultural expansion.

Even though the model used in the analysis is imperfect and the data base it uses is approximate (see Section 1.6), the simulation experiments performed with the model yield, in my view, useful insights into the working of the Indian economy, because the model includes the essential structural features of the economy relevant for (agricultural) policy analysis. However, the results of the simulation exercises are not meant to serve as substitutes for critical and comprehensive thinking and common sense. In Keynes's (1936:297) words, 'The object of our analysis is, not to provide ourselves with a machine, or method of blind manipulation which will furnish an infallible answer, but to provide ourselves with an organised and orderly method of thinking out particular problems; and, after we have reached a provisional conclusion by isolating the complicating factors one by one, we then have to go back on ourselves and allow, as well as we can, for the probable interactions of the factors amongst themselves. This is the nature of economic thinking.' It is in this sense that economic modelling deserves careful attention.

In Chapter 5, the general equilibrium model's data base is presented in some detail, informing the reader about the parameter values which were used in the model exercises and about the reliability of the data on which these parameter values are based. The principal sources of data on production, income and employment on which the bulk of the model's parameter values are based, are the input–output table for 1978–79, data from the 1985–86 annual survey of industries, and national accounts data for the period 1985–1989, all three published by the Central Statistical Organisation (CSO). Taken together with data from various other sources, they were reconciled within the framework of a social accounting matrix (SAM) bringing together in a coherent and consistent way, on the one hand, data on production and income generation and, on the other hand, data on income received and spending and saving patterns (Keuning and De Ruijter, 1988). Evidently, consistency does not imply accuracy and, hence, I consider it required to report on the reliability of the data used in the analysis.

The transactions recorded in the input–output table supposedly correspond to market transactions, although it is clear that not all output is marketed. A major example is provided by the output of subsistence farming (Thamarajakshi, 1977). Farm output should conceptually be evaluated at prices which accrue to the producer at the first transaction. In practice, however, this is not possible, as the producer disposes of the product at different stages, the more important of which are (*i*) sales at village farm sites, (*ii*) sales at nearby and distant markets at different points in time, and (*iii*) retentions for consumption and other uses such as seed, feed, *etc.* in the producer households (CSO, 1989d:50). Ideally, each transaction should be evaluated at each stage of disposal at the corresponding price, but little information is available to make this possible. However, studies show that the disposal of output by producer households is concentrated in the primary markets during peak marketing periods (Gulati and Sharma, 1990). It is for this reason that the value of agricultural output is imputed on the basis of output estimates which are evaluated at state average prices worked out as a weighted average of district level prices during the peak marketing period. With respect to the industrial sectors, the input–output table distinguishes 66 manufacturing sectors which include practically within each sector registered and unregistered economic activities. Registered activities include factories in which the manufacturing process is carried on with the aid of power and which employ on an average twenty or more persons, as well as those in which the manufacturing process is carried on without the aid of power and which employ 100 persons or more, and all electricity undertakings (CSO, 1989c). Detailed time–series data on registered industrial production, value added, and employment on a uniform basis are available only through the

Annual Survey of Industries (ASI). Data on unregistered production do not exist at the same level of detail and for a similar period, so that, for the unregistered sector, I had to rely on the national accounts data. These data on unregistered manufacturing are based on the results of the National Sample Survey (NSS) which provides comprehensive data on principal characteristics of the household manufacturing sector only once in five years. This gives rise to the problem of preparing the estimates for the intervening years. Accordingly, the data on the unregistered component of production and employment are anything but comprehensive. As regards the services and other sectors, there are no regular time series of data on many of these sectors including construction, trade, hotels and restaurants, transport and other services (Gupta, 1989:237). The national accounts estimates of these sectors are based on decennial population census data and on limited information on average per capita earnings (CSO, 1989d:162).

As a result of the difficulties encountered in collecting detailed data on a large number of economic activities, particularly in the unregistered sectors, the input–output and national accounts data suffer from a certain degree of unreliability, which is partly reflected in the sometimes large statistical discrepancies reported by the CSO. However, it is easier to detect inadequacies than correct them and, hence, in the absence of anything better, these data formed the basis for the construction of the SAM and for deriving most of the model's parameters. Two things need to be stressed. First, in view of the above discussion, the model's data base is best to be regarded as being a 'stylised', but in my opinion valid, representation of the Indian economy. Second, as the unavoidable limitations in accuracy of the data call for great care in drawing conclusions from the results, I considered it important to evaluate the sensitivity of the model results to changes in its key parameters. The results of this sensitivity analysis are also reported in Chapter 5.

1.7   *Policy Focus*

The time frame of the general equilibrium model is one to five years, covering the period 1985 to 1989. This time period was chosen for essentially two reasons. First, I felt it to be important to examine the consequences of (agricultural) policy intervention in the short as well as medium term, because of possible differences in the effects over time. Second, the period is long enough so that the effects of the policies adopted can be felt, and yet not so long that it lies beyond the planning horizon of policy-makers. In fact, the time period exactly corresponds to the Seventh Five Year Plan period (1985–90) which is the time frame adopted in much of Indian policy-making.

The model was used to track the Seventh Plan period, the simulated values of the different variables describing the reference path of the economy. The results of (counterfactual) simulation experiments with the model, based on pre–specified changes in exogenous (agricultural) policy variables, were compared to this reference path, providing insight into the effects of policy changes and into the constraints, set by private sector behaviour, and determining the feasibility of the (agricultural) policy. In this way the effects of a large number of policies were to some extent quantified. The agricultural policy instruments, the economy–wide effects of which were to be explored with the help of the model, were not difficult to chose, as there exists a general consensus in the large literature on the management of India's agricultural economy on which instruments are important (Krishnaji, 1990). Hence, I included in the analysis procurement/minimum support prices and procurement quantities, food subsidisation under the Public Distribution System (which takes the form of subsidised prices as well as quantities of foodgrains issued), the fertiliser subsidy scheme, and public investment in irrigation and other agricultural infrastructure. To appreciate the degree of government involvement in the agricultural sectors, I shall consider each of these four instruments in somewhat more detail.

Taking public procurement first, this policy is implemented by the Food Corporation of India (FCI) which is the sole agency of the central government to purchase, store, transport and distribute foodgrains. The FCI has its offices in almost all the States of the country and employs more than 70,000 persons. During 1987–88, the number of purchase centres operated for the procurement of rice was as high as 4,417. In the case of wheat, the total number of purchase centres exceeded 7,800. The FCI purchases foodgrains at prices fixed by the central government, while the quantum of procurement largely depends upon the volume of production and the difference between the market prices and the procurement prices. Since 1968–69 the FCI has purchased, as a matter of policy, all foodgrains offered to it at the procurement price, which consequently took on the role of minimum support price. The FCI's willingness to buy as much foodgrains as is offered to it, implies a source of perfectly elastic demand at the procurement price, with the result that the procurement price sets the floor to the market (Balakrishnan, 1991:51). In some markets, the FCI purchases directly from the producers, whereas in other markets state government agencies operate on behalf of the FCI. Procurement by the FCI as a proportion of total foodgrain production has shown an increasing trend, from about 9 per cent of foodgrain production in 1971–72 to 16 per cent in 1985–86, representing some 40 to 50 per cent of marketed surplus in the case of rice and wheat (Tyagi, 1990:33).

The foodgrains procured by the FCI are used in the operation of the public distribution system (PDS). The distribution of foodgrains takes place either through statutory rationing or through the sale of foodgrains through

17

controlled outlets. Statutory rationing is confined to the major industrial areas to ensure that industrial workers have a steady supply of foodgrains. Outside these areas, public distribution is effected through Fair Price Shops to meet the needs of the lower–income strata of the population. These shops are generally owned privately or cooperatively, the owners receiving a commission on the quantities sold by them. A Fair Price Shop usually caters to a population of about 2,000 persons. In 1988, the number of Fair Price Shops was about 350,000 of which nearly two–fifths were located in rural areas (Tyagi, 1990:38). In every village, town or city, all people, whether rich or poor, are entitled to draw supplies from these shops at issue prices, which are annually fixed by the central government and are uniform throughout the country. These issue prices are generally lower than the economic cost of the procured foodgrains (procurement price plus procurement and distribution costs) and, hence, the government incurs a consumer subsidy.

The fertiliser subsidy scheme which was initiated in 1977, is administered by the Ministry of Agriculture through the Retention Price Scheme (RPS). Under this scheme, a uniform price is charged to farmers across the country for any given amount of fertiliser. Domestic fertiliser subsidies arise because of the difference between the price assured to the domestic fertiliser industry inclusive of distribution costs, and the price at which fertilisers are sold to the farmers. Subsidies on imported fertilisers arise when the purchase prices of imported fertilisers plus distribution costs exceed the prices paid by farmers. With the expansion of irrigated area and the increased adoption of higher yielding varieties of crops, fertiliser consumption increased steadily, rapidly raising public expenditure on fertiliser subsidies. The RPS was also meant as an import–substitution programme, protecting domestic producers from external shocks and offering them a guaranteed return on capital employed (Datta–Chaudhuri, 1990:21). As a result, production capacity of the domestic fertiliser sector was able to increase rapidly to meet the growing demand. By 1989–90, India was the fourth largest producer of chemical fertilisers in the world.

The last policy instrument considered is public investment in agricultural infrastructure and, in particular, in irrigation. As the soil and climatic conditions in India allow for the production of only a single crop in the whole agricultural year from most of the unirrigated arable land resource, multiple cropping is largely dependent on irrigation (Dhawan, 1988:14). With the potential of extensive agricultural growth through area expansion being exhausted, a step–up in agricultural growth can only result from intensifying production, mainly by raising the number of harvests per year and by increasing per hectare yield levels through the adoption of higher yielding varieties. It is widely recognised that, in this process of intensification, irrigation is the critical factor, being a prerequisite for the use of chemical fertilisers and also often conditioning the successful adoption of higher yielding seed varieties. Two types of irrigation can be distinguished: on the one hand, (small–scale) groundwater irrigation consisting of dugwells and shallow tubewells, and, on the other hand, (large–scale) surface water irrigation which comprises both canals and tanks. Irrigation facilities may be either privately owned, as is generally the case for dugwells and shallow tubewells, or government and/or community operated, which is the case for canals, tanks, and deep tubewells. However, pumpsets and tubewells are quite indivisible investments that prove uneconomic for farmers below a certain farm size, unless they can surmount the investment indivisibility by cooperative efforts (Dhawan, 188:215). Furthermore, the private use of minor irrigation sources (wells, pumpsets, and tubewells) is conditioned by prior massive public programmes of rural electrification and other infrastructure–improving projects, making the profitability of private irrigation investment crucially dependent on past public investment. Mainly because of such indivisibilities, but also because of external benefits, much of the investment required to improve agriculture's relatively poor infrastructure has to come from the government. Agricultural infrastructure essentially is a public good[12] due to the fact that no single individual farmer nor small number of farmers has any obvious incentive to pay (part of) the costs of its provision (even though it may be possible to design an agreement on its supply such that all farmers receive significant net benefits), while none of the farmers can be excluded from the benefits arising from its provision. As such, irrigation infrastructure provides the paradigm case for government intervention.[13]

---

[12] In neoclassical welfare economics, public goods are goods characterised by (i) joint supply (i.e. once a unit of the good is made available to one individual, a unit of the same quality can be made available to other individuals at no extra cost) and (ii) external (dis–)economies (i.e. once a unit of the good is made available to one individual, a unit of similar quality not only can but must be made available to all other individuals). The latter characteristic is usually referred to as 'impossibility of exclusion'. Samuelson (1954) has shown that a perfectly competitive market economy cannot be expected to bring about a Pareto–optimal provision of public goods. Public goods thus give rise to so–called 'market failures'. According to Head (1974:82), 'of the two characteristics of a public good, impossibility of exclusion is the much more potent cause of market failure.'

[13] Knut Wicksell was the first to draw attention to the crucial role of large numbers in 'market failure' analysis, particularly in relation to the non–exclusion characteristic of public goods. As he pointed out, where the number of economic units is large (as in the case of private agriculture) and no economic unit is so large that its own contribution is significant or perceptible in relation to the total, no completely voluntaristic system of market–type agreements can reasonably be expected even to approximate the Pareto–optimal provision of public goods (Head, 1974:83–86).

The main conclusion from the simulation results is that, in India, the agricultural sector may constrain non–agricultural growth both from the demand side and the supply side. In particular, I find that, in the short run, when agriculture's price responsiveness is rather low, macro–economic policies such as a rupee devaluation or an increase in government transfers to non–agricultural wage earners lead to unexpected results in terms of inflation, the level of national income, and income distribution. According to the outcomes of the medium–run experiments, an industrialisation drive involving a re–allocation of public investment from agriculture towards non–agriculture will lead to stagflation, while a strategy of export–led industrialisation results in a substantial increase in inflation as well as a redistribution of income in favour of farmers. These findings suggest that the performance of the non–agricultural sectors is hindered both by too high a level of agricultural prices as well as by too low a level of these prices. Too high a level of agricultural prices which results from inadequate agricultural supply relative to demand, restricts the size of the domestic market for non–agricultural goods, because it forces consumers to spend more on agricultural goods. Too low a level of agricultural prices which may be due to increases in domestic agricultural supply through imports or public distribution, also reduces domestic demand for non–agricultural goods, this time because low prices lead to low levels of agricultural output and income and, hence, low levels of agricultural intermediate and final demand.

This agricultural constraint on non–agricultural growth is due mainly to the relative price–inelasticity and income–elasticity of consumer demand for agricultural products and the relatively low price elasticity of (aggregate) agricultural supply – particularly in the short run. The particular structure of consumer demand is related to the low level of per capita income and the relatively unequal distribution of income. Agriculture's low price responsiveness is related to such structural factors as the limited availability of irrigation facilities, which implies a limited scope for multiple cropping as well as a strong dependence on weather conditions, and the relatively small size of the majority of farm holdings, which forces a substantial proportion of farmers' households to produce for self–consumption rather than for market sale. Given these structural supply characteristics of agriculture and the existing pattern of domestic demand, it is difficult to accelerate the growth rate of real GDP, witness the fact that the growth rates of real GDP from the different experiments all fall within a relatively small range.

However, when a sufficient number of different agricultural policy interventions were applied simultaneously (for example, by combining a re–allocation of public investment towards agriculture with an increase in fertiliser subsidisation), so that there is, in effect, a fundamental change in agricultural policy, were deviations from the reference run more sizeable. The results thus suggest that the agricultural constraint can be loosened (and the country's macro–economic performance improved) only by changing the structural conditions for stepping–up agricultural growth and raising the sector's (short–run) supply–responsiveness. The required structural change can be more effectively brought about by a policy of public agricultural investment than by some of the agricultural price policy measures that are often recommended. The marginal returns (expressed as average annual incre– ment to real GDP over the five–year planning period) per rupee of public expenditure on public investment are found to be about twice as high as the marginal returns from a rupee spent on fertiliser subsidisation and about 25 per cent higher than the marginal returns to increased expenditure on public foodgrain procurement. Further, stepping up public foodgrain procurement is highly inflationary. Its impact on inflation can be contained by combining it with an increase in public foodgrain distribution, but only at the cost of significantly reducing its expansionary impact and of an increase in the government's budget deficit. Through depressing agricultural prices (and, hence, agricultural output) an increase in public foodgrain distribution is both deflationary and contractionay in the medium run, even yielding negative aggregate marginal returns. Distributionally, the benefits from an increase in fertiliser subsidisation accrue relatively equally to the three private income groups. In contrast, the benefits from increased public procurement are very unequally distributed, with farmers gaining substantially and non–agricultural wage earners even losing income in real terms. The above results cast serious doubt on the efficacy of agricultural price policy in a situation in which the government has little control over industrial prices (and wages), indicating that more is needed than providing farmers with higher crop prices. A policy of increased agricultural price incentives at best offers high growth at the cost of increased poverty (because of its considerably inflationary impact). Hence, the need for adequate public intervention must be recognised, especially in the restructuring of the agricultural sectors. This calls for an expanded programme of public agricultural investment, particularly directed at irrigation and other rural infrastructure.

On the whole, my results underscore, on the one hand, the difficulties of stepping–up the growth rates of manufacturing in a non–inflationary manner when no proper attention is being paid to the agricultural sector, and, on the other hand, indicate that there is considerable scope for raising industrial growth through an agriculture–demand led investment strategy – in Adelman's (1984) terminology. As such, the results reinforce the need for a careful analysis of the economy–wide impact of potential agricultural policy alternatives implying that, as far as the Indian economy is concerned, a partial–equilibrium approach to matters of agricultural policy is doomed to be faulty. As will become clear from the following chapters, any analysis of the management of the Indian agricultural economy should take account of the direct as well as indirect, and short–term as well as medium–term effects of agricultural policy interventions.

ALTERNATIVE THEORIES OF
AGRICULTURE-INDUSTRY INTERACTION

2.1   *Introduction*

Theoretical interest in the relationships between agricultural and industrial
growth started with the Physiocrats who were the first to maintain the
analytical division between agriculture and industry and to acknowledge that
the production relations in agriculture are different from those in
manufacturing (Bharadwaj, 1987). In fact, their *Tableau Economique* provided
the first macro-economic analysis of the relationship between the level of
agricultural surplus[1] which they regarded as the only (domestic) source of
investible resources, and the level of aggregate economic activity (Morrison
and Thorbecke, 1990). Later, when following the industrial revolution the
share of the industrial surplus increased and the quantitative dominance of
the agricultural surplus declined, came the so-called classical growth
theories of Malthus and Ricardo which focus on the problem of increasing
demand for food coupled with diminishing returns in agriculture. Their
theories predict that industrial growth must eventually stagnate, due to
agriculture using ever increasing resources with falling productivity. Ricardo
initially highlighted the conflict between agriculture (in particular, the
landlords whom he considered spendthrifts) and the rest of the economy.

---

[1] The Physiocrats defined agricultural surplus as the difference between the
'gross produce' of agriculture and 'productive consumption' by farmers. The
latter was thought to consist of material requisites of production and of
sustenance of labour employed in production. See Bharadwaj (1987).

Assuming that, in the short run, land is a fixed factor of production, he showed that rent resulted from fertility differences among land types or plots and is determined by the price of the agricultural commodity (instead of determining that price). Ricardo argued against restrictions on corn imports, because any such restriction would imply compensatory increases in domestic production to meet demand, necessitating moving on to inferior lands and, hence, leading to a change in income distribution in favour of landlords. This would seriously hinder industrial capital accumulation and growth.[2] Ricardo's analysis was criticised by Malthus who argued in favour of the Corn Laws. He held that a change in income distribution in favour of the landlords might be beneficial to the nation's welfare, because it augments the size of the domestic market for manufactures.

In this chapter, the twentieth–century literature, following in the tradition of Ricardo and Malthus, which is concerned with both describing and explaining the structural change from a low–income, predominantly agrarian economy to a higher–income, more diversified economy, is classified in three main categories, on the basis of what is assumed to be the main constraint to economic growth.[3] It is good note from the outset that the classification adopted is a reflection of the early disagreement between Ricardo who emphasized *supply - side* factors, and Malthus whose argument was based on the belief that cheap food would reduce economic activity from the *demand side* by curtailing landlords' spending. Major contributions to each of the theoretical approaches are reviewed in the following order: the classical theories in Section 2.2, major contributions of a post–Keynesian nature in 2.3, and, finally, contributions within the neoclassical approach in 2.4. Section 2.5 concludes.

---

[2] Agricultural production costs and prices will rise which implies that (given the level of wages to be determined by the costs of subsistence) industrial profit margins will be squeezed. The motive for industrial accumulation 'will diminish with every diminution of profit and will cease altogether when profits are so low as not to afford them [the manufacturers] an adequate compensation for their trouble and for the risks which they must necessarily encounter in employing their capital productivity' (Ricardo, *Principles*, Sraffa edition, p. 122, as quoted by Kaldor, 1986). Sooner or later the economy will enter the long–run equilibrium of the Stationary State. On the way to it, it appeared inevitable that a steadily rising proportion of resources should be absorbed in the purchase of food, leaving less available for everything else.

[3] It should be observed that most of the literature discussed refers to a closed economy. Hence, it is assumed that, while substitutes through foreign trade may be available, difficulties of export expansion and foreign exchange shortages may not allow such routes to be taken, making industrial growth to a large extent conditional on agricultural growth.

2.2 The Classical Approach:
Agriculture's Role in Relaxing the Savings Constraint

The 'classical approach' which is the subject of this section, refers to the Ricardian tradition that was sought to be revived by Lewis (1954) (see Chakravarty, 1979). I also include Preobrazhensky's (1965, first published in 1926) contribution as it is a major precursor of Lewis's line of thought, although more on Marxian than on Ricardian lines. The approach is called 'classical' because it shares with the classical writers such as Adam Smith, David Ricardo and Karl Marx, the belief that a particular social formation could be abstracted on the basis of empirical observations and viewed as a system governed by certain objective rules. In particular, the classical approach refers to theories in which savings act as a constraint on capital formation because the distribution of incomes is weighted in favour of classes with low propensities to save. Profits are generally assumed to be mostly saved and invested, hence the 'classical' emphasis on policies in favour of profit–receivers.[4] The 'classical' proposition that, in a closed economy[5] with a binding savings constraint, a rise in the savings rate calls for an increase in the net finance contribution from agriculture to industry, can be traced back to the work of nineteenth century political economists beginning with Ricardo's arguments in favour of the repeal of the Corn Laws, and to the twentieth century Soviet industrialisation debate with Preobrazhensky's 'law of primitive socialist accumulation.'

2.2.1 Preobrazhensky's Primitive Socialist Accumulation:
The Importance of the Terms of Trade

One of the first instances in which the interaction between agriculture and industry in economic growth assumed importance is in the economic debate concerning the financing of the First Five Year Plan of the Soviet Union. The debate occurred within the Bolshevik party following the introduction of the New Economic Policy (NEP) in the spring of 1921. The introduction of the NEP was a retreat to market forms after the attempt at central planning during War Communism which by the end of 1920 had brought the revolution to the brink of disaster (Day, 1975). The objective of the NEP was to direct the development of capitalism (which was deemed to some extent and for some time inevitable) into state capitalism. To this end, peasants were given the right to trade post–tax surpluses in exchange for manufactured goods and the majority of small enterprises were denationalised and leased either to local entrepreneurs or to cooperatives. Hence, the Soviet economy in the mid–1920s may be

---

[4] For a comprehensive and clear review of the work of 19th century classical writers, the reader is referred to Bharadwaj (1987).

[5] Or an economy facing a serious foreign exchange shortage.

regarded as consisting of two main sectors, one sector including all private economic activities which, at that time, mainly consisted of agriculture and foreign trade, the other sector including the state economy, which was based on collective ownership of the means of (primarily) industrial production. However, within a year of the NEP's introduction, the private sector had gained considerable command over the economy as private traders were displacing the cooperatives in the distribution of manufactured goods and state trading organisations were forced to participate in market transactions for supplies. It is in this context that Evgeny Preobrazhensky (1965) formulated the proposition of *Primitive Socialist Accumulation* that a surplus has to be extracted from agriculture to provide resources for industrialisation, by means of price controls on agricultural products and overvaluation of the domestic currency.[6]

Preobrazhensky belonged to the major critics of the NEP. In particular, he was fearful that the NEP might lead to a recovery of the private sector at the expense of the public sector. In his view, the state sector was not able to finance the whole of the investment needed for industrialisation through socialist accumulation (*i.e.* from the surplus product generated within the state sector itself) and, hence, needed part of the surplus product generated by the private sector. In particular, the socialised non–agricultural sector required cheap inputs and cheap wage goods from agriculture to keep up its profitability and hence the capacity to finance its investments. But, given the existence of a private agricultural sector, higher agricultural prices were needed, if peasants were voluntarily to deliver sufficient foodgrains and raw materials to the non–agricultural sector, and this would harm the industrialisation process. Against this background, Preobrazhensky argued that, in a closed economy, the only way for the state sector (*i.e.* industry) to expand is at the cost of the private sector through a process of unequal exchange of material resources in which the *losing* private sector (*i.e.* mainly agriculture) deliveres more resources than what it receives.[7] Specifically, by making the exchange of agricultural goods for essential industrial consumer goods unfavourable for farmers, they can be made to part with the amount of agricultural surplus required for (state) industrialisation. This can be done by administratively holding down agricultural prices or by imposing heavy

---

[6] Preobrazhensky had anticipated the dualism models of the post–war period and in particular their emphasis on intersectoral resources transfers, several decades before the original Lewis paper in 1954. Together with Nikolai Bukharin, Preobrazhensky belonged to the most prominent participants in the Soviet Industrialisation Debate in the 1920's that highlighted the role of the intersectoral terms of trade as a policy instrument for effecting a desired 'primitive socialist accumulation'.

[7] For Preobrazhensky, this unequal exchange of goods implied an unequal exchange of labour values (*i.e.* amounts of 'socially necessary' labour embodied in the exchanged goods).

indirect commodity taxes on essential industrial consumer goods bought by the farmers. Hence, keeping the prices of the private sector's products low relative to public sector's prices is what Preobrazhensky meant by primitive socialist accumulation.[8] His case rested on the following two arguments. First, to Preobrazhensky, a USSR 'surrounded by enemies' needed rapid industrialisation, presumably because of the need of military self–sufficiency and the impossibility of prolonged reliance on foreign countries for loans or even heavy industrial imports (Lipton, 1977:125). Second, he believed that agricultural output could be substantially increased with the introduction of a more rational farm organisation and, hence, that the required amount of agriculture's resources could be transferred to industry without negatively affecting agricultural output and raising the terms of trade for industry.[9]

Preobrazhensky's argument has been reformulated by Sah and Stiglitz[10] (1984) in a static two–sector (agriculture–industry) model with policy controlled terms of trade, in which the government also effectively controls the industrial real wage. The state's surplus all of which is supposed to be used for investment purposes, is equal to the difference between industrial output and wage payments to the industrial workers. Wages are fully consumed. The agricultural market is assumed to clear through adjustments of the industrial real wage enforced by the government, whereas market balance for non–agriculture follows from the assumption of savings–determined investment Because, in this model, a decrease in the relative price of the agricultural good will lead to a fall in agriculture's marketed surplus, and supply and demand balance in the agricultural market can be reinstated only by a decrease in the industrial real wage, turning the terms of trade against agriculture leads to increased state accumulation.[11] Sah and Stiglitz thus vindicate Preobrazhensky's proposition of primitive socialist accumulation, but in opposition to him this is possible only by squeezing the industrial workers (Dutt, 1988:48–49).

Mitra (1977) is concerned with generalising Preobrazhensky's model to the

---

[8] What Preobrazhensky (1926:84) meant by the law of primitive socialist accumulation is 'accumulation in the hands of the state of material resources mainly or partly from sources lying outside the complex of state economy.' Quoted in Mundle (1981:7).

[9] It is on this point that Preobrazhensky had a fundamental disagreement with Bukharin, according to whom the farmers would simply withdraw their supplies from the market if Preobrazhensky's scheme were to be rigorously imposed.

[10] Sah and Stiglitz treat Preobrazhensky's idea that the terms of trade should be shifted against agriculture as a problem in optimal taxation by manipulations of Lagrangian functions to find optimal tax rates for the peasantry and using a Bergsonian social welfare function and a given social value of marginal investment.

[11] This is true only under the assumptions made in the Sah and Stiglitz model. Rattsø (1988) questions these assumptions both on theoretical and empirical grounds for the case of India. He discusses three alternative sets of assumptions two of which are of a Keynesian type.

27

Indian situation and introduces a private industrial sector and foreign trade. While his modifications allow for a variety of outcomes, one implication of his analysis is clear: for an economy to accumulate and grow, some social classes must be made the victim of non–equivalent exchange. Non–equivalent exchange takes place *via* shifts in the intersectoral terms of trade which, in Mitra's view, is a political parameter controlled by class forces. The state is not neutral, but participates in this conflict over the terms of trade.[12]

2.2.2 *Lewis's Growth with Unlimited Supplies of Labour: The Importance of Agriculture's Labour Contribution*

By transferring relatively low–productivity labour from agriculture to non–agriculture which is assumed to have a higher level of labour productivity, an important slack in the economy can be taken up. This was first pointed out by W. Arthur Lewis (1954) in a model of a two–sector economy. One sector was a 'traditional', mainly agricultural sector, where the marginal product of labour is zero, or close to zero, and the average product is close to subsistence minimum. The other sector is an enclave of modern industries, including plantation agriculture, which is referred to as a 'capitalist' sector where labour is employed upto the point where its marginal product equals the wage rate. The non–agricultural wage rate is assumed constant in *real* terms at a level slightly higher than the average product in 'traditional' agriculture – the difference providing the incentive for migration of labour from agriculture to industry. At the initial configurations of sectoral capital stocks and real wage rate in the industrial sector, there is thus available an 'unlimited' supply of surplus agricultural labour. Lewis's labour surplus resembles Marx's reserve army, as labour can be drawn as necessary from both (Chakravarty, 1979a:79).

In Lewis's model, growth proceeds with the continuous reinvestment of the capitalist sector's profits or surplus. With each round of reinvestment, a part of surplus labour from the traditional sector is absorbed in the 'capitalist' sector according to the profit maximising principle of equalising the wage rate with marginal product. As this capital accumulation proceeds, the rising share of industrial production results in a rising share of profits in national income – with real wages remaining constant.[13] The transfer of

---

[12] According to Mitra, the post–1965–66 shift of the terms of trade in favour of agriculture has been dictated by the alliance of large farmers and urban high–income classes, with the support of the state – through price support policies and public procurement of foodgrains. Mitra's analysis led to a debate on the role of the intersectoral terms of trade in Indian development. Mitra's conclusion has been attacked by Tyagi (1979), Kahlon and Tyagi (1980), and Tyagi (1987). For a review, see De Janvry and Subbarao (1986) and Vittal (1986).

[13] It is a well–known fact that in economic growth the registered savings ratio tends to rise in line with the increase in the share of the modern industry in

labour also benefits agriculture which experiences an improved land–labour ratio. The amount of labour that can be transferred will depend on the amount of capital stock that is available in industry, the industrial capital–labour ratio, and the amount of 'surplus' labour in agriculture. The rate of transfer will depend on the rate of growth of industrial profits. This phase of economic growth will come to an end when the entire pool of surplus labour in agriculture is absorbed (*i.e.* the so-called Lewis turning point). Thereafter, the level of real wages will rise, as the supply elasticity of labour from agriculture to non–agriculture no longer is infinite and agriculture will start competing with industry for more labour.[14] Beyond this turning point, the labour supply curve slopes upward, wages are determined by conditions of labour demand and supply and capital–labour substitution becomes important.[15] Lewis's model is closed by fixing the real wage of industrial labour in terms of a consumption basket. A share of non–labour income in industry is saved and investment adjusts to exhaust savings which permits the economy to grow at a steady pace. This steady state is supply–constrained and has a predetermined income distribution.

With low wages in terms of food, unchanged terms of trade and an upward moving marginal productivity of labour function based on the accumulation of industrial capital, Lewis could argue that economic growth consists in the fact that a low saving economy is transformed into a high saving economy.[16] It is important to note that it is essential for his argument 'that the capital–output ratio is not allowed to rise so long as the real wage rate stays the same, which he thought that competitive conditions will ensure' (Chakravarty, 1984:32).

In its elementary form, the only transfer from agriculture to industry required to generate growth in the Lewis model is the transfer of surplus labour. The principal source of capital accumulation is the internal surplus

---

the national product. This is due to the organisational form of the industrial enterprise in which retained profits form a major part of the investment funds. The higher the share of modern industry in national output, the higher the share of profits and thus *ceteris paribus* the savings ratio.

[14] Lewis calls this phase of economic growth the "commercialisation of agriculture."

[15] Lewis's model assumes a gradual transition from a classical to a neoclassical regime. According to Taylor and Arida (1988:175), causality in Lewis's model 'is only one step away from neoclassical determination of the rate of growth by forces of production and thrift.'

[16] According to Lewis (1954), 'the central problem of economic development is to understand the process by which a community which was previously saving and investing 4 or 5 per cent of its national income or less, converts itself into an economy where voluntary savings is running at about 12 or 15 per cent of national income or more". The major source of savings is profit, and "if we find that savings are increasing as a proportion of national income, we may take it for granted that this is because the share of profits in the national income is increasing.'

of the industrial sector itself. However, when interpreted as *food advanced to workers*, industrial capital accumulation will be constrained by the size of agriculture's marketed surplus. Lewis does note that, in case the industrial sector can neither produce its own food nor import it from the rest of the world, not only labour but also marketed surplus of food would have to be drawn from the stagnant, traditional sector.[17] As the size of the industrial labour force increases, the industrial demand for food will rise, threatening a shift of the inter–sectoral terms of trade in favour of agriculture. The wage rate will rise in terms of industrial product, while remaining constant in terms of agricultural product. The share of profits in the industrial product will fall. In these circumstances, policy intervention aimed at preventing the terms of trade from shifting in favour of agriculture will become necessary to ensure a transfer of resources from agriculture to industry in order to keep the accumulation process moving.

Adopting the special case of the Lewis model where the industrial labour force is dependent on the marketed surplus of food crops from domestic agriculture for its subsistence, Chakravarty (1974) argued that, in India, the increasing excess demand for foodgrains started to pull the intersectoral terms of trade in favour of agriculture from the mid–sixties onwards. This shift of the terms of trade forced up the industrial product wage. Based on a time series of the income terms of trade constructed by Thamarajakshi (1969), Chakravarty argued that the shifting terms of trade have resulted in net income transfers to the agricultural sector.[18] Assuming that the savings rate is lower in agriculture than in industry[19], this transfer of income resulted in a decline in the aggregate rates of savings and investment and, consequently, a slowdown of the overall growth rate of the Indian economy.

2.2.3 *Fei and Ranis:*
The Importance of Agriculture's Net Finance Contribution

Formal presentations of Lewis's work started with Gustav Ranis and John C.H. Fei (1961; 1964) whose model has two turning points – when food supply begins

---

[17] For another formulation which emphasizes the role of the transfer of marketable surplus rather than net resources, see Nicholls (1963).

[18] Chakravarty's analysis is problematic on this point. According to Mundle (1981:14), the income terms of trade provide no indication of any net income flow between sectors. This follows from the definition of the income terms of trade as the marketed surplus of agriculture multiplied by the intersectoral net barter terms of trade. Hence, it is not a measure of the net flow of earnings between the two sectors, let alone the net flow of factor incomes.

[19] This assumption is based on rather weak statistical evidence. Further, there is no explanation why the savings out of agricultural incomes were not invested in agriculture itself, or deployed as investment in industry. Later, Chakravarty (1979) reformulated his position more clearly in terms of the willingness of agriculturalists to capitalise their surplus in the form of adding to directly productive investment.

to decline as labour is withdrawn from agriculture and when the marginal product of agricultural labour rises to the institutionally fixed non–agricultural wage rate.

Following Lewis, they assume that the land area is fixed and subject to diminishing returns to scale as the labour–land ratio rises and that agricultural labour is paid an institutionally determined wage rate. In these circumstances, in the early phase of growth, a part of agricultural labour can be transferred to industry without a resulting decline in agricultural production. Because (in the early phase) the internal surplus of the industrial sector is relatively small, net savings of the agricultural sector constitute the principal source of industrial accumulation.[20] The *first stage* of economic growth (which is equal to Lewis's model) is characterised by an infinitely elastic supply of labour to industry as long as the agricultural labour surplus persists. Fei and Ranis assume a constant institutionally determined wage rate in agriculture, arguing that 'As long as surplus labour continues to exist in the agricultural sector, there is no reason to assume that this social consensus changes significantly' (Fei and Ranis, 1964:22). To get a constant industrial product wage, *i.e.* an industrial wage in terms of manufactures, they also assumed a constant terms of trade between the sectors. Industrial production operates under constant returns to scale and the rate of technical progress is assumed to be constant as well as purely labour–augmenting. With all wage income assumed to be consumed and a constant fraction of profits saved and invested, growth takes place through the reinvestment of profits in industry and the transfer of labour with zero or near zero marginal productivity from agriculture. This transfer is completed when the surplus labour in agriculture is exhausted and the marginal product of its labour begins to rise. This is the *second phase* of economic growth in which industrial wages remain higher than both average and marginal agricultural product. Since the marginal product of agriculture is now positive, opportunity costs of a labour transfer from agriculture to industry are also positive. Hence, beyond the point where the marginal product of agricultural labour starts to increase, the fund of agricultural wage goods available for the industrial workers begins to fall. As a result, the relative price of food will rise and, consequently, the supply curve of industrial labour ceases to be completely elastic and begins to rise. Investment and the rate of economic growth will tend to fall. The economy will enter its *third* and final stage of full commercialisation when the marginal product of

---

[20] According to Fei and Ranis (1964:31), 'In a dualistic type of underdeveloped economy with a large subsistence agricultural sector, this sector must serve as a primary basis for the expansion of the economy. For this reason, when the economy gathers momentum, it is likely that Sa [agricultural savings] will constitute a major source of the economy's investment fund, dwarfing the savings of the industrial sector, S.'

agricultural labour becomes equal to the industrial wage. At this stage, continued economic growth becomes conditional on technological progress in agriculture required to raise agricultural productivity and offset the fall in agricultural surplus due to the transfer of labour to industry.

Balanced growth of both the industrial and agricultural sector is necessary to avoid stagnation of the overall rate of economic growth. Balanced growth in this case has two dimensions. *On the output side*, it means that each sector provides a market for the other sector's products and that each must grow in such a way that the terms of trade do not turn against either, thus affecting relative investment incentives. *On the input side*, the agricultural sector will provide workers for the growing industrial sector. Balanced growth implies that the two sectors grow in such a way that the industrial sector is able to absorb the precise number of new workers freed by the agricultural sector at a constant real wage, set by the average product in agriculture plus a constant margin. This is sometimes called the *employment* balance (Saith, 1985).

Fei and Ranis emphasize private entrepreneurship as the critical agricultural input (Dixit, 1973:342). In the first stage of economic growth, landlords are required to sell all their surplus in the market in order to keep both the industrial product wage and terms of trade constant, and to use a substantial part of their profits for investment in industry. In the following stages in which technical change becomes important to offset the fall in agricultural surplus due to the transfer of labour to industry, landlords will have to introduce new techniques. They will be induced to adopt new technology if the price of agricultural goods is allowed to increase initially or through subsidisation of input costs.

The main implication of Fei and Ranis's analysis, *i.c.* that, in its early stages, industrialisation requires a substantial net finance contribution from agriculture, is not supported by empirical evidence for Japan[21], the USSR and India as well as for a number of other countries.[22] Cross–country empirical studies of industrialisation experiences suggest that in fact there is no unique pattern of net resource transfer between industry and agriculture. For example, Mundle and Ohkawa's (1979) estimates for Meiji Japan indicate that, although agriculture's net finance contribution was very high as a proportion

---

[21] Fei and Ranis are not very specific in delimiting the scope of application of their model. However, they state (1964:263–64): 'The empirical support of both our theory and policy conclusions draw heavily on the experiences of nineteenth century Japan and contemporary India.'

[22] Estimates of intersectoral resource flows are available for a large number of countries including Taiwan (Lee, 1971), China (Ishikawa, 1967), Iran (Karshenas, 1989) and Kenya (Sharpley, 1976). Karshenas (1989) who provides a good review of a number of these studies, concludes that the net finance contribution of agriculture to the growth of other sectors appears to have been negative in most of the economies and for much of the observation period.

of agricultural value added (up to 20 per cent in the 1890s), it was much lower as a proportion of non–agricultural value–added, reaching a maximum of just over 8 per cent during the decade immediately preceding the First World War.[23] The same holds true for the Soviet Union during the 1920s, when investable resources to finance industrialisation were transferred from agriculture to industry by an attempt to turn the terms of trade against agriculture (as suggested by Preobrazhensky) and later by the collectivisation of agricultural production. Estimates, published by Ellman (1975), indicate that while there was a net resource outflow from agriculture during the First Five Year Plan period, the volume of this outflow was small compared to aggregate investment in industry. His estimates further show that food price–induced forced savings by the industrial working class supported the Soviet investment drive of the early 1930s, in contrast to Preobrazhensky's suggestion that the terms of trade be shifted against agriculture to extract an investible surplus. A third and final example considered here concerns India during 1951–52 to 1970–71. Estimates by Mundle (1981) show that, since 1955–56, agriculture's net finance contribution in real terms has been positive and relatively large in terms of agricultural value added, but as a proportion of the value added in non–agriculture, it reached a peak of only around 9 per cent during the early 1960s after which it declined to only 3 per cent in 1970–71.[24] According to Ishikawa (1967), under the typical initial conditions obtaining in contemporary Asian countries such as India and China, facts of demography and agro–climatic character require large–scale investments in agriculture, in particular by the state. Such a huge flow of (public) resources to agriculture is unlikely to be offset by a simultaneous outflow of agricultural commodities. Even in economies where agriculture's net finance contribution has been negative, the overall savings rate has increased

---

[23] Net agricultural savings was only one of the sources of financing investment for the non–agricultural sector, but it was not the only source or even the major source of financing non–agricultural investment during the critical half century of Japan's industrialisation. See Mundle (1985).

[24] The increase in net real resource outflow out of agriculture upto 1963–64 may be due to the public policy of food imports aimed at keeping constant the intersectoral terms of trade (which on the basis of relative productivity growth would have increased for agriculture). According to Mundle (1981), the drain of agricultural surplus during this period has led to certain imbalances which forced down industrial growth after 1965–66. On the one hand, the increasing transfer of surplus has restricted the home market for industrial products in agriculture, and on the other hand, it has restricted agricultural investment and, hence, potential agricultural growth. After 1965–66, the terms of trade were allowed to shift in favour of agriculture. Given inelastic food demand, rising agricultural prices have eroded the 'agricultural product wage' of industrial workers. According to Mundle, in combination with higher prices for agricultural raw materials, this has added up to wage–push, cost–push inflation. Together with the stagnation of consumer demand for non–agricultural products, these imbalances in the economy set in operation a retrograde motion, slowing down industrial growth markedly and changing the size (and eventually the direction) of the net resource flow.

as a result of the rising share of industrial output in national income and the relatively fast rates of productivity growth in manufacturing.

2.3   The Post-Keynesian Approach:
The Importance of Intersectoral Demand Linkages

For high–income economies, the possibility of *demand deficiency* along Keynesian lines is widely accepted. It is attributed to the insufficiency of investment in relation to the full–employment level of savings which may result from (among other things) the severance of those who are responsible for the decisions to save, from those who are responsible for the decisions to invest. In particular, the problem of effective demand is located in the assumed volatility in investors' expectations. According to Keynes, investment decisions are causally prior to savings decisions inasmuch as investment levels change with changes in the state of expectations, with consequent adjustments in savings levels (*via* the operation of the multiplier principle). Keynes rejected the idea that the rate of interest could be regarded as a price that served to equilibrate investment demand and savings supply. Instead, he developed the idea that the interest rate should best be regarded as the price for liquidity (Chakravarty, 1979a).

For low–income, relatively non–monetised economies, however, the problem of demand deficiency was generally held to be non–existent, both by Keynesian and neoclassical economists, though their reasons for neglecting the demand problem were different. According to most Keynesians, given a very low elasticity of output (due to the limited supply of non–labour resources), the multiplier mechanism did not have much application because with a rise in investment, the money multiplier may operate but the real multiplier will not and, hence, prices will rise.[25] According to Rakshit (1989:1–2), the genesis of this approach may be traced to the *General Theory* itself, where 'Keynes defines 'full employment' as that level of activity at which the effective demand elasticity of output and employment is zero. Hence the problem of demand deficiency à *la* Keynes is supposed to assume importance only when the 'full employment' level has been raised sufficiently through capital accumulation and other measures of economic development.' In the writings of classical and neoclassical economists, demand considerations are conspicuous by their absence, because Walras's Law and Say's Law were both considered to apply.[26] In contrast to the above views, the post–Keynesian theories of

---

[25] Rao (1952) considers the standard Keynesian remedy for unemployment – the generation of additional effective demand. In low–income economies, because of the inelasticity of capital goods supply, output cannot respond to the additionally created demand, and the multiplier has its impact on nominal values by simply driving up prices.

[26] Rakshit (1982:4) rejects this common opinion arguing that, even in a

economic growth which are the subject of this section, stress the possibility of demand deficiency and the resulting unemployment and underemployment, and, hence, emphasize the importance of intersectoral commodity demand linkages. Contributions include those by Paul Rosenstein–Rodan (1943), Ragnar Nurkse (1953) and Richard Kahn (1972) in the debate on balanced versus un-balanced growth, by Michał Kalecki in his lectures delivered in Mexico City in 1953, and by Nicholas Kaldor in his writings on income distribution and the terms of trade between economies exporting primary commodities and those exporting manufactures.

2.3.1 Rosenstein–Rodan, Nurkse and Kahn: The Possibility of a Coordination Failure

In a low–income economy, the expansion of the industrial sector may be constrained more by the weak incentive to invest due to limited demand than by a limited capital supply. Although the expansion of employment and income in one sector will certainly lead to a rise in demand, the individual investor will rightly expect that this increase in demand is not only for her product, since individuals tend to be generalists in consumption and, accordingly, may not want to expand production capacity. However, if there was a *simultaneous* expansion of several sectors (in contrast to the expansion of a single sector), the expansion of production, employment and income in different sectors would create demand for all the sectors, finding markets for all the goods and all investment worthwhile. Clearly, when nothing happens to solve this coordination failure, the economy will remain trapped in a 'vicious circle'. This point was stressed in the early debate on balanced growth by Rosenstein–Rodan (1943) whose widely known doctrine of the 'big push'[27] underlined the importance of threshold factors and indivisibilities in the process of economic development. It is in this sense that Rosenstein–Rodan seems to combine Keynes's notion of effective demand and Smith's emphasis emphasis on the size of the market in case production is characterised by increasing returns to scale (Young, 1928; Stern, 1989).

Rosenstein–Rodan's argument was developed further by Nurkse (1953) and Kahn (1972). Emphasizing the savings potential contained in 'disguised unemployment', particularly in agriculture, both Nurkse and Kahn proposed to

---

so–called barter economy, aggregate demand for commodities may fall short of full employment output due to the existence of non–reproducable assets such as land. In case of excess demand for land and given that land prices and interest rates are sticky, the economy will adjust in a Keynesian fashion through a decline in the level of production. According to Rakshit, stickiness of interest rates is found to be an important feature of peasant societies.

[27] In short, it can be said that the main conclusion of Rosenstein–Rodan's (1943) paper rested on the internalisation of external economies through planning a big push. See Chakravarty (1983) for a more detailed review of his work.

effect the required big push in investment through redeploying unemployed and underemployed labour to the production of capital, while at the same time redistributing consumption goods from agriculture to the newly employed. Nurkse emphasized that, in a low–income economy, a rise in capital accumulation may be interpreted in terms of either machines or food advanced to workers – two concepts which are closely interrelated as was stressed by Chakravarty (1987:60–61). When capital formation is interpreted as *food advanced to workers*, which is a very classical concept (Kaldor, 1967), it may be possible to increase the capital stock *via* the generation of productive employment in a situation of un– or underemployment of labour. Kahn (1972) argued that what this requires is a *redistribution* of consumption from those who are fully employed, to those who would have otherwise been unemployed or imperfectly employed without a *rise* in the level of total consumption being required. The success of this strategy depends on whether it will be possible to make 'the more priviliged, including those who enjoy full employment anyhow, consume less, so that the available supply of consumption goods could be spread out more evenly, with the result that total employment could be greater, and the rate of development speeded up' (Kahn, 1972:157). Nurkse (1953) thought of redeploying surplus labour in overpopulated agriculture to the production of social overheads such as infrastructure, without affecting agricultural output and without significant additional investment. The wage costs of this new employment could be met by procuring the transferred labourers' share of consumption from agriculture. Under certain assumptions, this method of capital formation can be shown to involve only a relatively small marginal increase in the required rate of financial savings.[28]

In later years, Nurkse was especially emphatic in stressing the importance of *opportunities* for profitable investment as a critical factor affecting the rate of industrial accumulation, with the investment opportunities being dependent on demand conditions. He gave the following concise statement of the problem: 'The trouble is this: there is not a sufficient market for manufactured goods in a country where peasants, farm

---

[28] There has arisen a controversy, however, over the quantitative significance of this type of capital formation and whether it can be realised without organisational changes in farm production and without generating an inflationary rise in food prices. If the newly created employment does not provide enough wage goods for its own maintenance, then this will reduce the consumption fund of wage goods available to the already employed. This latter group may react by pushing up its real income and thus may set in motion an inflationary spiral. A further drawback of this approach is that, in practice, there are only few instances where labour becomes productive without the assistance of capital. An increase in productive employment will generally demand a simultaneous increase in capital stock unless there is excess capacity. In case the economy operates at full–capacity level, the increase in its consumption fund has to be supported by a corresponding increase in its capital stock and the problem of time preference (present versus future consumption) arises.

36

laborers and their families, comprising typically two–thirds to four–fifths of the population, are too poor to buy any factory products, or anything in addition to the little they already buy. There is a lack of real purchasing power, reflecting the low productivity of agriculture' (Nurkse, 1959:41–42). In Nurkse's view, there is a clear conflict between the emphasis on agriculture's net finance contribution to industrialisation and the emphasis on increased agricultural purchasing power as a stimulus to industrialisation. He argued that the only way to resolve this conflict is through a process of balanced growth between agriculture and manufacturing, stating that 'the relation between agriculture and manufacturing offers the clearest and simplest case of balance needed for economic growth. In a country where the peasantry is incapable of producing a surplus of food above its own subsistence needs there is little or no incentive for industry to establish itself: there is not a sufficient market for manufactured goods. Conversely, agricultural improvements may be inhibited by a lack of market for farm products if the non–farm sector of the economy is backward or underdeveloped. Each of the two sectors must try to move forward. If one remains passive the other is slowed down' (Nurkse, 1961:251).

Basu (1984) provides a formalisation[29] of Nurkse's argument involving a fixed nominal wage rate and producers in two sectors who select production levels depending on wage costs and expected marginal revenues from expanding sales down kinked demand curves (Taylor and Arida, 1988:165). In these circumstances, the economy may arrive at an equilibrium in which not all available labour is employed and it is possible to move toward fuller employment by increasing production in both sectors in line with consumers' tastes. Such an expansion is at the heart of 'balanced growth'. Taking up Rosenstein–Rodan's argument in favour of a 'big–push', Murphy et al. (1989a, 1989b) show the importance of income distribution and the size of population in generating demand sufficiently large to make manufacturing profitable. In their model, complementarities between industrialising sectors work through the market size effect. An imperfectly competitive economy can be moved from a low–level equilibrium to a higher–level one only through a big push strategy in which many investments take place simultaneously. For industrialisation to take place, benefits from this investment boom must be equally enough distributed to create a large enough market for domestic manufactures.

2.3.2   Kalecki: The Threat of a Wage Goods Constraint

Michał Kalecki's (1976) main concern is with the possibility for and

---

[29] It is important to note that Basu's formalisation misses the essential element of Nurkse's argument. Basu stresses imperfect competition as a cause of an unemployment equilibrium, whereas Nurkse (and Rosenstein–Rodan) stressed indivisibilities and increasing returns to scale.

macro–economic consequences of growth in a low–income economy in which capital is in short supply and labour is underutilised. In so doing, he distinguishes between a *fixprice* manufacturing sector in which the price is determined as a markup over prime (variable) costs and output is determined by demand (allowing for excess capacity), and a *flexprice* agricultural sector with output given in the short run (Kalecki, 1943). In the trade of food and raw materials, supply and demand are supposed to rule. In manufacturing, prices are set by the producer, the profit margin depending on the *degree of monopoly* prevailing in the industry. According to Robinson (1977:10–11), 'What it means is the absence of price competition (...). The weaker is price competition in any market, the greater is the freedom of firms to set prices in excess of costs.' In view of the uncertainties faced in the process of price fixing, industrial oligopolists are supposed to seek viable rules of competitive behaviour that will realise the potential joint surplus of their concentrated industry.[30] They implicitly agree not to chase shifts in demand with price changes, upward or downward. Price changes in response to cost changes might be more acceptable as a fair play among competitors, because changes in input prices are likely to be experienced and perceived rather uniformly by them all.[31] Assuming that prices are administered, the degree of markup rigidity is explained by the degree of industrial concentration. Note that the share of gross profits in the product of industry is determined by the level of the markup (Kalecki, 1933, 1938).

Kalecki also makes a clear distinction between the saving and spending patterns out of different categories of income, notably wage income and markup income. Wages will be fully spent as they are received, while profits will be partly spent and partly saved. Kalecki was one of the first to emphasize that finance has to be available before investment begins, while savings come afterwards. He asserted that 'a rise in the rate of investment will increase the flow of wages which will be spent, and if the accompanying rise in profits causes an increase in spending out of dividends, profits will rise by so much more. Thus there is an increase in retained profits equal to the increased

---

[30] According to Kalecki (1971:44), '[t]he firm must make sure that the price does not become too high in relation to prices of other firms, for this would drastically reduce sales, and that the price does not become too low in relation to its average prime cost, for this would drastically reduce the profit margin.'

[31] An alternative explanation of price rigidity is provided by the customer market view of price behaviour in which price rigidity is interpreted as resulting from implicit contracts between firms and customers. These contract introduce a concept of fairness based on price stability, particularly in relation to changes in demand. Customers are valuable to sellers because of their potential for repeat business, which depends on the customers' satisfaction with previous purchases and the expectation that good perfor- mance will be maintained. Stable prices benefit the buyer through economising on the expenses of shopping, trying out products, and otherwise engaging in transactions. See Okun (1981) and Chatterji (1989).

outlay on investment' (Robinson, 1977:13). In Kalecki's model, sectoral investment levels are commonly given in the short run and independent from the level of savings in the long run. With the causality running from investment to savings, the problem of demand appears.

According to Kalecki, capital accumulation may be hindered by the following three major obstacles: (i) inadequate incentives to the private sector to increase investment at a desirable rate; (ii) lack of physical resources to produce more investment goods; and (iii) inadequate supply of necessities or wage goods to meet the demand increase resulting from the rise in employment. Much of Kalecki's work deals with the third obstacle of inadequate supply of wage goods. He argued that this obstacle can, in principle, be overcome by 'balanced growth' which implies that for any rate of growth of real national income, there must be a corresponding rate of growth in the supply of necessities (food).[32] The growth rate of food supply must be at least such that it can feed the additional population at old levels and also meet the extra food demand arising from increasing per capita incomes. This is the *food balance* which was formulated by Kalecki (1960) in terms of a minimum unique rate of growth of agriculture needed to sustain a predetermined growth rate of the economy as a whole. If agricultural growth falls below this minimum rate, it becomes an effective constraint to overall growth.[33] This to happen requires that (a) agricultural production is price–inelastic, at least in the short run, and (b) the wage rate in terms of wage goods (*i.e.* the *real* wage) is rigid downwards at least in non–agriculture, even though there may exist surplus labour in agriculture (Dutta, 1988). It is essential that the lower limit of industrial wages is denominated (at least partly) in terms of the agricultural commodity. Both the price–inelasticity of agricultural supply and the downward wage rigidity in terms of the agricultural good set an upper bound on the industrial wage fund and hence, on industrial employment. Scarcity of wage goods can exercise an upward pressure on the wage rate relative to the price of the manufactured good. To the extent that this increase is not associated with an increase in productivity, it squeezes profitability in the industrial sectors, eventually retarding industrial investment and growth. Kalecki's argument is of particular importance in a situation in which nominal wages are linked to

---

[32] 'Inflationary pressures may be avoided by planning an increase in the supply of necessities matching the demand for them, which will be generated by the planned increase in national income' (Kalecki, 1976:25).

[33] Kalecki thus regarded the demand problem to be an integral aspect of the supply constraints traditionally argued to be operating in a low–income economy. Kalecki's approach formed the basis of Prabhat Patnaik's (1972) argument that, in India, a slowly growing agriculture would impose strict limits on the growth of a capitalist economy and that these limits would make their presence felt through engendering a cyclical process of growth in booms and slumps.

consumer (food) prices. It has been shown by Cardoso (1981) that the economy will suffer from persistent inflation, if the agricultural price responds less rapidly to excess demand than does the money wage rate to shortfalls of the real wage rate below some postulated target level. This situation applies, however, only to the short run, since in any economy, the observed responses to inflation would be reductions in food stocks or extra food imports (Taylor, 1983:162–66). Still, the existence of wage indexation can be seen to generate extra inflation in the economy since a consumer price increase is transmitted onto wages which, in turn, lead to a higher output price (Okun, 1975). Kalecki's diagnosis that inflationary pressure arising from the inelasticity of wage goods output could co–exist with deficient demand for non–wage goods (in particular, capital goods) is one of the earliest references to the phenomenom that came to be known as 'stagflation'.

Although the policy implications following from Kalecki's model resemble those derived by Nurkse, they differ in two ways. First, in Kalecki's model, growth of agricultural production is not only constrained by technical factors, but also by institutional factors.[34] Consequently, an increase in the growth rate of agricultural output is not possible without land reforms and other major institutional changes.[35] The second difference is that, within Kalecki's approach, a rise in the price of the agricultural good may result in general inflation, assuming that workers in an effort to maintain their real wages, push up nominal wages and industrial producers respond by raising prices.

2.3.3 Kaldor: The Working of a Forced Savings Mechanism

Nicholas Kaldor (1976) discusses the constraints to economic growth in a world economy which compel the system to run below the level of full capacity utilisation. His argument is of importance because he assumes the world economy to consist of primary producing countries (agriculture) on the one hand and industrial countries (industry) on the other. In this set–up, continued and stable economic growth requires that the growth of output of the two (groups of) countries or sectors should be 'at the required relationship with each other – that is to say, the growth of the saleable output of

---

[34] In the context of India, Kalecki (1976:19) identifies as institutional constraints such factors as the structure of property rights, 'the operation of many farms under a system of disguised tenancy without security of tenure" and the "inherent poverty of small peasants enhanced by their dependence on the merchants and moneylenders.'

[35] According to Kalecki (1976:149), to achieve the degree of economic security required for undertaking basic improvements on their holdings, '[a] government corporation should buy and sell agricultural produce at fixed prices throughout the year thereby eliminating seasonal fluctuations. [....] The government should also grant through appropriate channels short or medium term credits to replace the activities of the money lender.'

agriculture and mining should be in line with the growth of demand, which in turn reflects the growth of the secondary (and tertiary) sectors' (Kaldor, 1989a:518). Hence, the issue is whether the growth of labour productivity in industry and services and the growth of land productivity in agriculture and mining are in an appropriate relationship to one another, which need not imply proportionality.[36] In neoclassical theory, such balanced growth is ensured by the price mechanism, more particularly by relative prices or the terms of trade between agricultural commodities and manufactured goods.

To assess the efficiency of the terms of trade mechanism, Kaldor looks at the nature of the markets for agricultural products and manufactures. In the agricultural market, the price is given to the individual producer and consumer, and it moves in response to market pressures. The industrial price is administered, i.e. fixed by the producers themselves[37], and the adjustment of production to changes in demand takes place, independently of price changes, through a stock adjustment mechanism.[38] The industrial price is not market clearing[39], since normally the typical producer operates at less than full capacity. She can increase production without incurring higher costs per unit and frequently benefits from reduced costs resulting from an increase in volume of production (due to increasing returns to scale, see Young, 1928; Kaldor, 1986; Weitzman, 1982).

Due to the asymmetric nature of the agricultural commodity market and the market for manufactured goods, the terms of trade are not allowed to operate efficiently (i.e. to reflect relative sectoral profitability). While a *fall* in the agricultural price may be effective in moving the terms of trade against agriculture, an *increase* in the agricultural price is not likely to be nearly as effective in moving the terms of trade in the opposite direction, since an agricultural price rise is easily transmitted onto the industrial price due to its cost–determined nature. To this should be added a price–induced increase

---

[36] Strict numerical proportionality is not required since the income elasticity of consumption demand for food is less than unity and that for manufactured goods and services greater than unity. Kaldor's main point is, therefore, 'valid in the sense that there is a 'warranted' relationship between them at any particular level of real income' (Kaldor, 1989:257).

[37] It generally involves some firm, or firms, assuming the role of a price leader which other manufacturers follow. From the consumers' point of view, there is not much difference whether they buy from a high cost or a low cost firm, the differences in efficiency are reflected, not in a difference in price (for goods of similar quality), but in a difference in profits per unit of sale of different producers.

[38] A fall in demand leads to an undesired (or involuntary, as the Keynesian term goes) accumulation of stocks, and *vice versa* if demand exceeds supply. The market thus operates via changes in quantities rather than in prices.

[39] This is not 'market clearing' in the neoclassical sense, since the actual production of the representative seller is below her optimum level of production at the prevailing price – i.e. below the level of production that would maximise her profits. See Kaldor (1989:259).

in wages resulting from the reluctance of (industrial) workers to accept a cut in their standard of living. It is not difficult to see why a shift of the terms of trade in favour of agriculture is not likely to last for long.[40] The important contrast between the two sectors resides in the fact that technical progress in agriculture and mining tends to get passed on to consumers in the secondary sector in lower prices, whereas in the industrial sector its benefits are retained within the sector through higher wages and profits (Kaldor, 1989:264). Hence, the market mechanism emerges as a highly inefficient regulator for securing continuing balanced growth between the two sectors. A fall in agricultural supply which should lead to a rise in the relative agricultural price and, hence, to an increase in agricultural supplies may result instead in inflation of the industrial price which will (wholly or partly) offset the improvement in the terms of trade, and lead to general recession in the (world) economy.

Kaldor's argument has been formalised by Molana and Vines (1989) in terms of a North–South model, and by Targetti (1985) and Thirlwall (1986) within the context of a growth model of an economy with two complementary sectors (agriculture and manufacturing). Thirlwall's paper provides an good illustration of the implications of Kaldor's approach, relevant within an agriculture–industry context. Thirlwall assumes that there exists surplus labour in agriculture so that the supply curve of labour to industry is infinitely elastic at some conventional wage. Industrial income is distributed over capitalists and workers classes of which the former are assumed to save and invest and the latter to wholly consume their incomes (see Kaldor, 1956). The industrial price is determined by a markup over variable costs. Agricultural growth depends on technical progress through the installation of capital goods obtained from the industrial sector in exchange for the agricultural surplus. The lower the industrial price is in terms of agricultural output, the faster will be the rate of growth of agricultural output and real income. A rise in industrial investment will lead to a rise in the markup rate (in line with the extra aggregate demand for industrial goods), and the nominal price of the industrial good. In response, the agricultural sector may consider increasing its supply at the existing nominal price, which will amount to *forced saving* in agriculture to finance its investment. If it resists such forced saving by attempting to raise the nominal agricultural price, the burden will fall on industrial workers who become the victim of Kaldor's forced saving mechanism. If, however, there is real wage resistance (as suggested by Kaldor), there exists a real danger of

---

[40] In Kaldor's (1989a:521) words: 'The industrial sector with its superior market power, resists any compression of its real income by countering the rise in commodity prices through a cost–induced inflation of industrial prices.'

inflation.[41]

2.4   *The Neoclassical Approach: Full Employment, Pareto Efficiency, and Price Distortions*

Mainly in reaction to the classical approach, neoclassically oriented economists have argued that the marginal product of agricultural labour is not zero, and that disguised unemployment and surplus labour do not exist. These criticisms were based on the 'efficient–but–poor' view of traditional agriculture associated with Theodore W. Schultz (1964) and others. The 'neoclassical' theory of economic growth in a dual economy consisting of agriculture and industry was first elaborated by Dale W. Jorgenson (1961). I also include contributions by J.M. Hornby (1968) and Kelley *et al.* (1972).

2.4.1   *The 'Efficient–but–Poor' Hypothesis*

In the neoclassical approach, it is assumed that agriculture – irrespective of whether it is 'traditional' or 'modern' – is subject to the dictates of perfect competition and Paretian efficiency. Farmers are viewed as constantly and efficiently maximising their utility as consumers and their profits as producers. Markets are believed to function impersonally, *i.e.* any individual can enter any market to buy the goods and services that she needs and to sell those that she produces on the same terms as any other individual. As a result, due to competition, the same price rules throughout the market for any good or service. Implicit and explicit markets are believed to exist to ensure full employment of all resources and their efficient utilisation leaving no room for surplus labour. This being the case, it follows that peasant farmers are poor, not because they utilise their resources inefficiently, but because of restrictions in the kinds and quantities of resources they command (the 'efficient but poor' concept). From this it can be inferred that, because peasant farmers are 'allocatively efficient', *i.e.* they are doing the best they possibly can with the resources at their disposal, they cannot raise their output except through technical innovation. It is claimed that the 'efficient but poor' hypothesis is supported by the results of a number of

---

[41] Thirlwall argues that diminishing returns in agriculture cause the terms of trade to move progressively against industry over the long run. This tendency can only be offset by increased availability of land and/or land–saving technical progress. According to Canning (1988:463), with increasing returns to scale in the industrial sector (a very Kaldorian characteristic), diminishing returns in agriculture need not be a barrier to growth. Economic growth may be unlimited, despite ever increasing demand for agricultural products and in the absence of technical progress in agriculture, 'if the increasing returns in the capital goods industries are sufficient to outweigh the diminishing returns to capital in agriculture.'

studies of traditional agriculture including the ones summarised in Schultz (1964).[42]

The 'efficient–but–poor' hypothesis has two important implications. First, given that the farmers are doing the best they can do with the available resources, the only way of improving agricultural performance is by equipping them with more productive resources. In other words, a technical revolution is essential. Second, (relative) prices are important for transforming agriculture, not only in generating short–run supply responses, but also in conditioning the investment climate and expectations of all decision–makers in the rural economy about the future profitability of activities in the sector. Relative factor scarcities which are reflected in relative factor prices, are held to (partly) determine the adoption and dissemination of new technology.[43,44] It is because of their function of price discovery that markets are important. Prices are regarded as signals to producers and consumers to adjust their behaviour towards equilibrium which is believed to be of enormous importance in inherently unstable, disequilibrated agricultural markets (Timmer, 1988).

In the belief that both private and public resources employed in agriculture are highly responsive to (relative) price signals, 'unfavourable' prices for agriculture (distorted by government intervention) are generally held responsible for slow agricultural growth. The key argument is that by depressing producer prices and thus distorting producer incentives, governments have prevented agriculture from growing as rapidly as would have been technically possible, given current scientific knowledge. Two types of distorsions are generally reported (Timmer, 1986): the underpricing of agricultural goods relative to world prices on the one hand, and the underpricing of agricultural goods relative to all other prices (including input prices) in the domestic economy on the other. Thus, 'for want of profitable incentives, farmers are not making the necessary investments, including the purchase of superior inputs' (Schultz, 1978:7).

---

[42] See Ghatak and Ingersent (1984) for a review and critical evaluation of these studies.

[43] A simple but often overlooked fact is that, for farmers to participate in the benefits of technical change, not only must the new technology be workable on their (often small) farms, but they must also be able to purchase the input that carries the new technology, and to finance possible complementary fixed capital investments (Timmer, 1988:312).

[44] Hayami and Ruttan (1985) go even further, making the generation of new technologies dependent on relative prices. In their view, 'induced innovation' leads scientists to develop mechanical technologies to raise labour productivity in labour–scarce economies, whereas scientists in land–scarce economies, such as those in Asia, develop biological–chemical technologies to raise output per hectare.

2.4.2   Neoclassical Two-Sector Growth Models:
The Importance of Supply-Side Factors

Schultz's emphasis on full employment, farmers' rationality and the superiority of market prices as a coordination mechanism led to the generation of a number of neoclassical two-sector growth models including those of Jorgenson (1961, 1966, 1967), Hornby (1968), and Kelley, Williamson and Cheetham (1972). These models are based on the hypothesis that full employment of the labour force is guaranteed by a flexible real wage rate. There is thus no gap between the industrial wage and the social opportunity cost of industrial employment, which means that withdrawal of workers from agriculture by industry necessarily reduces agricultural output (Marglin, 1966). Profit maximisation is assumed in both sectors. Supply and demand are determined by technology and the preferences of consumers.

Dale W. Jorgenson (1961, 1967) modified the original Lewis model to allow for the neoclassical determination of the real wage rate. He considered an economy in which agriculture produces with given land and labour endowments under diminishing returns to scale and industry produces with accumable capital according to a constant-returns-to-scale Cobb–Douglas production function. In the manufacturing sector, capitalists hire labour to produce in order to maximise profits. All profits are saved and invested. Jorgenson further assumed exogenously given rates of technological change for both sectors, a constant rate of growth of population (after an initial phase in which it increased with per capita income), and zero income and price elasticities of the demand for food. The growth rate of agricultural production is dependent on agricultural labour productivity, (neutral) technical progress, and population growth.

In Jorgenson's model, the necessary and sufficient condition for the emergence of a positive and growing agricultural surplus and, therefore, a necessary and sufficient condition for sustained economic growth is that the rate of growth of per capita agricultural output is positive. This, in turn, requires that $\alpha - \beta\varepsilon > 0$ – that is, that the rate of technical progress in agriculture (α) exceeds the exogenously determined rate of population growth (ε) multiplied by the elasticity of output with respect to land (β). An industrial labour force comes into being when agricultural output per head attains a certain critical value – that is, when agricultural output attains the minimum level necessary for population to grow at its maximum rate. The non-agricultural sector is economically viable only if there is a positive and growing agricultural surplus. The terms of trade play a passive role: they adjust to equate the income per head in the two sectors. Hence, the neoclassical model of Jorgenson points out that economic growth may be constrained by the rate of release of labour from agriculture. This conclusion is, of course, diametrically opposed to Lewis's view in which the transfer of surplus labour to the non–agricultural sector is limited by the demand for labour, which in turn is limited by the rate of industrial capital accumulation.

However, if $\alpha - \beta \varepsilon \leq 0$ – that is, if technological change in agriculture is not rapid enough relative to population growth, given the value of the elasticity of output with respect to land – the agricultural sector can never produce a food surplus and release labour for industry, and the (purely agricultural) economy will settle at a low–level equilibrium trap. To escape from this trap, changes in the rate of introduction of new techniques of agricultural production are required. In view of this result, Jorgenson attaches much importance to accelerating the rate of technical progress in agriculture – which had also been suggested by Schultz (1964). Jorgenson (1967) also emphasizes productivity growth in agriculture, analysing the rate of technical progress that would have to occur in the sector for it to produce sufficient food to meet industrial demand.

The linked problems of agriculture's marketed surplus and net finance contribution have been analysed in an optimising framework under conditions of steady growth by Hornby (1968). In this open–economy model, government sets the intersectoral terms of trade and effectively controls the industrial surplus. Via manipulation of the terms of trade, government influences the allocation of investable resources among agriculture, capital goods and industrial consumption goods so as to maximise growth. Optimal policy involves (i) relatively low food prices, but significant capital transfers to agriculture when the price elasticity of marketed surplus is small; here, free foreign trade is far from optimal; but (ii) if the elasticity is large, only little investment in agriculture is needed (Rao, 1986).

Kelley, Williamson and Cheetham's (1972) model is a generalisation of Jorgenson's model in the sense that their framework, with two exceptions, can be reduced to Jorgenson's by making restrictive assumptions on specific parameter values. In contrast to Jorgenson, in the model by Kelley et al., both sectors utilise labour and capital in production, although the specific manner in which these inputs are combined is different between sectors, and, second, the rate of population growth is endogenously determined.[45] The rates

---

[45] Important differences in assumptions on the parameter values include the following. First, Jorgenson assumed a Cobb–Douglas production function in both sectors, while Kellley et al. use a CES production function, with the substitution elasticity between capital and labour assumed to be larger than unity in agriculture and smaller than unity in industry. Second, Jorgenson assumes that the demand parameters are identical between sectors and, further, that all consumer expenditures above subsistence are devoted to goods produced in non–agriculture. In contrast, Kelley et al. assume that consumer demands are given by a linear expenditure system with different demand parameters for agricultural and non–agricultural consumers. Third, in the Jorgenson model, the non–agricultural wage and the agricultural opportunity cost (which includes the returns to labour and land) are equated, while in the Kelley et al. formulation capital returns and labour returns are both

of technical progress are exogenously given. Given perfect factor markets, labour will move from agriculture (where the amount of capital per worker and average productivity are relatively low) to industry and services (where capital per worker and average productivity are relatively high). Commodity markets are cleared by commodity prices, factor markets clear through wage and rental rates adjustment. The income earned on comparable types of labour and capital will be same in the two sectors, since in the long run labour and capital will be used in the sector where they earn the highest return. However, due to the inclusion of capital in the agricultural production function, their model has many feasible growth paths (for any given set of parameter values and initial conditions), while Jorgenson's model generates changes on a single time path.

With the help of their model, Kelley *et al.* analyse the effects of different patterns of (agricultural and non–agricultural) consumer demand – given full employment, constant returns to scale in both sectors, and the absence of foreign trade. They find that, if the income elasticity of demand for agricultural products is positive but less than unity, an acceleration in the rate of capital accumulation is sufficient to ensure GNP growth, industrialisation and urbanisation. According to their results, demand plays an important role in influencing the pattern (but not the *rate*) of growth and industrialisation through changes in consumer tastes (*i.e.* in parameter values), while an increase in the economy's savings parameters considerably raises the growth rates of capital stock and per capita output. Kelley *et al.* claim that the empirical validity of their neoclassical model is confirmed by a comparison of their model results with Japanese data drawn from the Meiji period.

2.5 *Summary and Policy Implications*

Starting from the *Tableau Economique* of the Physiocrats, there is a long tradition within economics, emphasizing asymmetries, both in production and in economic organisation, between agriculture and non–agriculture and their implications for economic growth (Ranis, 1988). In this chapter, I have classified major contributions within this tradition into three main approaches, depending on what they assumed to be the main growth constraint. At one extreme lie the *neoclassical* theories of economic growth in which the necessary supply adjustments during the growth process are brought about by the price mechanism, at the other extreme are the *post – Keynesian* theories which take into account some of the technological and institutional

---

equalised between sectors in equilibrium. Finally, Jorgenson assumes the rates of depreciation to be zero; in Kelley *et al.* they are positive.

constraints that arise in a growing economy. In between lie a number of important theories of supply–constrained growth which are more *classical* in spirit. Table 2.1 (below) summarizes the main assumptions underlying these three approaches.

The main presumption on which both the classical as well as the neoclassical approach is based, is that economic growth in a low income economy is exclusively dependent on supply–side factors. In particular, it is held that 'as a low income economy, in general, is one characterised by a low volume of capital stock, relative to labour, the rate of return on investment on the margin must be necessarily high thus helping to keep the inducement to invest at a high level' while, at the same time, '.... the ratio of consumption to income must be necessarily high, leaving very little scope for savings.' (Chakravarty, 1984:26). Taken together, these two presumptions imply that the level of aggregate demand will normally exceed the level of aggregate potential output. In these circumstances, the economy's growth rate depends on the rate of growth of its capital stock which, in turn, is constrained by the savings rate (investment being savings–determined). Hence, the economy is believed to operate subject to a *savings constraint*, which means that, initially, the savings rate is much too low relative to the investment effort envisaged.

The classical approach stresses the contribution which agriculture can make to relaxing this constraint, either through a net finance contribution to industrial investment or through a transfer of its labour surplus to industry. Its essential features may be summarised as follows. First, savings which originate mainly (or only) out of profit income, are all used for investment purposes by the same individuals (the capitalists) who save. Second, there exists surplus labour with a zero (or nearly zero) marginal productivity in agriculture. Finally, the real wage rate is assumed fixed, because it is 'institutionally determined' in terms of agricultural goods, and remains fixed so long as there is disguised unemployment in the agricultural sector.

The savings constraint is interpreted by neoclassicals as a limitation on capital formation arising from the unwillingness to defer current consumption. Emphasis is put here on the lack of adequate foresight (Chakravarty, 1987:92). In the neoclassical view, the economy always operates at its full capacity level, with the full employment of all factors of production ensured by adjustments in relative factor prices, leaving no room for surplus labour in agriculture. The real wage rate is assumed to be variable rather than fixed and the marginal productivity of labour is assumed to be always positive so that agricultural labour is never redundant. Savings–investment balance is established by adjustments in the rate of interest. On empirical grounds, the neoclassical approach initially claimed superiority over the classical model, in response to which it was developed, although the Japanese evidence which was cited in support of the neoclassical approach has been strongly

Table 2.1
Classification of Theoretical Approaches

Classical Approach
Production Conditions
Agriculture operates under diminishing returns to scale,
industry under constant returns to scale.
Labour Market
The agricultural labour market does not clear, the agricultural
wage being institutionally determined. The industrial labour
market clears, the real industrial wage being determined by
marginal productivity. Since the industrial labour supply is
infinitely elastic at the wage corresponding to the marginal
product, it remains constant – at a level slightly above the
agricultural wage.
Commodity Markets
The agricultural and industrial prices clear their markets.
Capital Market
There is no 'open' capital market, since all savings are used for
investment by the same individuals. Say's law is assumed to hold.
Only capitalists save (out of profits). Accumulation takes place
only in industry.

Neoclassical Approach
Production Conditions
Agriculture operates under diminishing returns to scale, industry
produces under constant returns to scale. Kelley, Williamson
and Cheetham assume constant returns to scale in both sectors.
Labour Market
The agricultural and industrial labour markets are price–
clearing, given technology and consumer preferences. With factor
prices being flexible, the economy operates always at full
employment.
Commodity Markets
The agricultural and industrial commodity markets are price–
clearing, given technology and consumer preferences.
Capital Market
Savings–investment balance is established through interest rate
adjustments. Hence, investment may be regarded as being
determined by savings and Say's law is believed to hold true.

Post–Keynesian Approach
Production Conditions
Agriculture operates under diminishing returns to scale, industry
produces under constant or increasing returns to scale.
Labour Market
The agricultural labour market does not clear, the real
agricultural wage is institutionally determined. The industrial
labour market also does not clear; there is nominal wage
indexation in the industrial sector.
Commodity Markets
The agricultural market is price–clearing. The industrial price is
administered, *i.e.* determined as a mark–up over variable cost.
The industrial market clears through quantity–adjustment, with
industrial supply being determined by demand.
Capital Market
The interest rate is not able to balance savings supply and
investment demand. Say's law does not apply. Income distribution
(with income being distributed between wages and profits and the
propensity to save out of profits being higher than out of wages)
is important in bringing about savings–investment balance (forced
savings).

criticised.[46] The neoclassical approach stresses the fact that, over time, when people and resources have time to shift in and out of agriculture, supply–rigidities disappear and agricultural supply becomes quite elastic. Supply of and demand for agriculture's produce will be balanced by the agricultural–industrial terms of trade which merely reflect relative sectoral productivities. Any shortages or slacks resulting from deviations from equilibrium growth are removed by price adjustments ensuring convergence to the equilibrium growth path. In the neoclassical approach, not much has been retained of the distinct institutional and technological features of the agricultural sector, distinguished by the classical approach.

The classical and neoclassical approaches have in common the assumption that Say's law holds and consequently the problem of demand deficiency does not arise. Production growth in non–agriculture is capacity–determined and all that is needed to ensure sustained growth is to increase the rate of industrial investment and, hence, the savings rate in the economy. Agriculture does not support industry by providing a market for its product, since the industrial sector has no market problem. This particular feature was already noted by Johnston and Mellor (1961)[47]. Only the negative impact of a worsening terms of trade for industry on the rate of industrial capital accumulation is explicitly recognised, but its positive effect on the demand for industrial goods resulting from higher agricultural incomes is neglected.[48]

Post–Keynesians have stressed the tension between agriculture's role as a source of surplus for industry versus its role as a source of effective demand. Because, at low levels of income, agriculture provides a potential mass market for manufactures, investment in agriculture is seen as *complementary* to raising industrial accumulation. The post–Keynesian approach has been concerned more with the short run in which agricultural supply is

---

[46] In particular, Marglin (1966) showed that some of the results which Jorgenson claimed for his model and which, he argued, better fitted the data for Japan were a consequence of his use of the Cobb–Douglas production function, assuming an elasticity of substitution between labour and capital of unity, while Dixit (1973) argued that Jorgenson mistakenly compared the long–run results of the neoclassical model to the short–run results of the classical model.

[47] They remark (1961:580) that 'one of the simplifying assumptions of the (Lewis) two sector model is that expansion of the capitalist sector is limited only by a shortage of capital. Given this assumption, an increase in rural net cash income is not a stimulus to industrialisation but an obstacle to expansion of the capitalist sector.'

[48] According to Targetti (1985:81), '[Lewis's] model is, in fact, unable to show that – in a closed market – the excess of industrial output over the investment in the sector must be sold to the agricultural sector. The terms of trade between the two sectors must play a double role, the first being to extract surplus from agriculture to industry, and the second being to, at the same time, create agricultural income which will be transformed into industrial demand. If it does not work properly, the phenomena of stagnation and inflation ("stagflation") can arise.'

believed to be relatively price inelastic. The different contributions to the post–Keynesian approach more or less share the following three characteristics. First, the rate of interest is not able to balance investment demand and savings supply. Instead, investment–savings balance is established through a change in the level of income and/or a shift in income distribution. In either case, investment may fall short of the full–employment level of saving. Second, the presence of 'true' uncertainty[49], increasing returns to scale and imperfect information in industry give rise to the adoption of specific behavioural rules including mark–up pricing and wage indexation, which contribute to reducing uncertainty and transaction costs. Relative prices will cease to be perfectly flexible and factors will no longer be perfectly mobile and substitutable between the two sectors. Finally, income distribution is important in determining the level of domestic saving (Kalecki, Kaldor) and the size of the market, particularly in the presence of increasing returns to scale (Rosenstein–Rodan, Nurkse, and Kahn). Taken together, these assumptions imply that the factor markets and the commodity markets are not price–clearing and quite different mechanisms come into play in order to achieve macro equilibrium. In a situation of less than full employment, the post–Keynesian approach emphasizes the importance of quantity clearing instead of price clearing, through Keynesian multiplier effects by which changes in aggregate demand lead to changes in aggregate supply, and/or Kaldorian distributional effects by which changes in the distribution of income lead to changes in aggregate savings (the forced savings mechanism). According to post–Keynesians, agricultural growth can augment the rate of economic growth if it serves to increase the size of the domestic market. When there exists a fairly rigid and large demand for the agricultural commodity and when its share in the average consumer's budget is large, a fall in the agricultural price will lead to substantial reallocations of budget expenditures. The resulting shift in consumer spending may have a major direct impact on total demand and utilisation of (industrial) capacity. If the inducement to invest in private industry hinges on the level of aggregate demand via profitability and capacity utilisation, then a rise in the size of the domestic market will provide a further stimulus to industrial output and investment.

Not surprisingly, the (agricultural) policy implications drawn from each of the three approaches differ considerably. For neoclassical economists, there is no need to treat agriculture differently from any other sector in the

---

[49] Post–Keynesians emphasize that many economic decisions have to be made in circumstances in which there is no information regarding future prospects and in which, therefore, there is thus no basis on which to form any calculable probability whatever (*i.e.* neither an objective nor a subjective probability distribution can be established). See Davidson (1991) for a discussion of probability theory in the light of uncertainty.

economy. Because farmers (as other economic agents) are held to behave in response to price signals – raising output and marketed surplus as prices rise and curbing supplies as prices fall – there is no rationale for an agriculture–industry distinction. Policy recommendations based on the neoclassical approach are primarily concerned with 'getting prices right'. Relative price distortions, as measured by deviations of domestic market prices from appropriately defined border prices, inevitably lead to a reduction in economic welfare because of dead–weight efficiency losses. Providing better incentives to agricultural producers is mainly a matter of permitting foreign prices to be more freely transmitted to the domestic economy. No policy efforts on behalf of agriculture's own modernisation are needed, because, in a market–oriented economy, relative prices will take care of the generation and dissemination of appropriate technical and institutional change which will carry the agricultural transformation further. In response to a few well–defined 'market failures' (Scitovsky, 1954)[50], government intervention may be required, but, in general, it will only lead to distorted relative prices which result in welfare losses – both in the short and long run.

In classical theories, manufacturing is viewed as the 'engine of growth' as it is characterised by economies of scale or economies of specialisation. Given the strategic role of manufacturing, government's role should be to direct resources into that sector, at a rate well above that indicated by the market rate of return on industrial investment, through a transfer of investable resources from agriculture to industry, at a rate well above the one which would have materialised without public intervention. Policy instruments which can be used to this end, include the intersectoral terms of trade which can be manipulated against agriculture, keeping effective protection low or negative for agriculture because of high nominal industrial protection, and direct taxation of agricultural income (Preobrazhensky and Lewis). Classicals were well aware of the fact that manipulation of the terms of trade against agriculture may negatively affect marketed surplus to the extent that the wage goods constraint on industrial investment becomes operative. According to Fei and Ranis, this situation may be avoided by a process of *balanced* growth through technological change and capital accumulation in both sectors (pushing outward both supply and demand curves for labour in the industrial sector). This will sustain investment incentives in both sectors, by leaving unchanged the intersectoral terms of trade, and by ensuring that agriculture will supply enough labour to satisfy the expansion of industry at a constant real wage.

---

[50] Scitovsky emphasizes externalities that prevent price signals from leading the economy to full employment. His main examples include economies of scale and monopoly power in trade.

Post–Keynesians regard industry's role in economic development to be pre–eminent, but nevertheless think agriculture to be a binding constraint. This is because if, at low levels of income, industrialisation raises the demand for agricultural products more than agricultural supply is able to expand, the attempt to increase industrial capital accumulation may fail through a terms–of–trade induced industrial profit squeeze. Only if agricultural supply is relatively elastic, this type of industrial capital accumulation can proceed a fair way from a low initial base without getting aborted through a price increase (Chakravarty, 1987:61). Given the asymmetries in price and wage formation in both sectors and given the low level of the price elasticity of agricultural supply, the market mechanism can only be relatively inefficient as compared to government intervention and regulation in coordinating investment plans between sectors and over time, redeploying surplus agricultural labour, generating required technological and institutional change, and preventing general inflation through agricultural price stabilisation. Post–Keynesians recognise the need for public action, especially for the restructuring of the agricultural sector, and often call for an expanded programme of public agricultural investment, aimed at improving and expanding agriculture's infrastructure including irrigation and electrification. Also of particular importance are expenditures for extension services or agricultural research and education that broaden the range of alternative production possibilities available to farmers and strengthen their capacity to make and execute decisions on the basis of more adequate knowledge of agricultural technology. Only then will reasonably high growth in agriculture also expand opportunities for industrialisation.

**INDIAN ECONOMIC GROWTH, 1950–1990:
SELECTED ISSUES**

3.1   *Introduction*

Taking the classification of theoretical approaches put forward in the
previous chapter as frame of reference, I try, in this chapter, to bring out
certain structural features of India's economy which are of relevance to the
formulation of the general equilibrium model. In so doing, it is pertinent to
ask how such a structure came into being, particularly against the background
of the systematic development strategy pursued by the country over the last
forty years. Therefore, this chapter discusses major aspects of Indian
economic growth and policy during the period 1950–51 to 1989–90, paying
particular attention to issues of agricultural policy. Section 3.2 considers
the period of the first Three Five Year Plans (1950–51 to 1964–65) which saw
the initiation of India's planned development strategy. The mid–1960s during
which the growth process was temporarily arrested, witnessed important policy
changes, particularly in the field of agriculture. These policy changes may be
interpreted as reflecting a shift from a classical approach, as embodied in
the Mahalanobis model, towards a more neoclassical approach, emphasizing
indirect controls such as fiscal and monetary incentives and (agricultural)
price policy. Section 3.3 deals with these policy changes and with macro–
economic aspects of the growth performance of the economy during the post–
1965–66 period. Section 3.4 discusses a number of important structural
aspects. Section 3.5 concludes.

3.2   The Nehru-Mahalanobis Strategy[1] of Growth: 1950-51 to 1964-65

In examining the country's economic structure, it is important to bear in mind that this structure has evolved over the years under the influence of the development strategy which started with the first Five Year Plans in the 1950s. In this period, Indian planning succeeded in bringing about a significant diversification of the industrial structure, avoiding uncontrollable inflationary pressures and large-scale foreign borrowing.

At the time the First Five Year Plan (1950-55) was launched, the economy was experiencing a severe food shortage. Not surprisingly, the First Plan[2] gave priority to agricultural growth and particularly to augmenting food production. A number of short term regulatory measures were taken to meet the acute food shortage including such measures as food procurement and demarcation of food zones.[3] A Grow More Food Campaign was initiated aimed at switching from cash crops to food crops, intensifying cultivation of land already under cultivation (through irrigation, better seed and manure and improved farming practices), and expanding area under cultivation.[4] Following the rapid increase in agricultural production due to a series of good monsoons in the early 1950s, attention shifted from agriculture to industry in the Second Plan. Planners argued that a change in the existing occupational pattern in the direction of greater employment in the industrial sector and in services was necessary to tackle the associated phenomena of mass poverty and unemployment effectively (Mahalanobis, 1955). Their view was based on long-term projections of national and per capita income, derived from the

---

[1] See Chakravarty (1987), Chapter 2, for a discussion of the genesis of the Nehru-Mahalanobis development strategy and an explanation of the structural constraints facing the policy makers in the early 1950s.

[2] Goals set for the First Plan (1950-55) were rather modest because there was a need of meeting the problems arising out of the war and partition. The goals included (i) increasing the level of national income from Rs. 91.1 billion (at 1952-53 prices) in 1950-51 to over Rs. 100 billion in 1955-56 (implying an annual growth rate of 2.1 per cent); and (ii) increasing the rate of investment in the economy from 4.9 per cent in 1950-51 to above 7 per cent of national income at the end of the plan period. Significantly, both goals were achieved without a price rise.

[3] Zoning refers to administrative measures that restrict the movement of foodgrains by private traders across a specified boundary, particularly between surplus states and deficit states, leaving scope only for government procurement and trade. The degree of restriction varied from period to period and between groups of states. The rationale for these restrictions was that they enabled the government to procure grain in the surplus states at a lower price than the price that would have prevailed if private traders had been free to transfer the foodgrains. In 1977, zoning was abolished.

[4] The results of this particular campaign were, however, disappointing in terms of growth of foodgrain production and damaging for the production of cotton and jute.

variant of the Harrod–Domar model underlying the First Plan.[5] Unlike the original model, the First Plan model assumed that actual output would be equal to potential output (or, alternatively, that the actual rate of savings would be equal to the warranted rate of savings). The projections showed that, to achieve a doubling of per capita income by 1973–74, the step–up in investment had to be larger in the Second (and Third) Plan periods than in later periods. Hence, the real break with the past had to come with the Second Plan (1956–61) which saw the articulation of the Nehru–Mahalanobis growth strategy. The Second Plan had the following four objectives:

(a) a sizeable increase in national income (of 5 per cent per annum) so as to raise the level of living;
(b) rapid industrialisation with particular emphasis on the growth of basic and heavy industries;
(c) a large expansion of employment opportunities; and
(d) reduction of inequalities in income and wealth and a more even distribution of economic power.

Planners believed that these goals could only be achieved by according primacy to industrialisation over agricultural development. They assumed that 'whereas agriculture was subject to secular diminishing returns, industrialisation would allow surplus labour currently underemployed in agriculture to be more productively employed in industries operated according to increasing returns to scale' (Chakravarty, 1987:9). Hence, to break the barriers to productivity increases, Indian planners advocated rapid diversification of the economy through a policy–induced acceleration of industrial growth.[6] In terms of the classification put forward in the previous chapter, the model embodied in the Second Plan – the so–called Mahalanobis model – belongs to the classical approach, as it was based on the presumptions that economic growth in a low–income economy is primarily supply–constrained by the inadequate size and composition of the initial material capital stock, and that capital accumulation is limited by the low capacity to save. Consequently, the principal policy questions were viewed as those pertaining to increasing the rate of savings[7] as well as bringing about its conversion into an appropriate mix of capital goods, consistent with a process of accelerated growth. It should be noted that Mahalanobis's model was in no way concerned with the

---

[5] See Bhagwati and Chakravarty (1969) for a survey of Indian plan models.

[6] According to Dantwala (1986:2), at that time, policymakers took care to emphasize that 'in an under–developed economy with low yields in agriculture, there is no real conflict between agricultural and industrial development. One cannot go far without the other; the two are complementary.'

[7] For the required level of investment to materialise in a non–inflationary way, the level of domestic savings had to increase. Realistically, planners sought an acceleration in the growth process through depressing incremental consumption rather than attempting to reduce the absolute level of consumption. In other words, the escape route from a low level equilibrium situation called for a marginal savings rate substantially higher than the average savings rate. See Chakravarty (1974).

Keynesian problem of demand deficiency, as he assumed the marginal propensity to save to equal the marginal propensity to invest. The latter variable was not treated as a behavioural variable, but rather as a variable reflecting the allocational decisions of the planners (Chakravarty, 1976). The idea was that the public sector (in which industrialisation was intended to take place) was going to be largely self–financing in the sense that accelerated public investment, financed by public savings, was likely to create large profits which were to be re–invested in the state sector.

In fact, the Second Plan model can be seen as a variant of the Lewis model. On the one hand, the variation relates to the two–sector disaggregation introduced by Mahalanobis (1955) who, adapting Marx's two departmental scheme, distinguished between capital goods producing capital goods, and capital goods engaged in the production of consumer goods. Mahalanobis argued that, from the point of view of maximising intertemporal welfare in a nearly closed economy, inter–sectoral consistency over time demanded that the productive capacity of the capital goods producing industries would have to rise at an accelerated rate in order to convert the increase in savings into additional real investment (Chakravarty, 1987:12). In other words, the basis for industrialisation was in building ahead of demand in the capital goods sector, because, according to the Planning Commission (1956:25), 'if indus-trialisation is to be rapid enough, the country must aim at developing basic industries and industries which make machines to make the machines needed for further development.' In effect, the Nehru–Mahalanobis strategy was primarily a strategy of industrialisation which hoped to succeed by forging strong industrial linkages, both backward and forward. This type of industrialisation could not be left to the market as private investment would not come forth in sectors which were essential to the accelerated growth of the economy, but which required large–scale investments with long gestation lags. Therefore, key sectors such as iron and steel, coal, power, mineral oils, machine tools, and transport were made the exclusive domain of public sector enterprises. A massive step–up in public investment was planned to close such infrastructural gaps as could hamper industrial growth, and to contribute to the growth of the protected home market, directly through purchases of commodities and in-directly through the creation of additional incomes. Further, to ensure that private investment funds would be utilised in accordance with the invest-ment–mix corresponding to the planned pattern of industrialisation, a wide range of indirect controls on the capacity creation of the private corporate sector were introduced. The active role allotted to the state by Mahalanobis is the second difference between the Second Plan model and Lewis's model in which the capitalists in the 'modern' sector are the main actors (Chakravarty, 1987:14). In fact, in both models, it is assumed that investments are savings–determined, but, while Lewis justified this assumption by pointing out that all profits are saved and invested by the urban capitalists, Mahalanobis argued that the profits made by public enterprises were to be saved and converted into investment by the government.

Apart from its reliance on the profits of public enterprises, the Nehru–Mahalanobis strategy, from the outset, relied on foreign aid as a source of investment finance.[8] To take care of the growing requirements of capital goods and heavy intermediates, it was, according to Chakravarty (1979:1229), decided 'to follow a two–pronged strategy which relied on the building up of a capital goods base at an accelerated rate while relying on an inflow of foreign aid during an intervening period.' It was generally felt that the supply elasticities of Indian exportables were rather low as the infrastructural support base was not adequate enough for a major export thrust. Besides, the balance of payments position was such that it was impossible to import the necessary 'machines' by increasing export earnings without excessively depressing the country's terms of trade. Based on this elasticity pessimism,[9] the possibilities for rapidly building up a domestic capital–goods producing sector with the help of imported machines were believed to be restricted (in a situation without foreign aid). As it was felt that the economy would likely continue to suffer from a foreign exchange constraint until an adequate potential for exporting domestically manufactured goods had been developed, an import substitution strategy was initiated as part of the Second Plan. The strategy consisted of a widening and intensification of the protection offered to domestic manufacturing, through the institution of quantitative restrictions on imports, and an across–the–board increase in tariffs, supplementary to a licensing framework. During the period 1950–65, import growth was high due to the rapid growth of domestic demand in import intensive sectors (particularly the capital goods industry), and because there was an increasing need to meet domestic food shortages through imports. By 1965–66, imports had been restricted almost entirely to capital goods, maintenance inputs, and food, which taken together accounted for about 94 per cent of total imports. Over the same period, the growth of exports was low (about 2.5 per cent per year) and its composition remained virtually unchanged, with agricultural products and agro–based manufactures accounting for over 70 per cent of export revenues. Hence, during much of the period upto 1965–66, foreign assistance substituted for export expansion as a source of foreign exchange. The rapid increase in gross domestic investment from 11.8 per cent in 1950–51 to 15.9 per cent in 1960–61

---

[8] Reliance on foreign aid was particularly high during the Second Plan period when as much as 28 per cent of gross domestic investment was financed by a foreign capital inflow (compared to an average share of only 11 per cent during the post–independence period as a whole). See Table 3.1.

[9] Note that there was more than 'elasticity pessimism' that was at issue. The basic argument ran in terms of 'ability to transform', that is, it included the infrastructural constraint to a major export thrust. See Chakravarty (1987:69).

Table 3.1
Aggregate Savings and Capital Formation
(Rs. crores at current prices)

	1950 –51	1960 –61	1970 –71	1980 –81	1985 –86	1986 –87	1987 –88
Gross Domestic Saving	975	2063	6783	28773	55150	63426	66650
– Households	718	1362	4873	21835	41143	50484	54773
– Private Corporate	89	276	657	2284	5415	4924	5684
– Government	168	425	1253	4654	8592	8018	6193
– as % of GDP	10.4	12.7	15.7	21.0	21.0	21.6	20.0
Gross Domestic Capital Formation	1034	2583	7379	31016	68010	71408	74405
– Private Sector	775	1441	4571	17016	37313	36153	38619
– Public Sector	259	1142	2808	14000	30697	35255	35786
– as % of GDP	11.0	15.9	17.1	22.8	25.9	24.3	22.4
of which:							
Change in Stocks	160	427	1074	9029	13005	7947	4548
– as % of GDP	1.7	2.6	2.5	6.6	5.0	2.7	1.4

Source: CSO (1989a; 1990).

(Table 3.1) was financed by a rise in the rate of gross domestic savings (from 10.4 per cent to 12.7 per cent during the same decade) and by a sharp rise in foreign savings, mainly foreign aid.

During 1950–65, industrial growth was high, although falling short of the Plan targets (Table 3.2), and the country's industrial structure became more diversified, with the share of capital goods industries in manufacturing production increasing from 4.7 per cent in 1950–51 to 11.8 per cent in 1960–61 and the corresponding share of consumer goods industries declining from 48.4 to 37.3 per cent during the same period.[10] The combined share of manufacturing, electricity, gas and water supply, and construction in GDP at factor cost rose from 15.0 per cent in 1950–51 to 22.8 per cent in 1965–66, whereas the share of agriculture, forestry and fishing declined from 55.4 to 43.3 per cent over the same period. With the pattern of consumer demand remaining more or less unchanged and, if anything, changing in favour of agricultural goods (Mundle, 1975), the industrial diversification was largely due to the unbalanced pattern of public investment, strongly favouring the basic and capital goods sectors. Public sector capital formation registered a rapid rate of increase of over 10 per cent per annum during 1955–56 to 1964–65.

The growth of public industrial investment could be maintained at fairly

---

[10] The shares of industries in total manufacturing are reported in the Reserve Bank of India Reports on Currency and Finance. The trend of changes in the sectoral composition continued during the 1960s, the share of capital goods industries amounting to 15.3 per cent and the share of consumer goods industries to 31.5 per cent in 1970–71.

Table 3.2
Growth Rates of Industrial Production
(per cent per annum)

		Target	Actual
1st Plan	(1950–51 to 1955–56)	7.0	7.3
2nd Plan	(1955–56 to 1960–61)	10.5	6.6
3rd Plan	(1960–61 to 1965–66)	11.0	9.0
Annual Plans	(1966–67 to 1968–69)	–	2.0
4th Plan	(1968–69 to 1973–74)	12.0	4.7
5th Plan	(1973–74 to 1978–79)	8.0	5.9
6th Plan	(1979–80 to 1984–85)	8.0	5.9
7th Plan	(1984–85 to 1989–90)	8.7	8.5[1]

Note: (1) Average of the first four years of the Seventh Plan period.
Source: Planning Commission.

high levels without generating undue inflationary pressure, because, upto the early 1960s, the trend rate of agricultural growth was generally high, although exhibiting considerable fluctuations around the trend. During 1950–51 to 1965–66, the annual growth rate of foodgrain production was 2.9 per cent and of commercial crop production 3.5 per cent (Table 3.3). Whenever agricultural supply fell short of demand, inflation could be contained at a low level by allowing for extra food imports which were available on concessional terms. Planners' resort to imports to keep food prices low helped to maintain a low product wage[11] in industry which may have stimulated industrial private investment. Furthermore, agricultural growth which resulted mainly from expansion of cultivated area – through land reclamations operations, a reduction in fallow lands and an appreciable decline in culturable waste through new irrigation projects and adoption of soil conservation measures – required relatively little investment means. Given its low capital requirements, agricultural production did not compete in any significant way for scarce investible resources, which could primarily be used for industrialisation.

With respect to the agricultural sectors, the longer–term perspective underlying the first Five Year Plans was based on the awareness that major institutional changes were required to raise agriculture's production potential. The unequal distribution of assets (land) and income and the unequal access to inputs such as credit and education, were regarded as serious impediments to an agricultural productivity increase. The awareness of the need to alter the distribution of assets (in particular, of land) was

---

[11] The 'product wage' involves the deflation of money wages by the price index of industrial products and, hence, is clearly linked with profitability. See Chakravarty (1987:95).

60

Table 3.3
Compound Growth Rates of Area, Production and Yield of Principal Crops

Crop	1949–50/1986–87			1949–50/1964–65			1967–68/1986–87		
	Area	Prod	Yield	Area	Prod	Yield	Area	Prod	Yield
Rice	0.88	2.52	1.61	1.33	3.49	2.13	0.63	2.54	1.93
Wheat	2.67	5.95	3.20	2.68	3.99	1.27	2.23	5.48	3.17
Jowar	−0.21	1.19	1.40	0.99	2.50	1.50	−0.65	1.24	1.90
Bajra	0.21	1.74	1.55	1.08	2.34	1.24	−0.79	−0.15	0.56
Maize	1.65	2.51	0.85	2.66	3.87	1.18	−0.08	0.98	1.07
Coarse Cereals	−0.07	1.28	1.21	0.90	2.23	1.29	−0.92	0.44	1.32
Total Cereals	0.76	2.98	1.86	1.30	3.24	1.68	0.28	2.90	2.19
Pulses	0.32	0.34	0.19	1.90	1.39	−0.22	0.44	0.68	0.32
Foodgr.	0.67	2.70	1.76	1.41	2.93	1.43	0.31	2.76	2.32
Sugarcane	1.86	2.97	1.15	3.27	4.26	1.12	1.49	2.63	1.13
Oilseeds	0.91	1.89	0.71	2.69	3.11	0.20	0.15	1.53	1.20
Cotton	0.36	2.35	1.99	2.47	4.56	2.04	−0.12	2.11	2.22
Jute	0.95	1.62	0.71	3.86	4.20	0.73	0.89	2.57	1.40
Non-Food	1.06	2.59	1.13	2.52	3.54	0.93	0.49	2.47	1.48
All Crops	0.75	2.62	1.57	1.61	3.13	1.30	0.36	2.62	2.05

Source: Ministry of Agriculture (1986b).

reflected in a chapter on 'Land Reform and Agrarian Reorganisation' included in the Second Plan. The objectives of land reforms according to the Planning Commission (1956:178) were 'firstly, removal of such impediments to agricultural production as had arisen from the character of the agrarian structure; and secondly, creation of conditions favourable for speedily evolving an agrarian economy with high levels of efficiency and productivity.' The main idea was that ceilings should be imposed on private land ownership (of individual or family holdings), and the excess over these ceilings taken over by the state and redistributed among small farmers and the landless. The second part of the reformist strategy, the Community Development Programme, was expected to help transforming the agricultural production base through institutional reforms and, in particular, through cooperativisation of the rural economy. During the 1950s, the number of rural cooperatives rapidly increased, their membership increasing from 4.4 million persons (or 5 per cent of the rural labour force) in 1950–51 to 17 million persons (or 12 per cent of the rural labour force) in 1960–61. The Community Development Programme also contained an important agricultural extension component aimed at spreading knowledge about the 'appropriate' agricultural practice.

Landowners were, however, able to evade the various forms of regulatory legislation and as a result no radical restructuring of rural property relations was carried out. The proportion of agricultural households belonging to the smallest farm–size class (smaller than 1 hectare) to all households increased from 31.4 per cent in 1953–54 to 36.8 per cent in 1960–61. The proportion of area owned by these households to total area increased from 1.4 per cent in 1953–54 to 1.6 per cent in 1960–61. Over the same period, the proportion of large farm households (larger than 15 hectares) to all agricultural households fell from 10 to 7.7 per cent. The proportion of area owned by these households to total area declined from 52.5 per cent to 45.5 per cent. These figures indicate that the reforms actually carried out did little for the small farmers and the landless, but they did bring about, though with much regional variation, a fairly substantial shift of land from the very big landlords to better–off farmers and lower–level intermediaries. Hence, through the redistribution of land, the reforms did contribute a 'real element of dynamism by restricting landlordship largely to the village level, establishing greater proximity between ownership and cultivation of land' (Sen, 1981:173).

Of other redistributive policies which could have been pursued from independence onwards, direct taxation of agriculture was of minor importance. Taxes on land revenue and agricultural income were comparatively low. In terms of agricultural GDP, the direct tax rate was 1.1 per cent in 1950–51 and 1.6 per cent in 1960–61, whereas the aggregate direct tax to GDP rates were 8.4 per cent and 10.8 per cent, respectively. In the early 1960s, demands for higher taxation of agricultural income met with strong resistance, as, by that time, there existed a strong lobby of those who had gained from the earlier land and tenure reforms 'which could not only voice farm interests, but also block threats to it' (Sen, 1981:176).

During the first three years of the Second Plan, domestic foodgrain production remained almost stagnant which led to the adoption of the Intensive Agricultural District Programme (IADP). The main thrust of the programme was to concentrate efforts on crops and areas which have the highest potential for an increase in food production. Important features of the programme are the development of a package of improved agricultural practices for each crop, and credit assistance to cultivators to make possible the purchase of the necessary inputs. What was new, was the programme's 'almost single–minded' concentration on increasing the use of modern inputs, particularly fertiliser. In 1964–65, the original programme was extended from the original 15 IADP districts to 114 districts and termed as Intensive Agricultural Area Programme (IAAP). By 1966–67, this programme covered about 10 per cent of cultivated area. Despite a substantial increase in the use of 'new' inputs in the project districts, the results were disappointing. The yields achieved in the IADP districts showed no statistically significant differences with the yield levels obtained in adjoining districts (which served as control areas), whereas the variability of IADP yields was higher than that in non–IADP districts.

Table 3.4
Basic Statistics on Foodgrains in India, 1951–88

	Gross Output[1]	Internal Procurement[1]		Net Imports[1]		Issues[1]	Public Stocks[1]	Per Capita Net Avail[2]
1951 – 52	50.8	3.8	(7.5)	4.8	(9.4)	8.0	1.3	395
1955 – 56	68.1	0.1	(0.1)	0.6	(0.9)	1.6	0.9	428
1960 – 61	76.7	1.3	(1.7)	5.1	(6.6)	4.9	2.8	448
1965 – 66	89.4	4.0	(4.5)	7.4	(8.4)	10.1	2.1	480
1966 – 67	72.3	4.0	(5.5)	10.3	(14.4)	14.1	2.2	408
1967 – 68	74.2	4.5	(6.1)	8.7	(11.7)	13.2	2.0	402
1970 – 71	99.5	6.7	(6.7)	3.6	(3.6)	8.8	5.6	450
1975 – 76	99.8	9.6	(9.6)	7.5	(7.4)	11.3	7.9	407
1980 – 81	109.7	11.2	(10.2)	– 0.3	–	15.0	11.7	417
1985 – 86	150.4	20.1	(13.4)	– 0.4	–	15.8	25.2	454
1986 – 87	143.4	19.7	(13.6)	– 0.1	–	17.6	23.6	476
1987 – 88	140.4	15.7	(11.2)	– 0.4	–	18.3	9.4	472
1988 – 89	170.3	14.1	(8.3)	1.9	(1.1)	18.3	7.4	441

Notes: (1) in millions of tonnes; (2) per capita net availabilty in grams;
       (3) figures in brackets represent percentages of gross output.
Source: Ministry of Agriculture (1988); Economic Surveys, various issues.

During 1950–1965, the real impetus to agricultural growth was provided by a fairly massive scheme of public investment in large-scale multipurpose irrigation projects, which, besides dovetailing into industrialisation plans by generating substantial amounts of electricity, created in 15 years a larger irrigation potential than that built up in 150 years of colonial rule (Sen, 1981:174). The annual expansion of irrigated area amounted to 2 per cent during 1950–59 and to 2.8 per cent during 1960–69. The share of public sector outlays on agriculture and irrigation was as high as 36.9 per cent in the First Plan. It was reduced to 21.9 per cent in the Second Plan, following the reduction of the estimates of the capital–output ratios in agriculture for the Second and Third Plans. Agricultural capital–output ratios were revised downwards following agriculture's impressive growth record during the First Plan period, when overall agricultural production responded quickly to a series of good monsoons and foodgrain production recorded a growth rate of 5.2 per cent per annum. This relative de–emphasis (in terms of public investment) on agriculture in the Second Plan suggests that planners treated agriculture as a *bargain sector*, 'a sector with large unexploited potential which can provide the requisite surplus with relatively low investment and in a comparatively short time after, of course, a certain minimum infrastructure has been developed.'[12] However, foodgrain production during the Second Plan did not increase at the same rate as in the First Plan. 1957–58 was a particularly bad agricultural year, with a fall in foodgrain output by 5.5 million tonnes from the previous year. Foodgrain imports were stepped up from 1957 onwards to maintain the per capita availability at the level of the closing years of the First Plan. At the time that the domestic public distribution scheme had become largely administered through imports (Table 3.4), serious concern about the country's dependence on food imports led to the formulation of self–sufficiency in foodgrains as one of the major objectives in the Third Plan in 1960.

3.3   *Economic Growth and Policy*: 1965-66 *to* 1989-1990

During the Third Plan period, the potential for extensive agricultural growth became largely exhausted. Increasingly, marginal, less fertile lands were brought under cultivation, which contributed to a deceleration of the agricultural growth rate. In 1966–67, due to severe droughts, foodgrain production dropped dramatically by 17 million tonnes from the peak production of 89.4 million tonnes in 1965–66, and foodgrain imports reached an all–time high of 10.3 million tonnes (Table 3.4), aggravating the prevailing balance of payments crisis. Following the drought period of 1965–67, there were many new initiatives in the field of agricultural policy, which eventually led to the adoption of the so–called New Agricultural Strategy which aimed at reducing agriculture's vulnerability to adverse weather conditions and improving its productivity.

3.3.1   *The New Agricultural Strategy*

The new strategy aimed at rapid technological modernisation of agriculture, deliberately concentrating investments in crops and areas where returns were expected to be relatively high and certain. In particular, the new strategy aimed at spreading the water–seed–fertiliser technology to areas where irrigation was already advanced. The adoption of the new technology by farmers was to be achieved through a policy package consisting of three elements, *viz.* output price policies, input price subsidies, and a public distribution policy, which tried to contain foodgrain prices at affordable levels while at the same time ensuring that producers did not suffer on account of volatile output prices and high input prices. The policy change articulated the government's belief that a 'positive' agricultural price

---

[12] The expression 'bargain sector' is due to S.R. Sen (1966:3–4), 'The Strategy for Agricultural Development', quoted in Chakravarty (1987:94).

policy is an effective instrument to stimulate output growth and influence its composition, implicitly assuming that agricultural output and marketed surplus do respond sensitively and regularly to price stimuli. The policy change coincided with the emergence of a 'positive' price policy as the dominant agricultural policy instrument following the publication of Theodore Schultz's (1964) study of traditional Indian agriculture. In this study, Schultz formulated the 'efficient but poor' hypothesis, according to which peasant farmers are poor, not because they utilise their resources inefficiently, but because of restrictions in the kinds and quantities of the resources they command. The finding that peasant farmers were allocatively efficient, implied that they could not increase their production except through technical innovation. Here, price policy was expected to be of help, since it can be used so as to provide an incentive to the farmers to adopt higher–risk new technology and to cover possible hazards of higher input costs and output–price instability.

Hence, procurement pricing was the first element of the new strategy to be adopted. From 1965 onwards, every season, the procurement prices of wheat and rice, the major foodgrains, were set by the central government on the basis of the recommendations of the Commission of Agricultural Costs and Prices (CACP) which was established in 1965 as the Agricultural Prices Commission. As its primary task the commission has to fix two sets of administered prices, procurement prices[13] and minimum support prices[14], which were designed to reduce price uncertainty for farmers and to promote the adoption of new technology. Normally, the procurement price is lower than the market price, but higher than the minimum support price. However, the distinction between these two types of administered prices began to get blurred very early. In the marketing season of 1967–68, when, following the introduction of the New Agricultural Strategy, the first real breakthrough in wheat production was achieved and the market price of wheat tended to fall below the level of the procurement price, the government took the significant decision to support the market at the level of the procurement price rather than the lower minimum support price (Balakrishnan, 1991:50). This was a major precedent. Minimum support prices were no longer announced for wheat from

---

[13] The procurement price is the price at which the government announces its intention of purchasing certain specified quantities of foodgrains. Procurement prices are announced just before the harvest, when information on the nature of crop is available to the government.

[14] Minimum support prices were in the nature of a long–term guarantee as they were meant to cover all production costs, including the imputed value of family labour and depreciation of farm assets, and yield a profit. The government is committed to buy at the minimum support price whatever quantities the producer offers to sell at her own initiative at the end of the harvest. Minimum support prices are announced on the eve of the sowing season and serve the purpose of an insurance.

the crop year 1968–69 onwards and for paddy from the mid–1970s onwards. Presently, minimum support prices are not announced for either crop, the government having undertaken to support the market at the level of the procurement price (Tyagi, 1990:30).[15]

Procurement/minimum support prices are fixed on the basis of data on costs[16] collected from different states, allowing for a fair return of 10 to 12 per cent on the comprehensive cost estimate which covers the full costs of production including the imputed value of family labour. During the late 1970s, a new element entered the price fixation process, the principle of parity, by which procurement prices are revised upwards in accordance with the rise in the costs of inputs, irrespective of output and stock levels. The parity principle was justified on the following two grounds (Bharadwaj, 1989). First, unfavourable terms of trade would inhibit investment in agriculture and hinder the advancement of new technology, which increasingly relies on industrial inputs. Second, with the achievement of higher yield levels, the rapid growth of agricultural output would tend to depress agricultural prices relative to industrial prices, unless supported actively to maintain parity. The principle was sanctified by the renaming of the Agricultural Prices Commmission as the Commission on Agricultural Costs and Prices in the early 1980s.

While the CACP is responsible for advising the government on matters of procurement pricing, the Food Corporation of India (FCI), established on 1 January 1965, is solely responsible for purchasing, storing, transporting and distributing foodgrains. Through its procurement and buffer–stock policy, the FCI tries to bring about a reasonable degree of intertemporal price stability. It procures/purchases foodgrains at procurement/minimum support prices and issues these to state governments at wholesale prices which do not cover the full economic costs. Five alternative systems have been used by the central government and the states to obtain grain for the public distribution system: outright acquisition of stocks from traders; monopsony purchase, under which

---

[15] In years of poor harvest, when the procurement price is below the market price, levies are imposed and farmers are obliged to sell a part of their production at the procurement price to government agencies. The difference between the two prices constitutes a tax on the farmers. In years of abundant harvest, the reverse holds true and farmers are in fact subsidised.

[16] The Agricultural Prices Commision uses a cost concept which covers all items of cultivation cost including the computed value of inputs owned by the farmers such as the rental value of owned land and the interest on fixed capital. Other items included are (*i*) the value of hired human labour; (*ii*) the value of hired bullock labour; (*iii*) the value of seed; (*iv*) the value of manure; (*v*) the value of owned bullock labour; (*vi*) the value of owned machine labour; (*vii*) irrigation charges; (*viii*) the value of fertilisers; (*ix*) land revenue cesses and other taxes; (*x*) hired machine charges; (*xi*) depreciation on implements and farm buildings; (*xii*) interest on working capital; (*xiii*) miscellaneous expenses; (*xiv*) rent paid for leased–in land; (*xv*) imputed value of family labour; (*xvi*) value of insecticides and pesticides. See Kahlon and Tyagi (1983).

the farmers are allowed to sell grain only to the government or its agents; a compulsory progressive levy on farmers, traders, or millers, which requires them to deliver to the government a proportion of their output or turnover; preemptive purchases in the market, with the government exercising the legal right of prior purchase of any amount of grain sold in the market at the going price; and open market purchases at the going price without preemption or compulsion. States have used different systems, except the last, for different crops, and changed these systems from year to year. The obvious reason for the exclusion of the last system of competitive open–market purchase is that, under conditions of shortage, the government can purchase the foodgrain quantities it requires, in competition with private trade, only at high prices. The time profile of public procurement is evident from the figures in Table 3.4. Procurement was rather low in the 1950s, when imported foodgrains were available on concessional terms, and started to increase in the early 1960s. Following the introduction of the New Agricultural Strategy, public procurement increased even further to meet the requirements arising out of the operation of an expanding public distribution system and the maintenance of a sizeable buffer stock, especially in the context of declining imports (Balakrishnan, 1991:39).

The second element of the new strategy – input (price) subsidies – was mainly concerned with credit subsidies and fertiliser subsidies. Credit assistance which was sought to be accelerated through a number of measures including the nationalisation of banks, was mainly provided to finance privately or community–owned irrigation works such as tanks, tubewells, and other items of minor irrigation[17] from which particularly small farmers were expected to benefit. With the new strategy, the emphasis of public investment shifted from public sector directed and financed major and medium irrigation works to minor irrigation which was mostly privately developed with private funds, assisted by government and institutional subsidiary finance. The fertiliser subsidy was a result of a two–pronged strategy to raise the level of agricultural output through the increased use of modern inputs which increased the productivity of land, and to encourage the domestic fertiliser industry to increase its output and capacity.

Finally, the New Agricultural Strategy aimed at controlling the distribution of foodgrains through operating a public distribution system (PDS) for which the FCI is responsible. Public distribution serves the aim of protecting vulnerable sections of the population from rising food prices by issuing foodgrains at a subsidised price. As part of the PDS, consumers in

---

[17] Minor irrigation schemes include all groundwater schemes (dugwells, shallow tubewells and pumpsets) and surface water schemes which consist of storage tank and lift irrigation schemes.

major cities[18] are provided ration cards against which they are entitled to purchase upto a certain quantity of foodgrains at prices below the market prices. These issue prices (the price at which foodgrains are issued to the States and Union Territories for sale in the ration and Fair Price Shops) are fixed on the recommendation of the CACP. From Table 3.4, it can be seen that, excluding the year 1951–52 when public distribution was exceptionally large, the magnitude of the PDS (expressing public issues as a proportion of the net availability[19] of foodgrains) increased steadily over time. It will be recalled that this has been an objective of food policy ever since the mid–1960s.

What were the effects of the New Agricultural Strategy ? Despite the shift towards higher yielding varieties and the increased use of chemical fertilisers, the post–green revolution period did not record a substantial increase in growth rates of crop production over and above the growth rates recorded in the earlier period, wheat being the only exception. In fact, the annual growth rate of aggregate agricultural production declined from 3.1 per cent during 1949–50 to 1964–65 to 2.6 per cent in the period 1967–68 to 1986–87 (Table 3.3). This decline in agricultural growth is to be attributed mainly to the decline in the growth rate of commercial crop production, which did not experience a major technological breakthrough, from 3.5 per cent per annum in the previous period to 2.5 per cent per year. The decline was particularly large for sugarcane, oilseeds, and fibres. Foodgrain production as a whole maintained a growth rate similar to the one it recorded during 1950–1965. The growth rate of foodgrain output did not significantly decline due to two compensating factors, *viz.* the increase in the growth rate of wheat production and, in addition, an increasing contribution of other rabi[20] food crops in total foodgrain production. The growth rates of almost all crops other than wheat including pulses and coarse cereals – jowar (sorghum), ragi (finger millet), barley and bajra (pearl millet), which are the main staples of the lower income groups – marginally declined after the mid–1960s.

During the post–green revolution period, the amplitude of output fluctuations for all crops, except wheat, increased significantly when compared to the pre–green revolution period. Rao *et al.* (1988) show that the increase in variability is highest in the case of oilseeds, followed by coarse cereals, pulses, and rice, whereas wheat shows the lowest variability. The

---

[18] Until the 1970s, the PDS was largely confined to the urban population, but, during the 1980s, some state governments (*i.c.* those of Kerala, Gujarat, Tamil Nadu, Andhra Pradesh and Karnataka) have extended the scheme to include rural low–income groups on a regular basis.

[19] Net availability is defined as gross output plus net imports minus the change in government stocks.

[20] Rabi refers to crops sown in autumn, following the kharif harvest. Kharif crops are sown during the early rains and harvested as the monsoon rains slacken in August, or sown during mid–monsoon for harvest during the dry season. Kharif crops are mainly rainfed. Rabi crops are more irrigated.

variability in rabi foodgrains which are dominated by wheat, is lower than that in kharif foodgrains.[21] The increase in instability of crop production is to be attributed to, on the one hand, the increase in regional concentration of crop supply, and, on the other hand, to a shift in cropping pattern towards higher–yielding, but simultaneously more rainfall–sensitive crops and crop varieties. As regards the first factor, the green revolution has been confined mainly to wheat as well as to the better endowed regions and the larger farmers (Rao, 1975). This has led to the situation in which the bulk of foodgrain supply has become concentrated in only a few states. Hence, according to the Seventh Plan (1985:1), 'there is a serious regional imbalance in the impact of the green revolution in that less than 15 per cent of the area under foodgrains accounts for 50 per cent of the increase in foodgrains production in the post–green revolution period.' Although these states are relatively well–endowed with irrigation facilities, their agricultural production is not immune to a bad monsoon. States such as the Punjab and Haryana are mainly irrigated by canals, the potential of which ultimately depends on rainfall. With respect to the second factor, the following two observations can be made. First, the rising importance of yield – a more unstable component than area – as a source of post–1965 agricultural growth has contributed to an increase in output fluctuations. Moreover, the instability in area itself has increased and synchronised or correlated movements in area and yield have become more pronounced in the post–green revolution period (Rao et al., 1988:36–43), contributing to the rise in output fluctuations. Second, the availability of higher yielding varieties, public promotion of wheat–oriented irrigation, and price supports favouring wheat have encouraged a shift in the use of land to wheat. Table 3.5 shows that, with regard to the allocation of irrigated area, there has been a dramatic shift in favour of wheat, from 15.1 per cent in 1960–61 to 32.1 per cent in 1986–87. The share of rice in irrigated area recorded a spectular decline from 44.7 per cent in 1960–61 to 32.1 per cent in 1986–87. These shifts in the distribution of irrigated area across crops may explain the rise in variability in output in the case of rice and the decline in variability in the case of wheat.

Another important issue is whether the 'positive' agricultural price policy adopted since the mid–1960s has been effective in inducing the desired

---

[21] Rao et al. (1988) have computed the standard deviation in annual per cent changes in crop output as indicator of the instability in aggregate crop output. Their results are: The standard deviation in annual output growth rates of rice increased from 10.0 during 1950–65 to 13.9 during 1966–85; of coarse cereals, from 8.0 to 13.2; of oilseeds, from 9.3 to 16.9; and of pulses, from 12.0 to 16.3. The standard deviation of wheat output growth declined from 11.5 to 11.2 over the same period. Growth rates of kharif foodgrains registered a standard deviation of 13.9 during 1968–85, whereas the standard deviation of rabi output growth was 9.8 in the same period.

Table 3.5
Cropped Area, Irrigated Area and Area under HYV
(million hectares)

	1950 -51	1960 -61	1970 -71	1980 -81	1986 -87
Net sown area	118.8	133.2	140.8	140.3	140.1
Area sown more than once	13.1	19.6	25.0	32.8	36.8
Gross cropped area	131.9	152.8	165.8	173.1	176.9
Percentage shares:					
– Rice	23.6	22.3	22.6	23.3	23.3
– Wheat	7.6	8.5	11.0	12.8	13.1
– Other food	45.5	44.9	41.8	37.8	35.6
– Commercial crops	23.3	24.3	24.6	26.1	28.0
Net irrigated area	20.9	24.7	31.1	38.8	43.0
Area irrigated more than once	1.7	3.3	7.1	11.1	12.6
Gross irrigated area	22.6	28.0	38.2	49.9	55.6
Percentage shares:					
– Rice	43.8	44.7	37.5	32.8	32.1
– Wheat	15.1	15.1	26.0	31.3	32.1
– Other food	22.3	19.1	15.3	11.3	10.6
– Commercial crops	18.8	21.1	21.2	24.6	25.2
Area under HYV	–	–	15.3	43.1	55.4
– Rice	–	–	5.6	18.2	23.0
– Wheat	–	–	6.5	16.1	19.4
– Jowar	–	–	0.8	3.5	5.5
– Bajra	–	–	2.1	3.6	5.3
– Maize	–	–	0.5	1.6	2.2

Note: (1) Provisional; (2) Target.
Sources: Ministry of Agriculture (1985; 1986a; 1986b);
Ministry of Finance (1990).

quantity responses. That incentive price policy alone is not effective in inducing supply responses appears clearly from the trends in cropping patterns that emerged after 1965–66. Specifically, despite high price levels, area under pulses, jowar, bajra, and oilseeds appears to have declined, and despite higher relative prices of rice as compared to wheat, the increase in acreage under wheat has gone up much faster (Table 3.5). Factors including the degree of commercialisation of agricultural production and the availability of infrastructural facilities (including the efficient delivery of inputs) complementary to higher yielding seed varieties and fertilisers, may have limited the price–responsiveness of agricultural supply during this period. With respect to the first factor, studies of the supply response of agricultural producers to relative price movements suggest that crops can be ranged along a subsistence–commercial continuum with their responsiveness to relative price movements increasing with the degree of commercialisation (Krishna, 1967). Subsistence grain crops respond little to relative price variations, whereas crops grown both for subsistence and for sale – wheat, rice, and maize in surplus areas, and sugarcane – have a higher supply response. Not surprisingly, commercial fibres have the highest elasticities. Because the degree of commercialisation differs between households as their market involvement is not uniform (Narain, 1961; Patnaik, 1975) and hence supply responses differ considerably at the micro–level, the aggregate (macro) outcome of a policy–induced change in relative agricultural prices is not clear at forehand. In the case of crops, wholly or almost wholly marketed, the price elasticities of output would more or less correspond to the elasticities of marketed surplus. But when a substantial part of the produce is for self–consumption, the marketed surplus response will differ from the output response. Ahluwalia (1979) even found a negative and statistically significant short run elasticity of the marketed surplus of foodgrains with respect to relative prices, suggesting that the income effect on the consumption of foodgrains is stronger than the substitution effect. In general, with the econometric knowledge as to how foodgrain output responds to relative price changes being scanty and not suggesting a relatively large supply response,[22] it would seem that the role of price policy is confined to the more commercialised surplus producers in technically advanced regions with well established trading networks, who organise their production mainly for profit in exchange (Bharadwaj, 1989). With respect to the second factor – the infrastructural support base – Krishna and Chhibber (1983) found the supply elasticity of wheat with respect to irrigation to be 1.5 times higher than the supply elasticity of wheat with respect to its relative output price. Similar results bringing out that the elasticity of output is higher with respect to technology variables (such as irrigation) than with respect to price variables, are reported by Bhide et al. (1986), Gulati (1987), and Gulati and Sharma (1990). It would seem thus that agricultural price policy is effective only when a certain minimum infrastructural support base exists.

The New Agricultural Strategy also resulted in large increases in costs of cultivation per hectare which were not matched by a corresponding rise in productivity per hectare. In 1970–71, farmers spent on average Rs. 272 on inputs (including capital consumption) to obtain Rs. 1,250 as output per hectare of gross cropped area. In 1984–85, an expenditure of Rs. 460 was incurred to obtain Rs. 1,665 as output, both at 1970–71 prices. The growth of the cost of inputs used per hectare has been more than double that of the value of output.[23] The rise in costs is the result of the shift from low–cost

---

[22] For estimates of the short–run and long–run price elasticity of agricultural supply, see Table 3.8 (below).

[23] Rao (1983) observes that output–input ratios at constant (1960–61) prices declined between 1960–61 and 1979–80 from 4.6 to 3.6 (by 22.5 per cent) in agriculture. Nadkarni's (1988) estimates of the agricultural output–input ratio in constant (1970–71) prices show a similar decline from 4.6 in 1970–71

self–produced inputs to high–cost capital–intensive market inputs.[24] Of the total increase in input cost (valued at 1970–71 prices) between 1970–71 and 1984–85, the increase in three major industrial inputs – fertilisers, pesticides, and diesel – constituted 64.6 per cent. While these three inputs accounted for 16.2 per cent of total input costs in 1970–71, their share increased to 35.1 per cent in 1984–85 at constant prices. Labour costs per unit of output have declined both as a proportion and in absolute terms[25] and have actually exercised a dampening influence. The fall in output–input ratio's at constant prices is particularly disquieting because of its following two effects:

(a) a *cost–push* effect on the economy, as agriculture's output consists of either food or raw materials which enter into the cost of labour maintenance and industrial production; and

(b) an effect on agricultural income as agricultural value added declines relatively to input cost[26]; with the proportion of value added in total output declining, prospects of growth of agricultural income and employment cannot be bright unless technological breakthroughs take place to lower the per unit costs significantly.

It is sometimes argued, notably by Krishnaji (1988), that the guarantee of a return over and above the costs, provided by the public procurement price, has ensured that there is no disincentive to choosing high cost technologies. The method of cost–plus pricing underlying procurement prices has enabled farmers to transfer cost increases onto agricultural prices, often pushing these prices to levels which the market finds difficult to sustain. In turn, high agricultural prices have been compensated for by increases in food subsidies under the public distribution system.

A final result of the New Agricultural Strategy is the sharp increase in public food stocks. It is well known that these surpluses are a result of large increases in output in certain well–endowed regions in the country. Five states – Punjab, Haryana, Uttar Pradesh, Andhra Pradesh, and Maharashtra – with a share of 40.5 per cent of total gross cropped area accounted for 68 per cent of the incremental output in foodgrains since the green revolution (Kumar, 1990:502). Substantial increases in administered prices (which emerged to meet increasing costs and, for wheat, were above the open market prices in some years) facilitated the increase in internal procurement of food in these

---

to 3.6 in 1984–85.

[24] These figures suggest that, so far, technological change occurring in Indian agriculture defies the customary definition of technological progress, *i.c.* an upward shift in the production function implying that a higher level of production is achieved at a given input level, *e.g.* at a lower per unit cost.

[25] The compensation of employees (excluding mixed income of self–employed) per Rs. 100 worth of output declined from Rs. 16.9 in 1970–71 to Rs. 15.1 in 1984–85 at current prices. See Nadkarni (1988:A–116).

[26] It should be noted here that the cost increases are in real terms, independent of inflation rates and the terms of trade of agriculture.

states.[27] Food stocks rose from an annual average of 1.2 million tonnes in the 1950s, to 2.6 million tonnes in the 1960s, 10.1 million tonnes in the 1970s to 25 million tonnes in 1985–86, with no comprehensive plan for their disposal (Vittal, 1986). On the one hand, foodstocks were not used to step up investment (in Nurkse's sense), because of the perceived uncertainty regarding the continuation of both food and foreign exchange reserves. Apparently, a rise in public investment was believed to lead to uncontrollable inflationary pressures in the event of rapid exhaustion of food stocks and depletion of foreign exchange reserves would make it difficult to relieve this situation via food imports (Mitra and Tendulkar, 1986:27). On the other hand, foodstocks were also not used to bring down prices during years of good harvest. During those years, the surpluses went into public stocks. Consequently, market prices for foodgrains remained steady when production was rising and increased when shortfalls in harvests occured. Not only market prices, but also procurement and issue prices portrayed such staircase type of movements since they were either kept stable or revised upwards irrespective of production levels (Krishnaji, 1988:62). Since the procurement price was an assured support price, market price movements closely followed those of the former. In fact, there appears to be a mutually re–inforcing tendency between the market price and the support price to rise.[28] Through an increase in industrial wage costs, a high agricultural price may lead to a rise in prices of industrial goods entering as inputs into agricultural production. Hence, production costs in agriculture increase and so does the support price, because of the parity principle which assures that purchase prices fixed by the CACP were in general close to the weighted average costs of production for the two main staple foodgrains – rice and wheat. The rising support price, in turn, raises the floor for the market price.[29]

---

[27] The fact that rice began to be produced as a summer crop in the predominantly wheat–consuming north–western part of India in the early 1970s also contributed to the rise in food stocks.

[28] According to estimates by Balakrishnan (1991:91), the use of procurement prices as a market support mechanism has led to a market price higher than would have prevailed in the absence of such intervention. The suggestion that procurement prices may affect market prices was first made by Mitra (1978:112): 'It is as if what the Government does or does not do is in the nature of an early warning signal for others. If the Government raises administered prices, it stimulates prices over the entire range of market operations; if it marks down administered prices, its decision acts as a depressant which again casts its spell over the rest of the market. As long as the belief is promoted that the Government is the price–setter, whatever the objective reality in the initial stages, the administered price becomes, after an interval of time, the actual price–setter for all effective purposes.'

[29] Prabhat Patnaik (1981) was one of the first to consider the inflationary consequences of procurement price changes. His argument rested, however, primarily on the possibility of excessively large speculative stock build–ups engendered by procurement price increases.

3.3.2   Post-1965 *Economic Policy and Performance*[30]

No consistent strategy came in the field of industrial development after the breakdown of the ambitious industrialisation programme of the Second and Third Plans. This vacuum in policy making became obvious when the country declared a 'plan holiday' in the late 1960s. To resolve (part of) the economic crisis of 1965–66 and 1966–67, a fair degree of trade liberalisation[31] was introduced along with a large devaluation of the Rupee in 1966. The combination of export growth following the devaluation and continued import restriction led to a sharp reduction in the trade deficit from a high of Rs. 905 crores in 1966–67 to Rs. 178 crores in 1969–70. Whereas foreign demand marginally increased, private domestic demand for industrial consumer goods suffered from a major decline due to the worsening terms of trade *vis-à-vis* agriculture for industry. The fall in domestic demand was augmented by a considerable decline in public investment which – through the multiplier mechanism – led to the emergence of further idle capacity in the capital goods and other sectors, pushing down gross profit margins because of the possible increase in overhead charges and the prices of raw materials. Public investment was cut primarily in response to fiscal pressures which arose because, following the droughts, public expenditure increased, whereas revenue fell, partly because of the slowdown of industrial production and partly because customs revenues fell. The growth rate of public investment declined from 11.6 per cent per annum in the first half of the 1960s to 4.6 per cent per annum in the subsequent decade. The decline in the growth rate of public investment was particularly concentrated in infrastructural investment (including irrigation), the rate of growth of public infrastructural investment declining from 16.7 per cent during 1956–65 to only 2.1 per cent during 1965–75.

The immediate effect of the fall in domestic final demand was a decline in industrial capacity utilisation rates. Capacity utilisation in capital goods industries declined from 85.9 per cent during 1960–65 to 66.4 per cent during 1966–70; underutilisation of capacity was also widespread in basic

---

[30] Important characteristics of an economy and of the policy measures affecting its performance are often best understood when examined in the context of how it copes with exogenous changes, such as a harvest failure. Therefore, this section examines the effects of and policy responses to the major agricultural supply shocks which have occurred (sometimes simultaneously with a major change in the international environment) since the mid–1960s. The figures mentioned in the text were taken from the National Accounts Statistics.

[31] This liberalisation of imports was gradually reversed during the late 1960s. In the event, liberalisation of imports could not go very far because of the foreign exchange constraint – there was no significant increase in the flow of foreign aid consequent on the Rupee devaluation. Further, exports also did not increase as much as anticipated, the reasons of which are much debated. See Chakravarty (1987:69–70); P. Sen (1986); and Bhagwati and Srinivasan (1975).

industries.[32] Over the medium term, the decline in public investment demand led to a fall in the annual growth rate of industrial production from 9 per cent during the Third Plan period to 4.7 per cent during the Fourth plan period (Table 3.2). In particular, the heavy industries sector was hit by the decline in (public) investment demand: the annual growth rate of basic goods production declined from 11 to 5.9 per cent and the annual growth rate of capital goods manufacturing fell from 15.4 to 6.6 per cent. Obvious attempts to encourage investment by the private corporate sector, including a delicensing of some industries, and low (and sometimes negative) levels of real interest rates did not induce the desired response. Private investment failed to pick up in spite of the policies designed to remove all possible constraints and create an environment conducive to growth (Nayyar, 1978).

It was only in the 1970s, and particularly after 1975–76, that the industrial sectors showed signs of recovery. Before that, during 1972–75, the economy experienced a severe shortfall in agricultural production. On average, agricultural production was about 5 per cent below the trend levels, leading to a rise of the inflation rate from 7.5 per cent in 1970–73 to 20 per cent in 1973–75. Inflationary pressures were strengthened by the oil–price shock which raised international crude oil prices by a factor of four between September 1973 and April 1974, and by a steep rise in defence expenditure following the creation of Bangladesh in 1971. The economy was able to adjust to these changes in external environment relatively rapidly. The current account deficit of Rs. 455 crores in 1973–74 was converted to a surplus of Rs. 1146 crores in 1976–77. The other sign of recovery was the decline in the inflation rate. Prices fell during 1975–76 and grew at an annual rate of only 2.4 per cent over the next three years. The rapid recovery was aided by a combination of favourable factors (see Sen, 1986), *viz.*

(a) 1975–76 witnessed a bumper harvest with agricultural output rising by 13.8 per cent over the previous year and by 4 per cent over the trend level. Agricultural prices dropped by over 7 per cent. During 1975–80, a large foodgrain stock was built up, amounting to over 30 million tonnes (*i.e.* several months' supply); the agricultural–industrial terms of trade fell, restraining overall inflation;

(b) India was able to get relatively easy access to external funds to meet the increased trade balance deficit following the oil price increase. During 1973–75, about 43 per cent of the trade deficit was financed by low or unconditional short–term loans from the IMF;

(c) exports grew rapidly over this period; export earnings increased by more than 20 per cent per year during 1972–73 to 1978–79. The volume growth was much lower, amounting to 9 per cent per annum. Export growth was increased through bilateral trading arrangements with the Comecon countries and in response to increased demand from the oil producing

---

[32] There has been a great deal of controversy about the causes of this deceleration in the rates of Indian industrial growth. Ahluwalia (1985) provides a comprehensive review of the debate in the light of India's industrial performance. Original contributions to the discussion include: Bagchi (1970); Patnaik (1972); Chakravarty (1974); Raj (1976); Shetty (1978); Nayyar (1978); Mundle (1985); and recently Kumar (1988).

countries; and

(*d*) a positive side–effect of the oil–price increase was the migration of Indian labour to the Gulf countries and the consequent remittances to India by them.

Government's response to the oil price increase of 1973–74 consisted mainly of a contractionary stance in fiscal and monetary policy aiming at short–run stabilisation. For example, interest rates were revised upwards to historically high levels, private consumption expenditure was reduced through a series of fiscal and other measures including the freezing of all wages in the public sector, and export growth was encouraged by a real exchange rate depreciation. However, the burden of the expenditure adjustment fell on public investment, and on public investment in agriculture in particular. Its share in total public investment declined from 12.9 per cent in 1969–70 to 9.4 per cent in 1975–76. Further measures included an increase in the domestic price of petroleum products to check the growth of demand for imported oil. Imports of crude oil remained at a more or less stable level during the three–year period 1974–75 to 1976–77. Imports of nitrogenous fertilisers declined in 1976–77 and 1977–78 as compared to 1974–75 and 1975–76, whereas its domestic production went up by 80 per cent during the three years after 1973–74. Since the success of the New Agricultural Strategy was crucially dependent on the adequate availability of chemical fertilisers, their supply was not allowed to decline. The country's response to the oil crisis was to step up the pace of import substitution in the domestic production of fertilisers. Whereas the imports of fertilisers grew at an average annual rate of 4.2 per cent between 1969–79, domestic production grew at 13.6 per cent per annum.

In the event, the strong dose of demand management proved excessive because subsequent conditions in weather and the external environment turned out to be favourable (Mitra and Tendulkar, 1986). Public foodgrain stocks increased considerably, because the bumper harvests of 1977–78 and 1978–79 caused the government support price for wheat to become a binding floor on the farm–gate price. The unanticipated growth of private remittances led to the accumulation of comfortable foreign exchange reserves. The trade deficit marginally declined, mainly as a result of stagnant import volumes due to slow growth of domestic investment demand. Other reasons for the decline of the balance of trade deficit were the greater domestic production of machinery and capital goods as a result of earlier industrialisation,[33] and export promotion through diversification of goods and markets as also through government subsidies and other incentive schemes. It is interesting to note that, during

---

[33] In non–electrical machinery, for example, the proportion of imports in total supply declined from 66 per cent in 1959–60 to 31 per cent in 1979–80; in electrical machinery and chemical products, the decline was from from 38 per cent and 30 per cent, respectively, to 10 per cent and 19 per cent, respectively. There are exceptions: import dependence in case of edible oils increased during the same period. See Ahluwalia (1985).

this period of recovery from the combined oil and agricultural crisis of 1973, real interest rates were extremely high, following their upward revision in 1974–75 coupled with the decline in the inflation rate (Sen, 1986).

The year 1979–80 marks another watershed in Indian economic growth, witnessing both an agricultural failure as well as the second oil–price shock. Inflation increased from 4.8 per cent in 1978–79 to 17.5 per cent per year during 1979–82. In contrast to the fast recovery of the first oil–price shock, adjustment was slow in the early 1980s, although the initial conditions were more favourable at the time of the second oil shock than at the time of the first one. On the eve of the second oil shock, both the foodgrain and foreign exchange reserves were high and inflation had come down to less than 10 per cent. This time, however, adjustment was hindered by a number of unfavourable factors including:

(a) access to external funds was much more restricted. A large part of the current deficit had to be borrowed under the high conditionality Extended Fund Facility arrangement of the IMF[34];

(b) the flow of workers' remittances from the Gulf stagnated, although remaining at high levels; and

(c) due to the world recession, export growth dropped from 9.4 per cent per year in volume terms during 1973–79 to only 3.6 per cent during 1979–82. Import volumes increased. Principal imports included machinery, fertiliser, and petroleum products, with a combined share of 60 per cent of the total. The deficit on the trade balance increased from Rs. 108 crores in 1977–78 to Rs. 5967 crores in 1980–81, amounting to 4.4 per cent of GDP.

Immediate adjustment was aided by a reduction in oil–based imports made possible by the rise in indigenous oil production, and by a recovery of agricultural production after the drought of 1979–80. Inflation–fighting through deflationary measures still dominated official thinking, but the comfortable foodstocks and foreign exchange position kept the deflationary measures at a less rigorous level (Datta–Chaudhuri, 1990). Although public investment expenditure was reduced in order to avert inflationary imbalance, the cutback was not as severe as in 1973–75.

In addition to the short–run stabilisation policy, this time the policy response concentrated on the medium run, emphasizing policies of trade liberalisation and domestic deregulation. With respect to the former, already from the end of the 1970s onwards, imports of raw materials and components were significantly liberalised. In the 1980s, the list of readily importable items was considerably increased and imports in general were made easier. In 1985–86, the government launched a wide array of export promoting measures, including the initiation of a more competitive exchange rate policy. Trade liberalisation was supplemented by domestic liberalisation which brought, in

---

[34] Although the arrangement was terminated prematurely, over 1980–84, India obtained SDR. 4.7 billion from the IMF, representing over 50 per cent of the cumulative current account deficit (Sen, 1986:6).

1982[35], a significant change in the industrial licensing policy: industrial capacity of licensed units was to be annually refixed on the basis of the highest production achieved during the five years preceding the year of reference – even if such production exceeded previously licensed capacity. Consequently, in case of units which were able to attain higher and higher levels of output, the industrial licensing requirement was no longer a binding constraint. However, with the liberalisation, the balance of payments problems increased, mainly due to relatively low rates of export growth (3 per cent over the Sixth Plan period). Problems were exacerbated by (EAC, 1989):

(a) the plateauing of domestic oil production in the face of continually increasing domestic demand for oil–products;
(b) the levelling–off of workers' remittances from abroad;
(c) the steep increase in debt service payments following the rise in foreign borrowing; and
(d) the drought of 1987–88 which entailed large–scale imports of food and other essential commodities.

Although the drought was severe with as many as 21 out of 35 rainfall sub–divisions having received deficient or scanty rainfall, agricultural production declined with 2 per cent which is a small decline as compared to the decline due to the drought of 1979–80, when kharif and rabi foodgrain output fell by as much as 19 per cent and 13.7 per cent respectively. In 1987–88, the impact of the drought was particularly felt in kharif production which is still largely dependent on rainfall. In response to the drought, the following measures were taken:

(a) foodstock operations, relief employment programmes, and measures to boost up rabi production. A Special Foodgrain Production Programme was designed to capitalise on identified sources of immediate agricultural growth. The fall in kharif foodgrain production of over 9 per cent was to a considerable extent offset by an increase of 2 per cent in rabi foodgrain production. Foodgrain requirements could be met largely from internal public stocks which were built up in earlier years. Stocks were run down from a level of over 23.3 million tonnes in June 1987 to 8.1 million tonnes in September 1988 to meet the demand pressure arising from the drought;
(b) these measures were supplemented by fiscal and monetary policies designed to finance the substantial additional expenditure on drought and food relief without generating undue inflationary pressures.
(c) a rise in external assistance helped financing the additional imports of edible oils and pulses necessitated by the drought.

These measures had a significant dampening effect on inflation, which could be contained at a level of 10.4 per cent (in terms of the wholesale price index)

---

[35] During 1951–1982, the licensing system remained unchanged although it was recognised that in practice its operation was characterised by problems relating to administrative delays and lack of flexibility. The Fourth Five Year Plan (1970:302) explicitly recognised this first set of problems, saying that 'detailed controls not only put considerable strain on the administrative machinery, but led to delayed implementation. Further, the controls did not always secure the objectives for which they were designed.' For a review of industrial licensing policies, see Ahluwalia (1985) and Chandrasekhar (1988).

during 1987–88 as compared to 21 per cent following the previous major drought of 1979–80. Industrial growth remained largely unaffected by the agricultural supply shortfall. The government's budgetary position, public foodstocks and foreign exchange reserves were, however, negatively affected. Favourable monsoons enabled the rapid recovery of the economy in 1988–89 when GDP in real terms recorded a growth rate of 10.4 per cent, agricultural production grew by 20.8 per cent, and industrial growth was 8.8 per cent. Inflation was contained at 5.7 per cent in terms of the wholesale price index. The favourable monsoons resulted in a large increase in foodgrain production, from 140.4 million tonnes in 1987–88 to 170.3 million tonnes in 1988–89 (*i.e.* a 21.3 per cent increase, see Table 3.4). Despite high export growth and a good harvest, pressures on the balance of payments kept on increasing due to a spillover of drought related imports of essential commodities from 1987–88, and strong demand for imports generated by the recovery in production during 1988–89 (EAC, 1989:4).

How is the rapid recovery from the 1987–88 drought to be explained ? According to some commentators, notably Kumar (1990) and Sen (1988), the resilience of the non–agricultural sectors to the drought of 1987–88 can be related to two factors, *viz.* the fact that, during the period 1980–1987, aggregate consumption had become less intensive in food, which contributed to a dampening of agricultural price increases, and the moderately expansionary fiscal policy stance adopted by the government, the impact of which was to contain the decline in aggregate demand and, hence, limit the recessionary consequences of the drought. Both factors need some further explanation.

With respect to the first factor, according to national accounts data, the share of food consumption in aggregate private consumption fell from 53.5 per cent in 1980–81 to 49.7 per cent in 1987–88. While it can be argued that this decline in the aggregate average budget share of food reflects an Engel effect, with consumers diversifying away from basic necessities to other commodities, such a trend would seem unlikely to manifest itself given the *absolutely* low level of per capita food consumption (see Table 3.4). What may be a more plausible explanation is that the lower–income groups, particularly those employed in agriculture and the non–registered non–agricultural sectors, were forced to cut down on essential expenditure, because of their slowly growing real incomes, while the middle and higher–income groups, enjoying higher rates of real income growth, were able to increase their consumption demand for non–foodgrains.[36] Evidence from the National Sample Surveys

---

[36] Further indirect evidence of an industrial production pattern that is skewed in favour of the richer sections of society and in particular of the urban middle class is provided by the pattern of industrial growth during the 1980s which indicates that, to a greater extent than ever before, industrial production has been propelled by a fast rate of increase in the demand for consumer durables. See EAC (1989:6).

indicates that the real incomes per worker in the unregistered manufacturing sectors have indeed declined during much of the 1980s (Sen, 1988a), while there is also evidence suggesting that, in agriculture, the compensation of employees has remained stagnant, while the share of rent, interest and profit increased (Kumar, 1990). An important factor explaining the low real income growth for wage earners in agriculture and the non-registered manufacturing sector relative to overall real income growth is the absence of nominal wage indexation arrangements in these sectors, while (unionised) wage earners in registered manufacturing were able to get their real wage losses due to inflation compensated for by (nominal) wage increases. It is argued that due to the redistribution of income and purchasing power and the ensuing decline in the share of food in private consumption, inflationary shocks were heavily dampened, with the cost borne largely by the non-indexed wage earners in the agricultural and unregistered industrial sectors (Sen, 1986).

The second factor explaining the rapid recovery of the 1987–88 drought is related to the expansionary fiscal policy response. It will be recalled that the general response to earlier agricultural supply shocks was to cut public expenditure (particularly public investment) in order to curb demand and, hence, contain inflationary pressures.[37] However, the fiscal policy response to the agricultural shortfall of 1987–88 was expansionary, largely taking shape in the running down of public food stocks and other relief operations. The government was able to respond in this way because of the huge foodgrain stocks stored by the FCI (see Table 3.4). A measure of the degree of fiscal stimulus imparted by the central government is given by the excess of total expenditure over revenue receipts which was much higher in 1987–88 (9.1 per cent of GDP) than in 1979–80 (6.6 per cent). With aggregate demand kept more or less intact, the industrial sectors were able to continue their high rates of growth and remain relatively insulated from the adverse effects of the drought. Hence, the fact that the economy was able to adjust to the 1987–88 drought, avoiding both a two-digit inflation and an adjustment recession that followed earlier droughts, is (partly) to be attributed to the higher public deficit.

Against this background, a distinguishing feature of the economy's performance during the post-green revolution period is the gradual decline in the growth rate of public investment, particularly public investment in

---

[37] In the years following the crises of 1972–75 and 1979–80, this type of demand management proved excessive, suggesting that a fiscal policy response of such a contractionary type is correct only in a situation in which there is a physical limit to the availability of agricultural goods – as was the situation following the droughts of 1965–67. In a situation in which agricultural supplies, over and above production, can be made available either through imports or by running down stocks (as was the case in 1972–75 and 1979–80), the correct fiscal policy response to a temporary agricultural shortfall might have been of a more expansionary nature (Sen, 1988:734).

agriculture and infrastructure (Shetty, 1990). The annual growth rate of public infrastructural investment fell from 12.5 per cent during 1950–51 to 1964–65 to 6.1 per cent during 1966–67 to 1986–87. Apart from a general slowdown, the growth rate of public investment showed strong fluctuations over the post–green revolution period. For example, in real terms, it declined from about 10 per cent per annum during the triennium ending 1971–72 to –0.8 per cent per annum during the three–year period ending 1973–74. It declined again from 10.8 per cent per annum during 1975–76 to 1977–78 to 4.1 per cent during the triennium ending 1979–80. During the 1980s, the investment growth in real terms in infrastructural sectors further stagnated. Growth rates of public sector capital formation in agriculture show similar fluctuations as those of public infrastructural investment, declining after a drought period and not regaining its earlier level. National accounts data show that, following the recessionary years 1979–1982, public sector investment in agriculture declined in real terms from an average of Rs. 1,789 crore per annum during the triennium ending 1982–83 to Rs. 1,511 crore (at 1980–81 prices) per year during the triennium ending 1987–88.

The tendency of the growth rate of public investment to decline was strenghtened by growing pressures on the public budget, particularly during the 1980s, when the balance on the revenue account, which is equal to the difference between public current revenue and public current expenditure, deteriorated, showing an increasing deficit from 1983–84 onwards. In Chakravarty's (1987:78) words, 'the government budget has come under pressure even when the government is faced with a favourable succession of good monsoons – again a matter of some contrast with the pre–Green Revolution years, when government resources dipped only when harvests failed on a large enough scale'. As a result, the proportion of public investment that could be financed by public savings declined. In effect, the public sector, whose savings increased less than proportionately to its investment, became obliged to increasingly rely on borrowing from the private sector and in particular from the household sector, where much of the increase in savings took place (see Table 3.1). The fall in public sector savings can be partly attributed to the sharp increase in current expenditure on fertiliser and food subsidies.[38] Subsidy expenditure on fertilisers has been rising ever since the introduction of the fertiliser subsidy scheme in 1977. It increased from Rs. 603 crores in 1979–80 to as much as Rs. 3995 crores in 1990–91, amounting to about 38 per cent of total subsidy expenditure. It is noteworthy that, although public agricultural expenditure increased, there has been hardly any attempt at

---

[38] The other two items responsible for the increase in public current expenditure are interest payments and defence expenditure. The increase in interest payments is related to the growing borrowing requirements of the government. The share of interest payments in the Centre's revenue expenditure has increased from 20.7 per cent in 1981–82 to 26.1 per cent in 1988–89.

raising resources from agriculture through direct taxation, while large parts of agriculture have prospered and a large class of well–to–do farmers has come up. The PDS also places a heavy burden on the government budget. In 1985–86, food subsidies (which are equal to the difference between the procurement price and the issue price of foodgrains) amounted to 33.5 per cent of subsidy expenditure. The costs of the PDS are even larger on account of storage and administration costs. According to some commentators, the government itself contributed to the growing budgetary pressures by protecting the private agricultural sector from all risks, including risks of losses through an imbalance between supply and demand. If there is a chance of excess supply, the public sector buys off the stocks of the agricultural sector at procurement prices which comfortably cover the costs of the latter. At the same time, the government cannot resist pressures to supply necessities (foodgrains) at reasonable prices.[39] Caught in the dichotomy of subsidising the consumption of essential commodities while at the same time guaranteeing agricultural profit margins, the government was forced to curtail its investment expenditure (Patnaik, 1981).

This particular pattern of public investment growth has had two negative consequences. First, it contributed to the length and severeness of the recessionary periods following the agricultural supply shocks of 1972–75 and 1979–80 through directly reducing domestic demand for basic and capital goods and indirectly curbing the growth rate of the demand for domestic manufactures (Mitra and Tendulkar, 1986). Secondly, it negatively affected capacity creation in certain crucial infrastructural sectors such as power, transport and irrigation, which in effect limit the potential for raising the rate of agricultural growth. In view of the fact that, in periods of economic upswings, demand for agricultural products generally increases more than agricultural supply and, hence, agricultural prices increase, triggering–off an economy–wide inflationary process and forcing a reduction in public investment and expenditure aimed at holding the price level (Chakravarty, 1987:78), it seems reasonable to conclude that, in a medium–run sense, the most proximate supply constraint on Indian growth is still the agricultural one (Sen, 1990).[40]

---

[39] Furthermore, government has no control over the private producers using receipts from sales of stocks to the government for speculation in essential commodities. In P. Patnaik's (1981) view, attempts by the government to expand its investment will be counteracted by the private sector through stock speculation. Paradoxically, the private sector is in a position to speculate due to the liquid resources which it has acquired through sales to the public sector.

[40] For the period 1952–53 to 1975–76, results of Sen's (1981) model simulations show that much higher GDP growth than actually observed would have been feasible on the basis of actual savings rates and import capacity (determined by the available amount of foreign exchange). The economy was therefore supply–constrained by the actual rate of agricultural growth. Given the

3.4   Post-1965-66 *Economic Performance*: *Structural Characteristics*

The previous section examined the short-run effects of as well as policy responses to the major agricultural supply shocks, which have occurred during the post-green-revolution period, to highlight certain features of the country's economic structure and macro-economic policy regime. In this section, I try to draw out the implications of this discussion in terms of the economy's structure.

3.4.1   *Agricultural Structure*

Despite the heterogeneity which characterises Indian agriculture,[41] I believe that certain aspects of it are amenable to the sort of aggregate analysis which is the subject of the present study. Specifically, I believe that it is possible to argue that the price-responsiveness of aggregate as well as cropwise agricultural supply is relatively low, in particular in the short run. Table 3.6 presents a large number of econometric estimates of the price elasticity of agricultural supply, both in the aggregate and cropwise. Although the short-run estimates included in the table vary a great deal in size, depending on the type of crop under consideration and on the time period of estimation, the bulk falls within only a relatively limited range, between 0.1 and 0.5. Hence, it seems reasonable to conclude that agriculture's short-run price response is typically small. Corresponding long-run elasticities are generally higher, but they are still considerably below unity. It can also be seen that, in the short run, the price elasticity of aggregate agricultural supply tends to be lower than cropwise price-elasticities which is due to the fact that the growth in one crop takes away resources which are fixed in the short run, from other crops (Binswanger, 1991).

The relatively low level of aggregate price responsiveness can be related to the following two distinct features of agricultural production: first, the small size of agricultural holdings, and, second, agriculture's low irrigation coverage. With respect to the first factor, according to the 1981 Agricultural Census, in 1980-81, the number of agricultural holdings in the country was

---

latter, the maximum rate of GDP growth possible given the actual rates of savings could not be reached without incurring very high rates of inflation, unless implausible additions were made to the import capacity. The agricultural constraint is due to Kalecki (1955). An agricultural or 'food' bottleneck as the main operative constraint was already much emphasized by Vakil and Brahmananda (1956) who were heavily influenced by the work of Nurkse (1953).

[41] See Bhalla and Tyagi (1989) for a district-level study of agricultural growth which brings out its heterogeneity, both cropwise and region-wise.

Table 3.6
Price Elasticities of Selected Crops

Crop	Period	Short Run	Long Run	Source
Aggregate	1952–74	0.20/0.30	0.30	Krishna (1982)
	1954–77	0.28/0.29		Chhibber (1988)
	1955–76	0.24		Bapna (1981)
	1961–81	0.13		Binswanger, Khandker and Rosenzweig (1989)
Barley	1950–82	0.38		Bhide *et al.* (1989)
Cotton	1950–82	0.09		Bhide *et al.* (1989)
Groundnut	1950–82	0.08		Bhide *et al.* (1989)
Jute	1950–82	0.25		Bhide *et al.* (1989)
Maize	not given	0.12		Narayana *et al.* (1991)
Rice	1957–70	0.45	0.85	Krishna & Raychaudhuri (1980)
	1964–75	0.19		Sirohi (1984)
	1950–82	0.04		Bhide *et al.* (1989)
Sugarcane	1950–82	0.28		Bhide *et al.* (1989)
Wheat	1957–69	0.22		Krishna & Raychaudhuri (1979)
	1960–78	0.33	0.47	Roy & Subramanian (1983)
	1961–78	0.58	0.58	Krishna & Chhibber (1983)
	1964–75	0.12		Sirohi (1984)
	1965–79	0.27	0.68	Gulati (1987)
	1950–82	0.20		Bhide *et al.* (1989)

Note: The estimates by Chhibber (1988), Bapna (1981), and Binswanger, Khandker and Rosenzweig (1989) are taken from Binswanger (1991).

89.4 million operating on 162.8 million hectares of land, with an average farm size of only 1.8 hectares (Table 3.7). Marginal holdings, defined as those operating on less than one hectare, accounted for 56.6 per cent of total holdings, while small holdings (1 to 2 hectare) constituted another 18 per cent. Taken together, marginal and small holdings operated only about 26 per cent of total area, while large holdings accounting for 2 per cent of total holdings, controlled nearly 23 per cent of all operated area. The small size of many holdings is the primary factor keeping most farmers at the subsistence level of production (Tyagi, 1990:56). This is reflected by the fact that the percentage of area under food crops, largely grown for own use, on marginal and small holdings is much higher than the percentage of area devoted to these crops on large farms (Table 3.7). Most (marginal and small) farmers have little scope to expand (food) production sufficiently to generate a marketable surplus, retaining most of their produce for home consumption. This implies that, while, as producers, these farmers gain from a rise in the price of their crops, they lose as consumers. Following a rise in agricultural prices, many marginal and small farmers will not be able to wholly postpone increases in their consumption by raising their marketed surplus, but will shift from production for the market to production for self–use. It is for this reason that subsistence crops respond little (or, sometimes, even 'perversely') to

Table 3.7
Distribution of Holdings by Major Size-Groups, 1980–81
(number and area)

Size–Group	No. of operational holdings (millions)	% to total	Area (million hectares)	% to total	% of Area under Food	% of Area under Irrig.
Marginal (<1 ha)	50.58	56.6	19.73	12.1	88.6	34.8
Small (1 to 2 ha)	16.10	18.0	23.01	14.2	85.2	28.6
Semi–medium (2 to 4 ha)	12.48	14.0	34.53	21.2	82.0	25.1
Medium (4 to 10 ha)	8.08	9.0	48.32	29.7	77.5	20.3
Large (>10 ha)	2.15	2.4	37.17	22.8	73.2	12.5
Total	89.39	100.0	162.76	100.0	80.3	22.5

Source: Ministry of Agriculture (1986).

relative price variations (Ahluwalia, 1979).

With respect to the second factor, from Table 3.5, it can be seen that, in the 1980s, the aggregate irrigation coverage (*i.e.* the ratio of gross irrigated to gross cropped area) amounts to about one third. Cropwise irrigation coverage varies a great deal – between 75 per cent in wheat production to about 10 per cent in other foodgrains production. It is also well–known that the proportion of irrigated to total area is higher for small than for large farms (Table 3.7). Irrigation is important because it makes possible the inter–season transfer of water, enabling the growing of more than one crop in a year on the same plot of land – in a situation in which the climatic and soil conditions do not allow multiple cropping on most of the unirrigated land resource. The increase in irrigation has also raised the rate of adoption of higher yielding seed varieties and resulted in a re–allocation of area across crops and an intensification of the usage of inputs such as fertilisers. It is against this background that the price-responsiveness of irrigated agriculture is found to be considerably higher than that of unirrigated agriculture (Binswanger, 1991). Hence, agriculture's price responsiveness is constrained by its limited irrigation coverage.

3.4.2   Structure of Domestic Demand

It will be clear from reading Section 3.3.2 that a change in foodgrain availability has strong repercussions not only on foodgrain prices, but also on the general price level and the overall level of economic activity. This impact is directly related to the structure of Indian consumer demand, which is characterised by the following six features:

(*a*)   an absolutely low level of average per capita food consumption: the growth rate of foodgrain production has just kept ahead of the rate of population growth, enabling the per capita net availability of foodgrains to increase from 395 grams in 1951–52 to 441 grams in 1988–89 (Table 3.4) which is low, both in absolute terms and in comparison with other low-income countries (Kumar, 1990);

(b) relatively high average budget shares for food: consumption data made available by the National Sample Organisation show that, on average, 30 per cent (rural) and 14 per cent (urban) of consumer expenditure is on cereals and pulses only (see Table 3.8); total expenditure on food amounts to about 59 per cent (rural) and 52 per cent (urban) of total consumer expenditure; it is well-known that the lower-income groups spend an even larger proportion of their incomes on food; these figures imply that the domestic market for many non-agricultural consumer goods is rather narrow;

(c) rural (or agricultural) demand constitutes about 70 per cent of total demand for industrial consumer goods (Table 3.8);

(d) relatively high marginal budget shares and expenditure elasticities of food: for the lower income groups, marginal budget shares of foodgrains are found of the order of 0.42 (rural) and 0.26 (urban); expenditure elasticities on foodgrains are significantly higher for lower-income groups as compared to higher-income groups, being as high as 0.78 for the lowest rural income earners and 0.58 for the lowest urban income group as compared to 0.23 (rural) and 0.16 (urban) for the highest income group (see Table 3.9);

(e) relatively low own-price elasticities of foodgrain demand, both for low and high income groups, implying that foodgrain demand is relatively insensitive to price changes (Table 3.9); and

(f) relatively high cross-price elasticities of foodgrain demand, particularly for lower and middle income groups, which implies that price increases for foodgrains will have a considerable depressing effect on the demand for other commodities (Table 3.9).

Taken together, the six characteristics of consumer demand imply that, whenever the incomes of the lower-income groups increase and part of their latent demand becomes effective demand, the impact on the aggregate level of foodgrain demand will be tremendous. In view of agriculture's low short-run price-responsiveness, it is doubtful whether the increase in domestic foodgrain production will be of a corresponding size. Imports may add to food supply in order to match the rise in demand, but they have large opportunity costs in terms of foreign exchange foregone. In case the demand increase is not fully matched by the expansion of supply, food prices will rise, which (given the relatively low own-price elasticity of food demand and the high cross-price elasticities) will lead to a significant reallocation of consumer expenditure from non-food to food products. This particular structure of consumer demand has a number of important implications. First, it implies, *ceteris paribus*, that, to provide a cushion in years of drought, large foodstocks must remain an integral part of the economic system, diverting resources away into procurement and stockholding. Second, at the low levels of income earned by the majority of the population, it may prevent a diversification of consumer expenditure that could potentially expand the domestic market for industrial consumer goods. Finally, it implies that the country is only self-sufficient in foodgrains *given* the current level and distribution of income.

Table 3.8
Structure of Private Consumption, 1977–78

	Rural:		Urban:	
Commodity groups:	Average Budget Share	Share in PFCE	Average Budget Share	Share in PFCE
Cereals & Cereal Substitutes	0.275	0.861	0.126	0.139
Pulses	0.022	0.817	0.014	0.183
Milk & Milk Products	0.084	0.751	0.078	0.249
Edible Oils	0.032	0.735	0.032	0.265
Meat, Fish & Eggs	0.040	0.724	0.043	0.276
Other Food Products	0.139	0.636	0.225	0.364
Non–Agr. Products	0.409	0.705	0.482	0.295
Total	1.000	0.739	1.000	0.261

Note: PFCE is private final consumption expenditure.
Source: Planning Commission (1979).

Table 3.9
Marginal Budget Shares (μ_i), *Income Elasticities* (ε_i) *and Own and Cross-Price Elasticities of Foodgrains* (ε_{fi})

Commodity Group	Lower μ_i	ε_i	ε_{fi}	Middle μ_i	ε_i	ε_{fi}	Higher μ_i	ε_i	ε_{fi}
Rural									
Foodgrains	0.42	0.78	−0.44	0.18	0.44	−0.32	0.07	0.23	−0.16
Milk	0.10	2.26	−1.17	0.16	1.83	−0.62	0.07	0.65	−0.15
Ed. Oils	0.03	1.25	−0.64	0.03	1.01	−0.34	0.02	0.84	−0.20
Meat,Eggs	0.03	1.34	−0.70	0.04	1.26	−0.42	0.01	0.51	−0.12
Sugar,Gur	0.03	1.54	−0.80	0.04	1.26	−0.43	0.02	0.72	−0.17
Other Food	0.11	0.87	−0.46	0.11	0.87	−0.29	0.07	0.62	−0.14
Clothing	0.09	1.90	−0.99	0.16	1.78	−0.60	0.15	1.18	−0.27
Fuel,Light	0.05	0.63	−0.33	0.05	0.82	−0.28	0.02	0.48	−0.11
Oth.N.Food	0.12	1.46	−0.76	0.24	1.73	−0.58	0.56	2.07	−0.48
Urban									
Foodgrains	0.26	0.58	−0.57	0.12	0.39	−0.41	0.03	0.16	−0.26
Milk	0.11	2.01	−0.52	0.14	1.43	−0.29	0.09	0.80	0.20
Ed.Oils	0.04	1.11	−0.29	0.03	0.75	−0.15	0.01	0.45	−0.06
Meat,Eggs	0.04	1.45	−0.38	0.05	1.28	−0.26	0.02	0.62	−0.08
Sugar,Gur	0.04	1.45	−0.38	0.03	0.86	−0.17	0.01	0.48	−0.06
Other Food	0.15	1.01	−0.26	0.15	0.97	−0.20	0.11	0.76	−0.10
Clothing	0.07	2.19	−0.57	0.13	1.99	−0.40	0.12	1.39	−0.17
Fuel,Light	0.07	0.79	−0.20	0.05	0.75	−0.15	0.03	0.53	−0.07
Oth.N.Food	0.22	1.64	−0.43	0.31	1.52	−0.31	0.56	1.73	−0.22

Note: Marginal budget shares, income elasticities, own and cross price elasticities were estimated as parameters of a LES.
Source: Radhakrishna (1978).

A final point needs to be made here concerning the change in the structure of intermediate demand, brought about by the increase in agricultural demand for industrial inputs including fertilisers, pesticides, pumpsets, and electricity during the green revolution period (Section 3.3.1). The substantial increase in purchased inputs in agriculture from manufacturing industries and services means that agriculture–industry input–output linkages have become two–way now to a much greater extent than ever before. Whereas Manne and Rudra could argue, in 1965, that, in India, industrial growth had a largely autonomous character because flows between industry and agriculture were not sufficiently strong, any current analysis of Indian economic growth needs to take into account the impact of agriculture's demand for non–agricultural inputs (Chakravarty, 1987:25). The greater use of energy and of oil–based fertilisers further led to a substantial increase in the import intensity of agricultural production, as a result of which, agricultural production has become far more sensitive to fluctuations in world market prices than ever before.

3.4.3   *Structure of Manufacturing*

Following the launching of the Nehru–Mahalanobis development strategy in the 1950s, entry into the sectors earmarked for private enterprise came to be determined by the procedure of 'licensing' by which the government controlled the creation and expansion of production capacity. It is generally understood that government controls and licensing policies have reinforced the already existing oligopolistic industrial structure, which, in turn, has often led to the creation and maintenance of excess idle capacity (Ghose, 1974; 1974a; 1974b). With the data pointing to a marked product–wise concentration over a wide range of industries (Table 3.10),[42] it would be agreed upon that, in terms of conventional indicators of market structure, Indian manufacturing may be described as oligopolistic.[43]

---

[42] I will not deal with the causes of industrial concentration here. The reader is best referred to Hazari (1966) and Ghose (1974).

[43] Already before independence, India's private industrial sector was characterised by a high degree of industrial concentration both in terms of market shares and in terms of capital stock. In 1964, the Monopolies Inquiry Commission reported that of a total of 1,298 commodities under study, 87.7 per cent were produced by oligopolists; 437 commodities were produced by only one firm and 229 commodities by two firms each. Hazari (1966) identified 20 large industrial houses which controlled a significant part of the private corporate sector over the years 1951–58. Other evidence on industrial concentration is provided by Sawhney and Sawhney (1974), Katrak (1980), Chandra (1981), and Chandrasekhar (1988). In terms of the share of the top 4 enterprises in total output, Chatterji (1989) considers the degree of industrial concentration to be high (over 75 per cent) in iron and steel industries, paper industries, and chemicals, and medium (60 to 75 per cent) in general engineering.

Table 3.10
Market Concentration in Selected Manufacturing Industries

Industry	Number of Products	Number of Products where Top Four Firms Control:	
		100% of Output	>75% of Output
Automobiles	104	96 (94)	101 (99)
Drugs & Pharmaceuticals	97	90 (93)	96 (99)
Insecticides & Plastics	114	105 (92)	113 (99)
Acids, Fertilisers & Other Chemicals	132	116 (88)	130 (98)
Tools	66	54 (82)	65 (98)
Light Mechan. Engineering	93	74 (80)	89 (96)
Instruments	19	15 (79)	19 (100)
Industrial Machinery	71	54 (76)	70 (99)
Alcohol & Organic Chem.	27	20 (74)	25 (93)
Metallurgical Industries	71	50 (70)	67 (94)
Rubber Manufactures	75	50 (67)	74 (99)
Mineral Industries	52	29 (56)	43 (83)
Electrical Engineering	39	17 (44)	33 (85)
Leather Manufacturing	9	4 (36)	8 (87)

Source: N.S. Siddhartan (1980), 'Technology, market structure and the deceleration in the growth of capital stock in Indian engineering industries' (mimeo), quoted in Mundle (1981).
Note: Figures in parenthesis give percentages of corresponding totals of number of products.

With respect to industrial prices, the high degree of industrial concentration in the registered sectors suggests that market prices are controlled or *administered* in one way or another, implying that increases in input costs and/or wages resulting from agricultural price rises may be transmitted onto industrial output prices. Empirical evidence in support of this proposition is given, *inter alia*, by Chatterji (1989) who found that prices are almost entirely cost–determined, based on a fixed mark–up over costs, while demand factors have no significant role to play.[44] Given the large proportion of raw material costs in total variable costs of manufacturing, fluctuations in industrial prices are to a considerable extent due to fluctuations in agricultural prices. According to Chatterji (1989:159), '...,
it remains true that increasing the supply of food and raw materials adequately would considerably dampen inflationary pressures. In this respect, the Indian case is different [from industrialised capitalist economies] because it is neither wage nor profit inflation which is important but the

---

[44] Chatterji (1989) provides a comprehensive and detailed analysis of industrial price formation in India on the basis of data, covering the period 1947–1976, relating to all registered industry as well as to six broad industry groups. Katrak (1980) and Balakrishnan (1991) report similar findings.

inflation in the price of wage goods and industrial raw materials.'

The co-relation between fluctuations in agricultural prices and industrial prices is strengthened by the fact that changes in the wage rates earned in registered manufacturing are themselves directly related to agricultural price changes. Reflecting the oligopolistic structure of the industrial product markets, workers in registered manufacturing are widely organised in labour unions and their wages are determined within the framework of institutionalised collective bargaining (Subramanian, 1977). Empirical evidence for the registered industrial sectors indicates that nomninal wage rates are primarily determined in response to changes in the price of wage goods, reflected by changes in the consumer price index (Krishnamurty, 1985). Nominal wages are indexed to the consumer price index in which foodgrains have a relatively large weight, through the system of dearness allowances (or cost of living allowances), which make up approximately one third of total earnings. However, compensation is seldom the full amount of the price rise and, hence, although money wages tend to rise automatically with increases in the cost of living, a real wage fall is built into the system in periods of rising prices.

3.5   *Implications for Model Construction*

It is time now to bring together the various threads of the above discussion and to ask what its implications are for the construction of the general equilibrium model. The general view I arrive at from the discussion of the previous sections, is that the growth performance of the Indian industrial sector, over the last two decades at least, has not been in conformity with the widely held belief that its production is supply– rather than demand–constrained – a belief that formed the basis of the Nehru–Mahalanobis strategy of growth (see Section 3.2).

This lesson was brought home by the sharp deceleration of industrial growth in combination with the rise in inflation during the second half of the 1960s, which is generally held to be caused by the substantial decline in public investment demand aimed at curbing demand and, hence, containing inflationary pressures following the droughts of 1965–66 (Section 3.3.2). Throughout the period 1967–1971 the government remained reluctant to step up investment lest it trigger off an inflationary spiral (in spite of the existence of considerable excess capacity in the capital goods sector). Private investment demand is believed to have declined following the shift in the terms of trade against industry, implying a reduction in the opportunities for profitable industrial investment. Similar adjustment recessions which resulted from a decline in public investment, aimed at containing agricultural price rises, and a decline in private investment, following the deterioration of the terms of trade for manufacturing, were experienced after the droughts of 1972–73 and 1979–80 (see Section 3.3.2).

But even apart from the sharp declines in the levels of industrial activity following these drought periods, for the major part of the 1970s and early 1980s, industrial performance is characterised by the existence of widespread excess capacity and slow growth due to deficient demand. An important indication of this demand deficiency is given by the sharp increase in inventories during this period which has taken place because of the absence of a profitable market (see Table 3.1). Most notable is the sharp increase in public food stocks (Table 3.4) which resulted from government's attempt to keep up effective demand for foodgrains (Section 3.3.1). It will be recalled that effective demand for foodgrains has been low, because, given the need to pay a remunerative price to farmers, a price support scheme, which prevents the price of food from falling, has had to be maintained. As was argued in Section 3.3.2, a telling manifestation of the low level of demand for food is to be found in the muted price response to the drought of 1987–88 (Kumar, 1990). Had effective demand been more evenly distributed, region–wise and across income groups, the country might well have experienced a sudden and unprecedented rate of inflation, once the fall in agricultural output had occurred, which would in all probability have been extremely difficult to contain through supply management. The data on the structure of consumer demand – referred in Section 3.4.2 – reveal just how rapid price increases would have been in case of a less skewed distribution of incomes.

In this context, it is important to recall from the previous chapter that, in the classical and neoclassical approaches, the problem of demand deficiency is defined away, either by assuming that savers are necessarily the same as investors (the classical assumption) or, alternatively, by evoking the equilibrating role of the rate of interest, which is the neoclassical assumption (Chakravarty, 1979:1237). Given that the bulk of gross domestic savings is done by the household sector, with an increasing part of these household savings being held in the form of financial rather than real assets (Rakshit, 1988:325), and given that public investments exceed public savings to a significant extent (Table 3.1), the classical assumption that savers are the same as investors, becomes untenable. This conclusion is also drawn by, *inter alia*, Rakshit (1989:4), noting that 'an important implication of these developments in respect of savings propensities and financial intermediation is the widening (if not total divorce) between acts of investment and acts of savings.' With respect to the neoclassical assumption, the discussion of the economy's growth performance during the last two–and–half decades in Section 3.3.2 sheds some light on the interest elasticity of private investment demand. Specifically, it was found that, with the deceleration of industrial growth during 1967–74, lack of sufficient investors' confidence led to the insufficiency of investment in relation to the full–employment level of

91

savings, even though real interest rates were low and sometimes even negative. It was also found that private investment demand increased following the recovery from the 1973–74 crisis, in the face of substantial increases in real interest rates. Taken together with the increase in the financial savings of the household sector, these observations suggest that financial savings require the existence of sufficient private investors' confidence to be useful, since they do not create their own demand. This renders the neoclassical approach irrelevant because of its reliance on the interest rate as the equilibrating force behind the investment–savings balance.

It is for the above reasons that, within the framework of a mixed economy, it is no longer adequate to rely merely on supply–oriented models such as the ones proposed by adherents of the classical and neoclassical approaches. However, it is not that supply limitations are unimportant, as it will be clear from Section 3.3.1 that agricultural production is supply–constrained. The point is that, when devising a non–inflationary investment programme, the Indian government cannot ignore demand factors, as it was the weak incentive to invest by both the public and private sector which, during much of the period 1965–1980, imposed a demand–side constraint on the rate of economic growth (Chakravarty, 1979), while it was the strong increase in domestic private consumer demand (particularly for consumer durables) as well as the rise in export demand, which contributed to the acceleration of the growth process during the 1980s (EAC, 1989). Further evidence in support of a post–Keynesian specification of the investment–saving process was given in Section 3.3.2, where it was suggested that at least part of the increase in savings during the post–green revolution period was financed through income–distributional changes, leading to reductions in the consumption of the lower–income groups (particularly, agricultural labourers, small farmers, and workers in the unregistered sectors). Hence, the model includes independent investment demand functions, both for the public and private sectors, requiring savings to adjust *via* a change in the level and/or distribution of income in order to establish the *ex – post* investment–savings equality.

The other implications for the formulation of the general equilibrium model drawn from the previous sections include:

(1) Key areas of the economy were reserved for the public sector which explains the importance of public investment for understanding economic fluctuations. The model should allow for public investments to be complementary to private investments, particularly in agriculture.
(2) Given the importance of public expenditure (and in particular of public investment), the model should incorporate the major sources of public revenue, *viz.* tax revenues and profits from public enterprises. A detailed specification of the public budget is required.
(3) Within the part of the economy left to the private sector, market forces are regulated to a fairly large degree by public intervention. In the largely private agricultural sector, the degree of policy intervention is quite high on account of procurement policies, input subsidies (particularly fertiliser subsidies), the public distribution system, and

public investment in irrigation. In foreign trade, private sector activity is to a considerable degree restricted by a quota policy and licensing.

Given agriculture's importance to economic growth in the short and medium run, the sectoral disaggregation of the model should at least distinguish between agriculture and non–agriculture, and, within agriculture, between food and non–food production. With respect to the agricultural sectors, one may note that:

(1) The short–run supply response of agricultural output with respect to the agricultural price is relatively low (Section 3.4.1). In the short run, agricultural output is consequently quite independent of demand conditions.

(2) The agricultural sector is a source of instability in the economy, because agricultural output strongly fluctuates with changing weather conditions (Section 3.3.2). Changes in agricultural supply induce strong price fluctuations, because the demand (especially for foodgrains) is relatively price inelastic (Section 3.4.2).

(3) The substantial increase in inputs in agriculture from manufacturing industries and services means that any current analysis of Indian economic growth needs to take into account the impact of agriculture's demand for non–agricultural inputs (Section 3.3.1).

(4) Changes in agricultural market prices are closely correlated to changes in procurement/minimum support prices. Market prices are free to fluctuate in response to prevailing supply–demand conditions, but will never fall lower than the support prices. The adoption of a price–support policy has thus introduced a downward rigidity in agricultural market prices which may produce a ratchet effect whereby over time the support price as a floor is pulled upwards by a rising market price (Section 3.3.1).

(5) As agriculture has become more import–dependent than before, mainly following the rise in (imported) fertiliser consumption, agricultural policy alternatives can only be evaluated within an open–economy frame-work (Section 3.4.1).

(6) With the potential for extensive agricultural growth being exhausted, an increase in agricultural growth can only result from intensifying production, which means raising the number of harvest per year and increasing per hectare yield levels. Irrigation is the critical factor in this process of intensification, being a prerequisite for the use of chemical fertilisers and conditioning the successful adoption of higher yielding crop varieties. It is for these reasons that the model should distinguish between irrigated and unirrigated cultivation and incorporate the impact of (public and private) agricultural investment *via* irrigation and agriculture's cropping intensity on crop outputs.

Relatively low and variable capacity utilisation rates in the manufacturing industries represent a problem for a neoclassical formulation of the supply side of these sectors (Rattsø, 1988). Other significant features of industrial performance include:

(1) Cost plus pricing seems to give a realistic description of pricing behaviour in the non–agricultural sectors (Section 3.4.3). Oligopolistic market structures in the registered non–agricultural sectors explain for this mark–up pricing. Industrial mark–up rates are found to be reasonably stable. Industrial mark–up pricing also explains for the high correlations found between agricultural price changes and industrial price changes.

(2) The main determinant of non–agricultural money wage levels seems to be

93

the consumer price index. This appears to be fairly plausible because, even though the economy as a whole has surplus labour, those employed in (registered) manufacturing are quite well organised (Section 3.4.3). At the same time, large sections of the population (*i.c.* those employed in agriculture and the non–registered manufacturing and services sectors) have almost no indexation.

In my view, these are the main 'stylised facts' regarding the Indian economy which need to be incorporated in the general equilibrium model.

A COMPUTABLE GENERAL EQUILIBRIUM MODEL
FOR INDIA'S SEVENTH PLAN PERIOD, 1985-90

4.1   *Introduction*

Given the importance of the agricultural sector in the Indian economy, any
policy intervention that affects the growth rate of agricultural output and
income will have significant spill–over effects in the rest of the economy. To
quantify these economy–wide effects of agricultural policies rather than their
effects on the agricultural sector itself, a computable general equilibrium
model was constructed to simulate their macro–economic, income–distributional
and sectoral growth effects over the short and medium term. This chapter is
devoted to a discussion of that model. It is organised as follows. Section 4.2
discusses a number of important empirical and theoretical aspects of the
general equilibrium approach. The main assumptions of the model are clarified
in Section 4.3. In Section 4.4, the agricultural policy issues addressed by
the model are discussed. Section 4.5 presents the components of the general
equilibrium model and the agricultural production submodel. A summary is given
in Section 4.6.

4.2   *The Computable General Equilibrium Approach*

Section 4.2.1 compares the computable general equilibrium approach adopted
here to the alternative macroeconometric approach in terms of numerical specification. Section 4.2.2 briefly reviews the main theoretical specifications
which can be given to computable general equilibrium models.

4.2.1 *Numerical Specification*

The relevant literature[1] broadly distinguishes between two alternative approaches to applied economy–wide modelling, *viz.* the macroeconometric and the general equilibrium approach, although the boundary lines between the two categories are somewhat blurred and some (but as yet not many) models would have to be classified into both of them.[2,3] To explore the differences between the two approaches in more detail, consider the following system of n equations[4]

$$(4.2.1) \qquad F \; (y, \; X; \; \beta, \; \varepsilon) = 0$$

where y is a vector of endogenous variables, X is a vector of exogenous variables, β is a vector of unknown parameters, and ε is a vector of n stochastic disturbances of either known, partially known, or unknown distribution (Lau, 1984).

To prevent all misunderstanding, it should be noted that I use the term 'macroeconometric model' here in a restricted sense, indicating those models the parameters of which are estimated from observed data through statistical techniques, while the term 'general equilibrium model' is used in its most general sense, to cover any other numerically quantified closed system of simultaneous equations; the solution to that system of equations, if it exists, is the solution of general equilibrium.[5] As such, the distinguishing

---

[1] The reader may be referred to Powell (1981) and Challen and Hagger (1983) whose classification of macroeconomic modelling is widely used. A similar classification can, for example, be found in Dervis *et al.* (1982), Borges (1986), and Capros, Karadeloglou and Mentzas (1990).

[2] Examples of such models include the general equilibrium (energy) model of the economy of the United States of America developed by Jorgenson and various associates which is based on full econometric estimation of the parameters of the various submodels (see Jorgenson, 1984), and the agricultural policy model constructed for India by Narayana *et al.* (1987) of which a large number of parameters are based on econometric estimation.

[3] A comparison of the two modelling approaches is complicated by the fact that varying and often conflicting theoretical specifications can be accommodated in both the macroeconometric model and the general equilibrium model. The paper by Capros, Karadeloglou and Mentzas (1990) is problematic on this point. They compare two small–scale models – a macro–econometric and a general equilibrium model – which were estimated from a similar data base. Their macroeconometric model is specified as a Keynesian (in the sense of Hicks) macro–model, whereas their general equilibrium model is specified along Walrasian lines. What they are comparing, in effect, are two conflicting theoretical approaches instead of two alternative modelling approaches.

[4] For a detailed discussion of the problems involved in the numerical specification of general equilibrium models, see Mansur and Whalley (1984). Lau (1984) provides a critical comment.

[5] According to this definition, the Walrasian system is simply a particular example of general equilibrium, where the system of equations refers to demand and supply in individual markets and their simultaneous interaction, with the

feature of macroeconometric models is that the structural relations are not deterministic, because, with certain exceptions, the most important of which are purely definitional relationships, they contain a so–called 'random disturbance' – the vector ε in (4.2.1). These random disturbances are viewed as a set of stochastic variables, $e.g.$ as a set of variables covered by some joint probability distribution (Challen and Hagger, 1983). They are included in the model to allow for non–systematic influences of one sort or another in the relationships.[6] Typically, a distribution[7] is specified for the unknown ε in equation (4.2.1) and β is estimated from the resulting system of equations, using all available observations on y and X. Only if the data are consistent and complete, a macroeconometric model will be able to keep a complete balance between supply and demand in all sectors, satisfying the general equilibrium constraints in the benchmark period; otherwise, inconsistencies will emerge. Hence, if the macroeconometric approach is used, then, in general,

$$(4.2.2) \qquad F\ (y,\ X;\ \hat{\beta},\ \varepsilon) \neq 0$$

for the benchmark period (where $\hat{\beta}$ is the estimated vector of parameters).

The second or general equilibrium approach has its origins, on the one hand, in the work by Arrow, Debreu and others dealing with the theoretical Walrasian general equilibrium model, and, on the other hand, in the Leontief input–output model. In fact, the computable general equilibrium models reported here extend Leontief's empirical work on linear models based on fixed input–output coefficients[8] by closing the 'circular flow–of–incomes' from demand to production to income and back to demand, incorporating endogenous consumer and producer behaviour, usually expressed in endogenous factor and commodity prices.[9] The first contribution to this approach is Johansen's

---

auctioneer managing the process of adjustment to the equilibrium position in each market. See Hansen (1970).

[6] One such influence which is reflected in the set of random disturbances is the 'omitted–variables' error.

[7] Indeed, the specification of the probability distribution of these disturbances and of the exogenous variables is part of the model (Fischer et $al.$, 1988).

[8] In the original static input–output model, only one technique exists for producing each output, with input requirements per unit of output kept fixed and final demand exogenous; there is no joint production. See Bulmer–Thomas (1982).

[9] The term 'computable general equilibrium model' is generally used to denote those general equilibrium models which do not allow for joint production and for switches between activities. The term 'applied general equilibrium models' has been used to describe models based on activity analysis which generalizes the production structure by representing it in terms of activities. In these models, joint production is permitted and there may be more than one activity producing the same output. For a discussion of 'applied general equilibrium models', see Fischer et $al.$ (1988).

(1960) model of the Norwegian economy (see Rattsø, 1982). In the last decade, in numerous empirical applications, the computable general equilibrium approach was adopted to study a broad range of issues including income distribution, agricultural and resource economics, and international trade.[10]

In contrast to the macroeconometric approach, the general equilibrium approach integrates the behaviour of individual agents or groups of agents into a consistent framework by à *priori* imposing constraints (or system requirements) on the economic system as a whole (Fischer *et al.*, 1988). A typical example of such a constraint is the requirement that markets clear, either by quantity or price adjustment. For instance, in the case of price adjustment in a competitive commodity market, although all agents are affected by the market price, no agent is able to influence it individually, the price being determined by the system requirement of supply–demand balance.[11] This consistency property requires the general equilibrium modeller to start from a complete and consistent data set. To this end, a standard practice of 'calibration' has evolved, which means that parameter values of demand and production functions are selected which enable the model to exactly reproduce the constructed data set as a 'base' solution to the model – on the assumption that there are no changes in policies from those in operation in the base period. As such, computable general equilibrium models are non–stochastic – in contrast to macroeconometric models. In terms of equation (4.2.1), the disturbance term ε is set equal to zero and β is solved from the resulting system of equations using a single observation of y and X, implicitly assuming that no factors other than those already included in the model have affected and will affect the values of the endogenous variables. It is evident that if the 'calibration' approach is used to derive $\hat{\beta}$, then

$$(4.2.3) \qquad F \ (y, \ X; \ \hat{\beta}, \ 0) = 0$$

In this way, the general equilibrium constraints are satisfied. However, apart from the consistency requirement, there is a practical problem of empirical estimation which has led to the practice of 'calibration'. General equilibrium models are generally characterised by a higher degree of sectoral

---

[10] For a review of computable general equilibrium models, see Shoven and Whalley (1984), Borges (1986), De Janvry and Sadoulet (1987), Decaluwé and Martens (1988) and Sherman Robinson (1988).

[11] In this context, Mansur and Whalley (1984:84) remark that 'at an aggregate industry level input prices are unlikely to be exogenous, and exogenously given factor endowments introduce additional cross–equation restrictions (among different sectors), particularly across errors.' Hence, to obtain consistent estimates of the general equilibrium model's production parameters, this simultaneity should be taken into account. In practice, this may prove difficult.

desaggregation than macroeconometric models.[12] This makes their empirical estimation on the basis of time–series data rather difficult because the necessary data often do not exist for more than one or two points in time. Therefore, most computable general equilibrium models can be said to 'involve dimensionalities that are quite outside those which econometricians are used to, and estimation of all model parameters using a stochastic specification and time series data is usually ruled out as infeasible' (Mansur and Whalley, 1984:69). Accordingly, model builders within the general equilibrium approach do not emphasize forecasting to the same extent as those within the macroeconometric approach. Instead, they have concentrated on preserving sufficient transparancy and simplicity of structure to enable a clear exposition of the mechanisms generating any simulated result (S. Robinson, 1988).

4.2.2   *Theoretical Specifications*

In this section, the different theoretical approaches discussed in Chapter 2, *viz.* the classical, neoclassical and post–Keynesian approaches, will be compared in terms of differences in computable general equilibrium model specification. In so doing, I will compare the alternative approaches, firstly, in terms of their macro–economic assumptions – particularly with respect to the savings–investment relationship[13] or 'macro–economic closure' – and, secondly, in terms of their micro–economic assumptions.

General equilibrium implies macro–economic equilibrium, *i.e.* that total savings equal total investment in terms of current prices. Sen (1963) showed that, in a closed economy with a neoclassical production function, it is possible only by coincidence, given predetermined levels of real investment and public consumption, to pay production factors the value of their marginal product, while simultaneously maintaining full employment of these production factors, because the general equilibrium model has more equations than unknowns. As such, the modeller has to drop one of the equations, or introduce some other 'unknown' into the system in order to render it mathematically

---

[12] It should be observed, however, that the difference in level of sectoral desaggregation is not an inherent difference between the two approaches, because, in principle, desaggregated macroeconometric models can be constructed, whereas the econometric estimation of the parameters of a general equilibrium model is not impossible (Jorgenson, 1984).

[13] Within the framework of an aggregated general equilibrium model, Taylor and Lysy (1979) show that the features of medium–run growth of an economy depend substantially on the manner in which savings and investment are brought into equality within each temporary equilibrium, making it the key element in any computable general equilibrium model. Their point of departure was the insensitivity of income distribution to policy changes in the models of Adelman and Robinson (1978) and Taylor *et al.* (1980).

determined.[14] Hence, the classical, neoclassical or post–Keynesian approaches may be viewed as different ways of rendering a general equilibrium system mathematically determined. Because the classical approach (in which investments are savings–determined) may be regarded as a 'special case' of the neoclassical model, the comparison will be limited to only the neoclassical – in particular the Walrasian – and the post–Keynesian approaches.[15]

In the Walrasian approach[16], full employment of factors of production is maintained by freely varying prices. Real wages or rents paid to production factors are determined by their respective marginal productivities and their relative availability, so that with full employment all income flows are determined from the side of supply. Investment is brought into equality with planned savings through some mechanism outside the system, *e.g.* the interest rate. In most neoclassical general equilibrium models, the adjustment process is not explicitly discussed, but *no independent investment equation is introduced*. With earnings given, the total amount saved is determined by behavioural parameters, and investment is assumed to adjust to saving. This assumes that 'full employment investment and saving could *always* be brought into equality at a rate of interest at or above the minimum interest rate at which the liquidity preference becomes perfectly elastic – a problem that worried Keynes.' (Sen, 1963:55). Hence, in a Walrasian model, there is no possibility of unemployment of factors of production. Say's law always holds true.

In the post–Keynesian approach, the distribution of income is institutionally determined. Rather than assuming that it can be derived from the nature of technology of the production process and the economy's given endowment of production factors, post–Keynesian theory treats the distribution of income as a variable directly linked to the institutional factors determining a division of income between various income categories, particularly between wages and profits (Eichner and Kregel, 1975). Hence, the marginal productivity conditions by which real wage rates and profit rates are determined in neoclassical general equilibrium models are dropped in most

---

[14] Following Sen, there is a large literature on different closure rules including Taylor and Lysy (1979) and Adelman and Robinson (1988). The results of a general equilibrium model are sensitive to the model's theoretical specification. See Rattsø (1982) and Decaluwé *et al.* (1988) for simulation exercises under alternative theoretical specifications.

[15] In this section, I am only able to deal with some of the differences between the various approaches to computable general equilibrium modellling. A more extensive treatment of the various approaches to general equilibrium modelling can be found in Taylor (1983) and Sherman Robinson (1988).

[16] For an introduction and survey of computable general equilibrium models of the Walrasian type the reader may be referred to Shoven and Whalley (1984) whose discussion is limited to modelling efforts in the fields of taxation and international trade, and Borges (1986) who gives an assesment of the types of policy issues which could be addressed with a Walrasian general equilibrium model.

post–Keynesian models. Further, following the classical proposition, post–Keynesians assume that the propensity to save out of profits is higher than the propensity to save out of wage income (Kaldor, 1956; Pasinetti, 1962). While Pasinetti attributes the higher propensity to save out of profit income to people in the higher income brackets (normally wealth owners), Kaldor (1966:310) explicitly rejects this idea and regards 'the high savings propensity out of profits as something which attaches to the nature of business income.'[17] In contrast to neoclassical models, post–Keynesian models include *an independent investment equation* in which investment is determined by (long–term) expectations, nonmarket considerations, and in some cases the rate of interest. Savers abstaining from present consumption do not simultaneously place specific orders either for future consumption or for capital goods, but instead they acquire generalised stores of value which they can spend when they please on what they please. In these circumstances, planned savings equal planned investment only by coincidence. In effect, this divorce of saving from contemporaneous investment imposes on capital and commodity markets too large a burden of coordination (Tobin, 1983:14). Because relative prices, including the interest rate, are slow to adjust, the equality between investment and saving is brought about instead by a change in income distribution. For instance, if real investment exceeds planned savings, the income distribution will shift to the income category with the higher saving propensity so as to permit the necessary investment finance to come forth.[18] The extra saving is in some sense unintended and is often called 'forced saving' for that reason (Kaldor, 1956).

Neoclassical and post–Keynesian approaches differ not only with respect to the manner in which *macro*–economic equilibrium between saving and investment is brought about, but also with respect to their *micro*–economic foundations.

Neoclassical micro–economic theory postulates individual economic agents who, given their endowments of productive resources and wealth and given market prices, atomistically maximise their utilities (as consumers) and/or profits (as producers) in a world without uncertainty and (socio–economic) group interests. Economic agents are assumed to be price–takers; market power is absent. Market prices, equating demands and supplies and governing quan-

---

[17] In both cases, the post–Keynesian treatment of savings is at variance with the neoclassical life–cycle theory of saving in which individuals, who regard saving as deferred consumption, aim at an optimal spread of consumption over their life time. See Van Ewijk (1989:12–15) for a review of these alternative views on differential savings.

[18] In the commodity markets, the excess demand for investment goods leads to rising prices. Hence, real wages fall, while, due to mark–up pricing, profit incomes are not affected. Because the (marginal) propensity to consume out of profits is supposed to be less than the propensity to consume out of wages, this shift in income distribution reduces aggregate demand and restores equilibrium between aggregate demand and supply.

tities produced, bought, and sold by all agents, are determined simultaneously for all commodities and resources. The neoclassical model encompasses intertemporal choices, time–consuming production technologies, and risk about the future by a simple ingenious expedient, namely extending the list of commodities, prices, and markets by distinguishing the dates and contingencies in which commodities are to be delivered (Tobin, 1983). With frictionless, costless, simultaneously cleared auction markets for all commodities, there is no need for money holdings to bridge gaps between sales and purchases or to mitigate costly searches for advantageous transactions and there is thus no need for making binding nominal contracts.

Because the underlying theoretical structure of Walrasian general equilibrium models is so firmly rooted in neoclassical micro–theory, they are often used in the (comparative static) welfare analysis of a particular policy change, with particular emphasis on its aggregate efficiency impact. Such welfare analysis usually relies upon a comparison between an existing, 'before–policy–change' equilibrium and a counterfactual equilibrium computed with modified policies. The measures most widely used are Hicksian compensating variations which take the new equilibrium incomes and prices and ask how much income must be taken away or added in order to return agents to their prechange utility level, and Hicksian equivalent variations which take the old equilibrium income and prices and compute the change needed to achieve new equilibrium utilities (Shoven and Whalley, 1984:1014). For the economy as a whole, the welfare consequences of any policy change are measured by aggregating the compensating or equivalent variations over the different household groups in order to assess whether the gainers could compensate the losers. In effect, one is using the (possibly weighted) sum of individual utilities as a social welfare function. The theoretical shortcomings of this particular social welfare function and of social welfare functions in general are, of course, well known (see Samuelson, 1947).

The excess demand functions of a Walrasian general equilibrium model have two important properties. First, they are homogeneous of degree zero in all prices and income, and, second, they are not independent (Hansen, 1970). The second property implies that in accordance with Walras' law[19], for any allowable price vector $(p_1, ..., p_n)$, there are only $(n - 1)$ independent excess demand equations to determine $(n - 1)$ *relative* price ratios. The first property of zero homogeneity of the excess demand functions implies that if a vector $(p_1, ..., p_n)$ constitutes a solution to the system of n excess demand

---

[19] In the simplified version of a pure exchange model (which is due to Hicks), Walras' Law states that the following identity holds as an aggregate budget restriction: $\Sigma_i \, p_i(x_{di} - x_{si}) = 0$, where x_{di} is demand for commodity i and x_{si} is supply of commodity i. The identity states that at any set of prices, the total value of consumer expenditures equals consumer incomes. See Hansen (1970).

equations, any vector λ $(p_1, ..., p_n)$ will also constitute a solution. Only relative prices are of importance in such a model; the absolute price level has no impact on the equilibrium outcome. In order to determine the absolute price level, a wide variety of price normalisation equations by which the price of a particular commodity – the numéraire commodity – is fixed, have been used in Walrasian computable general equilibrium models.[20] The choice of the numéraire commodity does not affect any of the real variables in the model. Another approach to determining the absolute price level is to add a monetary side to the model in which the absolute price level is determined endogenously (Adelman and Robinson, 1978). In the Walrasian approach, it is thus assumed that money is neutral, *i.e.* that 'Whatever functions money may perform, whatever holdings agents may therefore desire, the *real* equilibrium must be independent of the stock of money as measured in its own nominal units' (Tobin, 1983:9). Money neutrality underlies the 'classical dichotomy' which separates the determination of real variables and relative prices from the determination of the absolute price level.[21] In a Walrasian model in which prices and wages are flexible and markets are price–clearing, the macro–economic variables are determined by the outcome of the (micro–economic) general equilibrium model. Specifically, micro–economic behaviour is not affected by changes in the rate of inflation.

By contrast, the fundamental assumption of post–Keynesian micro–economic theory is that micro–economic behaviour is affected by uncertainty[22] about macro–economic variables such as the inflation rate and about such variables as future proceeds. Particularly, investment is a highly hazardous business, a 'gambling decision', for business people at the time of their decisions do not know whether they will make profits or not in future years. Following Keynes, post–Keynesians emphasize the essential unpredictability of future returns on investment. This may explain why agents deciding on investment often adopt certain rules or norms on 'proper' financial behaviour. A well–known example of such a convention is the emphasis on the pay–back period criterion[23] rather than the (neoclassical) present value criterion in the explanation of investment behaviour (Kaldor and Mirrlees, 1962). Because of the uncertainty, rules–of–thumb, practical modes of behaviour, must be devised. These rules may include mark–up pricing rules and wage indexation formulas, and/or

---

[20] Johansen (1960) fixed the wage rate and thus expressed all prices in terms of wages. Dervis *et al.* (1982) propose to use an aggregate wholesale price index.

[21] The classical dichotomy is the rationale of the quantity theory of money, the proposition that absolute prices are proportional to the stock of nominal money.

[22] What is meant here is 'true' uncertainty. See *e.g.* Davidson (1991).

[23] The pay–back period criterion implies that investment is related to the (undiscounted) prospective returns within a certain time horizon.

institutional arrangements such as publicly guaranteed minimum support prices, social security schemes, and (nominal) wage negotiation. Post–Keynesians stress 'reasonableness', that is to say, acting sensibly with given information (Harcourt, 1985:132). Generally, this brings them to postulate expectations as being formed adaptively.[24]

These rules–of–thumb, just because they have to be based on expectations which can come badly unstuck, may prove to be a very unstable basis for economic growth. In a world of uncertainty where the future is not merely a random draw from a given and unchanging probability distribution and in which production takes time, the most efficient way to organise production is via forward monetary contracts (Davidson, 1978). If contracts are made in terms of money, then nominal magnitudes matter and money affects real decisions.[25] For post–Keynesians, '*binding* nominal contractual commitments are a sensible method for dealing with true uncertainty whenever economic processes span a long period of calendar time. These legal arrangements permit agents to protect themselves to a large extent against the unpredictable consequences of current decisions to commit real resources towards production and investment activities of long duration. (...) By using fixed forward money contracts requiring performance and payment at specified future dates, entrepreneurs (and households) can efficiently control the sequencing use of, and payment for, resources in time–consuming production and exchange processes. The use of overlapping money contracts permits agents to cope with the unknown by controlling their cash flow position over time. When prediction is not possible, such control is eminently desirable in a money–using economy' (Davidson 1991:137–138)

The next main point is the importance of socio–economic relationships and

---

[24] Many economists nowadays postulate 'rational' expectations, implicitly earmarking adaptive expectations as being 'irrational'. In view of the available empirical evidence on expectation formation, it is not at all clear why the assumption of rational expectations is so often preferred to the assumption of adaptive expections. Various studies that were carried out on the formation of expectations (using samples of expert opinions or household samples) reject the hypothesis of 'rational' expectations and conclude that, if anything, expectations seem to be formed adaptively (Jonung and Laidler, 1988). Hence, there have to be other reasons for the popularity of the rational expectations postulate. Martin Paldam's (1989:340) appears a reasonable explanation. In his view, many economists have grown accustomed to using 'rational expectations' because (*i*) it allows them to use all kinds of intellectually gratifying mathematical exercises, (*ii*) it allows them to make economic theory 'real' in the longer run, and (*iii*) it makes it easy to keep institutional and sociopolitical reasoning out of their models.

[25] This was recognised by Arrow and Hahn (1971:356–7): '... the terms in which contracts are made matter. In particular, if money is the goods in terms of which contracts are made, then the price of goods in terms of money are of special significance (nominal magnitudes matter!).' Arrow and Hahn demonstrate that if contracts are made in nominal terms (so that nominal magnitudes affect real magnitudes), then the existence theorems of Walrasian general equilibrium break down.

institutions in post–Keynesian theory. Post–Keynesians, following the classical tradition, look at the behaviour of groups and their functions in an economy. Economic agents are regarded as members of particular socio–economic groups including capital–owners, entrepeneurs, or employees, which share particular interests in common and articulate these interests *via* particular organisations such as farmers' organisations or unions of employers. For post–Keynesians, nominal prices and wages are under varying degrees of control by different socio–economic groups in the economy. Consequently, nominal price and wage changes are viewed as the outcome of distributional conflict between these groups, depending on the relative strength of one group *vis* – à – *vis* other groups. Particularly in manufacturing, individual firms (or at least the price leaders) have discretion and rely on mark–up pricing rules because of oligopolistic interdependence. Profit maximisation, at least in its simplest forms, is rejected, for the following reasons: 'the complementarity of inputs ... precludes the estimation of marginal products for individual inputs; and the inability to define ... a demand curve for individual firms means that marginal revenue product curves cannot be estimated' (Asimakopulos 1980–81:164). Due to the nominal rigidities, the excess demand functions in the post–Keynesian models are not homogeneous of degree zero in prices. This implies that, in these models, the nominal side and the real side of the economy are interlinked. There is no need for a numéraire, since the absolute price level is already determined.

Table 4.1 summarizes the main differences between computable general equilibrium models of the neoclassical versus the post–Keynesian type. The discussion above has concentrated on a comparison of the most extreme version of the neoclassical model – the Walrasian one – with the post–Keynesian model. Apart from the Walrasian approach, the neoclassical approach encompasses two other major strands of thought (S. Robinson, 1988), *viz.* the elasticity pessimist, and the (temporary) disequilibrium approach, characteristics of which are also listed in Table 4.1. These two categories of general equilibrium models are classified as neoclassical because of the fact that, in these models, investments are determined by savings in contrast to what happens in post–Keynesian models. The elasticity pessimist approach (as summarised by Dervis *et al.*, 1982) overlaps with the Walrasian approach, although, in empirical application, markets adjust less flexibly in elasticity pessimist models than in Walrasian models due to low elasticities of substitution between commodities and/or production factors. The real difference within the neoclassical approach resides in the distinction between Walrasian models and elasticity pessimist models on the one hand and temporary disequilibrium models on the other. In the latter models including those by Barro and Grossman (1971) and Malinvaud (1977), nominal prices are, for reasons left unexplained[26], stuck at values other than the Walrasian general equilibrium solution.[27] Economic agents – consumers, producers, employees – may be constrained in their demands and supplies by the actual transactions they are able to perform at these wrong prices. They cannot effectuate their 'notional' demands and supplies (*i.e.* the transactions they would choose to make at these prices if constrained only by their endowments) because the given rigid prices will not clear the markets. But the markets will nonetheless clear at some vector of quantities, which replace prices as the equilibrating variables, resulting in a 'disequilibrium' solution. Price and wage rigidities are regarded as short–run phenomena which will disappear in the medium to long run. Disequilibrium situations are therefore confined to the short run only.

Applying the fixed–price variable–quantity calculus to a large number of markets simultaneously, disequilibrium models permit a number of possible outcomes (Malinvaud, 1977). First, an underconsumptionist regime may prevail when firms are rationed both in their demand for labour and in their supply of goods. Second, 'Keynesian' unemployment[28] may occur when suppliers are rationed in both the market for goods and the market for labour. Labour is unemployed and firms do not sell more because of lack of effective demand. When labour is not fully employed and firms sell all their supply, a regime of classical unemployment prevails. Finally, when demand exceeds supply in all markets, there is overall inflationary pressure. Because prices do not rise, but remain sticky, the regime is called 'repressed inflation'. There exists, in fact, a fifth regime – Walrasian equilibrium – which will prevail only whenever nominal prices are, by coincidence, stuck at the values of the Walrasian general equilibrium solution.

---

[26] Some authors, notably Leijonhufvud (1968), explain the price rigidities in terms of the high information costs associated with adjusting prices quickly and continuously. A similar approach is taken in the so–called menu–cost theory. See Gordon (1990).

[27] Note that classical general equilibrium in which the real industrial wage is fixed, with the corresponding labour supply assumed infinitely elastic at the exogenous wage, may be classified under the (temporary) disequilibrium approach.

[28] The disequilibrium approach, however, misses the central point of Keynesian logic, *i.c.* that there could be an underemployment equilibrium even if prices happened to be the 'right' ones for full Walrasian equilibrium.

Table 4.1
Classification of Computable General Equilibrium Approaches

1. Neoclassical	2. Post–Keynesian
– *Savings determine investments (Say's law holds true).* – *There is need for a numeraire.* – *Neoclassical micro – economic behaviour is postulated. There is no true uncertainty.*	– *Investments determine savings.* – *There is no need for a numeraire.* – *Post – Keynesian micro – economic behaviour is postulated in which uncertainty about macro – economic variables such as the rate of inflation affects economic decision making at the micro – level.*
– *Economic agents are regarded as atomistic individuals. The notion of socio – economic group interests is absent.* – *The distribution of income is explained solely by the availability of variable factor inputs and their marginal productivity.*	– *Economic agents are viewed as belonging to particular socio – economic groups, e.g. capital – owners in contra-distinction to employees.* – *Markets are 'imperfect' with monopolistic elements. The distribution of income is institutionally determined.*
a. Walrasian – *All markets are price – clearing. Economic agents are pricetakers.* – *Full employment prevails.* – *Elasticities (particularly of substitution between factors of production and/or between tradables and non – tradables) are significantly different from zero.*	 – *There is no tendency to full employment.*
b. Elasticity–Pessimist – *Substitution elasticities are low in a number of important relationships.*	
c. Temporary Disequilibrium Approach – *Markets do not work 'properly' (generally due to government intervention) or are not present at all. There exist nominal rigidities in the economy. Rationing of economic agents produces spillover effects in other markets. Unemployment may arise. Disequilibria are, however, confined to the short run.*	

4.3   The Main Assumptions of the Model

Because the term 'general equilibrium' is, in this study, conceived of in a specific sense, Section 4.3.1 begins by explaining exactly what is meant. The 9–sector classification used in the model is discussed in 4.3.2. The general equilibrium model itself is the subject of the next two sections. It consists of two parts, *viz.* a static within–period equilibrium model built around a social accounting matrix with nine production sectors and three income categories which is discussed in Section 4.3.3, and a between–periods part which is discussed in 4.3.4.

4.3.1   The Concept of General Equilibrium

Following the terminology suggested by Frisch[29], one can say that if there is no tendency for the variables in a model to change, given the model's data, then the system of variables is in equilibrium (Hansen, 1970:4). This definition brings out the essentially dynamic nature of equilibrium, because to determine whether there is any tendency to change, one must first study the forces of the system and determine the equilibrium conditions. Probably the most common definition of equilibrium conditions in economics is the equality of the quantity in demand and the quantity in supply. This definition presumes that if the quantity in demand does not equal the quantity in supply, the price will tend to change – a presumption which has found explicit expression in Walras' excess demand hypothesis for price changes. Alternatively, one may define equilibrium as the equality between the demand price and the supply price. If the demand price does not equal the supply price, producers will change the quantity in supply. This is Marshall's excess price hypothesis for quantity changes (Hansen, 1970). Every definition or, rather, condition of equilibrium, thus presumes a particular adjustment process in which either prices or quantities change towards equilibrium.

In the model, aggregate demand for commodity i, x_{di} ($i = 1, .., 9$) is made up of intermediate demand, consumption demand, investment demand, demand for additional stocks, and export demand, or

$$x_{di} = \sum_{j=1}^{9} \alpha_{ij} x_{sj} + c_i + g_i + i_i + \Delta\, stk_i + e_i \qquad i = 1, ..,9.$$

where x_{si} is domestic supply of commodity i, α_{ij} are input–output coefficients, c_i is private consumption demand for i, g_i is public consumption demand for i, i_i is gross domestic investment demand for i, $\Delta\, stk_i$ is the

---

[29] See R. Frisch (1935–36), 'On the notion of equilibrium and disequilibrium', *Review of Economic Studies*, volume 3. Quoted in Hansen (1970).

change in stocks of i, and e_i is export demand for i. Aggregate supply of good i consists of domestic supply of i plus imports of i, m_i. In real terms, general equilibrium requires that all excess demands be zero or

$$x_{di} - x_{si} - m_i = 0 \qquad\qquad i = 1, ..,9.$$

General equilibrium is defined as a set of prices and quantities such that all excess demands for commodities and services are zero. Prices (in agriculture) and quantities (in non–agriculture) are the equilibrating variables of the model, while zero excess demands are the equilibrium conditions or system constraints which the model has to satisfy. General equilibrium as defined above has the following two implications:

(i) supply also equals demand for the economy as a whole, which implies that, *ex – post*, GDP (at current prices) is equal to aggregate domestic final demand (at current prices) plus the difference between exports and imports valued respectively at f.o.b. prices and c.i.f. prices; and

(ii) *ex – post* gross national savings (defined as the sum of gross domestic and foreign savings) are equal to gross domestic investment.

The notion of general equilibrium used here does not imply full employment of factors of production.

4.3.2 The Model's Sector Classification

The sectoral desaggregation of the model was deliberately chosen to highlight the main links between agricultural activities and the rest of the economy. The production and demand sides of the model distinguish the following nine sectors (where each sector is treated as if it produces a single, homogeneous commodity):

(1) *rice* which includes paddy and rice milling;

(2) *wheat* including wheat and wheat flour milling;

(3) *other food crops* which include jowar (great millet), bajra (bulrush or spiked millet), maize, gram and pulses;

(4) *commercial crops* including sugarcane, groundnut, raw jute, raw coffee, tea and coffee plantation, rubber and tobacco plantation;

(5) *other agriculture* which consists of milk and animal products, animal services, forestry and logging, and fishing;

(6) *fertiliser industries*;

(7) *basic, intermediate and capital goods industries* which include minerals, chemicals and chemical products, heavy industries, construction, electricity, gas and water supply;

(8) *consumer goods industries* which include agro–industries producing food products, beverages, textiles, and leather products; and

(9) *services* including storage, trade, banking and insurance, real estate, educational and medical services, public administration and defence.

It can be seen that, within agriculture, a distinction was made between 'crop agriculture' ($i = 1, .., 4$) and other agriculture ($i = 5$), and that, within 'crop agriculture', foodgrain production ($i = 1, 2, 3$) is distinguished from non–foodgrain production ($i = 4$). Food crops are important items of consumption, whereas commercial crops are mainly used as intermediate inputs in agro–based industry and for exports. It is important to distinguish between rice and wheat on the one hand and other food crops on the other hand, because the rate of adoption of high yielding varieties is much higher in the case of rice and wheat as compared to other food crops. Rice and wheat are also the main fertiliser consuming crops (accounting for more than 60 per cent of total fertiliser use). The breakdown of manufacturing into consumer goods (sector 8) on the one hand and basic, intermediate and capital goods (sector 7) on the other is based on the criterion of the dominant use pattern of the gross output of these sectors. For present purposes, what is important is that the consumer goods sector is largely made up of agro–based industries in contrast to the basic, intermediate and capital goods sector which is an important supplier of inputs and capital goods to agriculture. Fertiliser manufacturing (sector 6) is distinguished as a separate sector as it produces a major input into agriculture. Finally, a services sector (being the rest of the economy) is included. Manufacturing and services include both registered and unregistered production units.

4.3.3   The Static Within–Period Equilibrium Model

The static within–period model is based on the static general equilibrium model documented in Taylor (1983), Taylor, Sarkar, and Rattsø (1984) and Rattsø (1986; 1988a; 1989). The present model is different from these earlier contributions in a number of important respects, *viz.* the treatment of the agricultural sectors (particularly in terms of short–run supply response), the behaviour of the government sector (in particular with respect to the agricultural sectors), the degree of sectoral detail, and the reference period. It is based on the following assumptions:

(i) Investment decisions are separated from savings decisions. In fact, investment decisions are causally prior to savings decisions in the sense that changes in investment levels lead to consequent adjustments in savings levels.[30] Different private investment functions are assumed for the

---

[30] No common understanding of the savings–investment relationship has emerged out of the macroeconometric models of the Indian economy. For example, Bhattacharya (1984) and Krishnamurty (1985) assume that investments are determined by savings in contradistinction to Pandit (1985) who applies a Keynesian multiplier framework in which manufacturing output adjusts to demand, and Srivastava (1981) who adopts an IS–LM approach.

agricultural and non–agricultural sectors. Private agricultural investment reacts positively to changes in the one–period lagged value of the agricultural–non–agricultural terms of trade and the one–period lagged amount of public investment in agriculture. Private investment in manufacturing and services is positively related, firstly, to sectoral mark–up income which represents the availability of internal investment funds[31] and, secondly, to public investment in the previous period. This specification was chosen since a 'crowding–in' effect of public investment on private investment is acknowledged by many authors including Srinivasan and Narayana (1977) and Chakravarty (1987), while other studies have shown the relative importance of internal funds in financing investment demand per sector (Krishnamurty, 1985; Bhattacharya, 1984; Lahiri *et al.*, 1984). For fertilisers, no private investment demand function is included as this sector is largely a public sector and as such is modelled as belonging to the public domain.

(*ii*) The supply of agricultural products is endogenously determined in contrast to the general equilibrium models developed by Taylor (1983), De Janvry and Subbarao (1986), Sarkar and Panda (1991) and Rattsø (1989) in which short–run agricultural supply response is absent. Agricultural prices are in principle allowed to fluctuate to clear the market. Price adjustment in the case of rice and wheat is subject to a lower bound defined by the level of procurement prices. In case the market price falls below this lower bound, the procurement price becomes a minimum support price and government procurement is increased to raise the market price to the level of the minimum support price.

(*iii*) All production for self–consumption is valued at market prices.

(*iv*) Non–agricultural prices are assumed to be determined by Kaleckian cost–plus rules. Output of the non–agricultural sectors is determined by sectorwise demand, presupposing underutilisation of their production capacities. Only in case the level of demand exceeds the maximum level of output given installed capacity, the mark–up rate will adjust. Otherwise, mark–up rates are assumed constant (Chatterji, 1989). The fertiliser price is kept fixed for policy purposes. In case fertiliser demand exceeds production capacity, fertiliser supply will adjust through extra imports.

(*v*) The real and nominal sides of the economy are linked through the fixing (in nominal terms) of the non–agricultural nominal wage rates, the

---

[31] The specification of the non–agricultural investment demand functions may be related to Kalecki (1971) who regards profits as more important factors influencing investment demand than interest rates and changes in output (Sawyer, 1985:168). Kalecki's theory is based on the following considerations. First, capital market imperfections may make profits important as a source of finance and as an influence on the availability and cost of external finance. Second, in an uncertain world, future profitability may be gauged in part by current profitability. Finally, changes in profitability, leading to changes in desired capital stock, may lead to investment demand. See Kalecki (1971), Chapter 15.

procurement prices for foodgrains, and the exchange rate.

(*vi*) Value added accrues to agricultural and non–agricultural income earners. Non–agricultural income includes wage income and profit income. Income distribution determines savings and consumption. Average savings rates differ between the three income categories, *viz.* agriculturalists, non–agricultural wage earners and non–agricultural profit recipients. Marginal propensities to consume differ between agricultural and non–agricultural consumers.

(*vii*) With respect to foreign trade, world market prices are taken as given and the nominal exchange rate is assumed exogenous. Part of imports is treated as complementary, the other part as competitive. Competitive imports and exports are determined exogenously. 'The law of one price' is not imposed in the model and, consequently, domestic and border prices of imports and exports may differ. The price differential creates an income gain or loss which is registered on the expenditure side of the public budget. This implies that the government pays a variable import and export subsidy to firms, so that the latter can buy and sell at the same price at home and abroad (Taylor, 1983). It also implies that, for domestic producers, there is no difference between the domestic price and the world market price of their products and, hence, price–incentives to reduce imports or to step up export production are absent.

(*viii*) Only the real side of the economy is incorporated in the model, implicitly assuming passive money, *i.e.* the causality in the money supply process runs from money demand to money supply (Kaldor, 1982). Empirical evidence for India indicating that real factors predominate in aggregate and sectoral price changes can be found in Bhattacharya (1984), Singh (1989), and Balakrishnan (1991). In these studies, much of the inflation was found to be due to structural influences, *e.g.* crop failures, rather than to monetary operations.

4.3.4   *Medium–Run Adjustment Mechanisms*

In the between–periods part of the model, the exogenous variables and policy instruments are updated and the following four intertemporal adjustment mechanisms are specified, *viz.* (*i*) non–agricultural capital accumulation, (*ii*) non–agricultural nominal wage indexation, (*iii*) investment in irrigation, and (*iv*) cropwise area allocation.

(*i*) In non–agriculture, investment takes place even in the face of persistent idle capacity. Micro–economic justifications for the assumption that investment projects get undertaken even though firms are not operating at full capacity, include the building up of capacity ahead of demand to exploit decreasing capital project costs or to provide a margin of safety against a sudden upswing in sales (Taylor, 1985) and pre–emptive behaviour aimed at maintaining barriers of entry (Ghose, 1974a; Chandrasekhar, 1988).

(*ii*) Non–agricultural nominal wages are indexed to the consumer price index and to their one–period lagged values. The consumer price index is the weighted average of sectoral prices where the weights are defined by the consumption expenditures in each period.[32] This formulation of wage formation was adopted because most authors conclude that wage indexation to the con- sumer price index is the main explanation of wage growth, whereas changes in labour productivity are relatively unimportant (Subramanian, 1977; Lahiri *et al.*, 1984; Krishnamurty, 1985; Chatterji, 1989).

(*iii*) Public and private capital formation in agriculture is visualised as primarily resulting in the extension of gross irrigated area, either through direct investment in irrigation infrastructure or through investment in electrification, rural roads, *etc.* Hence, gross irrigated area is assumed to depend on the one–period lagged level of agricultural investment (the particular gestation lag–structure was adopted to fit the sequential framework of the model). In this way, agricultural capital formation is linked to productivity via irrigation which affects both the cropping intensity and the level of yields (Pandit, 1985).

(*iv*) With respect to agriculture, a Nerlovian partial adjustment model is postulated in which farmers are assumed to decide how much irrigated and non–irrigated area to allocate to crop *i* in period *t* depending on the one–period lagged price of crop *i* relative to the one–period lagged weighted average price of the other three crops, implicitly assuming that farmers' expectations are formed adaptively. Similar specifications of cropwise area allocation in Indian agriculture are used by Gulati (1987) and Bhide *et al.* (1989).

4.4   *Agricultural Policy Simulation Experiments*

The present model is meant for policy analysis. A change in policy may be introduced into the model by changing the values of some of the policy instruments. Scenarios with and without the policy change being implemented may be compared with scenarios where policies have remained unchanged – a scenario generated with the help of a model is characterised by the values of the exogenously specified parameters and policy instruments. The outcomes of the various scenarios which can be compared in terms of a number of indicators reflecting the various stated objectives, show the impact of the policy

---

[32] This particular index (the All–India Consumer Price Index) was chosen because most of the wage boards have related their recommendations regarding wage indexation (*via* a dearness allowance) to it. See Subramanian (1977:239–241)

change. Such a procedure raises the following three questions: (*i*) what should the reference scenario (the 'before–policy–change' scenario) look like; (*ii*) which policy changes are to be studied; and (*iii*) what indicators should one use to compare the outcomes ?

4.4.1 *The Reference Scenario*

As the present model is not meant for 'validation', the only purpose served by the reference scenario is to provide a bench mark relative to which policy changes are to be introduced and their impacts studied. Hence, the simulated course of the economy in the reference scenario for the period 1985–90 should not be regarded as a forecast of the likely actual course followed by the economy. The benchmark policy scenario was taken from the National Accounts Statistics and the Seventh Five Year Plan (1985–90) document which provide a detailed account of the values of the policy instruments.

4.4.2 *Agricultural Policy Alternatives*

The outcome of a specific policy change in terms of expenditure instruments depends on the way it is financed (*i.e.* on the particular combination of

Table 4.2
Policy Instruments included in the Model

Agricultural Policy Instruments

    Public Investment in Agriculture
    Public Procurement & Procurement Pricing ($i = 1, 2, 3$)
    Public Distribution & Issue Pricing ($i = 1, 2, 3$)
    Rural Employment Programmes
    Fertiliser Subsidy Rate
    Agricultural Producers' Subsidy Rates ($i = 1, .., 5$)
    Direct Tax Rate of Agricultural Income
    Indirect Tax Rates of Agricultural Goods ($i = 1, .., 5$)
    Public Consumption of Agricultural Goods ($i = 1, .., 5$)
    Exports of Foodgrains ($i = 1, 2, 3$)
    Imports of Agricultural Goods ($i = 1, .., 5$)
    Fertiliser Production

Other Policy Instruments

    Public Investment in Non–Agriculture ($i = 6, .., 9$)
    Non–Agricultural Producers' Subsidy Rates ($i = 6, .., 9$)
    Direct Tax Rate of Non–Agricultural Income
    Indirect Tax Rates of Non–Agricultural Goods ($i = 6, .., 9$)
    Public Consumption of Non–Agricultural Goods ($i = 6, .., 9$)
    Exchange Rate
    Public Employment
    Public Current Transfers

Table 4.3
Indicators for Comparison of Scenarios

Macro – Economic Indicators

      Gross Domestic Product at Factor Cost
      Gross Domestic Product at Market Prices
      Public Revenue Balance (Public Savings)
      Current Account Balance (Foreign Savings)
      Private Domestic Savings
      Gross Domestic Investment
      Consumer Price Index Number
      GDP Deflator
      (Functional) Income Distribution

Sector – Specific Indicators

      Sectoral Production Levels ($i = 1, ..., 9$)
      Commodity Prices ($i = 1, ..., 9$)
      Sectoral Nominal Wage Rates ($i = 6, ..., 9$)
      Government Nominal Wage Rate
      Sectoral Rates of Capacity Utilisation ($i = 6, .., 9$)
      Cropwise Yield Levels ($i = 1, .., 4$)
      Cropwise Per Hectare Fertiliser Consumption ($i = 1, .., 4$)

---

revenue generating instruments by which it is supported). Therefore, a *policy scenario* is defined in terms of a particular combination of both expenditure and revenue instruments. Table 4.2 lists the policy instruments included in the model. In particular, the model will be used to generate scenarios reflecting changes in the outlays on the four following agricultural policy instruments: (1) procurement and/or minimum support prices for some agricultural products; (2) fertiliser subsidies; (3) food subsidisation; and (4) public investment in irrigation. On the revenue side, different methods of financing each of the changes in a particular item of public expenditure can be formulated to study the impact of the method of financing on the outcome of the specific policy change.

4.4.3   Indicators for Comparison of Scenarios

For each year of simulation in a scenario, all the details required for a complete social accounting matrix are generated. To facilitate comparison, one needs to use some aggregate and some sector–specific indicators which reflect the aims of public policy. The effects of each of the policy scenarios will be examined in terms of the indicators listed in Table 4.3.

    Aggregate GDP at 1985 prices is used as an indicator of economic growth. In addition, the different scenarios may be compared in terms of the distribution of GDP across sectors and across the three income categories distinguished in the model. The size of the public revenue deficit in terms of

115

GDP is used as an indicator for comparison, since each of the scenarios will differently affect public revenues via changes in the distribution of incomes and the pattern of demand. Different policy scenarios will also differently affect the size of the current account balance in terms of GDP which provides another important macro–economic indicator. The consumer price index number and the GDP deflator are used as indicators of inflation. Important sector–specific indicators include the indices of prices and nominal wage rates, production levels, and rates of capacity utilisation.

4.5   The Computable General Equilibrium Model

This section discusses the components of the general equilibrium model constructed to assess income distribution and sectoral growth effects of alternative agricultural policies over the short and medium run. Section 4.5.1 discusses the agricultural production sub–model. The larger general equilibrium model of which agricultural production forms a part, is presented in Section 4.5.2. The equations of the complete computable general equilibrium model are given in Appendix 4.1. The list of symbols is given in Appendix 4.2. The solution strategy and the solution algorithm which were used to solve the set of nonlinear simultaneous (excess demand) equations are discussed in Appendix 4.9.

4.5.1   The Agricultural Production Sub-Model

Production of the four crop sectors, *viz.* rice, wheat, other food crops, and commercial crops, is determined by a two–stage procedure in which, first, their acreages are determined, and, next, their yield levels are established.

(i)   Determination of Aggregate and Cropwise Acreage

Net area sown represents the actual physical area under crops and orchards during the reporting year. By definition, gross cropped area during the reporting year is equal to the sum of net sown area and area sown more than once, *i.e.* that part of net sown area on which two or more crops are grown during the period of one agricultural year. Due to a considerable reduction in the potential for raising the amount of net area sown, gross cropped area can be raised only by raising the average cropping intensity (*i.e.* by increasing the extent of multiple cropping). Particularly after the mid–1960s, the potential for raising the amount of net area sown has become considerably limited, not to say exhausted. Consequently, in the model, net sown area is assumed exogenous[33], although not fixed.

Taking more than one crop on the same piece of land in the same agricultural year depends mainly on the availability of irrigation water through canals, wells, *etc.*, because rainfall is highly seasonal and undependable (Dhawan, 1988). Moreover, in many areas, because of the soil structure, the retentivity of soils is poor and the percolation is not adequate to enlarge the underground water resources. In areas of insufficient rainfall or soil with poor moisture retention, irrigation is essential if a second crop is to be grown in the dry season.[34] In turn, the extension of irrigated area is largely dependent on both public and private investment projects. In equation (4.1), total gross irrigated area in period t is made a function of agricultural investment in period $t-1$ and gross irrigated area in period $t-1$. The derivation of (4.1) is given in Appendix 4.3. Gross irrigated area represents the net irrigated area times the number of irrigated crops on it, one followed by the other, during a year. Net irrigated area refers to the physical area irrigated during an agricultural year, each hectare of which is only counted once even if two or more crops are irrigated in different seasons on the same land. The area irrigated more than once is the difference between the gross irrigated area and the net irrigated area.[35] Net irrigated area is assumed to be a constant proportion of gross irrigated area in (4.2).[36] Aggregate cropping intensity is specified as a function of the proportion of net irrigated area to net sown area in (4.3). Equation (4.4) is a definitional relationship, which states that gross cropped area under all crops is the product of net sown area and the aggregate cropping intensity. Gross non-irrigated area is the difference between gross cropped area and gross irrigated area in (4.5).

Next, both gross irrigated and non-irrigated area are allocated across the four crops under consideration. Assuming that the acreage allocation across crops responds to (expected) relative crop price changes, Nerlovian acreage response functions are used to determine the gross non-irrigated and

---

[33] As was done in the agricultural submodel of the modelframe used in the Seventh Plan.

[34] Other factors such as the development of seeds requiring shorter growing periods and mechanisation of farms to speed operations may also contribute to multiple cropping, but their contributions are still relatively inconsequential in most states in India (Narain and Roy, 1980).

[35] Note that it is erroneous to equate the difference between the total multiple cropped area and the area irrigated more than once with the entirely unirrigated multiple cropped area, because the difference includes (*i*) entirely unirrigated multiple cropped area, and (*ii*) area in which an additional crop is raised with the help of irrigation, the first crop being raised during the wet season. See Narain and Roy (1980).

[36] During the period 1980–81 to 1986–87, the ratio of net irrigated area to gross irrigated area did not show any significant change. It fluctuated between 0.77 and 0.78.

irrigated acreage for rice, wheat, other food crops, and commercial crops, in (4.7) and (4.8) respectively. Following Narayana *et al.* (1991), equations (4.7) and (4.8) are written in double–logarithmic form, assuming that the elasticity of acreage with respect to relative price remains constant throughout. Gross non–irrigated area is allocated across crops subject to the restriction that cropwise acreage adds up to aggregate gross non–irrigated area in (4.7). A similar additivity constraint is given in (4.8) for gross irrigated area. The price of crop *i* relative to the weighted average price of the three remaining crops is determined in (4.6). The derivation of the acreage response functions is discussed in Appendix 4.4. Gross cropped area under crop *i* is determined in (4.9).

(*ii*)   *Determination of Crop Yields*

For all crops and all types of crops, actual fertiliser application per hectare is determined by the ratio of the fertiliser price and the market price of the crop under consideration in (4.10) and (4.11), neglecting other important factors influencing a farmer's decision including her perception of risk, credit availability, and the fertiliser supply situation. Appendix 4.5 gives the derivation of the per hectare fertiliser demand functions. Note that these functions are double–logarithmic, presupposing a constant price elasticity of per hectare fertiliser demand.

Per hectare crop yields depend on such factors as the application of fertiliser, the type of seeds (local or high yielding variety), type and availability of irrigation facilities, climatic conditions, and the quality of soil (Fischer *et al.*, 1988:99). The first three factors are to some extent under the control of the farmer which together with the other 'natural' factors determine her agroecological resource endowment. Lack of aggregate data did not allow the inclusion of these factors for all crops in the model. Only in the case of rice and wheat, two types of yield functions are distinguished corresponding to two different cultivation regimes of seed variety and water use, denoted by k, *viz.* (*i*) yield of local and high yielding seeds sown on unirrigated land ($k = 1$); and (*ii*) yield of high yielding variety seeds sown on irrigated land ($k = 2$). It is thus assumed here that all high yielding variety seeds are grown on irrigated land. Equation (4.12) are the yield response functions to fertiliser application for the two cultivation regimes of rice and wheat; these functions exhibit decreasing returns to increased fertiliser input (Narayana *et al.*, 1991). The aggregate yield of crop i ($i = 1, 2$) is the weighted average of the k–types of yield as in (4.15), the weights being the proportion of area under the k–th type in the total area under crop i as defined in (4.13) and (4.14). For other food crops and commercial crops, no distinction has been made between cultivation regimes. Their yields are assumed to depend on the fertiliser application per hectare as in (4.16). The (double–logarithmic) yield response functions for other food crops and commercial crops of (4.16) do not exhibit decreasing returns to increased fertiliser input.

(iii)   Cropwise Production

For all four crops included in the model, both acreage and yield have been determined through (4.1) to (4.16). Production of crop i is determined as the product of area and yield in (4.17). The supply of other agricultural products is exogenous in (4.18). The cropwise amount of fertiliser consumption is determined in (4.19). In equation (4.20), the input–output coefficients α_{6i} are defined as the ratio of fertiliser input per unit of output of the four crop sectors.

   The agricultural production sub–model is summarised in the flow chart given in Figure 4.1. From the figure, it can be seen that agricultural production is determined simultaneously with the cropwise relative price of fertilisers, but with a one–period lag by agricultural investment. The short–run (or within–period) agricultural supply response thus operates solely through changes in relative fertiliser price, per hectare fertiliser input, and per hectare yield levels. In the static within–period model, both the amount of gross cropped area (which depends on one–period lagged agricultural investment) and the allocation of acreage across crops (which depends on lagged relative crop prices) are fixed.

4.5.2   The Remaining Part of the General Equilibrium Model

The agricultural production sub–model of Section 4.5.1 is only one of the 'blocks' of the general equilibrium model. The other blocks are: (i) non–agricultural prices, wages and production capacity; (ii) income generation and distribution; (iii) private saving and private consumption; (iv) investment; (v) export and import demand; (vi) public procurement, distribution and changes in stocks; (vii) the equilibrium conditions; (viii) government revenue and expenditure; (ix) national accounts identities; and (x) the intertemporal equations.

Figure 4.1
Flow Chart of the Agricultural Production Sub–Model

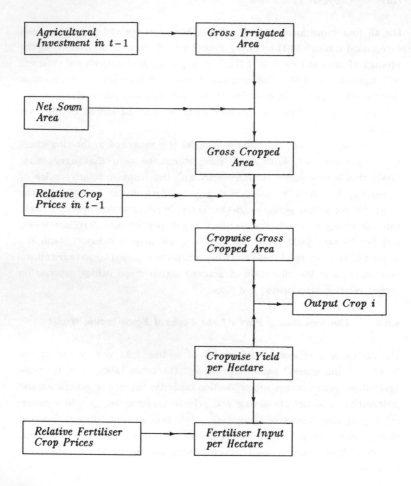

Non-agricultural prices are based on mark-up pricing rules as in (4.25). Non-agricultural production costs include wage costs and (domestic and imported) intermediate input costs.[37] Non-agricultural prices include terms for sales taxes as well as for subsidies. The mark-up rates are assumed fixed and initially do not change in response to changes in demand. This corresponds to the findings by Chatterji (1989), referred to in the previous chapter. Theoretically, there exist at least two conflicting explanations of mark-up pricing, *viz.* Kalecki's degree of monopoly approach and a marginalist approach, which are both discussed in Appendix 4.6. Non-agricultural nominal wages are determined in (4.23) as a function of the consumer price index and the one-period lagged nominal wage rate. Appendix 4.7 includes a short digression on nominal wage formation and gives the derivation of the wage indexation equations of (4.23). The consumer price index itself is given in (4.22) as the weighted average of consumer prices. Finally, consumer prices, which equal market prices plus a sales tax, are given by (4.21).

Production capacity of sector i ($i = 6,..., 9$) is determined as the product of its capital stock and output-capital ratio in (4.26). The output-capital ratio is determined at full capacity utilisation. Capital accumulation determines the production capacity for each sector, but the actual level of sectoral output is determined by demand (Rattsø, 1989). The average price of the capital stock of sector i – weighted by the proportion of the capital stock of sector i originating from sector j – is determined in (4.27). Agricultural depreciation outlays are given by (4.28). Aggregate non-agricultural depreciation is determined as a fixed proportion of the value of the non-agricultural capital stocks in (4.29).

(ii)   *Income Generation and Distribution*

As a variation on the post-Keynesian specification, an 'extended functional distribution of incomes' – in Adelman and Robinson's (1988a) phrase – is included in the model as it distinguishes between three income categories, *viz.* agricultural income, non-agricultural wage income and non-agricultural mark-up income. Each functional category of the income distribution is related to a set of economic actors (farmers, non-agricultural wage earners, and non-agricultural profit earners) which have different behaviour patterns and different partial controls over the system.

In (4.30), agricultural income equals value added from agricultural production adjusted for government procurement of foodgrains.

Non-agricultural wage income is defined as the sum of wage payments in

---

[37] Note that non-agricultural costs do not include working capital costs.

sectors 6 to 9, the government wage bill, transfer income from government (which mainly consists of wage payments) and net factor income from abroad (which mainly consists of foreign remittances) in (4.31).

For each non–agricultural sector, variable costs per unit of output are defined as the sum of domestic material input cost, wage cost and cost of imported inputs per unit of output in (4.32). Non–agricultural mark–up income is determined as the product of the mark–up rate and variable costs for sectors 6 to 9, net of private non–agricultural depreciation and inclusive of interest payments received from the government in (4.33).

(iv)   *Private Saving and Private Consumption*

Private savings out of net disposable income (*i.e.* income net of depreciation and direct taxes) are specified in (4.34) as a fixed proportion of disposable income. The savings rates are exogenously fixed and are assumed to differ between the three income categories. As such, private savings behaviour is grounded in post–Keynesian theory (see Section 4.2.2). Private consumption expenditure of agricultural and non–agricultural income earners is determined by subtracting savings from disposable income in (4.35) and (4.36), respectively.

Commodity–wise private consumption demand of agricultural and non–agricultural income earners is represented by a linear expenditure system in (4.37) and (4.38), where the consumption of the i–th commodity is responsive to both income above some 'floor'–level and prices. Marginal budget shares of commodity i are assumed to be different for expenditure from agricultural and non–agricultural income. The linear expenditure system takes account of food subsidies, both for agricultural and non–agricultural consumers. The derivation of the linear expenditure system inclusive of food subsidies is given in Appendix 4.8. Aggregate consumption of good i is the sum of agricultural and non–agricultural consumption in (4.39).

(v)   *Private Investment*

Keeping within the post–Keynesian approach, investment demand is separated from savings supply, firstly, by specifying public investment demand as being autonomous, and, secondly, by specifying independent private investment demand equations. Furthermore, the private investment demand functions are assumed to be different for agriculture and manufacturing. Private agricultural investment demand in real terms is assumed to respond positively to changes in the one–period lagged terms of trade between agriculture and industry, and to one–period lagged public investment in agriculture in (4.41). The terms of trade between agriculture and non–agriculture are defined in (4.40). Equation (4.42) relates real private investment demand in the manufacturing and services sectors to sectoral mark–up income and the one–period lagged value of real public investment. Public investment is treated as a policy variable as is its distribution between sectors. Aggregate real investment demand by sector of destination is given in (4.43). Real gross investment by sector of origin is derived from the investment demand by sector of destination through a matrix of partial capital coefficients representing the compositional structure of capital stocks by sector of origin in (4.44). This composition is assumed fixed.

(vi)   Foreign Trade

Exports are assumed exogenous in (4.45). Imports are assumed to consist of complementary imports of intermediate inputs and competitive final imports. Competitive imports are treated as exogenous in (4.46), implying that world supply of these commodities is infinitely elastic.

(vii)   Public Distribution and Stock Changes

The quantities and prices of publicly procured and distributed foodgrains are fixed by the government. Aggregate stock changes are the sum of public and private changes in stocks in (4.47). For the foodgrain sectors ($i = 1, 2, 3$), public stock changes in stocks are equal to the difference between public procurement and distribution in (4.48). For the remaining sectors, public stock changes are exogenous.

(viii)   Equilibrium Conditions

Commodity–wise aggregate demand is determined in (4.49). Equation (4.50) gives the excess demand equations for the nine sectors as the difference between aggregate demand and aggregate supply which in turn consists of domestic production and imports. The equilibrium conditions are that the excess demands be zero in (4.51). Note that the condition

$$(p_i - \overset{*}{p_i}) \geq 0 \perp (z_i - \overline{z}_i) \geq 0$$

is equivalent to

$$(p_i - \overset{*}{p_i}) \geq 0, \ (z_i - \overline{z}_i) \geq 0, \ (p_i - \overset{*}{p_i})(z_i - \overline{z}_i) = 0$$

(for the notation, see Fischer *et al.*, 1988).

The agricultural sectors are assumed to be price clearing. Price adjustment in the case of rice and wheat is, however, subject to a lower bound determined by the level of minimum support or procurement prices, $\overset{*}{p_i}$. In case the market price $p_i = \overset{*}{p_i}$ ($i = 1, 2$), adjustment will be brought about by public procurement changes. Government will step up actual procurement of these

Table 4.4
Equilibrium Conditions

$$(4.51) \quad ed_i = 0 \qquad\qquad\qquad\qquad\qquad\qquad i = 1, .., 9.$$

$$(z_i - \overline{z}_i) \geq 0 \quad \perp \quad (p_i - p_i^*) \geq 0 \qquad i = 1, 2.$$

$$(\overline{x}_6 - x_{s6}) \geq 0 \quad \perp \quad m_6 \geq 0$$

$$(\overline{x}_i - x_{si}) \geq 0 \quad \perp \quad \pi_i^* \geq 0 \qquad\qquad i = 7, 8, 9.$$

crops, z_i ($i = 1, 2$), over and above the fixed level of procurement, $\overline{z}_i$, raising the market prices to their assured minimum levels. Otherwise, actual government procurement z_i will equal $\overline{z}_i$.

Output of the fertiliser sector is determined by demand subject to a capacity constraint. If demand exceeds production capacity, supply–demand balance will be brought about additional competitive imports, which will otherwise be zero. Output of the other non–agricultural sectors ($i = 7, 8, 9$) is also determined by demand subject to a capacity constraint. If demand exceeds production capacity for these three sectors, their mark–up rates and hence their prices will adjust. Their mark–up rates are determined in (4.24) as the sum of an exogenously given part $\tilde{\pi}_i$ and an endogenous part π_i^*. In case demand is smaller than production capacity, π_i^* will be zero. In case demand exceeds production capacity, π_i^* will become greater than zero and π_i will rise.

(ix)   Government

The government collects taxes on incomes, intermediate inputs, consumer expenditure and imports. Revenue from indirect taxes is given in (4.52) and revenue from direct taxation of the three categories of income in (4.53). Public current revenue is the sum of revenue from indirect and direct taxes, and profits from public enterprises in (4.54).

Public current expenditure includes expenditure on producers', food, and export subsidies, procurement costs, final consumption, interest payments, current transfers, the public wage bill, and depreciation allowances in (4.55) through (4.60). Public consumption expenditure, public sector employment, interest payments and current transfers are treated as exogenous variables.

Net public saving (or the balance on the public revenue account) is determined as the difference between public revenue and expenditure in (4.61).

Table 4.5
Variables and Parameters to be Updated

Agricultural Production Submodel
　　　　　　　　　Net Sown Area (nsa)
　　　　　　　　　Production of Other Agriculture (x_5)

*General Equilibrium
Model*
　　　　　　　　　Labour Productivity $(\beta_i, \ i = 6, \ ..., \ 9)$
　　　　　　　　　Exports $(e_i, \ i \ = 1, ..., \ 9)$
　　　　　　　　　Export Prices $(p_{ei}, \ i = 1, \ .., \ 9)$
　　　　　　　　　Competitive imports $(m_i, \ i = 1, \ .., \ 9)$
　　　　　　　　　Import Prices $(p_{mi}, \ i = 7, \ 8, \ 9)$
　　　　　　　　　Public Stock Changes $(\Delta \ st_{gi}, \ i = 4, \ .., \ 9)$
　　　　　　　　　Private Stock Changes $(\Delta \ st_{pi}, \ i = 1, \ ..., \ 9)$
　　　　　　　　　Public Depreciation (DEP_g)
　　　　　　　　　Public Interest Payments $(GINT)$
　　　　　　　　　Agricultural Depreciation (DEP_a)
　　　　　　　　　Net Factor Income from Abroad $(FREM)$

(x)　　　*Accounting Identities*

Nominal GDP at factor cost and at market prices are given in (4.62) and
(4.63), respectively. Equation (4.64) determines the current account deficit
as the difference between (complementary plus competitive) imports and the
sum of export receipts, and foreign remittances. The savings–investment
balance is given in (4.65). It is not an independent equation as it can be
derived from the rest, but it has been included because it provides a
numerical check on the computations.

(xi)　　　*Intertemporal Equations*

Sectoral capital stock is determined as the sum of the previous period's
capital stock (minus depreciation) and gross investment by sector of
destination in (4.66). The opening stocks of the public sector are determined
in (4.67). The weights of the consumer price index are revised at the
beginning of each period in (4.68). Procurement prices which are revised
annually, are updated in (4.69). Finally, Table 4.5 gives the list of
exogenous variables and parameters which are updated between the two
periods.

125

4.6   *Summary*

To capture the economy–wide effects of agricultural policy interventions, a computable general equilibrium model was constructed to simulate their macro–economic, income–distributional and sectoral growth effects over the short and medium run. Not surprisingly, the focus on agriculture–non–agriculture relationships has conditioned the model specification. Specifically, the following linkages between agriculture and non–agriculture were included in the model:

(a) *final demand linkages, i.e.* the demand of agricultural income earners for industrial consumer goods and of non–agricultural income recipients for agricultural commodities in equations (4.37) and (4.38), (4.40), (4.41), (4.45) and (4.46);

(b) *intermediate demand linkages, i.e.* the demand of agricultural producers for industrial inputs and *vice versa* (represented by input–output relationships *via* which a price change of a particular input enters into the cost structure and price structure of purchasing sectors) in equations (4.10), (4.11), (4.25) and (4.49);

(c) *a wage goods linkage, i.e.* the effect of a change in food prices on wages and – through nominal wage indexation – on prices in all sectors of the economy in equation (4.21 to (4.23);

(d) *savings and investment linkages, i.e.* agriculture's net contribution to domestic savings over and above its own investment requirements, in equations (4.34) and (4.41);

(e) *fiscal linkages, i.e.* agriculture's net contribution to the public revenue deficit or surplus in (4.52) to (4.61);

(f) *balance of payments linkages* through agricultural exports and agriculture's direct and indirect import requirements in (4.64).

The model is used to assess the short–term as well as medium–term consequences of changes in agricultural policy on sectoral growth rates, the rate of inflation, the government budget, the country's balance of payments position, and the 'extended functional' distribution of incomes. It is clear that the macro–economic effects of a change in one or more of the policy instruments are largely determined by the interplay of the reactions of groups of private decision makers. The model was designed to capture these responses of private agents to public policy choices with respect to the agricultural sector, and the feedback effects of these responses, mostly through their effect on public revenues and expenditures. In the next chapters, the results of (counterfactual) simulation experiments performed with the model, based on pre–specified changes in (agricultural) policy variables, will be compared to the reference path, providing insight into the effects of policy changes and into the constraints, set by private sector behaviour.

Appendix 4.1
Equations of the General Equilibrium Model

The Agricultural Production Sub-Model

(4.1) $gia_t = \omega_0 + \omega_1 j_{a,t-1} + \omega_2 gia_{t-1}$

(4.2) $nia = \xi\, gia$

(4.3) $aci = \gamma_0 + \gamma_1 [nia/nsa]$

(4.4) $gca = aci * nsa$

(4.5) $ngca = gca - gia$

(4.6) $\tilde{p}_i = p_i \Big/ \sum\limits_{\substack{j=1 \\ j \neq i}}^{4} \zeta_j\, p_j$,   with $\zeta_j = \left[p_j\, x_{sj} \Big/ \sum\limits_{\substack{j=1 \\ j \neq i}}^{4} p_j\, x_{sj} \right]$

$j = 1,.., 4.$

(4.7) $\log ngca_{i,t} = \chi_{0i} + \chi_{1i} \log \tilde{p}_{i,t-1} + \chi_{2i} \log ngca_{i,t-1}$

$\sum\limits_{i=1}^{4} ngca_i = ngca$ $i = 1, .., 4.$

(4.8) $\log gia_{i,t} = \chi_{3i} + \chi_{4i} \log \tilde{p}_{i,t-1} + \chi_{5i} \log gia_{i,t-1}$

$\sum\limits_{i=1}^{4} gia_i = gia$ $i = 1, .., 4.$

(4.9) $gca_i = ngca_i + gia_i$ $i = 1, .., 4.$

(4.10) $\log fert_{ki} = \nu_{0ki} + \nu_{1ki} \log [p_6/p_i]$ $i = 1, 2.\quad k = 1, 2.$

(4.11) $\log fert_i = \nu_{0i} + \nu_{1i} \log [p_6/p_i]$ $i = 3, 4.$

(4.12) $yld_{ki} = \varepsilon_{0ki} + \varepsilon_{1ki} fert_{ki} - \varepsilon_{2ki} fert_{ki}^2$ $i = 1, 2.\quad k = 1, 2.$

(4.13) $\psi_{2i} = gia_i / gca_i$ $i = 1, 2.$

(4.14) $\psi_{1i} = 1 - \psi_{2i}$ $i = 1, 2.$

(4.15) $yld_i = \sum\limits_{k=1}^{2} \psi_{ki}\, yld_{ki}$ $i = 1, 2.$

(4.16) $\log yld_i = \varepsilon_{0i} + c_{1i} \log fert_i$ $i = 3, 4.$

(4.17) $x_{si} = yld_i\, gca_i$ $i = 1, ...,4.$

(4.18) $\quad x_{s5} = \bar{x}_{s5}$

(4.19) $\quad frt_i = fert_{1i} \, (gca_i - gia_i) + fert_{2i} \, gia_i \qquad\qquad i = 1, 2.$

$\quad\qquad frt_i = fert_i \, gca_i \qquad\qquad\qquad\qquad\qquad\quad i = 3, 4.$

(4.20) $\quad \alpha_{6i} = frt_i / x_{si} \qquad\qquad\qquad\qquad\qquad\qquad\quad i = 1, .., 4.$

Non–agricultural Price and Wage Equations

(4.21) $\quad p_{si} = (1 + \tau_{si}) \, p_i \qquad\qquad\qquad\qquad\qquad\qquad i = 1, .., 9.$

(4.22) $\quad cpi = \displaystyle\sum_{i=1}^{9} \omega_{ci} \, p_{si}$

(4.23) $\quad w_{i,t} = \theta_{0i} \, cpi_t^{\,\theta_{1i}} \, w_{i,t-1}^{\,\theta_{2i}} \qquad\qquad\qquad\qquad i = 6, .., 9, g.$

(4.24) $\quad \pi_i = \tilde{\pi}_i + \pi_i^{*} \qquad\qquad\qquad\qquad\qquad\qquad\quad i = 7, 8, 9.$

(4.25) $\quad p_j = \dfrac{(1 + \tau_j)(1 - \sigma_j)(1 + \pi_j)}{1 - \alpha_{jj}(1 + \tau_j)(1 - \sigma_j)(1 + \pi_j)} \left(\displaystyle\sum_{\substack{i=1 \\ i \neq j}}^{9} \alpha_{ij} p_i + w \beta_j + \alpha_{0j} rp_{mj} \right)$

$\qquad\qquad\qquad\qquad\qquad\qquad\qquad\qquad\qquad\qquad\qquad\qquad i = 6, ..., 9.$

Non–agricultural Production Capacity

(4.26) $\quad \bar{x}_i = K_i / \kappa_i \qquad\qquad\qquad\qquad\qquad\qquad\quad i = 6, ..., 9.$

Depreciation

(4.27) $\quad p_{ki} = \displaystyle\sum_{j=a}^{9} \vartheta_{ji} \, p_j \qquad\qquad\qquad\qquad\qquad\quad i = 6, 7, 8, 9, a.$

(4.28) $\quad Q_a = \delta_a \, p_{ka} \, K_a$

(4.29) $\quad Q = \displaystyle\sum_{i=6}^{9} \delta_i \, p_{ki} \, K_i$

Income Distribution

(4.30) $\quad Y_a = \displaystyle\sum_{i=1}^{3} p_i (x_{si} - z_i) + \sum_{i=1}^{3} p_i^{*} z_i + \sum_{i=4}^{5} p_i \, x_{si} - \sum_{j=1}^{5} \sum_{i=1}^{9} p_i \, \alpha_{ij} \, x_{sj}$

$\qquad\qquad - \displaystyle\sum_{i=1}^{5} r \, p_{mi} \, \alpha_{0i} \, x_{si} - \sum_{i=1}^{5} p_i \, t_i \, x_{si} + \sum_{i=1}^{5} p_i \, s_i \, x_{si} - Q_a$

$$(4.31) \quad Y_w = \sum_{i=6}^{9} w_i \beta_i x_{si} + w_g l_g + \overline{V} + r F$$

$$(4.32) \quad v_{cj} = \sum_{i=1}^{9} \alpha_{ij} p_i + w_j \beta_j + \alpha_{0j} r p_{mj} \qquad\qquad i = 6, \ldots, 9.$$

$$(4.33) \quad Y_z = \sum_{i=6}^{9} (\pi_i v_{ci} x_{si} - N_{gi}) - \phi_z Q + V$$

Private Saving

$$(4.34) \quad S_i = \overline{\sigma}_i (1 - t_{di}) Y_i \qquad\qquad i = a, w, z.$$

Private Consumption

$$(4.35) \quad D_a = (1 - \overline{\sigma}_a)(1 - \tau_{da}) Y_a$$

$$(4.36) \quad D_n = (1 - \overline{\sigma}_w)(1 - \tau_{dw}) Y_w + (1 - \overline{\sigma}_z)(1 - \tau_{dz}) Y_z$$

$$(4.37) \quad c_{ai} = \gamma_{ai} - f_{ai} + (\mu_{ai}/p_{si})(D_a + \sum_{i=1}^{9} p_{si} f_{ai} - \sum_{i=1}^{9} p_{si} \gamma_{ai})$$
$$i = 1, \ldots, 9.$$

$$(4.38) \quad c_{ni} = \gamma_{ni} - f_{ni} + (\mu_{ni}/p_{si})(D_n + \sum_{i=1}^{9} (p_{si} - p_i) f_{ni} - \sum_{i=1}^{9} p_{si} \gamma_{ni})$$
$$i = 1, \ldots, 9.$$

$$(4.39) \quad c_i = c_{ai} + c_{ni} + f_{ai} + f_{ni} \qquad\qquad i = 1, \ldots, 9.$$

Private Investment Demand

$$(4.40) \quad \hat{p} = \sum_{i=1}^{5} \varphi_i p_i / \sum_{i=6}^{9} \xi_i p_i,$$

$$\text{with } \varphi_i = \left[p_i x_{si} / \sum_{i=1}^{5} p_i x_{si} \right], \; \xi_j = \left[p_i x_{si} / \sum_{i=6}^{9} p_i x_{si} \right]$$

$$(4.41) \quad j_{pa,t} = \varphi_{a1} [\hat{p}_{t-1}]^{\varphi_{a2}} [j_{ga,t-1}]^{\varphi_{a3}}$$

$$(4.42) \quad j_{pi,t} = \varphi_{i1} \left[Y_{zi,t} / p_{ki,t} \right]^{\varphi_{i2}} \left[j_{gi,t-1} \right]^{\varphi_{i3}}$$

$$\text{where } Y_{zi} = \pi_i v_{ci} x_{si} - N_{gi} \qquad i = 7, 8, 9.$$

$$(4.43) \quad j_i = j_{gi} + j_{pi} \qquad\qquad i = 6, 7, 8, 9, a.$$

$$(4.44) \quad i_i = \sum_{j=a}^{9} \vartheta_{ij} j_j \qquad\qquad i = 6, 7, 8, 9, a.$$

Export and Import Demand

$$(4.45) \quad e_i = \bar{e}_i \qquad\qquad i = 1, .., 9.$$
$$(4.46) \quad m_i = \bar{m}_i \qquad\qquad i = 1, ..5, 7, 8, 9.$$

Changes in Stocks

$$(4.47) \quad \Delta st_{gi} = z_i - f_{ni} - f_{ai} \qquad\qquad i = 1, 2, 3.$$

$$\Delta st_{gi} = \Delta \overline{st}_{gi} \qquad\qquad i = 4, .., 9.$$

$$(4.48) \quad \Delta st_i = \Delta st_{gi} + \Delta st_{pi} \qquad\qquad i = 1, .., 9.$$

Excess Demand Equations

$$(4.49) \quad x_{di} = \sum_{j=1}^{9} \alpha_{ij} x_{sj} + c_i + g_i + i_i + \Delta st_i + e_i \qquad i = 1, .., 9.$$

$$(4.50) \quad ed_i = x_{di} - x_{si} - m_i \qquad\qquad i = 1, .., 9.$$

Equilibrium Conditions

$$(4.51) \quad ed_i = 0 \qquad\qquad i = 1, .., 9.$$

$$(z_i - \bar{z}_i) \geq 0 \perp (p_i - p_i^*) \geq 0 \qquad\qquad i = 1, 2.$$
$$(\bar{x}_6 - x_{s6}) \geq 0 \perp m_6 \geq 0$$
$$(\bar{x}_i - x_{si}) \geq 0 \perp \pi_i^* \geq 0 \qquad\qquad i = 7, 8, 9.$$

130

Government Revenue

$$(4.52) \quad R_1 = \sum_{i=1}^{5} \tau_i \, p_i \, x_{si} + \sum_{i=6}^{9} \tau_i \, (1 + \pi_i) \, v_{ci} \, x_{si} + \sum_{i=1}^{9} \tau_{si} \, p_i \, c_i$$

$$+ \sum_{i=1}^{9} (p_i - r \, p_{mi}) \, m_i$$

$$(4.53) \quad R_2 = \tau_{da} \, Y_a + \tau_{dw} \, Y_w + \tau_{dz} \, Y_z$$

$$(4.54) \quad R = \sum_{i=1}^{2} R_i + \sum_{i=6}^{9} N_{gi}$$

Government Expenditure

$$(4.55) \quad U_1 = \sum_{i=1}^{5} \sigma_i \, p_i \, x_{si} + \sum_{i=6}^{9} \sigma_i \, (1 + \pi_i) \, v_{ci} \, x_{si}$$

$$(4.56) \quad U_2 = \sum_{i=1}^{3} (p_{si} - \bar{p}_i) \, f_{ni} + \sum_{i=1}^{3} p_{si} \, f_{ai}$$

$$(4.57) \quad U_3 = \sum_{i=1}^{9} (p_i - r \, p_{ei}) \, e_i$$

$$(4.58) \quad \overline{U} = \sum_{i=1}^{3} U_i$$

$$(4.59) \quad Z = \sum_{i=1}^{3} (p_i^* - p_i) \, z_i$$

$$(4.60) \quad G = \sum_{i=1}^{9} p_i \, g_i + \overline{U} + V + \overline{V} + Z + w_g \, l_g + (1 - \phi_z) \, Q$$

Government Saving

$$(4.61) \quad S_g = R - G$$

Gross Domestic Product

$$(4.62) \quad Y_f = Y_a + Y_w + Y_z + Q_a + \phi_z \, Q + w_g \, l_g + \sum_{i=6}^{9} N_i$$

$$(4.63) \quad Y_m = Y_f + R_1 - \overline{L}$$

Current Account Deficit

$$(4.64) \qquad H = \sum_{i=1}^{9} r\, p_{mi}\, m_i + \sum_{i=1}^{9} r\, p_{mi}\, \alpha_{0i}\, x_{si} - \sum_{i=1}^{9} r\, p_{ei}\, e_i - r\, F$$

Savings – Investment Balance

$$(4.65) \qquad S_a + S_w + S_z + S_g + H + Q_a + Q = \sum_{i=1}^{9} p_i\, i_i + \sum_{i=1}^{9} p_i\, \Delta\, st_i$$

Intertemporal Equations

$$(4.66) \qquad K_{i,t+1} = (1 - \delta_i)\, K_{i,t} + j_{i,t} \qquad\qquad i = 6, ..., 9, a.$$

$$(4.67) \qquad z^*_{gi,t+1} = z^*_{gi,t} + \Delta\, st_{gi,t+1} \qquad\qquad i = 1, .., 9.$$

$$(4.68) \qquad \omega_{ci,t+1} = [p_{i,t}\, c_{i,t}]/[D_{a,t} + D_{n,t}] \qquad\qquad i = 1, .., 9.$$

$$(4.69) \qquad p^*_{i,t-1} = \lambda_{0i}\, p^{\lambda_{1i}}_{i,t}\, \hat{p}^{\lambda_{2i}}_{i,t} \qquad\qquad i = 1, 2.$$

Appendix 4.2
List of Variables and Parameters

a = agricultural.
g = government.
w = non–agricultural wage income.
z = non–agricultural mark–up income.

Agricultural Production Sub – Model

α_{6i}	Amount of fertiliser input required per unit of output of crop i, $i = 1, .., 4$ (endogenous)
aci	Aggregate cropping intensity (endogenous)
$fert_i$	Fertiliser consumption per hectare of crop i, $i = 3, 4$. (endogenous)
$fert_{ki}$	Fertiliser consumption per hectare of crop i, $i = 1, 2$, seed–water variety k, $k = 1, 2$. (endogenous)
frt_i	Aggregate fertiliser consumption by crop i, $i = 1, .., 4$ (endogenous)
gca	Gross cropped area in ten million hectares (endogenous)
gca_i	Gross cropped area under crop i in ten million hectares, $i = 1,..,4$ (endogenous)
gia	Gross irrigated area in ten million hectares (endogenous)
gia_i	Gross irrigated area under crop i, $i = 1, .., 4$ (endogenous)
j_a	Aggregate agricultural investment (endogenous)
ψ^a_{ki}	Proportion of area under crop i and seed–water variety k, $i = 1, 2$, $k = 1, 2$ (endogenous)
$ngca$	Aggregate gross non–irrigated area in ten million hectares (endogenous)
$ngca_i$	Gross non–irrigated area under crop i in ten million hectares (endogenous)
nia	Net irrigated area in ten million hectares (endogenous)
nsa	Net sown area in ten million hectares (exogenous)
$\tilde{p}_i$	Relative price of crop i with respect to the weighted average price the competing (three) crops, $i = 1, .., 4$ (endogenous)
p_i	Market price of crop i, $i = 1, .., 5$ (endogenous)
p_6	Market price of fertilisers (endogenous)
x_{si}	Level of sectoral production, $i = 1,..., 5$ (endogenous)
$\bar{x}_{s5}$	Exogenous level of sector 5 production.
yld_i	Yield per hectare under crop i, $i = 1, .., 4$. (endogenous)
yld_{ki}	Yield per hectare under crop i, $i = 1, 2$, of type k, $k = 1, 2$. (endogenous)

ζ_i	Weight of crop i in relative price of crop j ($j \neq i$) (endogenous)

Multi − Sector Model

c_i	Total consumption expenditure by sector, $i = 1, .., 9$ (endogenous)
c_{ai}	Consumption expenditure from agricultural income, $i = 1,.., 9$ (endogenous)
c_{ni}	Consumption expenditure from non−agricultural income, $i = 1,.., 9$ (endogenous)
cpi	Consumer price index (endogenous)
D_a	Consumer demand from agricultural income (endogenous)
D_n	Consumer demand from non−agricultural income (endogenous)
e_i	Export earnings by sector, $i = 1, .., 9$ (endogenous)
$\bar{e}_i$	Exogenous levels of export earning, $i = 1, .., 9$
ed_i	Excess demand for good i, $i = 1, .., 9$ (endogenous)
F	Net factor income from abroad (exogenous)
f_{ai}	Food distribution under food for work programmes, $i = 1, 2, 3$ (exogenous)
f_{ni}	Issue of foodgrains from fair−price shops, $i = 1, 2, 3$ (exogenous)
G	Public expenditure (endogenous)
g_i	Public consumption of good i (exogenous)
H	Current account deficit or foreign savings (endogenous)
i_i	Real investment by sector of origin, $i = a, 6, 7, 8, 9$ (endogenous)
j_i	Real investment by sector of destination, $i = a, 6, 7, 8, 9$ (endogenous)
j_{gi}	Real public investment by sector of destination, $i = a, 6, 7, 8, 9$ (exogenous)
j_{pi}	Real private investment by sector by destination, $i = a, 7, 8, 9$ (endogenous)
K_i	Real capital stock by sector, $i = 6, .., 9, a$ (endogenous)
l_g	Government employment (exogenous)
m_i	Competitive imports of good i, $i = 1, .., 9$ (endogenous)
$\bar{m}_i$	Exogenous level of competitive imports of good i, $i = 1, .., 5, 7, 8, 9$
N_{gi}	Revenues from public enterprises, $i = 6, .., 9$ (exogenous)
p	Agricultural−non−agricultural terms of trade (endogenous)
p_i	Market price of commodity i, $i = 1,..., 9$ (endogenous)

p_i^*	Procurement/minimum support price of crop i, $i = 1, 2, 3$ (endogenous for $i = 1, 2$; exogenous for $i = 3$)
$\bar{p}_i$	Subsidised consumer price of commodity i, $i = 1, 2, 3$ (exogenous)
p_{ei}	Export price of good i, $i = 1, ..., 9$ (exogenous)
p_{mi}	Import price of good i, $i = 1, ..., 9$ (exogenous)
p_{ki}	Price of the capital stock in sector i, $i = a, 6, 7, 8, 9$ (endogenous)
p_{si}	Consumer price of good i, $i = 1, .., 9$ (endogenous)
Q	Aggregate non–agricultural depreciation (endogenous)
Q_a	Agricultural depreciation (endogenous)
r	Nominal exchange rate (exogenous)
R	Public revenue (endogenous)
R_1	Indirect tax receipts by government (endogenous)
R_2	Direct tax receipts by government (endogenous)
Δst_i	Aggregate change in stocks, $i = 1, .., 9$ (endogenous)
Δst_{gi}	Change in public stocks, $i = 1, .., 9$ (endogenous)
$\Delta \overline{st}_{gi}$	Exogenous change in public stocks, $i = 4, .., 9$
Δst_{pi}	Change in private stocks, $i = 1, .., 9$ (exogenous)
S_i	Private savings, $i = a, w, z$ (endogenous)
S_g	Public savings (endogenous)
π_i	Mark–up rate in non–agriculture, $i = 6, ..., 9$ (endogenous)
$\tilde{\pi}_i$	Endogenous part of the mark–up rate in non–agriculture, $i = 6, ..., 9$
$\overline{U}$	Public subsidy expenditure (endogenous)
U_1	Public expenditure on producers' subsidies (endogenous)
U_2	Public expenditure on food subsidies (endogenous)
U_3	Public expenditure on export subsidies (endogenous)
V	Interest payments from the government to non–agricultural mark–up income earners (exogenous)
$\overline{V}$	Transfer payments by the government to non–agricultural wage earners (exogenous)
ω_{ci}	Weights in the consumer price index, $i = 1, .., 9$ (endogenous)
v_{ci}	Variable costs per unit of output, $i = 6, .., 9$ (endogenous)
w_i	Nominal sectoral wage rate ($i = 6,..., 9$) (endogenous)
w_g	Nominal public sector wage rate (exogenous)
x_{si}	Domestic production of commodity i, $i = 1,..., 9$ (endogenous)
x_{di}	Aggregate demand for commodity i, $i = 1,...., 9$ (endogenous)
$\overline{x}_i$	Production capacity in sector i, $i = 6, ..., 9$ (endogenous)
Y^i	Private income, $i = a, w, z$ (endogenous)
Y_f^i	Nominal GDP at factor cost at current prices (endogenous)

Y_m	Nominal GDP at market prices at current prices (endogenous)
z_i	Public procurement of crop i, $i = 1, 2, 3$ (endogenous)
$\bar{z}_i$	Exogenous public procurement of crop i, $i = 1, 2$
z_i^*	Level of public stocks, $i = 1, .., 9$ (endogenous)
Z	Cost of public procurement (endogenous)

Parameters

Agricultural Sub-Model

χ_{oi}, χ_{3i}	Constant, $i = 1, .., 4$
χ_{1i}	Elasticity of gross unirrigated area under crop i with respect to the one–period lagged relative price of crop i, $i = 1, .., 4$
χ_{2i}	Elasticity of gross unirrigated area under crop i with respect to the one–period lagged grossed cropped area under crop i, $i = 1, .., 4$
χ_{4i}	Elasticity of gross irrigated area under crop i with respect to the one–period lagged relative price of crop i, $i = 1, .., 4$
χ_{5i}	Elasticity of gross irrigated area under crop i with respect to the one–period lagged grossed cropped area under crop i, $i = 1, .., 4$
ε_{oi}	Constant, $i = 3, 4$
ε_{1i}	Elasticity of yield per hectare of crop i with respect to the fertiliser input per hectare, $i = 3, 4$
ε_{oki}	Constant, $i = 1, 2, k = 1, 2$
ε_{1ki}	Coefficient of the fertiliser response function, $i = 1, 2$, $k = 1, 2$
ε_{2ki}	Coefficient of the fertiliser response function, $i = 1, 2$, $k = 1, 2$
γ_0	Constant
γ_1	Coefficient relating irrigation intensity (nia/nsa) to average cropping intensity
ν_{0i}	Constant, $i = 3, 4$
ν_{1i}	Price elasticity of per hectare fertiliser consumption of crop i, $i = 3, 4$
ν_{0ki}	Constant, $i = 1, 2, k = 1, 2$
ν_{1ki}	Price elasticity of per hectare fertiliser consumption of crop i, variety k, $i = 1, 2, k = 1, 2$
ω_0	Constant
ω_1	Elasticity of gross irrigated area with respect to the one–period lagged level of real agricultural investment
ω_2	Elasticity of gross irrigated area in period t with respect to gross irrigated area in period $t-1$

ξ Constant proportion of net irrigated to gross irrigated area

Multi – Sector Model

α_{ij}	Input–output coefficient, $i = 1, .., 9$, $j = 1, .., 9$
α_{0j}	Input–output coefficient for intermediate imports, $j = 1, .., 9$
β_i	Sectoral labour–output coefficient, $i = 6, .., 9$
δ_i	Sectoral depreciation rates, $i = 6, ..., 9, a$
γ_{ai}	LES parameter of good i for agricultural income, $i = 1, .., 9$
γ_{ni}	LES parameter of good i for non–agricultural income, $i = 1, .., 9$
κ_i	Output–capital ratio, $i = 6, .., 9$
μ_{ai}	Marginal budget share of good i in agricultural expenditure, $i = 1, ..., 9$
μ_{ni}	Marginal budget share of good i in non–agricultural expenditure, $i = 1, .., 9$
ϕ_z	Share of private depreciation in non–agricultural depreciation
σ_i	Private savings rate, $i = a, w, z$
σ_i	Rate of producers' subsidy, $i = 1, .., 9$
τ_i	Indirect tax rate, $i = 1, .., 9$
τ_{di}	Direct tax rate, $i = a, w, z$
τ_{si}	Sales tax rate, $i = 1, .., 9$
π_i^*	Exogenous part of the mark–up rate in non–agriculture, $i = 6, ..., 9$
φ_{a1}	Constant
φ_{i1}	Constant, $i = 7, 8, 9.$
φ_{a2}	Elasticity of private agricultural investment with respect to the one–period lagged intersectoral terms of trade
φ_{a3}	Elasticity of private agricultural investment with respect to one–period lagged public investment
φ_{i2}	Elasticity of private investment with respect to sectoral mark–up income, $i = 7, 8, 9$
φ_{i3}	Elasticity of private investment wit respect to one–period lagged public investment, $i = 7, 8, 9$
ϑ_{ij}	Proportion of capital stock of sector j, $j = a, 6, 7, 8, 9$, originating in sector i ($i = a, 6, 7, 8, 9$)
θ_{0i}	Constant, $i = 6, .., 9, g$
θ_{1i}	Elasticity of the nominal wage rate with respect to the consumer price index, $i = 6, .., 9, g$
θ_{2i}	Elasticity of the nominal wage rate with respect to its one–period lagged value, $i = 6, .., 9, g$

Derivation of Equation (4.1)

Equation (4.1) is derived by applying the familiar Koyck transformation to the following equation:

(A.4.1) $\qquad gia_t = \alpha_0 + \overline{\omega}_1 j_{a,t-1} + \overline{\omega}_2 j_{a,t-2} + \overline{\omega}_3 j_{a,t-3} + \dots$

In (A.4.1), it is assumed that gross irrigated area depends on the level of real (public and private) agricultural investment in previous periods. Further, it is assumed that as one goes back into the past, the effect of agricultural investment on *gia* becomes progressively smaller. This implies that each successive $\overline{\omega}_t$ ($t = 1, .., \infty$) is numerically less than each preceding $\overline{\omega}_{t-1}$ or that

(A.4.2) $\qquad \overline{\omega}_t = \overline{\omega}_1 \lambda^t \qquad\qquad\qquad t = 0, 1, \dots.$
$\qquad\qquad\qquad\qquad\qquad\qquad\qquad\qquad 0 < \lambda < 1$

As a result of (A.4.2), the infinite lag equation of (A.4.1.) may be written as:

(A.4.1') $\qquad gia_t = \alpha_0 + \overline{\omega}_1 j_{a,t-1} + \overline{\omega}_1 \lambda\, j_{a,t-2} + \overline{\omega}_1 \lambda^2\, j_{a,t-3} + \dots$

Lagging (A.4.1') by one period, we obtain

(A.4.3) $\qquad gia_{t-1} = \alpha_0 + \overline{\omega}_1 j_{a,t-2} + \overline{\omega}_1 \lambda\, j_{a,t-3} + \overline{\omega}_1 \lambda^2\, j_{a,t-4} + \dots$

Multiplying (A.4.3) by λ and subtracting it from (A.4.1') yields

(A.4.4) $\qquad gia_t = \alpha_0 (1 - \lambda) + \overline{\omega}_1 j_{a,t-1} + \lambda\, gia_{t-1}$

which is equation (4.1) included in the model, with $\omega_0 = \alpha_0(1 - \lambda)$, $\omega_1 = \overline{\omega}_1$, and $\omega_2 = \lambda$.

Appendix 4.4
Derivation of the Nerlovian Acreage Response Functions

Well in advance of knowing what prices their resulting outputs will bring, farmers must make major decisions about what crops to grow and how many inputs to use in growing them. According to Nerlove's (1958) partial adjustment model, which underlies the acreage response equations included in the model, farmers are assumed to decide how much to grow of a crop *i* in period *t* on the basis of their expectations regarding the price of the particular crop during that period. In so doing, acreage is generally taken as a proxy for output, since it is, to a much greater degree than output, under the direct control of the cultivator and, thus, presumably a much better index of planned production (see Behrman, 1968:152–155).

A slightly modified version of Nerlove's acreage response model is presented in this appendix. Disturbance terms are not included in the derivation.[38] The symbols utilised throughout this appendix are all defined in the text (below).

Desired acreage of crop i in period t, denoted by $gca^*_{i,t}$, is assumed to be the following function of the anticipated relative price of crop i, $p^e_{i,t}$

$$(A.4.5) \qquad gca^*_{i,t} = \xi_i + \zeta_i \, p^e_{i,t}$$

where ζ_i, such that $0 < \zeta_i \leq 1$, is known as the coefficient of adjustment. In turn, the anticipated relative price of crop i in period t is formed adaptively, or

$$(A.4.6) \qquad p^e_{i,t} - p^e_{i,t-1} = \omega_i \, [p_{i,t-1} - p^e_{i,t-1}]$$

where ω_i, such that $0 < \omega_i \leq 1$, is known as the coefficient of price expectation. Expectations are revised each period by a fraction ω_i of the gap between the actual past price and its previous expected price. Equation (A.4.6) can be rewritten as

$$(A.4.6') \qquad p^e_{i,t} = \omega_i \, p_{i,t-1} + (1 - \omega_i) \, p^e_{i,t-1}$$

In each period, farmers are assumed to partially alter the gross acreage under crop i, gca_i, in response to the desired amount of acreage under crop i and to the acreage under crop i in the previous period:

$$(A.4.7) \qquad gca_{i,t} = \gamma_i \, gca^*_{i,t} + (1 - \gamma_i) \, gca_{i,t-1} \qquad 0 < \gamma_i < 1$$

where γ_i is the rate of adjustment which is often associated with technical and institutional factors. Substitution of (A.4.5) into (A.4.7) gives

$$(A.4.8) \qquad gca_{i,t} = \gamma_i \, \xi_i + \gamma_i \, \zeta_i \, p^e_{i,t} + (1 - \gamma_i) \, gca_{i,t-1}$$

and substitution of (A.4.6') into (A.4.8) yields

$$(A.4.9) \qquad gca_{i,t} = \gamma_i \, \xi_i + \gamma_i \, \zeta_i \, \omega_i \, p_{i,t-1} + \gamma_i \, \zeta_i (1 - \omega_i) \, p^e_{i,t-1}$$
$$+ (1 - \gamma_i) \, gca_{i,t-1}$$

---

[38] For a discussion of the assumptions that can be made about the nature of the reduced equation disturbance term, see Behrman (1968:172–179).

Lagging (A.4.8) by one period, multiplying it by $(1 - \omega_i)$ and substracting it from (A.4.9), we obtain

(A.4.10) $\quad gca_{i,t} = \gamma_i \, \xi_i \, \omega_i + \gamma_i \, \zeta_i \omega_i \, p_{i,t-1}$

$$+ [(1 - \gamma_i) + (1 - \omega_i)] \, gca_{i,t-1}$$

$$- [(1 - \omega_i)(1 - \gamma_i)] \, gca_{i,t-2}$$

Assuming that $\omega_i = 1$ (*i.e.* $p^e_{i,t} = p_{i,t-1}$), the lag 2 taken in gca_i may be ignored. Equation (A.4.10) may then be written as:

(A.4.11) $\quad gca_{i,t} = \xi^*_i + \zeta^*_i \, p_{i,t-1} + \gamma^*_i \, gca_{i,t-1}$

where $\xi^*_i = \gamma_i \xi_i \omega_i$, $\zeta^*_i = \gamma_i \zeta_i \omega_i$, and $\gamma^*_i = (1 - \gamma_i)$. These are the equations included in the agricultural submodel for gross irrigated and non–irrigated area.

The inadequacies of the Nerlovian approach should be made quite clear. First, the approach does not *explicitly* deal with factors other than relative prices which may affect farmers' production decisions to a similar or even greater degree than relative prices do. Non–price factors such as the availability of inputs complementary to land (including irrigation, fertilisers, extension, and credit), tenancy contracts which include arrangements concerning the cropping pattern, the sensitivity of the crop to variation in rainfall, and the existence of an ensured market outlet *via* public procurement agencies are not explicitly dealt with, although their net effect on area allocation is supposed to be captured in the γ_i coefficient.

Second, the approach does not explicitly distinguish between produced quantities and marketed quantities of a particular crop. Relevant to this distinction, of course, is whether or not the product may be consumed on the farm – as is the case for foodgrains (sectors 1 to 3). The distinction becomes less relevant, as the possibilities for on–farm consumption become more limited as may be the case for commercial crops.

Third, the approximation of planned production by cultivated area may be inadequate, since land is only one of many (sometimes substitutable) inputs in agriculture. Consequently, a decision to allocate a certain area of land to the production of a specific crop is consistent with a wide range of planned outputs.[39]

---

[39] Instead of considering only cultivated area as an indicator of planned production, one would prefer an index of all inputs to be devoted to the crop. This may prove difficult because most non–land inputs are varied across crops throughout the production period, *i.e.* they often are substitutable over time within the production period. See Behrman (1968:152).

Appendix 4.5
Derivation of the Fertiliser Demand Functions

The fertiliser demand functions of (4.11) and (4.12) can be derived as follows. It is assumed that (*i*) farmers aim at maximising their profits per hectare; (*ii*) there is a single variable factor, fertiliser, of which the price is given for all farmers, and (*iii*) technology is given by the per hectare production function of (4.11).

Farmers want to maximise their profits Π_i, defined here as gross value of output less the cost of variable fertiliser input, $p_6 \, fert_i$.

$$(A.4.12) \qquad \Pi_i(yld_i) = \max_{yld_i \geq 0} \; p_i \, \eta_{0i} \, fert_i^{\eta_{1i}} - p_6 \, fert_i$$

with

$$(A.4.13) \qquad yld_i = \eta_{0i} \, fert_i^{\eta_{1i}} \qquad\qquad \eta_{0i} > 0, \; 0 < \eta_{1i} < 1$$

Profit maximisation which requires $(\partial \Pi_i / \partial fert_i) = 0$, leads to the per hectare fertiliser demand function included in the model:

$$(A.4.14) \quad log \, fert_i = \left[\frac{1}{\eta_{1i} - 1} \right] log \left[\frac{1}{\eta_{0i}\eta_{1i}} \right] + \left[\frac{1}{\eta_{1i} - 1} \right] log \, (p_6/p_i)$$

$$= \nu_{0i} + \nu_{1i} \, log \, (p_6/p_i)$$

where $\nu_{0i} = \left[\dfrac{1}{\eta_{1i} - 1} \right] log \left[\dfrac{1}{\eta_{0i}\eta_{1i}} \right]$ and $\nu_{1i} = \left[\dfrac{1}{\eta_{1i} - 1} \right]$.

Note that $\nu_{1i} < 0$ because $(\eta_{1i} - 1) < 0$.

Appendix 4.6
On the Interpretation of the Mark–Up Rate

The idea that prices are based on a mark–up over cost and that price changes are closely linked with cost changes[40] was supported by the results of empirical studies of pricing behaviour by individual firms published in the 1930s (see Carlton (1989) for a review). Since then, numerous authors have advanced ideas in a similar vein, but usually they have confined their attention to firms' price formation without drawing the wider implications

---

[40] Particularly when the mark–up is thought to be fairly insensitive to changes in demand.

for macroeconomics. Cost–plus pricing implies that changes in demand do not necessarily lead to changes in price as is predicted by the 'traditional' theory of the firm as formulated by Robinson and Chamberlin. In these traditional models of monopolistic competition, firms are assumed to pursue a short run profit maximising strategy which implies the equalisation of marginal revenue and marginal cost. Further, firms are assumed to know with *certainty* their demand and cost functions. Since each period of time is assumed to be independent (in the sense that decisions taken do not affect the behaviour of the firm in other periods), short run profit maximisation also implies the maximisation of profits in the long run.

Kalecki (1943), in contrast, tried to derive a pricing rule for a particular industry on the basis of the pricing behaviour of individual firms. He argued that industrial firms typically sell in oligopolistic markets and do not act atomistically, but are aware of and concerned about the reactions of competitors. In these circumstances, firms are faced with conditions of uncertainty in setting their prices, with respect to both the immediate and the longer–run consequences of their actions. In practice, they do not posses the necessary information about the demand curves and price elasticities they face, since neither consumers' preferences nor competitors' reactions can be established with *certainty* (nor can probability distributions be established over all possibilities which could give rise to behaviour based upon as–if certainty). Therefore, marginal revenue schedules are difficult to determine, and the marginal rule impossible to operate. Hence, Kalecki (1971:44) concludes that, even though firms may be constantly striving for profits, 'in view of the uncertainties in the process of price fixing it will not be assumed that the firm attempts to maximise its profits in any precise sort of manner.' In Kalecki's view, a firm arrives at a price for one of its products by adding a mark–up to its average variable costs in order to cover overhead costs and realise some profit. The mark–up reflects the influences resulting from imperfect competition or oligopoly or what Kalecki called 'the degree of monopoly'. The more imperfect the market conditions faced by the firm, the stronger its position vis–à–vis other firms in the same industry and potential entrants in terms of costs, product differentiation, *etc.*, *ceteris paribus*, the higher the firm's mark–up. Kalecki's price equation has been reformulated by Cowling (1981) in the context of oligopolistic firms producing differentiated products.[41]

The marginalist reaction to Kalecki's theory attempted to assimilate the cost–plus pricing model within the terms of neoclassical theory. A cost–plus

---

[41] Kalecki's degree of monopoly theory has been subject to many criticisms into which I will not go as they have been extensively dealt with by Sawyer (1985:28–36). Irrespective of these criticisms, Kalecki's theory of price formation is important for its attempt to treat firms as *price makers* in *uncertain* circumstances.

pricing model which predicts a constant profit margin came to be regarded as a special case of marginal cost pricing where the goal of the firm is long run profit maximisation and where average (and marginal) costs and the price elasticity of demand are constant over the relevant range of output. It is implicitly assumed that firms guess at the value of their price elasticity of demand and give up the notion of short–run profit maximisation. Given these conditions, a rise in demand would lead to an increase in output but no change in price.

Formally, the mark–up equation is derived from the familiar profit maximisation condition that marginal revenue equals marginal cost. Given that total revenue r_i of sector i is equal to price p_i times output x_{si}, marginal revenue is derived as follows:

(A.4.15) $\qquad mr_i = (dr_i / dx_{si}) = p_i + x_{si}(dp_i/dx_{si})$

Using the definition of the price elasticity of demand for commodity i, $\varepsilon_i = -(\partial x_{si}/\partial p_i)(p_i/x_{si})$, equation (A.4.15) can be rewritten as

(A.4.16) $\qquad mr_i = p_i [1 - (1/\varepsilon_i)]$

The necessary condition for profit maximisation is that marginal cost equals marginal revenue. Over the flat stretch of the average cost curve, average cost ac_i is equal to marginal cost. This implies that

(A.4.17) $\qquad p_i [1 - (1 / \varepsilon_i)] = ac_i$

Solving this equation for p_i yields the following expression for the industry's mark–up rate π_i

(A.4.18) $\qquad (1 + \pi_i) = [\varepsilon_i / (\varepsilon_i - 1)]$

or equivalently

(A.4.18') $\qquad \pi_i = [\varepsilon_i / (\varepsilon_i - 1)] - 1$

This equation is based on Lerner's mark–up rule[42] which states that an industry will set its mark–up over marginal cost such that $[(p_i - mc_i)/p_i] = (1/\varepsilon_i)$, where $|\varepsilon_i| > 1$.[43] The constant elasticity assumption ensures that the price will not be affected by demand changes.

---

[42] Lerner, A. (1934), 'The concept of monopoly and the measurement of monopoly power', *Review of Economic Studies* 1.

[43] Given that $ac_i > 0$, mr_i must be positive for profit maximisation. This implies that profits can be maximised only if $|\varepsilon_i| > 1$. See Koutsoyannis (1981:278).

Appendix 4.7
Nominal Wage Indexation

In registered manufacturing and services, the wage typically consists of payment under three headings: (*i*) the basic wage, (*ii*) an end–of–the year profit sharing bonus, and (*iii*) a monthly dearness allowance.

In a broad sense, the 'bonus' component represents the adjustment of the wage rate for increases in labour productivity. Quantitatively, it is only a small part (about 4 per cent) of total wage income (Chatterji, 1989:43). Because of its relatively little importance, the 'bonus' component (or the labour productivity component) has been omitted from the wage indexation equations. The system of cost of living allowances known as dearness allowance makes up approximately one third of total wage income. Although there is only scattered information regarding the amounts paid as dearness allowance and its method of payment in particular industries, the evidence that is available indicates that it has become more and more common to link the dearness allowance to the consumer price index. According to Subramanian (1977:246), parties involved in the wage determination process (including the so–called wage boards) committed themselves to a system of 'an *automatic* link between dearness allowance and the consumer price index, so that neutralisation of the rising cost of living to a substantial, though not always full, degree has now become standard practice wherever in organised industry capacity to pay permits periodical adjustment of dearness allowance.' The dearness allowance payable to workers is calculated every month on the basis of the number of points by which the consumer price index has risen above some agreed–upon base index and on the number of days worked in a month. All employees working the same number of days in a month get the same amount of dearness allowance, irrespective of their individual wage rates.[44] Although the calculation of the rate of dearness allowance varies greatly between sectors, compensation is seldom for the full amount of the consumer price increase. Therefore, although money wages tend to rise *automatically* with increases in the cost of living, a real wage fall is built into the system of wage adjustment in periods of rapidly rising prices.

Nominal wage indexation *via* dearness allowances can be expressed in a partial adjustment framework analogous to Nerlove's acreage response functions by (re–)formulating it in terms of a sector–specific bargaining process between employees (probably represented by labour unions) and employers. Employees in sector i ($i = 6, .., 9, g$) strive after some 'desired' nominal wage rate in period t, $w^*_{i,t}$, by relating it to the expected consumer

---

[44] Consequently, workers in the lower wage groups receive a higher proportion of their basic wages as dearness allowance than those in the higher wage groups (Subramanian 1977:211).

price index cpi_t^e:

(A.4.19) $$w_{i,t}^* = \gamma_{0i} + \gamma_{1i}\, cpi_t^e \qquad\qquad 0 < \gamma_{1i} < 1$$

where γ_{1i} reflects the degree of indexation desired by the employees. Their consumer price expectations are formed adaptively:

(A.4.20) $$cpi_t^e - cpi_{t-1}^e = \rho_i\,[cpi_t - cpi_{t-1}^e] \qquad\qquad 0 < \rho_i \le 1$$

where ρ_i is the coefficient of price expectation. In each period t, nominal wage rates are formed on the basis of the previous period's wage rate (the basic wage) and the wage rate desired by the employees:

(A.4.21) $$w_{i,t} = \pi_i\, w_{i,t}^* + (1 - \pi_i)\, w_{i,t-1}$$

The coefficient π_i, such that $0 < \pi_i < 1$, is the rate of adjustment which reflects the bargaining power of employees *vis-à-vis* employers. Substitution of (A.4.19) in (A.4.21) gives:

(A.4.22) $$w_{i,t} = \pi_i\gamma_{0i} + \pi_i\gamma_{1i}\, cpi_t^e + (1 - \pi_i)\, w_{i,t-1}$$

and of (A.4.20) in (A.4.22) yields:

(A.4.23) $$w_{i,t} = \pi_i\gamma_{0i} + \pi_i\gamma_{1i}\rho_i\, cpi_t + \pi_i\,\gamma_{1i}(1 - \rho_i)\, cpi_{t-1}^e$$
$$(1 - \pi_i)\, w_{i,t-1}$$

Lagging (A.4.22) by one period, multiplying it by $(1 - \rho_i)$ and subtracting it from (A.4.23) yields:

(A.4.24) $$w_{i,t} = \pi_i\gamma_{0i}\rho_i + \pi_i\gamma_{1i}\rho_i\, cpi_t + [(1 - \rho_i) + (1 - \pi_i)]\, w_{i,t-1}$$
$$- [(1 - \rho_i)(1 - \pi_i)]\, w_{i,t-2}$$

Assuming that $\rho_i = 1$, or that $cpi_t^e = cpi_t$, we get

(4.23) $$w_{i,t} = \theta_{0i} + \theta_{1i}\, cpi_t + \theta_{2i}\, w_{i,t-1}$$
$$=$$

where $\theta_{0i} = \pi_i\gamma_{0i}$, $\theta_{1i} = \pi_i\gamma_{1i}$, and $\theta_{2i} = (1 - \pi_i)$. Note that both $0 < \theta_{1i} < 1$ and $0 < \theta_{2i} < 1$.

Appendix 4.8
Derivation of a LES inclusive of Food Subsidies

Inclusion of consumer subsidies alters the commodity–wise demand functions of the familiar linear expenditure system (Stone, 1954). This will be demonstrated by working through the utility maximisation by non–agricultural and agricultural consumers when the consumer subsidies are included in their budget constraints. Note that it is assumed in the model that all consumer subsidies are spent on food. Non–agricultural consumers receive an *issue* of foodgrains, f_{ni} ($i = 1, 2, 3$), at a subsidised price $\bar{p}_i$ and agricultural consumers earn food–for–work cereal compensations of quantity f_{ai} ($i = 1, 2$) at zero price. f_{ni} is zero for $i = 4, ..., 9$. f_{ai} is zero for $i = 3, ..., 9$.

The Stone–Geary utility function of agricultural (a) and non–agricultural (n) consumers, u_k ($k = a, n$), may be written as follows

(A.4.25) $\qquad u_k = \sum_{i=1}^{9} \mu_{ki} \, log \, (c_{ki} + f_{ki} - \gamma_{ki}) \qquad\qquad k = a, n.$

$$\mu_{ki} > 0, \; (c_{ki} + f_{ki}) > \gamma_{ki} \, , \; \Sigma_i \, \mu_{ki} = 1.$$

where c_{ki} represents the quantity consumed (apart from subsidised consumption) of good i ($i = 1, ..., 9$), f_{ki} represents the consumer subsidy for commodity i, and the γ_{ki} are often interpreted as representing quantities of 'committed' consumption although there is no requirement that any γ_{ki} be positive. The μ_{ki} may be thought of as 'marginal budget shares', *i.e.* marginal propensities to consume out of 'supernumerary' expenditure, so that $\Sigma_i \, \mu_{ki} = 1$. The γ_{ki} are assumed to be independent of income and prices. The utility function is concave provided all μ_{ki} are nonnegative and provided aggregate agricultural or non–agricultural consumer expenditure is no less than $\Sigma_i \, p_i \gamma_{ki}$ so that $(c_{ki} + f_{ki}) \geq \gamma_{ki}$ for all i. The utility function has to be concave for a maximum to exist.

Utility is maximised subject to a linear budget constraint (including the consumer subsidies) which is defined in terms of an exogenously given level of total expenditure on all commodities, *i.e.*

(A.4.26) $\qquad \sum_{i=1}^{9} p_{si} c_{ki} + \sum_{i=1}^{9} \bar{p}_i f_{ki} = D_k \qquad\qquad k = a, n.$

where D_k is aggregate agricultural or non–agricultural consumer expenditure. The use of the equality of (A.4.26) implies that consumers always attain the upper boundary of their opportunity set. This will happen *if* the consumers cannot completely satisfy all their wants within the budget constraint. There is always some good more of which is desirable and there is no room for 'satisficing' behaviour. Furthermore, implicit in the linear budget constraint is the assumption of efficient markets with negligible transaction costs.

146

Hence, the use of a linear budget constraint rules out possible non-linearities, indivisibilities, and interdependencies which may characterise consumers' decisions (Deaton and Muellbauer, 1980:14–20).

Noting that private expenditure on subsidised consumer items is equal to the 'market value' of $p_{si}f_{ki}$ minus subsidy expenditure $(p_{si} - \bar{p}_i) f_{ki}$, or

$$\sum_{i=1}^{9} \bar{p}_i f_{ki} = \sum_{i=1}^{9} p_{si} f_{ki} - \sum_{i=1}^{9} (p_{si} - \bar{p}_i) f_{ki} \qquad k = a, n.$$

one may rewrite equation (A.4.26) as

$$(A.4.26') \quad \sum_{i=1}^{9} p_{si}(c_{ki} + f_{ki}) = D_k + \sum_{i=1}^{9} (p_{si} - \bar{p}_i) f_{ki} \qquad k = a, n.$$

The Lagrangean expression for maximisation of u_k subject to the budget constraint of (A.4.26) is:

$$(A.4.27) \quad v_k = \sum_{i=1}^{9} \mu_{ki} log\ (c_{ki} + f_{ki} - \gamma_{ki}) + \lambda_k \{D_k - \sum_{i=1}^{9} p_{si} c_{ki} - \sum_{i=1}^{9} \bar{p}_i f_{ki}\}$$
$$k = a, n.$$

The first order conditions derived from $(\partial v_k / \partial c_{ki} = 0)$ lead to the following expressions for μ_{ki} :

$$(A.4.28) \quad \mu_{ki} = \lambda_k\ p_{si}\ (c_{ki} + f_{ki} - \gamma_{ki}) \qquad k = a, n.$$

Imposing the normalisation condition that the sum of the μ_{ki} equals 1, equation (A.4.28) becomes

$$(A.4.29) \quad 1 = \sum_{i=1}^{9} \mu_{ki} = \lambda_k \sum_{i=1}^{9} p_{si} (c_{ki} + f_{ki} - \gamma_{ki}) \qquad k = a, n.$$

The Lagrange multiplier λ_k is given by

$$(A.4.29') \quad \lambda_k = 1 / \sum_{i=1}^{9} p_{si} (c_{ki} + f_{ki} - \gamma_{ki}) \qquad k = a, n.$$

The value of the Lagrange multiplier λ_k is the amount by which the maximand would increase given a unit relaxation in the constraint (a unit increase in D_k) or, in other words, the marginal utility of total expenditure. One must bear in mind, however, that the utility function has no observable unit of measurement so that the amount of utility that an extra Rupee will buy is conditional on the normalisation selected for the utility function.

Substitution of equation (A.4.29') for λ_k in (A.4.28) and substitution for $\Sigma_i p_i(c_{ki} + f_{ki})$ from (A.4.26') gives us the following demand function for commodity i

$$(A.4.30) \qquad c_{ki} = \gamma_{ki} - f_{ki} + (\mu_{ki}/p_{si}) \{D_k + \sum_{i=1}^{9} (p_{si} - \bar{p}_i) f_{ki} - \sum_{i=1}^{9} p_{si}\gamma_{ki}\}$$

$$k = a, n.$$
$$i = 1, ..., 9$$

Noting that food–for–work compensations are given against zero price, utility maximisation by agricultural consumers subject to their budget constraint will give the following commodity–wise demand functions ($k = a$):

$$(A.4.30') \qquad c_{ai} = \gamma_{ai} - f_{ai} + (\mu_{ai}/p_{si}) \{D_a + \sum_{i=1}^{9} p_{si} f_{ai} - \sum_{i=1}^{9} p_{si}\gamma_{ai}\}$$

$$i = 1, ..., 9$$

Equation (A.4.30) forms a system of 18 expenditure equations or Engel curves which are linear in income and prices and correspond to Stone's (1954) LES (after substituting for $f_{ki} = 0$). Differentiation of (A.4.30) with respect to aggregate expenditure D_k gives the expenditure elasticity of demand (of consumer group k) for commodity i:

$$(A.4.31) \qquad \varepsilon_i^k = (\partial c_{ki}/\partial D_k)(D_k/c_{ki}) = (\mu_{ki} D_k/p_{si} c_{ki}) = \mu_{ki}/\phi_{ki}$$

where $\phi_{ki} = p_{si} c_{ki}/D_k$ is the average budget share of commodity i. The uncompensated own price elasticities ε_{ii}^k of consumption demand for good i can be derived by differentiating (A.4.30) with respect to p_{si}, assuming that $\partial D_k / \partial p_{si} = 0$.

$$(A.4.32) \qquad \varepsilon_{ii}^k = (\partial c_{ki}/\partial p_{si})(p_{si}/c_{ki}) = -\varepsilon_i^k \sigma^k + \mu_{ki} \left[\frac{(f_{ki} - \gamma_{ki})}{c_{ki}} \right]$$

where σ^k, the 'supernumerary expenditure ratio' (Taylor, 1979:221), is defined as

$$\sigma^k = \left[D_k + \sum_{i=1}^{9} (p_{si} - \bar{p}_i) f_{ki} - \sum_{i=1}^{9} p_{si}\gamma_{ki} \right] / D_k$$

The reciprocal of σ^k is sometimes called the Frisch parameter. Cross–price elasticities ε_{ij}^k ($i \neq j$) can be obtained as follows:

$$(A.4.33) \qquad \varepsilon_{ij}^k = (\partial c_{ki}/\partial p_{sj})(p_{sj}/c_{ki}) = \varepsilon_i^k \left[\frac{p_{sj}(f_{kj} - \gamma_{kj})}{D_k} \right]$$

The linear expenditure system is generally considered to be rather restrictive. In fact, the LES of (A.4.30) satisfies the following three theoretical restrictions (Deaton and Muellbauer 1980:65):

(1) an adding up restriction which says that the total value of demand be equal total expenditure;

(2) a homogeneity restriction according to which the demand functions be homogeneous of degree zero in total expenditure and prices; this restriction is also known as 'the absence of money illusion', since the units in which prices and aggregate outlay (or budget size) are expressed, have no effect on purchases; and

(3) a symmetry restriction saying that the cross price–derivatives of the (Hicksian) demand functions are symmetric, *i.e.* a compensated Rupee per unit increase in p_{si} should increase the quantity bought of commodity j by a number equal to the increase in quantity of commodity i bought consequent on a compensated rupee per unit increase in p_{sj}.

The adding up and homogeneity properties of the LES are consequences of the specification of a linear budget constraint. Symmetry, on the other hand, derives from the assumption that consumer preferences are consistent, which means that for any three vectors of goods, $\mathbf{q}^i$ ($i = 1, 2, 3$), in the consumers' choice set, if $\mathbf{q}^1 \geq \mathbf{q}^2$ and $\mathbf{q}^2 \geq \mathbf{q}^3$, then $\mathbf{q}^1 \geq \mathbf{q}^3$ (Deaton and Muellbauer, 1980:27).

Equations (A.4.32) and (A.4.33) show why additivity is both so useful and so restrictive. Additivity is useful because, apart from the parameter σ^k, knowledge of expenditure elasticities alone is sufficient to determine all the own and cross price elasticities. Consequently, almost no relative price information is required in order to estimate price elasticities.

Additivity is restrictive because it rules out inferior goods and any complementarity among goods, imposing substitutability only. Equation (A.4.31) shows that inferiority ($\varepsilon_i^k < 0$, *i.e.* the purchase of good i declines absolutely as aggregate consumer expenditure D_k increases) can only occur for goods with μ_{ki} negative. But this violates concavity and would lead to the good having a positive own price elasticity in (A.4.32). Further, for concavity to hold, no two goods may be complements.

A third restriction of the LES is that it has the property of approximate proportionality between price and expenditure elasticities, whereas there is no à *priori* reason to believe that price and expenditure elasticities should be proportional. The approximate proportionality can be explained as follows. Since all marginal budget shares μ_{ki} are positive and add to unity, each is of the same order of magnitude as the reciprocal of the number of goods included in the demand system. Hence, if the number of goods is large, ε_{ii}^k, becomes, to a reasonable degree of approximation,

(A.4.32') $\qquad \varepsilon_{11}^k \approx - \varepsilon_i^k \, \sigma^k$

This approximate proportionality of expenditure and own price elasticities in practice tends to be quite accurate even for eight or ten commodities.

These restrictions of the LES imply that 'its application must be restricted to those cases where its limitations are not thought to be serious. Even then, care must be taken in interpreting the results and a careful distinction drawn between properties of the model, imposed à priori, and properties of the data' (Deaton and Muellbauer, 1980:66). However, additivity may not be an inappropriate assumption for sufficiently broad groupings of commodities. The restrictive LES specification also may not be unrealistic when the range of income variation is small (Radhakrishna, 1978).

Appendix 4.9
Solution Strategy and Solution Algorithm

Following Adelman and Robinson (1978), a distinction can be made between a solution strategy and a solution algorithm. A solution strategy is defined by its purpose which is to establish numerically a set of nonlinear functions (i.c. excess demand equations) whose simultaneous solution is required. The solution strategy serves a purely calculational purpose and has as such no economic meaning. A solution algorithm, on the other hand, is a computation technique for solving the set of simultaneous nonlinear equations (established by the solution strategy) numerically.[45]

The most efficient solution strategy of the present model seems to be to separate the within–period and the between–period models. The between–period model can be solved straightforwardly equation by equation, because it represents a recursive set of equations. The solution strategy of the static within–period model is discussed below.

Solution Strategy

I have used the solution strategy described by Taylor (1983:69) which starts from a set of 'starting values' for agricultural prices and non–agricultural levels of production. The strategy uses both a Gauss–Seidel algorithm and a Newton type of solution procedure. The Newton type algorithm is discussed below. Schematically, the solution strategy works as follows:

(1) Start from initial values for agricultural prices and non–agricultural outputs.

---

[45] Dervis et al.(1982) discuss the existing solution algorithms used to solve CGE models. See also Challen and Hagger (1983).

(2) Determine new non–agricultural commodity prices *via* (4.21) to (4.25).

(3) Compute new levels of agricultural production based on new relative fertiliser prices through (4.10) to (4.20).

(4) Determine commoditywise intermediate and final demand *via* (4.27) to (4.49).

(5) Determine commoditywise excess demand in (4.50).

(6) If the excess demand of commodity *i* differs from zero by more than a prespecified level of tolerance, adjust its supply to its demand and return to (4); this procedure is known as the Gauss–Seidel iteration method; note that agricultural prices are not adjusted. Otherwise, *i.e.* if the excess demands have converged, continue to (7).

(7) Compare the resulting agricultural demand levels to the levels of agricultural supply generated by the agricultural production submodel in (3). If the absolute values of agricultural excess demands exceed a prespecified level of tolerance, adjust the agricultural prices *via* a Newton procedure and return to (2). Otherwise, *i.e.* if the excess demand have converged, stop.

Solution Algorithm

The Newton procedure uses the matrix of numerical derivatives of the system of excess demand equations with respect to each one of the equilibrating variables – the Jacobian – in the adjusting process. The basic procedure to numerically solve the system of excess demand equations may be set out as follows (note that the notation is unique to this appendix).

Let

(A.4.34) $\qquad f_i\,(p_1,\,p_2,\,...,\,p_5) = 0 \qquad [\text{or } f\,(p) = 0\,] \qquad i = 1,\,..,\,5.$

where p_i denotes the price of the *i*–th commodity and f_i denotes the excess demand for the *i*–th commodity. The value of the price vector p which satisfies the above system (assuming that there exists such a p) is called an equilibrium value of p and is denoted by $\overline{p}$. Assume that we know of an initial price vector p_k in the neighbourhood of the equilibrium price vector $\overline{p}$ – where k denotes the number of iterations which is initially set at zero.

The standard procedure to solve (A.4.34) is to take a linear approximation of the above system, *i.e.* by taking only the linear terms of the Taylor expansion of $f\,(p)$ about the initial price vector p_k and disregard the second and higher order terms, or

(A.4.35) $\qquad f\,(p_k + h) \approx f\,(p_k) + h\,f'(p_k)$

Supposing that we are able to chose h such that $f\,(p_k + h) = 0$, we get

(A.4.36) $f(p_k) + h\, f'(p_k) = 0$

which yields

(A.4.37) $h = -\left[f'(p_k) \right]^{-1} f(p_k) = -J^{-1} f(p_k)$

where $J = [j_{ij}]$ is known as the Jacobian matrix with element $j_{ij} = \partial f_i / \partial p_j$, evaluated at $p = p_k$.

The value obtained for h may now be used to calculate a new value for p, denoted by p_{k+1}:

(A.4.38) $p_{k+1} = p_k + h = p_k - J_k^{-1} f_k$

where an expression which is evaluated at the k–th iteration, is denoted by $f_k = f(p_k)$ and $J_k = J(p_k)$. One tests for convergence by substituting the newly obtained vector p_{k+1} back into $f(p)$. The iterative process continues until the values of the endogenous variables in successive iterations converge to a pre–specified level of tolerance $\overline{\varepsilon}$, such that $| f(p) | < \overline{\varepsilon}$.

Stability

Stability analysis is concerned with the question of whether p converges to an equilibrium value $\overline{p}$. A necessary and sufficient condition for local stability of (A.4.38) is that all the eigenvalues of J have negative real parts. If all non–diagonal elements of J are non–negative, this is will be the case if the trace of the Jacobian matrix is negative and if, at the same time, all principal minors alternate in signs as follows (see Samuelson, 1947:273):

(A.4.39) $j_{ii} < 0,$
$\quad \begin{vmatrix} j_{ii} & j_{ij} \\ j_{ji} & j_{jj} \end{vmatrix} > 0,$
$\quad \begin{vmatrix} j_{ii} & j_{ij} & j_{ik} \\ j_{ji} & j_{jj} & j_{jk} \\ j_{ki} & j_{kj} & j_{kk} \end{vmatrix} < 0, \ldots$

$$i \neq j, \; i \neq k, \; j \neq k.$$

The condition that $j_{ii} < 0$ says that an increase in the excess demand for commodity i will result in an increase in the equilibrium price of that good – which is an extension of the stability condition in isolated markets (see Hansen, 1970:34–35).

Note that condition (A.4.39) is sufficient to accomplish stability only if all $\partial f_i / \partial p_j > 0$ for all $i \neq j$ – a property of the Jacobian matrix which is known as 'gross substitutability'. Commodities i and j are said to be gross substitutes if an increase in the price of commodity i leads to an increase in the demand for commodity j. The 'gross substitutability' condition is not likely to be fulfilled in reality, since it conflicts with complementarities, which we know may be quite frequent. The present model, however, is locally stable in the sense that its Jacobian matrix has satisfied these conditions. This is to be attributed to the inclusion in the model of the linear expenditure system which rules out any complementarity among goods, imposing substitutability only.

NUMERICAL SPECIFICATION OF THE MODEL –
ESTIMATION AND CALIBRATION

5.1   *Introduction*

In assembling any economy–wide data base, inconsistencies emerge that require
one to make decisions about the relative reliability and accuracy of different
data sources. Such inconsistencies sometimes arise from differences in
coverage and accuracy, but, more often, they are due to variations in
definitions between the different sources. This chapter describes the method
which was used to generate the general equilibrium model's benchmark data set
for the base year 1985–86. The approach was to work within the framework of a
social accounting matrix (SAM). The major usefulness of a SAM is that it
brings together the accounts of each of the various economic actors whose
behaviour is to be modelled in a consistent framework. This consistency
property provides a useful check in reconciling data from disparate sources.
Section 5.2 describes the procedure followed in constructing the 1985–86 SAM.
Section 5.3 discusses the estimation and calibration of the remaining model
parameters. Finally, Section 5.4 presents the results of the sensitivity
analysis in which alternative values of key parameters were assumed and the
model results evaluated for their robustness.

5.2   *The Social Accounting Framework*

The method used to construct the SAM involved the following sequence of steps.
First, the production accounts based on input–output data were reconciled

(Section 5.2.1). Second, the income and expenditure accounts were reconciled with the production accounts (Section 5.2.2). In this procedure, the input–output table provided the starting point and was considered the controlling data source.

5.2.1   *Production and Value Added Accounts*

The most recent year for which detailed input–output data were available, was 1978–79. The 115 sector absorption and make matrices for 1978–79, published by the Central Statistical Organisation (*CSO*), were aggregated to the nine sector classification. Details of the mapping scheme are given in Table 5.1. With the help of the absorption matrix and make matrix, an industry by industry input–output table for 1978–79 was constructed.[1] Next, the 1978–79 matrix was updated to the model's base year 1985–86. Updating required detailed information for the year 1985–86. The major source of information on macro–economic variables are the consolidated accounts of the nation included in the *National Accounts Statistics* (*NAS*). These are reproduced in a modified format in Appendix 5.1 for 1985–86. The consolidated accounts provide the control figures of the macro–economic variables included in the 1985–86 input–output table and the SAM. The next step was to distribute the macro–economic aggregates across the nine model sectors, starting with (*i*) gross value added, (*ii*) gross production, (*iii*) net indirect taxes, and (*iv*) final demand.

(*i*)   *Gross Value Added*

The *NAS* give aggregate gross value addded (or GDP at factor cost) for agriculture, manufacturing, and services. For agriculture, disaggregrated figures of gross value added were not available. Therefore, aggregate agricultural gross value added was distributed across the five agricultural sectors in correspondance to their sectoral shares in agricultural gross value added in the 1978–79 input–output matrix.

The *NAS* provide disaggregated information on gross value added earned in non–agriculture. A complementary, even more disaggregated data source is the *Annual Survey of Industries* (*ASI*), which is also published by the Central Statistical Organisation. The *ASI* gives detailed information on about thirty selected characteristics of major registered industry groups upto the three–digit level of the National Industrial Classification Code. Gross value added earned in fertiliser industries was taken directly from the *ASI*. Gross

---

[1] See Bulmer–Thomas (1982), chapter 9, for details of the procedure which was followed to obtain a 'symmetric', industry by industry input–output table.

Table 5.1
Mapping Scheme for Sectoral Aggregation

Sector	115–sector classification *CSO* (1978–79)
1. Rice	001;
2. Wheat	002;
3. Other Food Crops	003 to 007;
4. Commercial Crops	008 to 017;
5. Other Agriculture	018 to 022;
6. Fertilisers	062;
7. Basic, Intermediate & Capital Goods	023 to 032, 046, 051 to 053, 056 to 061, 063 to 103, 106;
8. Consumer goods	033 to 045, 047 to 050, 054, 055;
9. Services	104, 105, 107 to 115.

Source: *CSO* (1989b).

value added of basic, intermediate and capital goods production and consumer goods production was taken from the *ASI* and the *NAS*. The *NAS* sectors electricity, gas & water supply, construction, mining, railways, and communication were classified as basic, intermediate and capital goods sectors. The *NAS* sector unregistered manufacturing was classified as belonging to the consumer goods sector. With the help of *ASI* data, the *NAS* figure for gross value added in registered manufacturing was distributed between basic, intermediate and capital goods on the one hand, and consumer goods on the other hand. Data on gross value added earned in services were taken directly from the *NAS*.

(ii)   *Gross Production by Sector*

The *NAS* provide data on cropwise gross production of the agricultural sectors and sectorwise gross production for registered manufacturing, construction, and mining. They do not provide any data on gross production in services, electricity, gas & water supply, railways, communication, and unregistered manufacturing.

For agriculture, the 1985–86 *NAS* gross production figures were adjusted upwards to include the output generated by secondary activities such as rice and wheat milling, which are not included in the *NAS* figures. The scaling factors were derived as the ratio of the value of gross production taken from the 1978–79 input–output table and the 1978–79 value of gross production given by the *NAS*. The *ASI* figures on gross production include only the registered part of manufacturing. Comparison of the gross production figures of basic, intermediate and capital goods industries and consumer goods industries

156

derived from the 1978–79 *ASI* with the corresponding figures derived from the 1978–79 input–output table revealed that unregistered manufacturing mainly belonged to the consumer goods sector. For services, the 1985–86 level of gross production was derived by applying the 1978–79 ratio of GDP to gross production to the 1985–86 *NAS* figure of GDP generated in that sector.

(iii)   Net Indirect Taxes

Net indirect taxes for 1985–86 were allocated to the different production sectors and the elements of final demand according to the percentage composition of the row of net indirect taxes in the 1978–79 input–output table.

(iv)   Final Demands

The next step was to determine the elements of the final demand matrix of the input–output table. Account 1, Appendix 5.1, provides the control totals of private final consumption expenditure, public final consumption expenditure, gross fixed capital formation, change in stocks, exports and imports, which add up to aggregate final demand (or GDP at market prices). Information about the sectoral composition of each of these final demand items was not available. For public consumption and gross fixed capital formation, the sectoral composition given by the 1978–79 input–output table was used to arrive at 1985–86 expenditure levels. *National Sample Survey (NSS)* data were used to establish the 1985–86 vector of private consumption by commodity on the basis of a linear expenditure system (see Section 5.3.2 and Appendix 5.2). Data on commodity–wise exports and imports from the *Economic Survey* (1988–89) were used to determine the sectoral composition of export and import flows. Finally, the 1985–86 vector of changes in stocks by sector is based on the 1985–86 SAM produced by Sarkar and Panda (1991) with additional information on changes in food stocks taken from the Ministry of Agriculture (1988). For all items of final demand, commodity–wise expenditure adds up to the control total given by Account 1, Appendix 5.1.

Given final demand, net indirect taxes, gross value added and gross production by sectors, the available supply of commodities for intermediate use by sector was determined as a residual. Given the 1978–79 matrix of input–output coefficients and the 1985–86 row and column sums of the intermediate flow matrix, sectoral demand for intermediate goods was determined by using the RAS method. Via this method the rows and columns of the intermediate input flows matrix (the input–output coefficients) were adjusted until the matrix converged on the pre–specified 1985–86 row and column control totals.

157

Finally, to arrive at the matrix of domestic input–output flows, the import content of each transaction (both for intermediate and final use) was separately identified with the help of an import flow matrix. The nine–sector import–flow matrix was constructed on the basis of the matrix on import transactions for 1979–80 (at 1979–80 prices) published in the *Technical Note on the Sixth Plan*. This 89 sector import–flow matrix was aggregated to the nine sector specification on the basis of the mapping scheme given in Table 5.2. Non–zero imports of paddy and services in 1985–86 which were zero in 1979–80, were assumed to be imported wholly for private consumption purposes. For the remaining sectors, the percentage composition of each row of imports from the import–flow matrix for 1979–80 was applied to the actual import values for 1985–86. Clearly, whatever biases that may have existed in the import–flow matrix included in the *Technical Note*, are translated into the import–flow matrix for 1985–86.

The matrix of intermediate imports for 1985–86 was subtracted from the aggregate intermediate input flow matrix to yield the matrix of *domestic* intermediate input flows. The sum of intermediate imports by sector was entered in a separate row in the input–output table, representing complementary intermediate imports by sector. The residual imports by sector were registered in the import column of the final demand matrix, representing competitive imports by sector.

Table 5.2
Mapping Scheme for Sectoral Aggregation of Import–Flow Matrix

Sector	89–Sector Classification
1. Rice	1;
2. Wheat	2;
3. Other Food Crops	3 to 6;
4. Commercial Crops	7 to 11;
5. Other Agriculture	12 to 15;
6. Fertilisers	47;
7. Basic, Intermediate & Capital Goods	16 to 19, 32, 36 to 38, 41 to 46, 48 to 68, 70 to 81, and 83;
8. Consumer goods	20 to 31, 33 to 35, 39, 40 and 69;
9. Services	82, 84 to 89.

Source: Planning Commission (1981).

158

5.2.2   *Income and Expenditure Accounts*

Section 5.2.1 yields a consistent set of production accounts (inclusive of intermediate deliveries) and aggregate value–added accounts. The next step was to generate a consistent set of disaggregated income and expenditure accounts. To this end, the following steps were taken: (*i*) distributing gross value added across the functional categories 'wages' and 'mark–up income' for each non–agricultural sector; (*ii*) introducing a government account; (*iii*) introducing a rest–of–the–world account; and (*iv*) incorporating a capital account which distinguishes between private domestic savings, public sector savings and foreign savings.

(*i*)   *Functional Distribution of Value Added*

Within agricultural income, no distinction was made between wage and mark–up income. Non–agricultural value added by sector was split into wage and mark–up income. For sectors 6, 7, and 8, the shares of wage income and mark–up income in aggregate value added were derived from the *CSO* (1989c). For sector 9, these proportions were taken from Sarkar and Panda (1991). Account 6, Appendix 5.1, gives the resulting distribution of private income.

(*ii*)   *Government Account*

Account 5, Appendix 5.1, presents the balance sheet of public sector revenues and expenditures. Government revenues include direct and indirect tax receipts and revenues from public enterprises. In the SAM, direct tax revenues were entered in the row of government income as a receipt and in the column of 'use of private income' as an expenditure.

Revenues from public enterprises were residually determined from Account 5, Appendix 5.1. As such, they include interest payments to government and government's miscellaneous receipts. The figure obtained corresponds to the figure given in World Bank (1989). The agricultural sectors are assumed not to contribute to direct public sector earnings from production. The share of the consumer goods sector in public enterprise revenue was taken from Sarkar and Panda (1991). Revenue from public enterprises was distributed across the remaining three sectors according to the sectoral distribution of gross profits of central government non–departmental enterprises given in World Bank (1989).

Government expenditure includes final consumption of goods and services, a wage bill, current transfers, interest payments, and subsidies. In the input–output table, government wage payments are registered as final consumption of services. In the SAM, the government wage bill was reallocated to the row of non–agricultural wage incomes.[2] Public sector consumption of services was reduced by the same amount, as were the levels of wage income and of gross production of the services sector. Public current transfers (mainly consisting of pensions and other social security payments) were added to non–agricultural wage income. Public interest payments were registered in the row of non–agricultural mark–up income. Finally, subsidy expenditure amounted to Rs. 8543 crores of which Rs. 1650 crores were food subsidies and Rs. 6893 crores were producers' subsidies. In the SAM, food subsidies were entered as a negative entry in the row of government income and in the column of use of private income. Producers' subsidies were allocated across sectors on the basis of the subsidy rates per unit of gross production given in Gupta (1989:468) and subtracted from the *net* indirect taxes by sector to yield the indirect tax flows. Rs. 542 crores of the producers' subsidies are export subsidies, given to the basic, intermediate and capital goods industries (Rs. 300 crores) and the consumer goods industries (Rs. 242 crores).

The difference between current public income plus depreciation and current expenditure (the gross revenue surplus of the government) of Rs. 8592 crores was entered in the row of gross savings (the capital account).

(iii)   Foreign Trade Account

Account 4, Appendix 5.1, gives the balance of payments for 1985–86. Imports amounted to Rs. 23260 crores of which Rs. 13364.6 crores were complementary intermediate inputs and Rs. 9895.4 crores were competitive imports. In the same year, the economy exported goods and services worth Rs. 15634 crores. Net current factor income from abroad (mainly consisting of workers' remittances from the Middle East) was Rs. 1392 crores and was entered in the row of non–agricultural wage incomes. The current account balance of Rs. 6234 crores (or foreign savings) was entered as a payment from the rest–of–the–world account to the capital account.

(iv)   Capital Account

In the capital account (Account 3, Appendix 5.1), all savings, domestic and foreign, are collected and spent on investment goods. The *NAS* give the 1985–86 control figures for private savings, public savings, and foreign savings, and for gross domestic capital formation. Aggregate savings were adjusted to include the errors and omissions reported in the *NAS*, leaving unchanged the level of gross investment. Within gross savings, the *NAS* estimates of public savings and foreign savings were preferred to the estimate of gross private

---

[2] As such, all government services are treated as 'pure' public goods on which no private expenditure is possible (*e.g.* defence).

savings. Private savings were determined as the difference between gross domestic capital formation on the one hand and gross public savings and foreign savings on the other. For private savings, the estimate obtained of Rs. 53184 crores is substantially higher than the *NAS* figure of Rs. 46558 crores. It corresponds, however, to Sarkar and Panda's (1991) estimate of Rs. 56771 crores for the same year.

5.2.3   *The Social Accounting Matrix*, 1985–86

Sections 5.2.1 and 5.2.2 have reconciled data from different sources in the six accounts included in Appendix 5.1. Inclusion of these accounts in the input–output framework yields the SAM of Table 5.3 which provides the benchmark data set used in the model exercises. Some of its details are worth pointing out. Note first that the first 9 columns give the cost structures of the producing sectors included in the model. Production costs include intermediate purchases, factor payments, (intermediate input) import costs, and indirect taxes less subsidies. Value added in the non–agricultural sectors is split into wage income, mark–up income and government income (revenue from public enterprises). Government income (row 11) further includes revenue from direct and indirect taxation; uses of government income including wage payments, transfer and interest payments, and subsidies, appear in column 11. Uses of private income are given in column 10. Only totals are shown in the SAM, although different consumption patterns for agricultural and non–agricultural households are postulated in the model (see Section 5.3.2). Transactions with the rest of the world are recorded in row 13 for intermediate imports and in columns 14, 15 and 16 for exports, competitive imports and exports subsidies. In 1985–86, the foreign exchange required to pay for imports (Rs. crores 23260) is provided for by export earnings (Rs. crores 15632), workers' remittances from abroad (Rs. crores 1392), and foreign savings or the current account deficit (Rs. crores 6234). Gross private savings amount to Rs. crores 53184 and gross public savings are Rs. crores 8592. The sum of the three savings sources is Rs. crores 68010 (row 12) which is equal to gross investment demand (*i.e.* the sum of columns 12 and 13).

Many of the model parameters including input–output coefficients, inter–mediate import coefficients, labour–output ratios, indirect and direct tax rates, and non–agricultural mark–up rates, and the base–year values of most of the exogenous variables such as government consumption, exports, final imports and stock changes were derived from Table 5.3. The values of the remaining model parameters were estimated as is explained in the next section.

161

Table 5.3

Table 5.3

A Social Accounting Matrix for India, 1985–86
(*Rs. Crores at Current Prices*)

		RICE 1	WHEAT 2	OTHER FOOD CROPS 3
01	RICE	885.5	35.1	3.4
02	WHEAT	4.0	864.2	3.6
03	OTHER FOOD CROPS	11.8	52.0	821.9
04	COMMERCIAL CROPS	31.7	39.6	70.3
05	OTHER AGRICULTURE	2030.7	1434.9	999.0
06	FERTILISERS	1205.9	957.9	105.5
07	BASIC, INTERM. & CAPITAL GOODS	1140.8	1013.9	299.2
08	CONSUMER GOODS	42.3	51.3	31.8
09	SERVICES	1429.6	996.0	389.2
10a	AGRICULTURAL INCOME	12054.0	5430.2	6577.0
10b	NON–AGRIC. WAGE INCOME			
10c	NON–AGRIC. MARK–UP INCOME			
10	PRIVATE INCOME	12054.0	5430.2	6577.0
11	GOVERNMENT INCOME			
12	GROSS SAVINGS			
13	INTERMEDIATE IMPORTS	430.8	284.2	108.6
14	PRODUCER/CONSUMER SUBSIDIES	– 430.2	– 456.1	– 149.4
15	EXPORT SUBSIDY			
16	INDIRECT TAXES		55.2	145.4
17	DIRECT TAXES			
18	GROSS PRODUCTION	18836.8	10758.4	9405.5

Note: One crore Rupees is equal to 10 million Rupees.

COMM. CROPS	OTHER AGRIC.	FERTI- LISERS	BASIC, INT. & CAPITAL GOODS	CONSUMER GOODS	SERVICES
4	5	6	7	8	9
27.2	222.0	0.0	61.6	188.2	181.2
28.7	179.1	0.0	14.7	171.9	73.9
68.5	868.7	0.0	31.8	271.7	216.2
759.2	7169.3	0.0	1215.3	6664.3	369.6
2533.0	44.4	3.6	2013.4	2414.3	1270.3
827.4	2.5	386.2	188.4	17.2	34.2
1066.5	408.8	1409.6	47108.6	4197.2	7187.5
43.5	3747.2	59.2	3327.3	17296.5	2312.1
1301.2	1837.1	1011.0	23239.5	7748.6	18730.7
32627.7	19848.1				
		245.5	22668.3	11089.1	35780.2
		321.4	17401.9	9433.8	26897.8
32627.7	19848.1	566.9	40070.2	20522.9	62678.0
		311.0	10467.0	988.0	4719.0
615.7		221.2	9611.9	621.8	1470.4
−517.9	−4.8	−1060.9	−2610.6	−378.9	−742.1
73.7	271.4	1217.4	18975.1	3805.7	3478.6
39454.4	34593.9	4125.2	153714.3	64529.4	101979.6

USE OF PRIVATE INCOME	USE OF GOVT. INCOME	GROSS FIXED INVESTMENT	CHANGE IN STOCKS	EXPORTS	less IMPORTS
10	11	12	13	14	15
16677.0	5.0		370.0	196.3	− 15.7
9425.4	6.2		54.9		− 68.3
7061.2	11.4		16.5		− 26.3
20420.3	0.3		457.7	2256.8	
20978.1	4.7	287.9	463.4	482.8	− 366.6
	32.8	115.6	251.7		
19057.1	7869.5	52345.1	9848.7	4834.9	− 4373.3
34452.8	196.0	316.2	1542.2	3186.7	− 2317.7
38437.3	3845.2	1940.2		4676.4	− 3602.3
	18869.0			1392.0	
	6115.0				
	24984.0			1392.0	
53184.0	8592.0			6234.0	
					− 13364.6
− 1650.0	8001.0				
	542.0				
8089.8					874.7
6574.0					
232707.0	60046.0	55005.0	13005.0	23260.0	− 23260.0

EXPORT SUBSIDY	INDIRECT TAXES	DIRECT TAXES	GROSS PRODUCTION
16	17	18	19
			18836.8
			10758.4
			9405.5
			39454.4
			34593.9
			4125.2
300.0			153714.3
242.0			64529.4
			101979.6
			76537.0
			96000.1
			60169.9
			232707.0
	36987.0	6574.0	60046.0
			68010.0
			0.0
			0.0
			542.0
			36987.0
			6574.0
542.0	36987.0	6574.0	

As far as possible, the remaining model parameters were estimated from time series data instead of taking them from the relevant econometric literature and/or basing them on own best judgement. In this section, the estimation results are presented and compared with the relevant econometric literature, from which it will become clear that there is often a great variation in estimation results. The (estimated) elasticities were 'calibrated' to the model's data base (see Section 5.3.7).

5.3.1   *Savings*

The average savings ratios of the three private income categories in the model were derived from the *NCAER* (1980) survey of household income. The cross–section data collected in this survey covering 5,125 households spread over the country, pertain to the agricultural year July 1975 to June 1976. According to the survey results, the average propensity to save of rural households and urban households was 0.16 and 0.22, respectively. These *NCAER* estimates were adjusted to consistency with the aggregate level of private household savings taken from the *NAS*. Private corporate savings were assumed to belong to savings from non–agricultural mark–up income.

Table 5.4 presents the 1985–86 levels of category–wise incomes, savings, and expenditure. Data on depreciation and direct taxes were taken from the *NAS*. It was assumed that part of agricultural income and of non–agricultural mark–up income is spent on depreciation, and that direct taxes are paid only from mark–up income.[3] Subtracting depreciation and direct taxes from gross value added gives net private disposable income which is either saved or consumed. Net private savings were distributed across the three income categories as in Table 5.4. Groupwise average savings propensities (defined as the ratio of net savings to net disposable income) are given in the table. The estimated average non–agricultural propensity to save is higher than the average agricultural savings propensity. This corresponds to findings by Krishnamurty and Saibaba (1981). The aggregate savings propensity of 0.18 equals the *NCAER* estimate.

5.3.2   *Private Consumption Demand*

The availability of the National Sample Survey (NSS) data on consumer expenditure since the early 1950s has stimulated a large number of studies

---

[3] This assumption may be justified on the following grounds: (*i*) agricultural income earners generally escape direct taxation; (*ii*) corporation taxes alone make up about 40–45 per cent of direct tax revenues; and (*iii*) from the larger part of wage income no direct taxes are paid.

Table 5.4
Private Income, Saving and Expenditure

	Gross Value Added	Depre-ciation	Direct Taxes	Net Disposable Private Income	Net Private Savings	Private Expenditure	Average Savings Rates
Y_a	76537	4923	0	71614	9064	62550	0.13
Y_w	96000	0	0	96000	18042	77958	0.19
Y_z	60170	9888	6574	43708	11267	32441	0.26
Σ	232707	14811	6574	211322	38373	172494	0.18

Source: Derived from *CSO* (1989a) and *NCAER* (1980).

Table 5.5
LES Parameters, 1985–86

Non-Agricultural Consumption	μ_{ni}	γ_{ni}	Uncompensated Own Price Elasticity	Expenditure Elasticity
Rice	0.0363	0.4891	−0.4381	0.8156
Wheat	0.0294	0.3612	−0.4476	0.8479
Other food crops	0.0242	0.1587	−0.3946	0.7500
Commercial crops	0.1160	0.5644	−0.5942	1.0520
Other agriculture	0.1282	0.5779	−0.6331	1.1183
Basic, Intermediate & Capital goods	0.1234	0.6859	−0.5318	0.9227
Consumer goods	0.2274	1.1398	−0.6347	1.0246
Services	0.3068	1.5700	−0.6636	1.0048

Agricultural Consumption	μ_{ai}	γ_{ai}	Uncompensated Own Price Elasticity	Expenditure Elasticity
Rice	0.0576	0.8193	−0.2266	0.3532
Wheat	0.0379	0.3393	−0.2957	0.5275
Other food crops	0.0270	0.3732	−0.2017	0.3536
Commercial crops	0.1040	0.5408	−0.4338	0.7247
Other agriculture	0.1565	0.3157	−0.6627	1.1816
Basic, Intermediate & Capital goods	0.1716	0.1202	−0.8444	1.5990
Consumer goods	0.2819	0.2646	−0.8301	1.5032
Services	0.1635	0.2082	−0.7523	1.3860

Note: Elasticities were 'estimated' from cross–section data.
     See Appendix 5.2.

estimating complete demand systems including those by Radhakrishna (1978), Radhakrishna and Murty (1980), the Planning Commission (1979), and the *NCAER* (1981). Most of these studies are confined to (linear) Engel curve analysis. Because the sectoral disaggregation of the available demand systems does not correspond to the present sector classification, and the earlier estimates do not explicitly include consumer subsidies, a linear expenditure system (LES) tailored to the present sector classification and inclusive of consumer subsidies was estimated for the base year 1985–86. The 'estimation' procedure is explained in Appendix 5.2. For agricultural and non–agricultural consumers, the estimated LES parameters μ_{ki} and γ_{ki} are presented in Table 5.5, together with the commodity–wise (uncompensated) own price elasticities and expenditure elasticities. Note that it is assumed that fertilisers are not used for purposes of final demand. From the table, it can be seen that the non–agricultural expenditure elasticity for four out of eight commodity groups slightly exceeds unity, categorising them as luxuries (*i.e.* those goods that take up a larger share of the budget as total expenditure increases). Luxuries include commercial crops, other agricultural products, consumer goods and services. Agricultural expenditure elasticities significantly exceed unity also in four out of eight commodity groups, *i.c.* for other agricultural goods, basic, intermediate and capital goods, consumer goods, and services.

5.3.3 *Estimates of Fixed Capital Stock, Depreciation Rates and Investment by Sector of Origin and Destination*

Base–year estimates of sectoral capital stocks were taken from the *CSO* (1988) which provides estimates of net fixed capital stocks as on the 31st of March, 1981. The estimates are based on the perpetual inventory method (PIM) which provides a correct picture of the replacement value of the capital stocks (Kumar *et al.*, 1987). With the help of the *NAS* (New Series) which provides figures on net sectoral investments and depreciation based on PIM, the *CSO* estimates for 1981 were updated to the base year 1985–86. Estimates of sectorwise capital stocks are given in Table 5.6. Sectorwise depreciation rates were determined as the ratio of depreciation allowances to gross fixed capital stock. The table also includes the capital–gross–production ratios used in equation (4.26).

In equation (4.44), investment by sector of destination is translated into investment by sector of origin through a matrix of fixed coefficients, ϑ_{ij}, representing the proportion of capital stock of sector j originating in sector i. Data on the vector of investment by sector of destination are available from the *NAS*. Estimates of the ϑ_{ij} for 1979–80 included in the *Technical Note to the Sixth Plan of India* were adjusted to yield the vector of investment by origin included in the SAM, assuming that investment in sector j is wholly spent on goods originating from the basic, intermediate and capital goods sector with the exception of the amount of investment by sector of

Table 5.6
Net Fixed Capital Stocks by Sector, 1985–86
(Rs. Crores at Current Prices)

	Net Fixed Capital Stock	Depreciation	Gross Fixed Capital Stock	Capital– Gross Production Ratio
a. Agriculture	76339	4923	81262	–
6. Fertilisers	1471	142	1613	0.29
7. Basic, Intermediate & Capital Goods	103722	9613	113335	0.47
8. Consumer Goods	30641	2769	33410	0.35
9. Services	162131	87	170889	1.27

Note: Gross fixed capital stock/maximum gross production. Maximum production is based on a capacity utilisation rate of 100 per cent.
Source: Derived from *CSO* (1988; 1989b) and Gupta (1989).

Table 5.7
Matrix of Composition of Sectoral Capital Stock

Sector	Proportion of Capital Stock of Sector j Originating in Sector i					Investment by Sector of Destination	Investment by Sector of Origin
	a	6	7	8	9		
a.	0.041	0.000	0.000	0.000	0.000	7500.0	303.5
6.	0.000	0.409	0.000	0.000	0.000	298.0	121.8
7.	0.960	0.591	1.000	0.933	0.896	22611.0	52202.0
8.	0.000	0.000	0.000	0.067	0.000	4980.0	333.2
9.	0.000	0.000	0.000	0.000	0.104	19616.0	2044.5

Note: a = Agriculture (Sector 1 to 5); 6 = Fertiliser; 7 = Basic, Inter-mediate & Capital Goods; 8 = Consumer Goods; and 9 = Services.

origin j itself as given in the SAM. The obtained ϑ_{ij} are given in Table 5.7.

5.3.4 The Agricultural Production Sub-Model

The behavioural and technical equations of the agricultural submodel were estimated by the ordinary least squares method, with the exception of the cropwise yield response functions of (4.12) for which no data were available. The estimation results are presented in Appendix 5.3. A number of the

Table 5.8.A
Cropwise Short-Run Price Elasticity of Gross Cropped Area

	Period of Estimation	Rice	Wheat	Other Food Crops	Comm. Crops
Own Estimates:					
Irrigated	1967 – 86	0.05	0.79	0.29	0.35
Unirrigated	1967 – 86	0.18	0.50	0.05	0.29
Bhide *et al.* (1989)	1950 – 82	0.04	0.20	0.38[1]	0.28[2]
Gulati (1987)	1965 – 79		0.27		
Krishna & Chhibber (1983)	1961 – 78		0.58		
Krishna & Raychaudhuri (1980)	1957 – 70	0.45	0.22		
Narayana *et al.* (1987)	*not specified*			0.12[3]	
Roy & Subramanian (1983)	1960 – 79		0.33		
Sirohi (1984)	1964 – 75	0.12	0.19		

Notes: (1) Refers to barley; (2) Refers to sugarcane; and (3) Refers to maize.

Table 5.8.B
Cropwise Long-Run Price Elasticity of Gross Cropped Area

	Period of Estimation	Rice	Wheat	Other Food Crops	Comm. Crops
Own Estimates:					
Irrigated	1967 – 86	0.06	0.82	0.37	0.40
Unirrigated	1967 – 86	0.20	0.60	0.04	0.37
Krishna & Chhibber (1983)	1961 – 78		0.58		
Krishna & Raychaudhuri (1980)	1957 – 70	0.85			
Roy & Subramanian (1983)	1960 – 79		0.47		

estimated equations require closer attention.

Estimation of the Nerlovian acreage response functions (4.7) for unirrigated area and (4.8) for irrigated area yields both short–run and long–run elasticities of (unirrigated and irrigated) area with respect to relative price. The obtained price elasticities are given and compared to estimates by other authors in Tables 5.8.A and 5.8.B. From these tables, it can be seen that the responsiveness of acreage to relative price differs considerably between crops. Price responsiveness is fairly high for wheat and for commercial crops – both irrigated and unirrigated. It is low for unirrigated other food crops and, surprisingly, for irrigated rice cultivation. The comparison of the present estimates with the estimates by Bhide *et al.* (1989) who have used the same method of estimation, reveals a pronounced difference only in the price elasticity for wheat. This difference may be due to the fact that the estimation period used by Bhide *et al.* includes part of the pre–green revolution period (1950–65) in which higher yielding wheat varieties were not yet available.

Fertiliser consumption per hectare under crop i is assumed to depend on the ratio of the fertiliser price and the price of crop i in (4.10) and (4.11). The estimated cropwise price elasticities of fertiliser demand have the correct sign and are significant at the 10 per cent level, with the exception of the elasticity for other food crops. The estimated price elasticities of fertiliser demand for rice and wheat of −0.30 and −0.39 respectively are comparable to earlier estimates (see Table 5.9). Estimation of fertiliser demand functions for each of the cultivation regimes of rice and wheat was not possible due to the absence of adequate data, so these elasticities were preselected. The values of these elasticities are also given in Table 5.9. For irrigated agriculture, the price elasticities of fertiliser demand are assumed to be considerably higher than those for unirrigated farming, although they are not as high as the ones employed by Narayana *et al.* (1987), who assumed the price elasticities of fertiliser demand to be −1.

Cropwise yields are determined as a function of fertiliser input via the yield response functions (4.12) and (4.16). Recent estimates of national yield response functions for major cereals are available in Narayana and Parikh (1987). Their estimation results for rice and wheat were calibrated to the model's data set (Appendix 5.3). The aggregate yield of rice and wheat is the

Table 5.9
Short-Run Elasticity of the Cropwise Fertiliser Demand
w.r.t. the Relative Fertiliser to Crop Price

		Own Estimates	Sidhu & Sidhu	Bhide *et al.*	Gulati & Sharma	Sirohi
Rice	Aggregate	−0.303*	−0.600			
	Unirrigated	−0.333*				
	Irrigated	−0.555				
Wheat	Aggregate	−0.394*	−0.400			
	Unirrigated	−0.227*				
	Irrigated	−0.650				
Other Food Crops		−0.146				
Commercial Crops		−0.328				
Aggregate					−0.476 −0.610	−0.110

(*) These elasticities were preselected.
Notes: (1) Sidhu and Sidhu (1984): they do not report the period of estimation; (2) Bhide *et al.* (1986): their period of estimation is 1966–1980; (3) Gulati & Sharma (1990): their estimation period is 1970–1987; and (4) Sirohi (1984): cross–section results, no period indicated.

Table 5.10
Land Use Statistics, 1985–86 (in 10 million hectares)

	Gross Cropped Area	Gross Irrigated Area	Area under HYV
Rice	4.0912	1.7704	2.347
Wheat	2.3074	1.7481	1.908
Other Food Crops	6.3076	0.4862	1.287
Commercial Crops	4.9222	1.4144	
All Crops	17.6284	5.4191	5.542

Source: Ministry of Agriculture (1986b).

weighted average of the k–types of seed–water variety, the weights being the proportion of area under the kth type (irrigated versus non–irrigated) in total area under crop i. The base–year proportions were taken from Table 5.10.

5.3.5 *Real Private Investment Demand by Sector*

Private investment demand in non–agriculture is specified as a function of one–period lagged public investment and of sectoral mark–up income. For basic, intermediate and capital goods and consumer goods, the estimated coefficient of one–period lagged real public investment is statistically significant and positive, reflecting a crowding–in effect of public investment on private investment. For services, the coefficient is statistically not significant at the 10 per cent level. The effect of mark–up income (as a proxy for the availability of internal funds) is significant and positive for consumer goods industries and services. Its effect was negative (which is difficult to explain) and not significant at the 10 per cent level for the basic, intermediate and capital goods sector. Accordingly, mark–up income was omitted from the investment function of the basic, intermediate and capital goods sector. Tables 5.11 and 5.12 compare the results with corresponding estimates by others.

For the five agricultural sectors taken together, private investment demand is determined as a function of the (one–period lagged) terms of trade between agriculture and non–agriculture and (one–period lagged) real public investment in agriculture. The estimated coefficients are both statistically significant. The estimated elasticity of private agricultural investment with respect to the lagged terms of trade is 1.22 which compares to Krishnamurty's (1985) estimate which is also above unity (see Table 5.13). The elasticity of

Table 5.11
Elasticity of Private Investment Demand
w.r.t. One-Period Lagged Public Investment by Sector

	Own Estimates	Chakravarty	Shetty
Agriculture	0.904	0.620	0.661
Basic, Intermediate & Capital Goods	0.412		
Consumer Goods	0.349		
Services	0.203		

Notes: (1) Chakravarty (1987): the estimation period is 1970–71 to 1982–83; and (2) Shetty (1990): the period of estimation is 1960–61 to 1986–87.

Table 5.12
Elasticity of Private Investment Demand
w.r.t. Mark-Up Income by Sector

	Own Estimates	Krishnamurty	Pandit	Lahiri *et al.*
Consumer Goods	0.371			
Services	1.438			
Manufacturing		1.59	1.11	1.28

Notes: (1) Krishnamurty (1985): the period of estimation is 1962–1980; (2) Pandit (1985): the estimation period is 1950–51 to 1977–78; and (3) Lahiri *et al.* (1984): their estimation period is 1950–51 to 1979–80.

Table 5.13
Elasticity of Private Agricultural Investment Demand
w.r.t. Lagged Public Investment in Agriculture and
w.r.t. the Lagged Intersectoral Terms of Trade

	Own Estimates	Krishnamurty
Public Investment	0.904	0.60
Terms of Trade	1.217	1.66

Note: (1) Krishnamurty (1985): the period of estimation is 1962–1980.

Table 5.14.A
Short-Run Elasticity of the Nominal Wage Rate
w.r.t. the Consumer Price Index

	Own Estimates	Krishnamurty	Lahiri *et al.*
Fertilisers	0.613		
Basic & Intermediate Goods			0.353
Capital Goods			0.500
Basic, Intermediate & Capital Goods	0.338		
Consumer Goods	0.243		0.527
Services	0.403		
Government	0.498		
Manufacturing		0.530	

Notes: (1) Krishnamurty (1985): the period of estimation is 1962–1980; and (2) Lahiri *et al.* (1984): their estimation period is 1961–1977; they give separate figures for capital goods industries and basic & intermediate goods industries.

Table 5.14.B
Growth Rates of Average Labour Productivity
(per cent per annum)

Fertilisers	8.8
Basic, Intermediate & Capital Goods	3.2
Consumer Goods	3.7
Services	3.7

private agricultural investment with respect to one–period lagged public agricultural investment is 0.9. Providing infrastructure for agriculture (particularly irrigation), public investment is found to have a strong complementary effect on agricultural private investment.

5.3.6   *Nominal Wage Indexation*

The main features of (registered) non–agricultural wage formation are incorporated in the model via the wage equations of (4.23). In these equations, the nominal wage rate is assumed to depend on the consumer price index (*cpi*), and on its one–period lagged value. The estimation results are given in Appendix 5.3. The estimated coefficients have the expected positive sign and are significant at the 5 per cent level. The short–run elasticities of the nominal wage rate with respect to the consumer price index are given in Table 5.14.A. It can be seen that these elasticities are smaller than unity, which reflects the fact that compensation is seldom for the full amount of the *cpi* increase. The present estimates turn out to be somewhat smaller than earlier estimates. The difference may be due to the difference in estimation period, presuming that the early 1980s have been a period of moderate nominal wage increases relative to the rise in the consumer price index.

Finally, Table 5.14.B presents the growth rates of labour productivity in the non–agricultural sectors which were estimated from *ASI* data for the period 1973–1985. The estimated growth rate of average labour productivity in the fertiliser sector turned out to be quite high, reflecting the increase in capital intensity of fertiliser production during the estimation period (see Section 6.2).

5.3.7   *Calibration*

To enable the static part of the model to exactly reproduce the benchmark SAM for 1985–86 (Table 5.3), the parameter estimates presented in the previous section were 'calibrated' to the model's data base. This 'static' calibration has to be distinguished from the 'dynamic' calibration which enables the model to reproduce a reference path for the period 1985–86 to 1989–90.

Calibration of the Static Model

Calibration of the static model means that parameter values of demand and production functions are selected which enable the model to exactly reproduce the constructed data set as a 'base' solution to the model, on the assumption that there are no changes in policies from those in operation in the base year. Formally, the general equilibrium model may be written as:

$$(5.1) \qquad F\ (X,\ y,\ z;\ \vartheta,\ \psi\ )\ =\ 0$$

where X, y, and z represent exogenous, endogenous and policy variables, respectively, ϑ is a set of exogenous parameters (mainly elasticities), and ψ is a set of calibration parameters (mainly constants). F is a multivalued function with the same dimension as y. In the calibration process, X and y are both treated as exogenous and are derived from the benchmark data set. ψ then is a function of ϑ, z, and the benchmark data set (Van der Mensbrugghe *et al.*, 1990). The two major weaknesses of this method of selecting parameter values are (*i*) the lack of any basis for a test of the specification; and (*ii*) the required preselection of elasticities.[4] To compensate for these weaknesses,

---

[4] Although no statistical tests can be performed, the value of the same tests in large scale econometric models may, however, also not be very considerable, especially if (as is often the practice) in order to get good fits, many of

during the calibration process, resort is usually made to sensitivity analysis in which alternative values of key parameters are tried and model results evaluated for their robustness (see Section 5.4).

Calibration of the Reference Run

For each year of the period 1985–86 to 1989–90, the model was calibrated to reproduce the actual course of the economy in terms of most of the endogenous variables. In terms of equation (5.1), in the calibration of the reference run, y and z are treated as exogenous, with X being a function of ϑ and ψ and the benchmark data set. Specifically, the calibration procedure involved the determination of the levels of commodity–wise changes in private stock so as to generate the reference price paths for the agricultural goods and the reference production paths for the non–agricultural commodities.[5] This particular calibration procedure was adopted due to lack of data on private stock changes by sector of origin. Its justification is that the 'calibrated' levels of private stock changes generating a 'realistic' reference run in terms of agricultural prices and non–agricultural commodities ought to resemble their 'actual' levels, presuming that the present general equilibrium model provides an adequate description of the Indian economy. The reference run resulting from this calibration procedure is discussed in Chapter 7, Section 2.

5.4   Sensitivity Analysis

Results from computable general equilibrium models are often presented as a single solution to a deterministic system. Nonetheless, there are several features of computable general equilibrium models which give rise to uncertainty concerning the reliability of the solution (Van der Mensbrugghe et al., 1990) including the values of key model parameters.[6] Hence, it is important to evaluate the sensitivity of the model results to changes in the values of key parameters. If the model is written as in (5.1), performing sensitivity analysis may be interpreted as involving changing a subset of the

---

the equations contain the lagged dependent variable or variables of doubtful economic merit on the right hand side. See Challen and Hagger (1983) for the practice of econometric modelling.

[5] In the literature, different exogenous variables are used for calibration. Rattsø (1989), for example, uses government procurement of foodgrains and exports of non–food agricultural products as calibrating variables. Savings rates are also frequently adjusted to generate a "realistic" time path as in Mitra and Tendulkar (1986).

[6] Although the results of computable general equilibrium models are also sensitive to the changes in model specification, no analysis of this issue is presented here.

parameters ϑ (*i.e.* important elasticities), re–calibrating the model to obtain a new set of parameters ψ (*i.e.* the model's constants), and then performing the simulation. This section presents the results of an analysis of the model's response to changes in four key parameter values, *viz.* cropwise price elasticities of fertiliser demand, nominal wage indexation coefficients, income elasticities of private investment demand, and the elasticity of gross irrigated area with respect to agricultural investment.

Before proceeding to the discussion of the results of the sensitivity analysis which are reported in Table 5.18, Appendix 5.4, it is worth making three observations. First, the coefficients of the cropwise yield response functions (4.12) and (4.16) are excluded from the sensitivity analysis, because (in my view) they are essentially reflections of technical production conditions dependent on climate and soil type and, hence, cannot be varied at will. Moreover, the parameter values included in the model were taken from Narayana and Parikh (1987) and are the most detailed and probably accurate figures currently available. Second, although the cropwise price elasticities of gross cropped area and the parameters of the consumption functions are important model parameters, they are not included in the sensitivity analysis, because the parameters values included in the model seem broadly in accordance with the findings in the relevant econometric literature (see in particular Radhakrishna, 1978; Bhide *et al.*, 1989; Narayana *et al.*, 1987). Finally, the results of the sensitivity analysis will be analysed only in a rather general way. For a more detailed discussion of the workings of the model, the reader is referred to the next chapter.

5.4.1   *Price Elasticities of Fertiliser Demand*

The cropwise price elasticities of fertiliser demand were selected for the sensitivity analysis because of their crucial role in agriculture's short–run supply response and in view of the variety of empirical estimates available in the literature (see Table 5.9). In experiment *SEN*–1, the price elasticities of fertiliser demand were set at –1 for *all* crops following Narayana *et al.* (1987), who in their agricultural policy model for India assumed (not estimated) these elasticities to be –1. In view of the available empirical evidence (see Table 5.9), I consider a price elasticity of fertiliser demand of –1 to be very high (in absolute terms) for rice and wheat and unrealistically high for other food crops and commercial crops, which are predominantly produced under rain–fed conditions.

As can be seen from Table 5.18, Appendix 5.4, the impact of *SEN*–1 is strongly deflationary (the average annual rate of increase of the consumer price index declines from 7.6 per cent in the reference run to 6.5 per cent in *SEN*–1) and only slightly expansionary (the average annual growth rate of real GDP at market prices increases from 5.7 per cent in the reference run to 5.9

per cent). With higher price elasticities of fertiliser demand and unchanged demand, the increase in agriculture's short–run supply response leads to higher crop outputs and a decline in the agricultural price increases in $SEN-1$ as compared to the reference run. Because of its impact on non–agricultural wages and prices, this relative decline in agricultural prices has an economy–wide deflationary effect. Its impact on non–agricultural production is twofold. On the one hand, it leads to a decline in agricultural income as compared to the reference run which results in a fall in agriculturalists' demand for non–agricultural goods. On the other hand, it leads to an increase in consumer demand for non–agricultural goods. The net effect is a slight increase in the growth rates of non–agricultural production and real income (mainly wage income) as compared to the reference run.

5.4.2   *Nominal Wage Indexation Coefficients*

The values of the elasticities of the nominal non–agricultural wages with respect to the consumer price index affect the economy's inflation–proneness to agricultural price rises, particularly in a situation of non–agricultural mark–up pricing. To study the sensitivity of the model results to changes in the values of these elasticities, the nominal wage indexation coefficients were raised by 10 per cent in $SEN-2$.

Not surprisingly, the increase in nominal wage indexation is considerably inflationary (the average annual rate of increase of the consumer price index rises from 7.6 per cent in the reference run to 9.4 per cent in $SEN-2$) and only slightly expansionary (the average annual growth rate of real GDP at market prices increases from 5.7 per cent in the reference run to 5.8 per cent in $SEN-2$). The increase in nominal wages raises demand which leads to agricultural price increases (relative to the reference run) since the short–run supply of agricultural goods is relatively inelastic. The agricultural price increases have two, partly offsetting, effects. First, they induce farmers to increase fertiliser use and raise crop outputs. With agricultural prices and crop outputs increasing, farmers' income increases and, hence, their demand for non–agricultural goods increases. Second, they force consumers to spend more on agricultural goods and to reduce their effective demand for non–agricultural goods. On balance, aggregate demand for non–agricultural products slightly increases, resulting in a modest rise in non–agricultural production and income in $SEN-2$ as compared to the reference run. Because the increase in inflation leads to the erosion in real terms of earnings and transfers which are assumed fixed in nominal terms (including government revenue from public enterprises and public transfers to wage earners), the expansionary effect of $SEN-2$ is further reduced.

5.4.3 Income Elasticities of Private Investment Demand

The major dynamic element in the model is investment. In agriculture, a step–up in investment leads to increased availability of gross irrigated area (see Section 5.4.4). In non–agriculture, an increase in investment raises productive capacity over time. About half of aggregate domestic investment is public investment which is assumed exogenous in real terms. The other half is private investment which is known for its volatility and is often regarded as the principal source of cyclical movements in the economy. To assess the impact on the economy of a less ambitious investment programme than that in the reference run experiment *SEN*–3 was performed in which the income elasticities of private investment demand in sectors 8 and 9 were reduced by 25 per cent.

In the medium run, *SEN*–3 leads to a sharp reduction in private investment demand in the consumer goods and services sectors resulting in a considerable decline in demand for capital goods and a fall in production of the basic, intermediate and capital goods sector which is the major sector of origin of investment goods. The decline in basic, intermediate and capital goods production is magnified by the multiplier mechanism to generate a lower level of income and aggregate demand than in the reference run. Hence, *SEN*–3 is deflationary. The average annual rate of increase of the consumer price index declines from 7.6 per cent in the reference run to 6.5 per cent in *SEN*–3. Agricultural prices decline more than non–agricultural prices, because the former are more sensitive to fluctuations in demand than the latter which are cost–determined. As a result, the fertiliser price increases relative to crop prices, inducing farmers to reduce their fertiliser use and leading to a decline in crop outputs in *SEN*–3 as compared to the reference run. With agricultural and non–agricultural production declining, *SEN*–3 is contractionary. The average annual growth rate of real GDP at market prices declines from 5.7 per cent in the reference run to 5.5 per cent in *SEN*–3.

5.4.4 Elasticity of Gross Irrigated Area with respect to Agricultural Investment

The elasticity of gross irrigated area with respect to agricultural investment is important in providing the medium–run link between public and private investment in agriculture and the amount of gross irrigated area. *SEN*–4 assesses the effects of a 10 per cent increase in this elasticity.

With unchanged public and private agricultural investment, *SEN*–4 results in an initial increase in gross irrigated area and an increase in crop outputs as compared to the reference run. Given demand, the increase in crop supply leads to a fall in crop prices which in turn has two effects. First, in the short run, it induces farmers to reduce fertiliser use, which, of course, negatively affects crop production. Second, it leads to a deterioration of the terms of trade for agriculture and, hence, to a decline in private agricultural investment. The decline in private agricultural investment negatively affects agricultural performance over the medium run. In effect, the impact of $SEN-4$ on agricultural production is only limited. The initial decline in crop prices has two, partially offsetting effects on non–agricultural production. On the one hand, it provides a stimulus to non–agricultural production because it enables consumers to raise their demand for non–agricultural goods. On the other hand, because it reduces agricultural income, it leads to a decline in agriculturalists' demand for non–agricultural products. In the event, as is clear from Table 5.18, $SEN-4$ has only a modest impact on the economy's performance during the Seventh Plan period: the average annual rate of inflation as measured by the consumer price index declines to 7.5 per cent, while the average annual growth rate of real GDP at market prices increases to 5.8 per cent (Table 5.18).

5.4.5   *Conclusions*

According to the results from the sensitivity analysis, changes in the values of one or more of the model parameters tend to have a larger impact on inflation than on growth. In particular, the evolution over time of agricultural prices which are determined by demand and supply, turns out to be rather sensitive to the model's parameter specification, while the time–paths of non–agricultural prices which are determined as a mark–up over wage and intermediate input costs, are affected to a much smaller extent. Because agricultural and non–agricultural prices respond differently to changes in parameter values, agricultural and non–agricultural production and income are differently affected, which, in turn, mitigates the impact of changes in parameter values on aggregate production and income in real terms. In other words, while a change in the model's parameters has a significant effect on inflation (either positive or negative) as well as on the *composition* of growth, its impact on the *rate* of growth is modest.

177

Consolidated Accounts of the Nation, India, 1985–86
(Rs. Crores at Current Prices)
Source: *CSO* (1989a)

	Account 1.	**Gross Domestic Product and Expenditure**	
1.1.		Net Domestic Product at Factor Cost	207848
1.2.		Consumption of Fixed Capital (Depreciation)	26215
1.3.		Indirect Taxes	36987
1.4.		*less* Subsidies	8543
1.5.		Gross Domestic Product at Market Prices	262507
1.6.		Private Final Cons. Exp.	172949
1.7.		Govt. Final Cons. Exp.	29174
1.8.		Gross Fixed Cap. Formation	55005
1.9.		Change in Stocks	13005
1.10.		Exports	15634
1.11.		*less* Imports	23260
1.12.		Expenditure on GDP	262507

	Account 2.	**National Disposable Income and Appropriation**	
2.1.		Government Final Consumption Expenditure	29174
2.2.		Private Final Consumption Expenditure	172949
2.3.		Net Domestic Saving	35561
2.4.		Appropriation of Disposable Income	237684
2.5.		Net Domestic Product at Factor Cost	207848
2.6.		Net Current Factor Income from Abroad	1392
2.7.		Indirect Taxes	36987
2.8.		*less* Subsidies	8543
2.9.		Disposable Income	237684

	Account 3.	**Capital Account**	
3.1.		Gross Domestic Capital Formation	68010
3.1.1.		Gross Domestic Fixed Capital Formation	55005
3.1.2.		Change in Stocks	13005
3.2.		Gross Accumulation	68010
3.3.		Net Domestic Saving	35561
3.4.		Consumption of Fixed Capital (Depreciation)	26215
3.5.		Current Account Balance (Foreign Saving)	6234
3.6.		Finance of Gross Accumulation	68010

Account 4. External Transactions

Current Transactions

4.1.	Exports of Goods and Services	15634
4.2.	Net Current Transfers from the Rest of the World	1392
4.3.	Current Receipts	17026
4.4.	Imports of Goods and Services	23260
4.5.	Current Account Balance (Foreign Savings)	−6234
4.6.	Disposal of Current Receipts	17026

Capital Transactions

4.7.	Current Account Balance (Foreign Savings)	−6234
4.8.	Net Capital Transfers from the Rest of the World	307
4.9.	Net Incurrence of Foreign Liabilities	4232
4.10.	Receipts	−1695
4.11.	Purchases of Intangible Assets not earlier classified from the Rest of the World	−
4.12.	Net Acquisition of Foreign Financial Assets	−1695
4.13.	Disbursements	−1695

Account 5. Public Sector Current Transactions

5.1.	Direct Tax Receipts	6574
5.2.	Indirect Tax Receipts	36987
5.3.	Revenues from Public Enterprises	16485
5.4.	Public Current Revenue	60046

5.5.	Final Consumption Expenditure	29174
5.5.1.	Expenditure on Goods and Services	11971
5.5.2.	Government Wage Bill	17203
5.6.	Subsidies	8543
5.7.	Interest Payments	6115
5.8.	Other Current Transfers	7622
5.9.	Public Current Expenditure	51454
5.10.	Public Savings (5.4 − 5.9.)	8592

Account 6. Private Income and Expenditure

1.	Agricultural Income	76537
2.	Non–Agricultural Wage Income	96000
2.1.	Non–government Wage Income	69783
2.2.	Government Wages	17203
2.3.	Public Current Transfers	7622
2.4.	Net Factor Income from Abroad	1392
3.	Non–Agricultural Mark–up Income	60170
3.1.	Public Interest Payments	6115
3.2.	Other Mark–up Income	54055
4.	Private Income	232707

5.	Private Final Consumption Expenditure	172949
6.	Private Savings	53184
7.	Direct Taxes	6574
8.	Use of Private Income	232707

Appendix 5.2
'Estimation' of the Parameters of the Linear Expenditure System

In Appendix 4.8, important properties of the linear expenditure system (LES) given by equation (A.4.30) were discussed. In particular, the adding up property of the LES was found to be rather restrictive, because it at once rules out inferior goods and any complementarity among goods. On the other hand, additivity proves very useful in empirical estimation of the LES parameters. The usefulness of additivity derives from the fact that, apart from the parameter σ^k, knowledge of expenditure elasticities alone is sufficient to determine all the own price elasticities as well as cross–price elasticities. As a result, almost no relative price variation in the data is required in order to 'estimate' price elasticities. The 'estimation' of the LES parameters μ_{ki} and γ_{ki} is, of course, largely by assumption (Deaton and Muellbauer, 1980:138–139).

Recall that differentiation of (A.4.30) with respect to aggregate expenditure D_k ($k = a, n$) gave the expenditure elasticity of demand (or *Engel* elasticity) for commodity i, ε^k_i, in (A.4.31). The expenditure elasticity of commodity i turned out to be equal to the ratio of its marginal budget share to its average budget share. Substituting the consumer demand equations of (A.4.30) into (A.4.31) yields the following expression for γ_{ki}:

$$(A.5.1) \quad \gamma_{ki} = f_{ki} - (\mu_{ki}/p_{si}) \sum_{i=1}^{9} (p_{si} - \bar{p}_i) f_{ki} + (D_k/p_i)(\phi_{ki} - \mu_{ki}\,\sigma^k)$$

where σ^k is the "supernumerary expenditure ratio" of which the reciprocal is known as the Frisch parameter. It follows from (A.5.1) that, once the marginal and average budget shares are known and a constant σ^k is assumed, all γ_{ki} are determined if values for the p_{si}, $\bar{p}_i$, D_k and f_{ki} are known.

It has been assumed that the σ^k is equal to 0.5 which is a reasonable assumption for an economy as the Indian (Ali, 1985). The level of total non–agricultural consumer expenditure D_n and D_a were taken from the SAM. Data on f_{ni}, f_{ai} and $\bar{p}_i$ were taken from the *Bulletin on Food Statistics* 1986, *Indian Agriculture in Brief* (22nd edition), and the *Economic Survey* 1988–89. These data were adjusted to consistency with the SAM, taking the total amount of food subsidy of Rs. 1650 crores as control figure. Table 5.15 gives a detailed picture of cropwise food distribution in 1985–86. f_{a1} was Rs. 216 crores and f_{a2} was Rs. 254 crores.

The marginal and average budget shares for agricultural (rural) and non–agricultural (urban) consumer groups were derived from the *NSS Report on Consumer Expenditure*, 42nd Round, which gives detailed commodity–wise consumption data for both rural and urban expenditure classes. From these cross–section data, average rural and urban budget shares were calculated as a weighted average of all rural and urban expenditure groups. The results are presented in Table 5.16. From the same cross–section data, marginal budget shares were estimated by ordinary least squares. The regression results (reported in Table 5.16) are satisfactory. The R^2 are high and the coefficients μ_{ni} and μ_{ai} have the right signs and are significant at the 99 per cent level of confidence. The negative intercept in the equations for commodities 5, 7, 8 and 9 identifies them as superior goods. This is more clearly reflected in the greater–than–unity expenditure elasticities for these commodities (see Table 5.5) which follow from (A.4.30), once marginal and average budget shares are known. Uncompensated own price elasticities of consumption demand followed from differentiating (A.4.30) with respect to p_{si}, assuming that $\partial D_k /\partial p_{si} = 0$, in (A.4.32). Differentiation of (A.4.30) with respect to price j $(j \neq i)$ yielded the uncompensated cross price elasticity in (A.4.33).

Uncompensated own–price elasticities are given in Table 5.5 and cross–price elasticities in Table 5.17. For five out of the 8 commodity groups considered, the numerical estimates of non–agricultural own price elasticities are smaller than –0.5 (Table 5.5). Cross–price elasticities turn out to be rather low, with the exception of the effects on the agriculturalists' demand for non–agricultural goods of a change in the price of rice and commercial crops and of the impact on the non–agriculturalists' demand for agricultural goods of price changes for consumer goods and services.

Table 5.15
Public Distribution of Foodgrains, 1985–86
(Rs. Crores at Current Prices)

	Public Distribution	Subsidy	Private Purchases
Rice	$p_{s1} f_{n1} = 2161$	$(p_{s1} - \bar{p}_1) f_{n1} = 687$	$\bar{p}_1 f_{n1} = 1474$
Wheat	$p_{s2} f_{n2} = 1857$	$(p_{s2} - \bar{p}_2) f_{n2} = 488$	$\bar{p}_2 f_{n2} = 1369$
Other food	$p_{s3} f_{n3} = 16$	$(p_{s3} - \bar{p}_3) f_{n3} = 5$	$\bar{p}_3 f_{n3} = 11$
All	$\sum_i p_{si} f_{ni} = 4034$	$\sum_i (p_{si} - \bar{p}_i) f_{ni} = 1180$	$\sum_i \bar{p}_i f_{ni} = 2854$

Source: Ministry of Agriculture (1986; 1986b); Ministry of Finance (1989).

Table 5.16
Estimates of Average and Marginal Budget Shares, 1985–1986

Non-Agricultural Consumption

	ϕ_{ni}	intercept	μ_{ni}	intercept	μ_{ni} (t–Ratios)	R^2
1. Rice	0.0445	9.84	0.0363	2.18	3.79	0.57
2. Wheat	0.0294	5.65	0.0250	2.45	5.09	0.70
3. Other food crops	0.0242	4.96	0.0182	2.85	4.92	0.69
4. Commercial crops	0.1160	4.19	0.1221	1.01	13.82	0.95
5. Other agriculture	0.1282	−1.57	0.1434	0.45	19.21	0.97
7 Basic goods *etc.*	0.1234	−2.10	0.1138	0.54	13.66	0.94
8. Consumer goods	0.2274	−8.25	0.2330	2.11	28.02	0.99
9. Services	0.3068	−12.71	0.3083	1.55	17.71	0.97

Agricultural Consumption

	ϕ_{ai}	intercept	μ_{ai}	intercept	μ_{ai} (t–Ratios)	R^2
1. Rice	0.1630	11.45	0.0576	1.90	4.04	0.60
2. Wheat	0.0719	4.00	0.0379	2.46	9.86	0.90
3. Other food crops	0.0763	6.45	0.0270	4.14	7.31	0.83
4. Commercial crops	0.1435	4.50	0.1040	1.54	14.99	0.95
5. Other agriculture	0.1324	−3.54	0.1565	1.07	20.00	0.97
7 Basic goods *etc.*	0.1073	−6.87	0.1716	0.78	8.19	0.86
8. Consumer goods	0.1876	−10.60	0.2819	2.39	26.88	0.99
9. Services	0.1179	−5.39	0.1635	2.59	33.12	0.99

Note: Average budget share were calculated and marginal budget shares were estimated from NSSO (1988).

Table 5.17
Uncompensated Own and Cross Price Elasticities

Non-Agriculture

Sector	1	2	3	4	5	7	8	9
1	0.438	0.014	0.013	0.045	0.046	0.055	0.091	0.125
2	0.023	0.448	0.013	0.047	0.048	0.057	0.094	0.130
3	0.020	0.013	0.395	0.041	0.042	0.050	0.084	0.115
4	0.028	0.018	0.016	0.594	0.059	0.071	0.117	0.161
5	0.030	0.019	0.017	0.062	0.633	0.075	0.125	0.172
7	0.025	0.016	0.014	0.051	0.052	0.532	0.103	0.142
8	0.027	0.018	0.016	0.057	0.058	0.069	0.635	0.157
9	0.027	0.017	0.015	0.056	0.057	0.067	0.112	0.664

Agriculture

Sector	1	2	3	4	5	7	8	9
1	0.227	0.019	0.022	0.032	0.019	0.007	0.016	0.012
2	0.071	0.296	0.033	0.048	0.028	0.011	0.023	0.018
3	0.047	0.019	0.202	0.032	0.019	0.007	0.016	0.012
4	0.097	0.038	0.045	0.433	0.038	0.015	0.032	0.025
5	0.158	0.062	0.074	0.107	0.663	0.024	0.052	0.041
7	0.214	0.084	0.100	0.145	0.085	0.844	0.071	0.056
8	0.201	0.079	0.094	0.136	0.080	0.030	0.830	0.053
9	0.185	0.073	0.087	0.126	0.073	0.028	0.062	0.752

Notes: 1. Figures along the diagonal represent own price elasticities and those off the diagonal are cross–price elasticities;
2. All entries have minus signs.

Appendix 5.3
Parameter Estimates

This appendix presents the estimation results (obtained by ordinary least squares) of most of the model parameters which could not be derived from the social accounting matrix. The 't' statistic is presented immediately below the estimated coefficient in parentheses. Significance at the 10 per cent level is denoted by one asterisk (*), at the 5 per cent level by **, and at the 1 per cent level by ***. The goodness of fit is represented by the adjusted multiple correlation coefficient ($\overline{R}^2$). The number of observations is given by n with the period in parentheses.

The Durbin–Watson (DW) statistic is presented to indicate serial correlation of errors. The DW–statistic may not be used to detect (first–order) serial correlation in autoregressive equations, because the computed DW value of such equations generally tends to equal 2, which is the value of DW expected in a truly random sequence (*i.e.* in the absence of first–order serial correlation). Durbin's h–statistic which provides a large–sample test of first–order serial correlation in autoregressive equations, is tabulated instead of the DW–statistic in the case of autoregressive equations. Since Durbin's h–test is meant for large samples, its application in small samples is not strictly justified (Gujarati, 1978). In those equations in which first–order autocorrelation was detected by either the DW or the h–test, the Cochrane–Orcutt method was applied so as to be able to apply OLS to a set of transformed data. In all cases, an error process AR(1) was used. I have not tried to remove possible simultaneity bias.

The Agricultural Production Sub-Model

The data used in the estimation of the equations of the agricultural submodel were taken from the following sources: (*a*) Bulletin on Food Statistics (various issues); (*b*) Estimates of Area and Production of Principal Crops in India (various issues); (*c*) Indian Agriculture in Brief (various issues), which are published by the Ministry of Agriculture, and from (*d*) National Accounts Statistics, published by the CSO; and (*e*) Economic Survey (various years), published by the Ministry of Finance.

The estimation results are as follows:

Gross Irrigated Area

$$(4.1) \quad gia_t = \underset{(3.992)^{***}}{1.317} + \underset{(2.721)^{***}}{0.614\ j_{a,t-1}} + \underset{(2.950)^{***}}{0.426\ gia_{t-1}} + \underset{(3.477)^{***}}{0.054\ \text{Time}}$$

$$\overline{R}^2 = 0.99,$$
$$h = -0.17,\ n = 26\ (1961–1986)$$

Net Irrigated Area

(4.2) $nia = 0.7904\ gia$ $n = 20\ (1967–1986)$

Average Cropping Intensity

(4.3) $aci = 0.473 \quad + 0.205\ (nia/nsa)$
$$\underset{(55.742)^{***}}{} \quad \underset{(15.079)^{***}}{}$$

$$\overline{R}^2 = 0.923,$$
$$DW = 2.45,\ n = 20\ (1967–1986)$$

Cropwise Acreage Response Functions

Cropwise irrigated and unirrigated acreage response functions of equations (4.7) and (4.8) were estimated simultaneously in a log–linear framework with additivity constraints, using Zellner's Seemingly Unrelated Regression Equations (SURE) estimation method (see Bhide *et al.*, 1989; Narayana *et al.*, 1987). A time variable was included in all acreage response equations. The estimation results are reported below.

All coefficients have the expected sign. The estimated elasticity of irrigated area under rice with respect to its relative price is not significant at the 10 per cent level of confidence. The estimated elasticity of gross unirrigated area under other food crops with respect to the relative price is also statistically not significant at the 10 per cent level. This may be explained by the fact that these crops are the least 'commercialised' of the four crops under consideration in the sense that they are to a relatively large extent cultivated for self–consumption.

Gross Non–Irrigated Area under Rice

$$\log ngca_{1,t} = \underset{(6.065)^{***}}{0.748} + \underset{(2.055)^{**}}{0.182 \log \tilde{p}}_{1,t-1} + \underset{(0.570)}{0.086 \log ngca}_{1,t-1}$$
$$+ \underset{(1.404)}{0.001\ \text{Time}}$$

$$\overline{R}^2 = 0.101,\ n = 20\ (1967–1986)$$

Gross Non–Irrigated Area under Wheat

$$\log ngca_{2,t} = -\underset{(2.865)^{***}}{0.177} + \underset{(3.525)^{***}}{0.499 \log \tilde{p}}_{2,t-1} + \underset{(2.020)^{**}}{0.163 \log ngca}_{2,t-1}$$
$$- \underset{(4.737)^{***}}{0.014\ \text{Time}}$$

$$\overline{R}^2 = 0.828,\ n = 20\ (1967–1986)$$

Gross Non–Irrigated Area under Other Food Crops

$$\log ngca_{3,t} = \underset{(11.632)^{***}}{2.545} + \underset{(1.490)}{0.053\ \log \tilde{p}_{3,t-1}} - \underset{(3.212)^{***}}{0.378\ \log ngca_{3,t-1}}$$

$$- \underset{(6.283)^{***}}{0.006\ \text{Time}}$$

$$\overline{R}^2 = 0.434,\ n = 20\ (1967–1986)$$

Gross Non–Irrigated Area under Commercial Crops

$$\log ngca_{4,t} = \underset{(7.720)^{***}}{0.973} + \underset{(4.141)^{***}}{0.291\ \log \tilde{p}_{4,t-1}} + \underset{(2.132)^{**}}{0.219\ \log ngca_{4,t-1}}$$

$$+ \underset{(1.371)}{0.001\ \text{Time}}$$

$$\overline{R}^2 = 0.585,\ n = 20\ (1967–1986)$$

Gross Irrigated Area under Rice

$$\log gia_{1,t} = \underset{(4.498)^{***}}{0.240} + \underset{(0.365)}{0.048\ \log \tilde{p}_{1,t-1}} + \underset{(0.901)}{0.161\ \log gia_{1,t-1}}$$

$$- \underset{(4.161)^{***}}{0.011\ \text{Time}}$$

$$\overline{R}^2 = 0.813,\ n = 20\ (1967–1986)$$

Gross Irrigated Area under Wheat

$$\log gia_{2,t} = \underset{(4.730)^{***}}{-\,0.467} + \underset{(5.213)^{***}}{0.787\ \log \tilde{p}_{2,t-1}} + \underset{(3.608)^{***}}{0.446\ \log gia_{2,t-1}}$$

$$- \underset{(4.746)^{***}}{0.038\ \text{Time}}$$

$$\overline{R}^2 = 0.960,\ n = 20\ (1967–1986)$$

Gross Irrigated Area under Other Food Crops

$$\log gia_{3,t} = \underset{(3.932)^{***}}{-\,0.307} + \underset{(2.281)^{***}}{0.294\ \log \tilde{p}_{3,t-1}} + \underset{(1.474)}{0.214\ \log gia_{3,t-1}}$$

$$- \underset{(2.412)^{**}}{0.008\ \text{Time}}$$

$$\overline{R}^2 = 0.259,\ n = 20\ (1967–1986)$$

Gross Irrigated Area under Commercial Crops

$$\log gia_{4,t} = \underset{(4.541)^{***}}{-\,0.349} + \underset{(3.482)^{***}}{0.353\ \log \tilde{p}_{4,t-1}} + \underset{(0.815)}{0.107\ \log gia_{4,t-1}}$$

$$+ \underset{(5.642)^{***}}{0.033\ \text{Time}}$$

$$\overline{R}^2 = 0.969,\ n = 20\ (1967–1986)$$

Cropwise fertiliser demand per hectare was estimated as a function of the relative fertiliser to crop price and a time trend. Time series data on cropwise fertiliser consumption were not available and had to be generated on the basis of some additional assumptions. In particular, it was assumed that total nitrogen use over time is allocated in the following fixed proportions between crops: 0.372 to rice; 0.298 to wheat; 0.12 to other food crops; and 0.21 to commercial crops (these proportions are given in Narayana and Parikh, 1987). Based on these proportions, time series of cropwise fertiliser consumption per hectare of rice, wheat, other food crops, and commercial crops were constructed for the period of estimation, 1966–67 to 1984–85. It was not possible to generate separate time series data of fertiliser application per irrigated hectare and per unirrigated hectare of rice and wheat. Consequently, the parameters of the per hectare fertiliser demand by k-th type seed–water variety of rice and wheat had to be preselected. The results obtained in this way are presented below. All per hectare fertiliser demand functions suffered from autocorrelation which led to the inclusion of an error process AR(1) in the estimation.

Not distinguishing between irrigated and unirrigated cultivation, the estimated per hectare fertiliser demand functions of rice and wheat are as follows:

$$\log fert_1 = -4.331 - 0.303 \log (p_6/p_1) + 0.086 \text{ Time}$$
$$(41.232)^{***} \quad (2.216)^{**} \quad (11.726)^{***}$$
$$\overline{R}^2 = 0.986,$$
$$n = 19 \ (1966\text{–}1984)$$
$$\text{Error Process} = \text{AR}(1)$$

$$\log fert_2 = -3.765 - 0.394 \log (p_6/p_2) + 0.077 \text{ Time}$$
$$(68.017)^{***} \quad (2.137)^{**} \quad (14.105)^{***}$$
$$\overline{R}^2 = 0.978,$$
$$n = 19 \ (1966\text{–}1984)$$
$$\text{Error Process} = \text{AR}(1)$$

The estimated per hectare fertiliser demand functions of other food crops and commercial crops are:

(4.11)
$$\log fert_3 = -6.117 - 0.146 \log (p_6/p_3) + 0.096 \text{ Time}$$
$$(51.825)^{***} \quad (1.257) \quad (11.684)^{***}$$
$$\overline{R}^2 = 0.984,$$
$$n = 19 \ (1966\text{–}1984)$$
$$\text{Error Process} = \text{AR}(1)$$

(4.11)
$$\log fert_4 = -4.879 - 0.328 \log (p_6/p_4) + 0.075 \text{ Time}$$
$$(37.470)^{***} \quad (2.612)^{**} \quad (8.451)^{***}$$
$$\overline{R}^2 = 0.985,$$
$$n = 19 \ (1966\text{–}1984)$$
$$\text{Error Process} = \text{AR}(1)$$

Only for other food crops which are mainly cultivated for own consumption and which have the lowest per hectare fertiliser input of the four crops under consideration, the estimated price elasticity of per hectare fertiliser demand is statistically not significant at the 10 per cent level. The price elasticities of fertiliser demand for the other three crops are statistically significant at the 5 per cent level.

Rice and Wheat Yield Response Functions by Cultivation Regime

The coefficients of the rice and wheat response functions by k-th cultivation regime were taken from Narayana and Parikh (1987). Their estimates are based on a large amount of experimental data of Simple Fertiliser Trials spread over various agro–climatic zones for various seed–water regimes. Experimental yield responses are usually believed to be higher than what can be realised in large scale adoption by farmers and, hence, would be too optimistic. Therefore, Narayana and Parikh made the experimental yield responses consistent with national time series data. The first coefficient on the right–hand side of (4.12) is the scaling factor, estimated to make the cross–section data consistent with national time series data.

$$(4.12) \quad yld_{11} = 0.424 \; [\; 1.823 + 16.56 \; fert_{11} - 79.99 \; (fert_{11})^2]$$

$$yld_{12} = 0.424 \; [\; 2.466 + 24.34 \; fert_{12} - 68.30 \; (fert_{12})^2]$$

$$yld_{21} = 0.741 \; [\; 0.835 + 18.35 \; fert_{21} - 81.84 \; (fert_{21})^2]$$

$$yld_{22} = 0.741 \; [\; 1.730 + 30.94 \; fert_{22} - 122.17 \; (fert_{22})^2]$$

For other food crops and commercial crops, the following yield functions were estimated:

Yield Function for Other Food Crops:

$$(4.16) \quad log \; yld_3 = \underset{(7.720)^{***}}{0.929} + \underset{(8.253)^{***}}{0.190 \; log \; fert_3}$$

$$\overline{R}^2 = 0.779,$$
$$DW = 2.14, \; n = 20 \; (1966–1985)$$

Yield Function for Commercial Crops:

$$(4.16) \quad log \; yld_4 = \underset{(25.060)^{***}}{2.049} + \underset{(8.800)^{***}}{0.175 \; log \; fert_4}$$

$$\overline{R}^2 = 0.801,$$
$$DW = 1.56, \; n = 20 \; (1966–1985)$$

Investment Demand

Data on private and public investment were taken from the *NAS* (New Series) at constant 1980–81 prices for the period of estimation 1962–1984. Investment in registered manufacturing was allocated across sectors 6, 7, and 8 on the basis of shares derived from the *ASI* for various years (in particular the period 1973–74 to 1985–86). The whole of investment in unregistered manufacturing was allocated to the consumer goods sector. Data on mark–up income were derived from the *ASI* and were deflated with the price–index number (1980–81 = 100) for investment expenditure. Estimation results are reported below. Note that a dummy variable for the years 1977 through 1980 was added to the private investment demand function, because these years were outliers (this was done following Krishnamurty (1985:35), according to whom private investment demand in these years may have been affected by the political uncertainty prevailing at that time). The dummy variable was found to be statistically not significant for the agricultural sectors and the services sector and was left out of the respective equations. Whenever it was required, first–order autocorrelation was corrected by an error process AR(1).

(4.42)
$$\log I^p_{7,t} = \underset{(5.378)^{***}}{4.451} + \underset{(4.260)^{***}}{0.412} \log I^g_{7,t-1} - \underset{(5.637)^{***}}{0.554} \text{Dum}$$

$$\overline{R}^2 = 0.724,$$
$$DW = 1.83, n = 23 \ (1962–1984)$$

$$\log I^p_{8,t} = \underset{(1.429)}{2.851} + \underset{(1.963)^{*}}{0.348} \log I^g_{8,t-1} +$$
$$\underset{(1.872)^{*}}{0.371} \log Y_{z8,t} - \underset{(2.704)^{**}}{0.157} \text{Dum}$$

$$\overline{R}^2 = 0.936,$$
$$n = 23 \ (1962–1984)$$
$$\text{Error Process} = \text{AR}(1)$$

$$\log I^p_{9,t} = \underset{(4.317)^{***}}{-7.055} + \underset{(1.627)}{0.203} \log I^g_{9,t-1} +$$
$$\underset{(6.140)^{***}}{1.439} \log Y_{z9,t}$$

$$\overline{R}^2 = 0.856,$$
$$DW = 1.89, n = 23 \ (1962–1984)$$

Equation (4.41):

$$\log I^p_{a,t} = \underset{(7.362)^{***}}{3.071} + \underset{(11.113)^{***}}{0.664} \log I^g_{a,t-1} + \underset{(5.431)^{***}}{1.444} \log p_{a,t-1}$$

$$\overline{R}^2 = 0.849,$$
$$DW = 1.71, n = 25 \ (1962–1986)$$

Data used in the estimation of the wage formation equations (4.23) cover the period 1968–69 to 1985–86. The indices of the nominal wage rate per person employed by sector were derived from the *ASI* as the ratio of 'total emoluments' to 'number of persons employed'. Total emoluments are defined as 'salaries and wages paid during the year to persons in employment'. The number of persons employed include 'all administrative, technical and clerical staff as also labour engaged in the production of capital assets for factory's own use'. The *cpi* was taken from the *NAS*. To some (particularly the neoclassically inclined), the absence of labour productivity from the equation may seem an important omission, but since the total explanation without it is as high as 0.99, it is unlikely that labour productivity would have shown up statistically (see Krishnamurty, 1985).

The estimated wage indexation coefficient for consumer goods industries is statistically not significant at the 10 per cent level which is not surprising, because this sector includes the whole of unregistered manufacturing. The estimated equation also suffers from first–order serial correlation. The elasticity of the nominal wage rate in the consumer goods sector with respect to the *cpi* of 0.24 is also much smaller than the corresponding elasticities of the other non–agricultural sectors and the public sector. The estimation results are:

$$\log w_{6,t} = 0.055 + 0.613 \log cpi_t + 0.506 \log w_{6,t-1}$$
$$\underset{(2.479)^{**}}{} \quad \underset{(3.264)^{***}}{} \quad \underset{(3.229)^{***}}{}$$
$$\overline{R}^2 = 0.985,$$
$$h = -1.568, \ n = 18 \ (1968–1985)$$

$$\log w_{7,t} = 0.073 + 0.338 \log cpi_t + 0.746 \log w_{7,t-1}$$
$$\underset{(5.660)^{***}}{} \quad \underset{(3.280)^{***}}{} \quad \underset{(8.823)^{***}}{}$$
$$\overline{R}^2 = 0.997,$$
$$h = 0.357, \ n = 18 \ (1968–1985)$$

$$\log w_{8,t} = 0.091 + 0.243 \log cpi_t + 0.819 \log w_{8,t-1}$$
$$\underset{(4.843)^{***}}{} \quad \underset{(1.158)}{} \quad \underset{(4.270)^{***}}{}$$
$$\overline{R}^2 = 0.984,$$
$$h = 1.800, \ n = 18 \ (1968–1985)$$

$$\log w_{9,t} = 0.081 + 0.403 \log cpi_t + 0.671 \log w_{9,t-1}$$
$$\underset{(6.503)^{***}}{} \quad \underset{(3.433)^{***}}{} \quad \underset{(6.659)^{***}}{}$$
$$\overline{R}^2 = 0.993,$$
$$h = -0.416, \ n = 18 \ (1968–1985)$$

$$\log w_{g,t} = 0.063 + 0.498 \log cpi_t + 0.677 \log w_{g,t-1}$$
$$\underset{(2.654)^{**}}{} \quad \underset{(3.060)^{***}}{} \quad \underset{(6.400)^{***}}{}$$
$$\overline{R}^2 = 0.993,$$
$$h = -1.139, \ n = 18 \ (1968–1985)$$

Procurement Pricing for Foodgrains

Procurement prices are determined by the government on the basis of recommendations given by the Commission of Agricultural Costs and Prices or CACP (see Section 3.3.1 for a discussion of the role of the CACP). However, it is not clear how each of the criteria ranging from the cost of production to international prices enters into the price fixation exercise. I took the view that, for rice and wheat, procurement price fixation can be explained by the one–period lagged market price (positively), the one–period lagged terms of trade (negatively), and the one–period lagged procurement price (positively). It was not possible to model procurement price fixation for rice econometrically. Consequently, the parameters of the procurement price for rice were assumed rather than estimated, taking the elasticity of the procurement price for rice with respect to its one–period lagged market price from Gulati and Sharma (1990) and the elasticity with respect to the one–period terms–of–trade from the procurement price equation for wheat.

Procurement Price of Rice

$$(4.69) \qquad \log p^*_{1,t} = 0.418 \quad + 0.450 \ \log p_{1,t-1} \ - 0.255 \ \log \hat{p}_{t-1}$$

The estimation results for wheat and other food crops are as follows:

Procurement Price of Wheat

$$(4.69) \qquad \log p^*_{2,t} = 5.016 \quad + 0.373 \ \log p_{2,t-1} \ -0.255 \ \log \hat{p}_{t-1}$$
$$\underset{(4.701)^{***}}{} \qquad \underset{(4.114)^{***}}{} \qquad \underset{(-1.484)^{*}}{}$$
$$+ 0.187 \ \log p^*_{2,t-1}$$
$$\underset{(1.189)}{}$$

$$\overline{R}^2 = 0.988,$$
$$h = 0.334, \ n = 13 \ (1975-1987)$$

Procurement Price of Other Food Crops

$$(4.69) \qquad \log p^*_{3,t} = 2.597 \quad - 0.420 \ \log \hat{p}_{t-1} \ +0.863 \ \log p^*_{3,t-1}$$
$$\underset{(1.141)}{} \quad \underset{(-1.007)}{} \qquad \underset{(7.813)^{***}}{}$$

$$\overline{R}^2 = 0.967,$$
$$n = 13 \ (1975-1987)$$
$$\text{Error Process} = \text{AR} \ (1)$$

Appendix 5.4
Results of the Sensitivity Analysis

Table 5.18 gives the results of four 'dynamic' experiments meant to test the model's responses to changes in the following key parameters:

Experiment SEN – 1: All Price Elasticities of Fertiliser Demand are Set at –1.

Experiment SEN – 2: All Nominal Wage Indexation Coefficients are Increased by 10 Per Cent.

Experiment SEN – 3: The Income Elasticities of Private Investment Demand are Reduced by 25 Per Cent.

Experiment SEN – 4: The Elasticity of Gross Irrigated Area with respect to Agricultural Investment is Raised by 10 Per Cent.

Table 5.18
Results of Sensitivity Analysis:
Average Annual Price and Wage Changes,
Average Annual Rates of Growth of Production and Income,
1984–85 *to* 1989–90 (in percentage change)

	Base Run	SEN–1	SEN–2	SEN–3	SEN–4
Price Changes					
Rice	8.0	6.9	10.0	6.8	7.7
Wheat	9.2	8.0	11.2	7.8	8.9
Other Food Crops	10.0	8.1	12.3	8.5	9.9
Commercial Crops	10.4	8.1	12.6	9.0	10.2
Other Agriculture	7.0	6.3	9.3	5.4	6.9
Fertilisers	5.2	4.7	6.5	4.6	5.2
Basic, Intermediate & Capital Goods	7.7	7.1	9.0	7.1	7.6
Consumer Goods	6.0	5.1	7.6	5.2	5.9
Services	5.5	4.9	7.1	4.8	5.5
Consumer Price Index	7.6	6.5	9.4	6.5	7.5
GDP Deflator	7.9	6.9	9.7	6.9	7.7
A–NA Terms of Trade	3.5	2.6	4.2	2.7	3.3

	Base Run	SEN–1	SEN–2	SEN–3	SEN–4
Nominal Wage Changes					
Fertilisers	7.5	6.6	9.8	6.6	7.4
Basic, Intermediate & Capital Goods	10.4	9.7	11.9	9.7	10.3
Consumer Goods	7.3	6.9	8.5	6.8	7.3
Services	8.1	7.5	9.8	7.4	8.1
Government	9.4	8.4	11.9	8.4	9.3

	Base Run	SEN–1	SEN–2	SEN–3	SEN–4
Production Growth					
Rice	1.9	1.9	1.9	1.8	1.9
Wheat	2.3	2.4	2.3	2.2	2.3
Other Food Crops	0.5	0.7	0.5	0.4	0.5
Commercial Crops	1.4	1.8	1.5	1.3	1.4
Other Agriculture	3.6	3.6	3.6	3.6	3.6
Fertilisers	4.4	5.1	4.7	4.1	4.4
Basic, Intermediate & Capital Goods	7.7	7.7	7.9	7.2	7.7
Consumer Goods	8.2	8.3	8.5	7.9	8.2
Services	8.3	8.3	8.5	7.9	8.3
Growth Rates of Income at 1985–86 prices:					
Agricultural Income	3.9	3.5	4.4	3.3	3.9
Non–agr. Wage Income	5.4	5.7	5.5	5.3	5.4
Non–agr. Mark–up Income	5.5	5.5	5.9	5.0	5.5
GDP at Factor Cost	5.2	5.2	5.3	4.9	5.2
GDP at Market Prices	5.7	5.9	5.8	5.5	5.8

Appendix 5.5
Values of the Model's Exogenous Variables
Which Are Not Included in the SAM

The static model

The static part of the general equilibrium model reproduces the benchmark 1985–86 SAM of Table 5.3. Following the convention for SAM accounting, apart from some government controlled prices, all prices including the nominal wage rates, foodgrain procurement prices, and the nominal exchange rate, are set equal to 1 in the base–year. Input–output coefficients, intermediate input import coefficients, and labour–output ratios can be calculated from the SAM. The consumption demand parameters are given in Table 5.5. The savings parameters are presented in Section 5.3.1.

Most of the exogenous variables are presented in the SAM: exports, competitive imports, stock changes, government consumption, government revenue from public enterprises, remittances, public wage transfers, and government interest payments. Information on public foodgrain procurement and distribution and issue prices of foodgrains is included in Table 5.15, Appendix 5.2. In 1985–86, net sown area amounted to 140 million hectares. Land use statistics are given in Table 5.10. Estimates of sectoral capital stocks and depreciation rates as well as of investment by sector of origin and destination are discussed in Section 5.3.3.

The Seventh Five Year Plan Reference Run

The reference run 1985–86 to 1989–90 is constructed to reproduce the evolution of the variables included in the national accounts and other statistical sources. The parameters of the static model are assumed to remain constant throughout the reference period. Table 5.19 presents time–series data on a number of exogenous variables, included in the model. Actual data were taken for as many years as possible. Due to lack of data at the time of the operationalisation of the model, most of the figures for 1988–89 and 1988–89 are projections, generated on the basis of their past five–year period growth rates. Table 5.20 gives the annual growth rates determining the time path of the remaining exogenous variables.

Table 5.19
Values of Exogenous Variables,
1986-87 *to* 1989-90

	1986 – 87	1987 – 88	1988 – 89	1989 – 90
net sown area	14.0	13.8	14.15	14.15
exchange rate (*index* 1985 – 86 = 1.000)				
	1.045	1.060	1.183	1.200
remittances	0.117	0.088	0.052	0.050
public transfers	0.915	1.086	1.500	1.600
govt. interest				
payments	0.763	0.972	1.235	1.550
export prices (*index* 1985 – 86 = 1.000)				
rice	0.949	1.028	1.093	1.148
wheat	0.997	1.090	1.093	1.148
other food crops	0.997	1.090	1.093	1.148
comm. crops	0.924	1.000	1.050	1.103
other agric.	0.996	1.083	1.150	1.208
export volume				
rice	0.043	0.070	0.035	0.035
wheat	0.000	0.000	0.031	0.030
other food crops	0.000	0.000	0.000	0.000
comm. crops	0.255	0.218	0.257	0.210
other agric.	0.130	0.106	0.103	0.100
import prices (*index* 1985 – 86 = 1.000)				
rice	0.814	0.901	0.901	0.946
wheat	0.814	1.064	1.064	1.117
other food	0.814	1.064	1.064	1.117
comm. crops	0.584	0.680	1.060	1.113
other agric.	0.969	1.064	1.218	1.279
import volume				
rice	0.000	0.000	0.000	0.000
wheat	0.000	0.000	0.000	0.000
other food crops	0.000	0.010	0.015	0.040
comm. crops	0.000	0.025	0.160	0.145
other agric.	0.000	0.010	0.090	0.090
real public investment				
agriculture	0.318	0.268	0.339	0.379
fertilisers	0.062	0.044	0.045	0.047
basic goods *etc.*	2.112	1.822	1.891	1.998
consumer goods	0.125	0.117	0.125	0.132
services	0.761	0.897	0.675	0.713

Continued overleaf.

Table 5.19
Concluded

	1986–87	1987–88	1988–89	1989–90
private stock changes				
rice	−0.013	0.038	0.025	0.008
wheat	0.019	0.074	0.018	0.007
other food	−0.048	−0.069	−0.037	−0.035
comm. crops	−0.190	−0.145	−0.253	−0.369
other agric.	−0.060	−0.015	−0.396	−0.325
fertilisers	0.006	0.006	0.006	0.020
basic goods *etc.*	0.395	0.530	0.600	0.850
consumer goods	0.330	0.390	0.650	0.650
services	0.320	0.200	0.600	0.600
public procurement				
rice	0.200	0.268	0.224	0.250
wheat	0.130	0.194	0.168	0.139
other food	0.000	0.001	0.000	0.006
public distribution (*urban*)				
rice	0.212	0.257	0.304	0.272
wheat	0.128	0.190	0.202	0.168
other food crops	0.001	0.005	0.016	0.004
public distribution (*rural*)				
rice	0.030	0.025	0.030	0.030
wheat	0.035	0.030	0.035	0.035

Table 5.20
Annual Growth Rates of Exogenous Variables,
1985-86 *to* 1989-90

real government consumption	8.0
nominal revenue of public enterprises	17.8
government employment	4.0
other agricultural production	3.6
non–agricultural exports	10.0
non–agricultural export prices	5.0
non–agricultural final imports	1.0
non–agricultural import prices	5.0

SHORT–TERM SIMULATION EXPERIMENTS

6.1   *Introduction*

This lengthy chapter describes the results of almost thirty short–run simulation experiments which were performed with the general equilibrium model constructed in the previous chapters. These short–term experiments are important not only for analysing the short–run implications of a particular policy change, but also as a basis for the selection of potentially desirable policy packages to be implemented in the 'dynamic' version of the model. Therefore, the results of the short–run experiments are examined before turning to the medium–term experiments in Chapter 7.

Chapter 6 is organised as follows. Section 6.2 discusses a number of short–term experiments which were performed to analyse the nature and importance of agriculture–industry linkages in the Indian economy. In 6.3, the economy–wide impact of changes in food and fertiliser subsidisation and foodgrain procurement are analysed. A comparison of the present model and the policy conclusions drawn from it with other studies addressing some of the same set of (policy) problems will be taken up after the discussion of the results from the medium–run experiments, *i.e.* in Chapter 8.

6.2   *Agriculture–Industry Interaction: The Short Term*

Section 6.2.1 discusses the simulation results of a number of experiments which were designed to trace out the short–run impact of agricultural performance on non–agricultural growth. Section 6.2.2 concludes.

6.2.1   *Simulation Results*

The simulation experiments reported below involve a change in only one exogenous variable or one policy variable or parameter at a time, assuming that any compensatory policy measures are absent.[1] Seven such experiments were performed, the outcomes of which are given in Table 6.1.

Experiment N-1
10% Reduction of Net Sown Area as a Consequence of Drought

From Chapter 3, it will have become clear that, in the Indian context, harvest failures due to drought are a major (and regular) example of an exogenous shock. To assess the economy–wide consequences of a harvest failure, experiment $N-1$ was performed in which net sown area was exogenously reduced by 10 per cent as a proxy for a drought. The decline in net sown area leads to a fall in the production of all crops. The fall in crop supply raises crop prices, particularly for foodgrains. Due to these crop price increases, agricultural income and demand rise, adding to consumer price inflation. Nominal wages in non–agriculture, which are indexed to the consumer price index, rise which further augments inflationary pressures in the economy. In effect, the consumer price index increases by 10.6 per cent and the GDP deflator by 10.4 per cent.

Except fertiliser production, all other non–agricultural production levels are negatively affected by the harvest failure. This negative impact is due to the following three factors. First, with crop supply declining, agriculture's demand for non–agricultural intermediate inputs declines. Second, with rising crop prices and given consumer budgets, the amount of fixed or 'committed' expenditure on foodgrains and commercial crops by (agricultural and non– agricultural) consumers increases, which reduces the amount of supernumerary expenditure[2] and leads to a fall in consumer demand for non–agricultural goods. Third, with the increase in the rate of inflation and the decline in mark–up income in real terms, real private non–agricultural investment demand declines. In effect, demand for non–agricultural products – apart from fertilisers – falls and, hence, the rates of capacity utilisation decline. The total result is that real non–agricultural wage income declines by 7.5 per cent and real non–agricultural mark–up income by 6.4 per cent as compared to the base run. The inflation leads to a redistribution of income from non–agricultural wage earners towards agriculturalists; the share in GDP at factor cost of agricultural income increases from 32.7 to 35.8 per cent,

---

[1] In particular, experiments $N-4$, $N-6$ and $N-7$ involve an expansionary policy change, the *ex – ante* negative impact of which on the government budget is not compensated for at forehand.

[2] Supernumerary expenditure refers to that part of consumers' budgets that is left over after consumers have paid for their 'fixed' expenditure. See Appendix 4.8, 'The Derivation of the Linear Expenditure System Inclusive of Food Subsidies.'

while the corresponding share of (imperfectly indexed) non–agricultural wage income declines from 37.2 to 35.4 per cent. The share of non–agricultural mark–up income also declines, *i.c.* from 23.1 to 22.3 per cent. Despite its positive impact on agricultural income, the aggregate impact of the harvest failure is contractionary. Real GDP at market prices declines by 2.8 per cent. The simulation results indicate that inflationary pressure due to the drought is heavily dampened by the following three factors. First, because nominal wage rate indexation in non–agriculture is less than perfect, real wage income gets eroded with inflation, containing the increase in consumer demand. The second dampening factor is the built–in fall in real private investment demand in the consumer goods and services sectors, which occurs when the mark–up income earned in these sectors declines in real terms. Finally, demand pressure is contained by the erosion of expenditure on transfers including public interest and transfer payments and revenue from public enterprises, which are assumed fixed in nominal terms.

The agriculture–induced inflation leads to a substantial decline of gross domestic fixed investment in real terms as is shown by the decline in its share in GDP at market prices from 21 to 19.9 per cent. The share in GDP of stock changes also marginally declines. With the decline in the share in GDP of gross domestic investment, *ex – post* investment–savings equality is re–established by a fall in the share in GDP of savings. The four savings sources distinguished in the model all suffer a decline. First, with the inflation, foreign savings decline as the deficit on the nation's current account as a proportion of nominal GDP at market prices improves; this is not surprising, because, since exports, final imports and the net inflow of factor payments are exogenous in real terms, the nominal exchange rate is fixed, and intermediate imports are dependent on real output levels, the share of the current account deficit (or foreign savings) in GDP declines with the inflation and with the decline in complementary intermediate imports (following the contraction). Second, public savings decline as the government's budgetary position deteriorates due to higher expenditure on food, fertiliser and export subsidies, final consumption, and government wages, and due to a decline in revenue from direct and indirect taxation and revenue from public enterprises.[3] Third, the share in GDP at market prices of net private savings declines, mainly due to the shift in income distribution in favour of the income category with the lowest saving propensity – agricultural income. Finally, with the rise in the rate of inflation, the share in GDP of depreciation allowances declines; this is due to the fact that depreciation allowances are tied to sectoral capital stocks which largely consist of capital goods (produced by sector 7), the price of which rises less than the general price level.

---

[3] Note that revenue from public enterprises is assumed fixed in nominal terms which implies that, with inflation, it gets eroded in real terms.

The simulation results show that, in the Indian context, a harvest failure will have considerable (negative) economy–wide effects which include a rise in inflation, a fall in real GDP, an increase in the public revenue deficit, an improvement of the nation's current account, a fall in real (private) investment, and a considerable redistribution of income in favour of agriculturalists. Comparing the outcome of the experiment to what actually happened following the drought of 1987–88, when aggregate agricultural production fell by over 2 per cent and inflation increased to 10.4 per cent, one may note that the extent to which inflationary pressure was dampened, has been somewhat larger in reality than in the simulation results. This is mainly due to the fact that, in the model, the degree of nominal wage indexation is overestimated by not distinguishing between registered and unregistered non–agricultural production.

Experiment N – 2:
10 Per Cent Increase in Net Sown Area

To evaluate the impact of a 'bumper' harvest, an experiment was performed in which net sown area was exogenously increased by 10 per cent. The increase in net sown area leads to a considerable increase in crop supply which, in turn, results in strong downward pressure on crop prices. However, due to a step–up in public procurement of rice and wheat, the market prices of rice and wheat do not fall below their minimum support prices. With some of the crop prices declining, consumers have to spend less in money terms on their fixed or 'committed' consumption plans, which increases the budgetary outlays available for 'supernumerary' expenditure. As a result, consumer demand increases for both agricultural and non–agricultural commodities, which leads to upward pressure on the price of other agricultural goods (the supply of which is relatively inelastic) and raises non–agricultural capacity utilisation, production and income. Despite the price increase for other agricultural products, the bumper harvest has a strong deflationary impact on the economy, the consumer price index declines by 3.9 per cent. With the decline in prices, real private investment demand in the consumer goods and services sectors rises, stimulating non–agricultural production. Real GDP at market prices rises by 2.6 per cent. Distributionally, agriculturalists are worst off. Despite the increases in crop production, their real income gains are eroded by the fall in prices of other food crops and commercial crops. Real agricultural income declines by 0.3 per cent. Following the increase in non–agricultural production and the deflation, the share in GDP at factor cost of non–agricultural wage income rises to 37.7 per cent.

With the deflation, the share in GDP at market prices of gross domestic investment rises from 25.9 per cent in the base run to 26.4 per cent. To finance the rise in gross domestic investment, savings increase in the following two ways. First, foreign savings rise with the deflation. Second, net public savings rise; the public revenue deficit declines mainly due to an increase in revenue from direct taxation (following the change in income distribution in favour of mark–up income), a decline in expenditure on export subsidies (with the deflation, domestic prices come more in line with world prices), and a rise in revenue from public enterprises which is assumed nominally fixed. Note that – although the share in GDP of net private savings is only marginally affected – its composition is changed considerably: the share in net private savings of savings from agricultural income declines from 23.6 to 22.8 per cent, while the share of saving from non–agricultural mark–up income increases from 47.0 to 47.5 per cent.

One important conclusion that emerges from a comparison of experiments $N-2$ and $N-1$ is that, in absolute terms, the impact on inflation of a fall in net sown area is much larger than that of a rise in net sown area. The main factor explaining this result is the existence of a minimum price support scheme for rice and wheat which prevents prices of rice and wheat to fall in experiment $N-2$.

Experiment N–3:
10 Per Cent Devaluation of the Rupee vis–a–vis Other Currencies

In this experiment, some of the domestic repercussions – particularly on effective demand and the distribution of income – are considered that might result from a devaluation of the Rupee. Before proceeding to a discussion of the simulation results, one should recall that, in the model, exports and final imports are exogenous and fixed in real terms. Imports required as intermediate inputs are tied in fixed proportions to sectoral output levels.

The devaluation leads to a rise in imported intermediate input costs, which, in agriculture, leads to a decline in income, while in non–agriculture it results in an increase in (mark–up) prices. Due to these two factors, the demand for agricultural products declines. While the fall in agriculturalists' income results in a fall in their demand for agricultural as well as non–agricultural goods, the tendency of demand to fall is strengthened by the fact that the increase in non–agricultural prices raises the amount of 'committed' consumer expenditure, which crowds out consumer demand for agricultural commodities. As a result, agricultural prices decline, with the exception of the prices for rice and wheat which – due to additional government procurement – remain at their minimum support levels. The net effect in terms of the consumer price index of the agricultural price decreases and the non–agricultural price increases is negative: the consumer price index declines by 0.3 per cent.

Apart from being (marginally) deflationary, the devaluation turns out to be contractionary; real GDP at market prices declines by 0.8 per cent. This decline can be attributed to two main factors. First, with respect to agricultural production, given the increase in the fertiliser price relative to the crop prices, per hectare fertiliser application declines, yield levels fall and crop output decreases. Second, concerning non–agriculture, the decline in agricultural (intermediate and final) demand contributes to the decline in non-agricultural capacity utilisation rates, production and income. With the fall in crop prices and the decline in crop output, agricultural income declines most – namely, by 1.3 per cent as compared to the base run. As a result, income distribution changes in favour of non-agricultural income.

With the deflation, the share in GDP at market prices of domestic investment increases. To restore the investment–savings equality, the share in GDP of savings increases in the following ways. First, given the model's assumptions, a devaluation of the Rupee leads to increased foreign saving. The reason is that the current account trade deficit is worth more domestically after a devaluation, implying a rise in foreign savings. It should be noted that the increase in foreign savings is partly offset by the decline in complementary imports of intermediate inputs which is due to the contraction. Second, with the devaluation, government saving increases because of higher revenue from import duties and because the expenditure on export subsidies required to make the Indian goods price–competitive on the world market is reduced. This is because, following the devaluation, the gap between domestic prices and world prices at an overvalued exchange rate has narrowed. Third, net private savings increase following the change in income distribution in favour of non-agricultural mark–up income. Finally, with the deflation, the share in GDP of depreciation allowances increases for reasons explained earlier (see $N-1$).

Under the model's assumptions of price–inelastic exports and imports, devaluation of the Rupee leads to increased saving which, in turn, leads to deflation, a fall in effective demand and contraction. Although many would question the extent to which I assume Indian exports and imports to be price–inelastic, there is empirical evidence that the present specification may not be too much besides the point (Ghosh, 1990). The simulation results also clearly indicate that agriculture and non-agriculture are differently affected by a devaluation.

Experiment N–4:
Reduction in the Direct Tax Rate on Non – Agricultural Mark – Up Income from 13.1 to 10.0 Per Cent.

In 1985, the advent of the new government ushered in a wide array of fiscal policy initiatives which together came to be known as the 'New Fiscal Policy' (Acharya, 1988:301–311). Among the measures taken, there were substantial reductions in the marginal tax rates for personal income, wealth and corporate incomes carried out in the 1985 Budget, which were meant to stimulate the economy from the demand side. With agricultural incomes remaining untaxed, the tax rate changes essentially concerned the non-agricultural sector. To assess the impact of the tax rate reduction, a policy experiment was performed in which the (average) direct tax rate on non–agricultural mark–up income was reduced from 13.1 per cent to 10.0 per cent.

The reduction in the direct tax rate raises disposable non–agricultural mark–up income which, in turn, leads to an increase in non–agricultural savings and consumption demand. With relatively inelastic crop supply, the increase in demand leads to a rise in crop prices which – through raising indexed nominal wages in non–agriculture – sets in motion an economy–wide inflationary spiral. As a result of the tax reform, the rate of inflation as measured by the consumer price index increases by 3.6 per cent. Because crop prices increase relative to the price for fertilisers, cropwise per hectare fertiliser application increases, raising crop yields and the levels of crop production. Following the increase in crop production, agriculture's demand for intermediate inputs other than fertilisers also increases. With the rise in agricultural prices and the increase in crop supply, agricultural income increases – by 3.7 per cent as compared to the base run – which augments the size of the domestic market for non–agricultural goods. As a result, non–agricultural production increases, which in the event raises non–agricultural mark–up income by 0.5 per cent. The income gain of non–agricultural wage earners is eroded by the agriculture–induced inflation. In fact, real wage income declines by 0.9 per cent as compared to the base run. In effect, the policy change is only slightly expansionary, real GDP at market prices increases by 0.9 per cent. Following the policy change, the share in GDP of gross domestic investment decreases from 25.9 to 25.3 per cent and, hence, the share of savings has to fall. Investment–savings balance is re–established in the following three ways. First, with the inflation, foreign savings decrease. Second, with the reduction in the direct tax rate, net public savings as a proportion of GDP decrease. Finally, due to the inflation, the share in GDP of depreciation allowances decreases. Note that the share in GDP of net private savings increases following the tax reform.

According to the above results, a reduction of the direct tax rate on non–agricultural mark–up income is both inflationary and expansionary. Distributionally, one would have expected non–agricultural mark–up recipients to benefit most from the tax reform, but, according to the simulation outcome, the agriculturalists are its main beneficiairies. Their share in GDP at factor cost increases from 32.7 per cent in the base run to 33.7 per cent.

Experiment N–5:
20% Increase in World Demand for Exports of Goods 7, 8, and 9

In a context where the need to earn foreign exchange to meet the country's import bill is large and the economy is operating at less than full capacity, an increase in export volume, whether due to a deliberate policy of export promotion or to a sudden rise in world demand, is generally regarded as being beneficial. To assess whether this argument holds for India, an experiment was performed in which the export volumes of basic, intermediate and capital goods, consumer goods, and services were exogenously raised by 20 per cent. It should be noted that these non–agricultural sectors all three suffer from considerable excess capacity.

Following the increase in export volumes, capacity utilisation rates in non–agriculture increase, which leads to an increase in their intermediate demand for agricultural commodities. Non–agricultural (wage and mark–up) incomes rise substantially, raising consumption demand for agricultural goods. Agricultural production expands, but not to the same extent as the demand for agricultural products increases, and, consequently, agricultural prices increase. The price increase of agricultural products varies from 7.9 per cent for wheat (the most price–responsive crop) to 12.8 per cent for other agricultural goods, the supply of which is price–inelastic. As a result, the consumer price index increases. Due to indexation, nominal non–agricultural wages also increase. In effect, the increase in export volumes leads to considerable inflation, the consumer price index increases by 6.3 per cent. Due to the fact that crop prices increase more than the fertiliser price, fertiliser use increases, raising crop yields and crop production. With the increase in crop supply and the rise in agricultural prices, agricultural income increases, which, via demand, provides a stimulus to domestic non–agricultural production. In effect, the impact of the export drive on real GDP at factor cost is expansionary. Distributionally, the farmers gain most from the non–agricultural export drive, their share in GDP at factor cost increases from 32.7 to 34.1 per cent. With the inflation and imperfectly indexed nominal wages, the relative income position of non–agricultural wage earners deteriorates; their share in GDP at factor cost falls from 37.2 to 36.2 per cent.

Due to the inflation, the share in GDP at market prices of gross domestic investment declines from 25.9 per cent in the base run to 24.8 per cent. Savings adjust in the following manner. First, the increase in exports leads to a considerable reduction in the nation's current account deficit or, in other words, to a fall in foreign savings. Second, with the inflation, the share in GDP of depreciation allowances declines as in experiment $N-1$. The share in GDP of net private savings marginally rises due to the redistribution of incomes following the policy change. Net public savings are the only savings source registering an increase. Net public savings increase due to the rise in revenue from direct and indirect taxation and the procurement tax.

According to the above results, a substantial increase in non–agricultural export volume is a mixed blessing on the economy. The export drive raises GDP in real terms, but also invokes a considerable increase in inflation and a sharp redistribution of income between agriculturalists and non–agricultural wage earners. The share in GDP at market prices of gross fixed investment declines from 21.0 to 20.1 per cent, which suggests that the export increase – through its negative impact on real investment – might negatively affect medium run growth. It has been argued by some that during the mid–1980s, when India achieved a fair measure of food self–sufficiency and was likely to meet a demand constraint for agricultural products, the emphasis in policy should have shifted towards industrialisation with an export market in view (Chakravarty, 1987:62). The outcome of the present experiment indicates that, even if the economy were to follow a policy leaning heavily on export promotion, its export performance will have to reckon with an important inflationary constraint arising out of an inadequate agricultural support base (Sen, 1981). Unless suitable domestic policies are followed, a rise in the rate of inflation will erode part of the income gain arising from the export increase, while at the same time eroding the country's competitiveness (Chakravarty, 1987:73).

Experiment N-6:
10% Increase In Public Transfer Payments to Non-Agricultural Wage Earners

The major (neo-)classical remedy for rectifying income distributional inequality is to redistribute through tax and transfer policies. Although the present model is not particularly well adapted to analyse the income distributional consequences of public transfer policies, it can be used to trace out the macro-economic impact of such redistributional policies. To this end, public transfer payments to non-agricultural wage earners were increased by 10 per cent.

With relatively inelastic agricultural output, the increase in public transfers which raises non-agricultural wage income and hence consumer demand for agricultural as well as non-agricultural products, is inflationary. The consumer price index increases by 1.9 per cent. The increases in crop prices relative to the fertiliser price raise crop production and lead to a rise in agricultural income. The home market for non-agricultural products expands, raising non-agricultural production capacity rates and, through the multiplier mechanism, real GDP at factor cost (by 0.4 per cent). The increase in inflationary pressure leads to a decline of gross domestic investment in real terms. As a proportion of GDP at market prices, gross domestic investment declines from 25.9 per cent in the base run to 25.6 per cent. The share in GDP of savings adjusts mainly through a decline in the share of net public savings (following the rise in expenditure) and of depreciation allowances (which declines with the inflation).

Due to the agriculture-induced inflation, the distribution of income changes in favour of agriculturalists and deteriorates for non-agricultural wage earners, the original and intended beneficiairies of the public transfer increase. Income redistribution programmes, where the redistributive gains are not erased by inflation, thus require a sharp increase in food availability, either from imports or from public distribution. The outcome of this policy experiment also indicates that 'self-sufficiency' in foodgrains is always defined in relative terms, that is, at the given level of demand arising from the given income distribution and the given level of purchasing power.

Experiment N-7:
10% Increase in Public Investment in Basic, Intermediate and Capital Goods Production

In a one–sector model of a closed economy, expansion of public investment will, in the short run, create additional demand for capital goods which will bring about a Keynesian multiplier increase in value added when there are no supply constraints. In a two–sector model of a similar economy, in which there is capacity underutilisation in non–agriculture while the agricultural sector operates subject to a supply constraint, the impact of an increase in public investment will be different, as has been observed by Kalecki. In his view, (public) capital accumulation may be hindered by an inadequate supply of wage goods to meet the demand resulting from the concomitant rise in employment. This so–called wage goods constraint, formulated by Kalecki in the early 1950s, was discussed in Section 2.5.3. It is important to emphasize that Kalecki's argument of a wage–goods constraint on industrial growth pre-supposes the existence of a foreign exchange constraint, which does not permit adequate imports of agricultural commodities (Sen, 1981).

To evaluate the impact of an increase in public investment on the economy, public investment in the basic, intermediate and capital goods sector was raised by 10 per cent. Its immediate impact is to raise the level of production of and value added earned in sector 7 which – via the input–output relationships – leads to a rise in production and income in other sectors too. The increase in income, in turn, leads to a rise in final demand, which enhances the multiplier process, set in motion by the policy change. In the event, the policy change is expansionary, real GDP at factor cost increases by 1.1 per cent. With relatively inelastic agricultural supply, it is also inflationary, the consumer price index increases by 2.9 per cent. Inflationary pressure is particularly strong in the agricultural markets. Distributionally, agriculturalists benefit most from the policy change, their share in GDP at factor cost rises from 32.7 to 33.4 per cent. The income share of non–agricultural wage earners declines by 0.6 per cent points.

Real private investment demand is eroded by the increase in the rate of inflation so that, the substantial increase in public investment not-withstanding, the share in GDP at market prices of gross domestic investment remains at the level of 25.9 per cent. However, the composition of savings changes as compared to the base run. First, following the policy change, the share in GDP of net public savings increases from –1.1 per cent to –0.8 per cent which is in particular due to the increase in government revenue from direct and indirect taxation. Second, with the inflation, the share in GDP of depreciation allowances declines. Finally, although the share in GDP of net private savings does not change in size, it changes in composition. Following the income redistribution in favour of agriculturalists, the share in net private savings of agricultural savings increases from 23.6 to 24.2 per cent, while the share of savings from non–agricultural wage income declines from 47.0 to 46.3 per cent. With respect to the balance on the nation's current account (or foreign saving), there are two forces which offset each other. On the one hand, with the rise in real GDP, complementary intermediate imports increase, raising foreign savings. On the other hand, with the inflation, the current account (denominated in a fixed exchange rate) improves, implying a reduction in foreign savings.

The outcome of the policy change suggests that the limited availability of agricultural goods – the main wage goods in the economy – may act as a constraint on non–agricultural investment in real terms and retard growth, as it puts upward pressure on prices and wages.[4]

6.2.2 Conclusions

The results of the experiments of Section 6.2.1 clearly indicate the importance of increasing the availability of agricultural products (particularly foodgrains) in achieving a desired rate of growth in the non–agricultural sectors in a non–inflationary way. This conclusion follows from the following observations:

1. An agricultural shortfall due to drought results in considerable inflation and erodes gross domestic fixed investment in real terms, apart from having a considerable negative impact on real GDP. Distributionally, farmers benefit most from an agricultural shortfall. A bumper harvest, on the other hand, is significantly deflationary and expansionary.
2. With a relatively inelastic (short–run) agricultural supply, macro–economic policies such as a devaluation or a reduction of the direct tax rate may have unexpected consequences including deflation and contraction (due to the devaluation) and inflation (due to the tax reform).
3. A sudden increase in (export or investment) demand for non–agricultural products leads to considerable inflation on account of the resulting increase in intermediate and final demand for agricultural goods and a redistribution of income in favour of agriculture.
4. A rise in redistributive income transfers has important macro–economic consequences, particularly in terms of inflation.

These results can be attributed to the fact that, in the short run, agriculture is not only a sector of relatively price–inelastic supply, but also one of relatively price–inelastic demand, while, at the low income levels, the income elasticities of the demand for foodgrains are high. These features imply that there is an asymmetry of adjustments on the demand and the supply side. While management of demand using fiscal policy instruments works

---

[4] Planners have been well aware of the possibility of a wage goods constraint on the growth of non–agricultural production and employment, as may be judged from the following quotation from the Seventh Plan Approach Paper, 'The growth in employment will be non–inflationary only if agricultural production, particularly food production, is augmented significantly.' (Planning Commission, 1984:1). This is, in fact, a restatement of Kalecki's assertion that the problem of financing Indian economic growth is essentially one of increasing the availability of agricultural supplies. It should be noted, however, that the Approach Paper is based on the belief that it is possible to step–up the rate of agricultural growth to the required extent.

Table 6.1
Results of the Non–Agricultural Experiments

	Base – Run	N–1	N–2	N–3	N–4	N–5	N–6	N–7
		percentage change from initial base – run values						
x_1	1.884	−3.0	4.6	−0.2	0.5	0.6	0.2	0.3
x_2	1.076	−0.8	1.4	−0.3	0.6	0.9	0.3	0.5
x_3	0.941	−9.8	9.1	−0.1	0.1	0.2	0.1	0.1
x_4	3.945	−6.6	6.7	−0.2	0.3	0.5	0.1	0.2
x_6	0.413	1.6	1.9	−0.9	1.5	2.6	0.8	1.4
x_7	15.093	−1.8	1.5	−0.7	0.7	2.5	0.4	2.3
x_8	6.453	−3.3	3.0	−1.1	1.7	4.3	0.9	1.5
x_9	10.198	−2.7	2.2	−0.8	1.3	3.7	0.7	1.6
p_1	1.0	20.8	0.0	0.0	5.3	9.0	2.8	4.5
p_2	1.0	6.0	0.0	0.0	4.7	7.9	2.4	3.9
p_3	1.0	76.8	−29.3	−2.3	6.7	11.5	3.5	5.8
p_4	1.0	32.4	−18.3	−2.0	6.4	11.6	3.3	5.6
p_5	1.0	−2.7	6.4	−2.8	7.3	12.8	3.8	6.4
p_6	1.0	4.2	−1.4	1.7	1.6	2.8	0.8	1.4
p_7	1.0	4.0	−1.4	1.8	1.5	2.7	0.8	1.3
p_8	1.0	9.5	−4.3	−0.2	2.8	5.0	1.5	2.4
p_9	1.0	4.7	−1.6	0.4	1.7	3.0	0.9	1.5
w_6	1.0	6.3	−2.2	−0.2	2.2	3.8	1.1	1.9
w_7	1.0	3.5	−1.2	−0.1	1.2	2.1	0.6	1.1
w_8	1.0	2.5	−0.9	−0.1	0.9	1.5	0.5	0.8
w_9	1.0	4.1	−1.4	−0.1	1.4	2.5	0.8	1.2
w_g	1.0	6.4	−2.2	−0.2	2.2	3.9	1.2	1.9
cpi	1.0	10.6	−3.5	−0.3	3.6	6.3	1.9	3.1
p	1.0	10.4	−3.9	0.0	3.4	5.9	1.8	2.9
		in constant prices						
Y_a	7.654	6.2	−0.3	−2.6	3.7	6.4	2.0	3.2
Y_w	8.699	−7.5	4.2	−0.9	−0.9	−0.5	−0.5	−0.2
Y_z	5.405	−6.4	4.2	0.0	0.5	2.5	0.3	1.5
Y_f	23.406	−2.9	2.7	−1.2	0.8	2.1	0.4	1.1
Y_m	26.251	−2.8	2.6	−0.7	0.9	2.2	0.5	1.3
		share in GDP at factor cost						
Y_a	0.327	0.358	0.317	0.322	0.337	0.341	0.332	0.334
Y_w	0.372	0.354	0.377	0.373	0.365	0.362	0.368	0.367
Y_z	0.231	0.223	0.234	0.234	0.230	0.232	0.231	0.232
ΣN_{gi}	0.070	0.066	0.071	0.071	0.068	0.065	0.069	0.068

Table 6.1 *Continued*

	Base–Run	N–1	N–2	N–3	N–4	N–5	N–6	N–7
		percentage of GDP at market prices						
S_p	14.62	14.55	14.64	14.57	14.76	14.65	14.67	14.62
S_g	−1.07	−1.60	−0.64	−0.89	−1.52	−0.76	−1.28	−0.82
H	2.37	2.12	2.50	2.59	2.32	1.42	2.35	2.38
$Q + Q_a$	9.99	9.77	9.94	10.23	9.76	9.52	9.86	9.74
I	20.95	19.91	21.21	21.41	20.45	20.06	20.69	21.07
$\Delta\, st$	4.95	4.93	5.23	5.09	4.87	4.77	4.91	4.85
		share in gross savings						
Y_a	0.133	0.154	0.126	0.127	0.141	0.146	0.137	0.137
Y_w	0.265	0.265	0.263	0.260	0.267	0.269	0.268	0.261
Y_z	0.166	0.167	0.165	0.163	0.175	0.174	0.168	0.166
H	0.092	0.086	0.095	0.098	0.092	0.057	0.092	0.092
S_g	−0.041	−0.064	−0.024	−0.034	−0.060	−0.031	−0.050	−0.032
$Q + Q_a$	0.386	0.393	0.376	0.386	0.385	0.384	0.385	0.376
		share in net private savings						
Y_a	0.236	0.263	0.228	0.232	0.242	0.248	0.240	0.242
Y_w	0.470	0.452	0.475	0.472	0.458	0.457	0.468	0.463
Y_z	0.294	0.285	0.297	0.296	0.301	0.296	0.292	0.295
		share in government expenditure						
$\Sigma_i p_i g_i$	0.190	0.187	0.192	0.197	0.189	0.188	0.188	0.189
$w_g l_g$	0.274	0.275	0.274	0.278	0.274	0.273	0.270	0.274
V	0.097	0.092	0.100	0.099	0.095	0.093	0.095	0.095
$\overline{V}$	0.121	0.114	0.124	0.124	0.119	0.116	0.130	0.119
$(1-\phi_z)Q$	0.181	0.178	0.183	0.188	0.180	0.179	0.179	0.180
Z	0.000	−0.013	0.000	0.000	−0.004	−0.007	−0.002	−0.004
U_1	0.101	0.102	0.102	0.103	0.102	0.104	0.101	0.103
U_2	0.026	0.034	0.017	0.027	0.029	0.031	0.027	0.029
U_3	0.009	0.031	−0.002	−0.016	0.015	0.023	0.012	0.014
		share in government revenue						
R_1	0.616	0.626	0.614	0.612	0.639	0.627	0.619	0.622
R_2	0.109	0.109	0.110	0.110	0.087	0.113	0.110	0.111
$\Sigma\, N_{gi}$	0.275	0.265	0.276	0.278	0.274	0.260	0.271	0.266

Note: for a list of variables included in the table, see next page.

Table 6.1
List of Variables

x_i	production of commodity i, $i = 1, .., 9$.
p_i	market price of commodity i, $i = 1, .., 9$.
w_i	nominal wage rate in sector i, $i = 6, .., 9$.
w_g	nominal wage rate in the public sector.
cpi	consumer price index.
p	GDP deflator.
Y_a	agricultural income (in constant prices).
Y_w	non–agricultural wage income (in constant prices).
Y_z	non–agricultural mark–up income (in constant prices).
Y_f	GDP at factor cost (in constant prices).
Y_m	GDP at market prices (in constant prices).
$\Sigma_i N_{gi}$	revenue from public enterprises.
S_p	net private savings.
S_g	net public savings.
H	current account deficit (foreign savings).
Q	non–agricultural depreciation.
Q_a	agricultural depreciation.
I	gross fixed capital formation.
$\Delta\ st$	change in stocks.
$\Sigma_i\ p_i g_i$	government consumption.
$w_g l_g$	government wage bill.
V	public interest payments.
$\bar{V}$	public transfer payments to non–agricultural wage earners.
$(1-\phi_z)Q$	public depreciation.
Z	cost of public procurement.
U_1	producers' subsidies.
U_2	food subsidies.
U_3	export subsidies.
R_1	indirect tax receipts.
R_2	direct tax receipts.

quite rapidly, supply–side adjustments requiring a reallocation of resources, investment for capacity expansion and so on, typically involve much more time to materialise. Thus, the speed of adjustment is typically much lower on the supply than on the demand side, especially in agriculture.

Of course, one can argue that – in contrast to what happened in the experiments – the government will respond to the inflation triggered off by an agricultural shortfall by increasing foodgrain availability, either by running down foodgrain stocks or by increasing imports. However, government's capacity to release food stocks or import foodgrains is often severely constrained. Consider the case of public food stocks which generally are not allowed to decline below the level needed to cover contingencies. Hence, in a situtaion of recurrent harvest failures, the government may show great reluctance in running down stocks (Krishnaji, 1990). If a demand increase for agricultural goods cannot be met internally, one may resort to importing agricultural commodities. This may not be feasible because of one or both of the following two reasons. First, if the magnitudes involved are large – as they are for large economies such as the Indian – the growth of agricultural imports will soon reach a point where the world market can no longer meet the country's excess demand for agricultural goods. This is because the amount of foodgrains traded internationally constitutes only a small part of the total domestic demand for foodgrains in large economies. For example, the total world trade in rice is only 10 to 15 million tonnes per annum, while India alone consumes about 65 million tonnes per year. This implies that a mere 10 per cent shortage in India amounts to nearly three–fifths of the total world trade (Bhalla, 1991). Second, the economy may not be able to earn enough foreign exchange to finance the required amount of agricultural imports, *i.e.* the so–called foreign exchange constraint may become binding, and, hence, the possibilities of transforming the domestic product–mix through international trade have to be regarded as limited (Sen, 1981).

In these circumstances, measures to increase non–agricultural production, employment and income without raising agricultural output are all inflationary. Therefore, the agricultural sector has to be able to increase its production at a correct proportion to the increase in real GDP to sustain the growth process in non–agriculture. Hence, at the policy level, agriculture's strategic role is paramount and the key question, therefore, is on the choice of policy instruments to be used to induce the required agricultural output increase. This question is addressed in the next section.

6.3 *Agricultural Policy Experiments: The Short Term*

Section 6.3.1 discusses the major instruments of agricultural price policy and raises a number of specific issues relating to the three subsidy schemes. In 6.3.2, the various policy scenarios are defined and their implications examined. Section 6.3.3 concludes.

6.3.1 Issues in Pricing and Subsidising

The experiments are grouped into three categories – fertiliser subsidy experiments, foodgrain procurement experiments, and food distribution experiments. This section describes the existing schemes as a background to the policy experiments in the next section.

(i) Fertiliser Subsidy

Government control in fertiliser distribution and pricing has been in existence ever since the establishment of the Central Fertiliser Pool in 1944. However, fertilisers were not subsidised until 1973–74, when following the rise in import prices of fertilisers, a subsidy was provided for the first time. Trends in the budget subsidy on fertilisers since 1973–74 are given in Table 6.2. In 1977, a fertiliser subsidy scheme was initiated via the Retention Price Scheme (RPS) for fertilisers. Under this scheme, the government fixes up 'fair' ex–factory prices for each type of fertiliser and for each fertiliser plant. The ex–factory price for a given product and plant is so fixed as to provide a return of 12 per cent (post–tax) on net worth on the basis of manufacturing units achieving the stipulated level of capacity utilisation of 80 per cent (recently revised to 90 per cent) and fulfilling the consumption norms regarding raw materials and maintenance costs. A uniform price inclusive of freight is charged to farmers across the country for any given amount of fertiliser. Under the RPS, the domestic fertiliser subsidy burden increased from Rs. 107 crore in 1977–78 to Rs. 1600 crore in 1985–86, in which year the share of fertiliser subsidy amounted to 41.5 per cent of total subsidy expenditure. The burden of fertiliser subsidies has increased further during 1985–86 to 1989–90 (Table 6.2). This increase in subsidy outlays has been the result of the rise in fertiliser consumption following the green revolution and a sharp rise in oil prices after 1979–80 (and again in 1990–91).

Under the RPS, there are three elements to the fertiliser subsidy. First, a subsidy is paid to the domestic producers of fertilisers equal to the difference between the retention price and the selling price of fertilisers. Second, a subsidy is paid to the farmers equal to the difference between the selling price and the import costs of fertilisers. The third element is the cost involved in the supply of fertilisers to the farmers including handling charges, freight charges, marketing expenses, and dealers' margins. The details of these three elements are not separately available. It is difficult to estimate them with accuracy because a major part of the fertiliser subsidy is in the form of intra–governmental transfers from the Department of Fertilisers in the Ministry of Agriculture to other public sector undertakings such as the Indian Railways, the Food Corporation of India, and Port Trust authorities. Only few estimates of the amount of subsidy received by the farmers are available of which those by Gulati and Sharma (1990a) are probably the most recent. They use international fertiliser prices as the opportunity costs faced by the economy, indicating the prices which the farmers would have paid under 'free trade'. In their approach, the fertiliser subsidy amounts to the difference between the international price and the price paid by the farmers, adjusted for transport costs. According to their estimates, 47.7 per cent of the average budget subsidy for fertilisers during 1981–82 to 1989–90 accrued directly to the farmers, the remaining 52.3 per cent going to the fertiliser industry and/or feedstock[5] supplying agencies.

Fertiliser policy has been governed by the twin objectives to make available fertilisers at a fair and affordable price to the farmers to encourage intensive, high–yielding cultivation, and to ensure fair returns on

***Table* 6.2**
Total and Per Tonne Subsidy on Domestic and Imported Fertilisers
(Rs. Crores)

| | Imported Fertiliser | | Domestic Fertiliser | | Total |
	Total	Per Tonne (Rs)	Total	Per Tonne (Rs)	
1973–74	33	265			33
1974–75	371	2316			371
1975–76	242	1555			242
1976–77	52	495	60	252	112
1977–78	159	1071	107	401	266
1978–79	169	848	173	588	342
1979–80	282	1406	321	1076	603
1980–81	335	1214	170	566	505
1981–82	100	490	281	687	381
1982–83	53	468	550	1249	603
1983–84	141	1041	900	1985	1041
1984–85	727	2006	1200	2317	1927
1985–86	450	1324	1600	2780	2050
1986–87	197	855	1700	2405	1897
1987–88	160	1626	2050	2875	2210
1988–89	250	1555	3000	3347	3250
1989–90 (BE)	530	–	3121	3320	3651

Source: Gulati and Sharma (1990a), Table (1).
Note: Per tonne subsidy on imported fertilisers is obtained by dividing total subsidy on imported fertilisers by imports of fertilisers in terms of nutrients. Similarly, per tonne subsidy on domestic fertilisers is obtained by dividing total subsidy on domestic fertilisers by total production of fertilisers in terms of nutrients. For 1989–90, per tonne subsidy on domestic fertilisers is based on targetted fertiliser production (BE = Budget Estimate).

---

[5] Feedstocks of fertiliser plants include natural gas, naphta, coal, and fuel oil. Production and pricing of most of the feedstocks are under government control.

Table 6.3
Regional Characteristics of Fertiliser Consumption, 1985-86

State	Fertiliser Consumption as % of All–India Fertiliser Consumption	Gross Cropped Area as % of All–India Gross Cropped Area	Per hectare Fertiliser Consumption (Kg./Hect.)
Andhra Pradesh	10.3	6.9	66.3
Assam	0.2	2.1	4.7
Bihar	5.7	5.9	48.9
Gujarat	4.8	5.8	40.2
Haryana	4.2	3.1	65.4
Himachal Pradesh	0.2	0.6	24.4
Jammu & Kashmir	0.3	0.6	35.7
Karnataka	6.3	6.6	48.4
Kerala	1.6	1.6	49.4
Madhya Pradesh	5.0	12.7	19.3
Maharashtra	7.7	11.6	31.6
Orissa	1.6	5.0	14.7
Punjab	12.6	4.0	157.4
Rajasthan	2.5	9.8	11.7
Tamil Nadu	7.7	4.0	99.4
Uttar Pradesh	22.5	14.3	78.7
West Bengal	4.7	4.3	52.1
All–India	100.0	100.0	48.4

Notes: (1) Figures on gross cropped area relate to 1984–85; (2) Figures on per hectare fertiliser consumption were estimated on the basis of area figures relating to 1983–84.
Source: Ministry of Agriculture (1986a).

Table 6.4
Fertiliser Use by Size of Farm, 1976-77

Size group	% of Irrigated Area with Chemical Fertiliser		% of Unirrigated Area with Chemical Fertiliser		% of Total Area Operated
Marginal (Less than 1 hectare)	17.1	(138)	17.8	(97)	10.7
Small (1.00 to 1.99 hectares)	16.7	(125)	15.1	(110)	12.8
Semi–medium (2.00 to 3.99 hectares)	24.2	(125)	24.0	(91)	19.9
Medium (4.00 to 9.99 hectares	28.2	(121)	27.0	(99)	30.4
Large (10 hectares and more)	13.7	(126)	16.1	(88)	26.2
All sizes	100.0	(126)	100.0	(97)	100.0

Note: Figures in parentheses are fertiliser intensities.
Source: Parikh and Suryanarayana (1989), Tables A.1 and A.2.

investment in fertiliser production to attract more capital to this sector. Both these objectives have been achieved to a great extent. With respect to the latter, particularly during the 1980s the RPS attracted higher investment by protecting industry from internal competition and from external shocks, and by offering a guaranteed return on capital employed; as a result, fertiliser production capacity registered a substantial expansion. With respect to the former objective, it must be remembered that it was not only the increase in fertiliser use that was responsible for the growth of agricultural output. Other factors including the expansion of irrigated area and the spread of higher yielding varieties contributed (probably more than fertiliser input) to agricultural growth. Fertiliser subsidies have not succeeded in spreading the use of fertilisers throughout the country. In 1985–86, three states, notably Uttar Pradesh, the Punjab, and Andhra Pradesh, accounted for 45.5 per cent of fertiliser consumption, while they had only 25.2 per cent of gross cultivated area (Table 6.3). Per hectare use of fertiliser also varied widely across states as is shown in the same table. The distribution of fertiliser use by farm size is given in Table 6.4. The differences in the intensities of fertiliser use by farmers of different size holdings that are shown in the same table, are small.

(*ii*)   *Procurement and Minimum Support Pricing*

It was not until 1965, when the Agricultural Prices Commission (APC) was established, that a cohesive and systematic fixation of support/procurement prices and quantities started. Since its inception, the APC has been recommending prices for various crops, the number of which has been increasing. Today, its recommendations cover 20 commodities which account for over 88 per cent of agricultural output in terms of value and over 80 per cent in terms of area. In 1980, the terms of reference of the commission were revised, stipulating that the commission should explicitly take into account the changes in the barter terms of trade between agricultural and non–agricultural products. In 1985, the commission was renamed as the Commission for Agricultural Costs and Prices (CACP). The commission bases its recommendations regarding the level of procurement prices on the following criteria: (*i*) cost of production; (*ii*) input–output price parity; (*iii*) trends in market prices; (*iv*) inter–crop price parity; (*v*) effect on the industrial cost structure; (*vi*) effect on the general price level; (*vii*) effect on the cost of living; and (*viii*) international market prices. How each of these criteria enters into the price fixation exercise is not spelt out by the CACP. On the basis of the CACP recommendations, the central government fixes the level of procurement prices.

Procurement prices are announced in advance of the crop output and serve the purpose of ensuring minimum support prices to farmers. Procurement prices may be regarded as an offer price at which the government is willing to buy

Table 6.5
Statewise Shares in Rice and Wheat Procurement
and in Total Public Distribution, 1985–86

	Rice Procurement as % of All–India Rice Procurement	Wheat Procurement as % of All–India Wheat Procurement	Share in PDS
Andhra Pradesh	16.0		8.8
Assam			4.3
Bihar			4.0
Haryana	10.6	22.2	
Karnataka			6.2
Kerala			10.1
Madhya Pradesh	5.8		2.5
Maharashtra			8.5
Punjab	42.5	61.5	1.4
Tamil Nadu	9.7		13.6
Uttar Pradesh	10.8	15.2	6.2
West Bengal	0.7		12.2

Note: Share in PDS refers to public distribution of rice and wheat.
Source: Ministry of Agriculture (1988a).

any amount of grain from the farmers in years of good harvest when, in the absence of support operations, the market prices may fall below the cost of production (Krishnaji, 1990). Usually, the market price of a particular commodity is not allowed to fall below this level. In years of poor harvest, when the procurement price is below the market price, levies are imposed and farmers are obliged to sell a part of their production at the procurement price to government agencies. The difference between the two prices constitutes a tax on the farmers. In years of abundant harvest, the reverse holds true and farmers are in fact subsidised. More often than not, the difference between the procurement price and the market price is not large enough during the post–harvest period to induce farmers to sell in the 'open market' instead of selling to the government. Farmers' decision to withhold their surplus in anticipation of selling it at a higher price in the lean season is strongly influenced by the costs entailed in retaining the stocks. Such costs include storage expenses, loss of interest, risk of fire, and adverse weather. Most farmers either are forced or find it profitable to sell soon after the harvest as is indicated by the market arrival pattern.[6] It is to be noted that procurement prices are generally higher than costs of production. Thus after having paid for all costs of production (including land rent, imputed family labour, interest on fixed capital, and depreciation allowances), farmers are given an extra margin. The underlying cost–plus

---

[6] More than 63% of wheat and 53% of rice arrives in the market during the first quarter of their respective marketing years. See Gulati and Sharma (1990).

method of procurement pricing has enabled farmers to transfer cost increases onto agricultural prices, often pushing these prices to levels which the market finds difficult to sustain. It is in this sense that the guarantee of a return over and above costs has ensured that there is no disincentive to choosing high–cost technologies. In turn, consumers (mainly urban) have been compensated for the rise in agricultural prices by increases in food subsidies under the Public Distribution System (PDS).

Over time, the scope of the public procurement system has steadily increased. Between 1965–66 and 1987–88, while output of wheat grew at an annual rate of 6 per cent, its procurement grew at an annual rate of 12.3 per cent. Corresponding figures for rice are 2.9 and 6.3 per cent respectively. The bulk of the procurement came from farmers in surplus areas, where the demand for self–consumption had already been met, and any further increase in output therefore had to be disposed of in the market. In deficit areas where the demand for self–consumption is relatively high, the rise in production did not lead to a commensurate increase in procurement. Table 6.5 gives the statewise distribution of rice and wheat procurement and distribution for the model's base year 1985–86. During most of the Seventh Plan period, this distribution changed only marginally.[7]

(iii)   Public Distribution Policy

The PDS was initiated in 1939 with the objective to check the speculative tendencies of grain merchants during the second world war. During the war and the immediate post–war years, severe shortages of essential commodities led to statutory rationing in metropolitan cities and major urban areas, with no private trade allowed in these commodities. Subsequently, almost all the committees and commissions that were set up to look into matters of foodgrain distribution emphasized and recommended its expansion and efficient functioning (Gulati, 1987:96). The sources of supply for the PDS are purchases from domestic producers (procurement) and imports. Imports constituted over 60 per cent of the grains distributed during thirteen of the seventeen years of the period 1951–1967, when access to concessional imports of foodgrains (mainly wheat) was available. During this period, domestic public purchases were limited to the needs of the PDS. The system of procurement changed radically under the New Agricultural Strategy with procurement prices taking on the role of support prices and government buying whatever is offered at the announced procurement price, regardless of the offtake from the PDS. The result has been the accumulation of huge stocks of foodgrains with the

---

[7] The Punjab, Haryana and Uttar Pradesh (mainly western) accounted for 99.3% of total procurement of wheat during the triennium ending 1988–89. The share of these states has remained high ever since the start of procurement operations. In the procurement of rice, Punjab, Haryana, Uttar Pradesh, and Andhra Pradesh had a share of 82% during the triennium ending 1985–86. See Gulati and Sharma (1990).

government, which are carried at a considerable cost in terms of storage and opportunity costs. Hence, the growth in food subsidies is not only due to the increase in issues, but also to the increased levels of public food stocks which are a result of the growing levels of procurement. The consumer subsidy is allocated to the Food Corporation of India to meet the costs of procurement, storage and distribution.[8]

As a part of the PDS, consumers in major cities are provided ration cards against which they are entitled to purchase upto a certain quantity of foodgrains at prices below the market prices. These issue prices (the price at which foodgrains are issued to the States and Union Territories for sale in the ration and 'Fair Price' Shops) are fixed on the recommendation of the CACP. Ration cards are issued to every urban consumer, irrespectively of income. During the 1980s, some state governments have extended the PDS to the rural areas on a regular basis (see Rao *et al.*, 1988:103–125).

6.3.2   Short-Term Simulation Results

In this section, the comparative statics implications of different agricultural policy options are examined in terms of their consequences for sectoral production, prices and wages, gross domestic product and its distribution, the balance on the public revenue account, the balance on the nation's current account, private savings, gross domestic investment, and the inflation rate. A catalogue of the short–term experiments is given in Table 6.6. The relevant indicators are given in Tables 6.8 (fertiliser subsidy experiments), 6.9 (procurement policy experiments), and 6.10 (food subsidisation experiments).

Experiment F – 1:
Increase in the Rate of Fertiliser Subsidy to 50 per cent

The level of fertiliser consumption in India was 48.4 kg. per hectare in 1985–86, which was low as compared to the consumption levels of other major agricultural areas of the world.[9] Even within India, there are large disparities in statewise consumption of fertilisers (Table 6.3). One may infer from these facts that there exists a large gap between actual and potential levels of fertiliser use. In these circumstances, lowering the price of fertiliser through subsidisation may induce an increase in the use of fertilisers. The first policy experiment traces out the effects of an increase in the fertiliser subsidy rate from 27.3 to 50.0 per cent.

---

[8] Currently, the central government procures and supplies essential commodities to States and Union Territories. These include wheat, rice, other cereals, sugarcane, imported edible oils, soft coke, kerosene oil, and controlled cloth. The present analysis is confined to foodgrains only.

[9] For example, 1985–86 per hectare fertiliser consumption in kg. was 55.5 in Bangladesh, 59.3 in Pakistan, 347.3 in Egypt, 134.9 in the United Kingdom, 182.6 in France and 122.1 in Italy. Source: Ministry of Agriculture (1988a).

Table 6.6
Catalogue of Short-Term Agricultural Policy Experiments

Designations	Descriptions

Fertiliser Experiments

$F-1$	$\sigma_6 = -0.5$
$F-1.1$	$\sigma_6 = -0.7$; $f_{ni} = 0$ for $i = 1, 2, 3$.
$F-1.2$	$\sigma_6 = -0.5$; j_{ga} is reduced.
$F-1.3$	$\sigma_6 = -0.5$; p_i^* is reduced by 15%.
$F-1.4$	$\sigma_6 = -0.5$; τ_z is increased.
$F-2$	$\sigma_6 = 0.0$;
$F-2.1$	$\sigma_6 = 0.0$; $(p_6/p_i) = 1$ for $i = 1, 2$.

Procurement Experiments

$P-1$	p_i^* is raised by 10% for $i = 1, 2$.
$P-1.1$	p_i^* is raised by 10% for $i = 1, 2, 3$; $\sigma_6 = 0$.
$P-2$	$\bar{z}_i$ is raised by 20% for $i = 1, 2$.
$P-2.1$	$\bar{z}_i$ and f_{ni} are raised by 20% for $i = 1, 2, 3$.
$P-3$	$\bar{z}_i = 0$ and $f_{ni} = 0$ for $i = 1, 2, 3$.
$P-3.1$	$\bar{z}_i = 0$ and $f_{ni} = 0$ for $i = 1, 2, 3$; $\sigma_6 = 0$.
$P-3.2$	$\bar{z}_i = 0$ and $f_{ni} = 0$ for $i = 1, 2, 3$; $\sigma_6 = -0.5$;

Food Subsidisation Experiments

$S-1$	$f_{ni} = 0$ for $i = 1, 2, 3$.
$S-1.1$	$f_{ni} = 0$ and σ_i is raised for $i = 1, 2, 3$.
$S-2$	f_{ni} is raised by 10% for $i = 1, 2, 3$.
$S-2.1$	f_{ni} is raised by 10% for $i = 1, 2, 3$ without minimum support pricing.
$S-2.2$	f_{ni} is raised by 20% for $i = 1, 2, 3$; $\sigma_6 = 0$.
$S-3$	$\bar{p}_i$ is reduced by 10% for $i = 1, 2, 3$.
$S-3.1$	$\bar{p}_i$ is reduced by 10% for $i = 1, 2, 3$; $\sigma_6 = -0.5$

Note: σ_6 is the rate of fertiliser subsidy; f_{ni} is the quantity of foodgrains issued from the Fair Price Shops; j_{ga} is real public agricultural investment; p_i^* is the procurement price of crop i; τ_z is the direct tax rate on non–agricultural mark–up income; $\bar{z}_i$ is the quantity of public procurement of crop i; p_6 is the market price for fertilisers; p_i is the market price of commodity i; and $\bar{p}_i$ is the subsidised consumer price of commodity i.

In the model, the fall in the market price of fertiliser relative to the market prices of crops induces farmers to apply more fertiliser per hectare of all crops. The increase in per hectare fertiliser input is highest in wheat production. As a result, crop yield levels and (with unchanged area allocation across crops) levels of crop production rise. The short–run (general equilibrium) elasticity of wheat production with respect to the (relative) fertiliser price is –0.24. Corresponding elasticities for all crops are given in Table 6.7.

In a partial equilibrium context, with demand remaining unchanged, an agricultural production increase will generally lead to lower agricultural prices. In a general equilibrium context, the extra production generates extra income and, hence, additional demand which puts upward pressure on agricultural prices, (to some extent) mitigating the initial price fall. Prices of other food crops, commercial crops, and other agricultural products (with no fertiliser response at all) increase. Through additional public procurement, prices of rice and wheat remain at their minimum support levels. Government procurement operations further augment the income earned in agriculture. Combined with the rise in agriculture's demand for non–agricultural intermediate inputs, the increase in agriculture's consumption and investment demand results in higher capacity utilisation rates in the non–agricultural sectors. Higher non–agricultural production results in higher wage and mark–up incomes and, hence, contributes to the increase in demand, both for agricultural and non–agricultural commodities.

Non–agricultural market prices (with the exception of the fertiliser price) slightly increase, mainly due to the rise in the price of other agricultural products (which are major inputs in consumer goods production) and the rise in (indexed) nominal wages. The GDP deflator increases by 1.6 per cent. In terms of the consumer price index, the inflation rate is 2.0 per cent. Real GDP at factor cost increases by 2.0 per cent. The agricultural sector benefits most from this increase, its share in GDP at factor cost increases from 32.7 to 33.4 per cent. Within the agricultural sector, the income gains are largely made in wheat cultivation which implies that additional income accrues to only a few states (including the Punjab, Haryana, and western Uttar Pradesh) in which wheat production is concentrated, and, within these states, to the larger, more commercialised farm households.

With the inflation, the share in GDP at market prices of gross domestic investment declines from 25.9 per cent in the base run to 25.7 per cent. The consequent decline in the share in GDP of savings can be attributed to two factors. First, net public savings decline (from –1.1 to –1.2 per cent of GDP). As a result of the rise in the rate of fertiliser subsidy, public current expenditure increases. This initial increase is augmented by the additional expenditure on procurement operations and (due to the production increases in sectors other than the fertiliser sector) on producers' subsidies. Second, with the inflation, the share in GDP of depreciation

Table 6.7
Elasticity of Crop Production with respect to Fertiliser Price

	Calculated from Table 6.8	Narayana & Parikh (1987)	Sirohi (1984)
Rice	−0.13	−0.207[*]	−0.177
Wheat	−0.24	−0.279	−0.120
Other Food Crops	−0.05		
Commercial Crops	−0.09		
Jowar		−0.016[*]	
Bajra		−0.019[*]	
Maize		−0.130	

(*) Determined on the assumption that the price elasticity of fertiliser demand is −1 for all crops.

allowances declines from 10.0 per cent in the base run to 9.8 per cent. The impact of the policy change on foreign savings consists of two opposing effects. On the one hand, with the rise in real GDP, complementary imports of intermediate inputs rise, which leads to a deterioration of the country's current account or, in other words, an increase in foreign savings. On the other hand, with the inflation, the share in GDP of foreign savings declines (see experiment $N-1$). The net effect of the policy change is a marginal increase in the share of foreign savings.

One may conclude that the effect of the policy change on crop production is far from impressive, as follows from the rather low elasticities of crop production with respect to the (relative) fertiliser price, and that an increase in the rate of fertiliser subsidy has a mixed impact on the country's macro–economy. What is particularly important is that, in a situation in which the government operates a procurement/minimum support price scheme, market prices for rice and wheat are not allowed to fall to the extent they would have declined in a situation without such a scheme. The difference in price between these two situations accrues as income to the agricultural sector and is paid for as a subsidy by the government. The income gains following the policy change are concentrated in wheat and (irrigated) rice production. It seems reasonable to conclude that a policy of increased fertiliser subsidisation will augment the already unequal regional and socio–economic distribution of agricultural income.

Experiment $F-1.1$:
Using the Expenditure on Food Subsidies for an Increase in the Rate of Fertiliser Subsidy instead of for the PDS

One may wonder what will happen when the resources allocated to the public distribution system are spent on fertiliser subsidies instead. In the model, subsidies can be eliminated either by eliminating the quota of subsidised food or, equivalently, by raising the subsidised prices to the level of market prices. In either case, the same budget expenditure is reallocated to increased government spending on fertiliser subsidies. The rate of fertiliser subsidy increases from 50 per cent to 72.3 per cent.[10]

The increase in the rate of fertiliser subsidy raises per hectare fertiliser consumption, raising crop yields, cropwise production and agricultural income (Table 6.8). The degree of capacity underutilisation in domestic fertiliser sector is not large enough to meet the increase in agriculture's demand for fertiliser inputs and the fertiliser demand in excess of domestic production capacity is met by additional imports. The rise in agricultural income leads to an expansion of the domestic market for final goods. As a result, capacity utilisation rates in the non–agricultural sectors improve. The increase in non–agricultural production generates additional wage and mark–up income, part of which is used for final demand. Specifically, demand for foodgrains increases following the elimination of food subsidies under the PDS, which leads to a strong upward pressure on food prices, the prices of rice and wheat increasing by more than 37 per cent. These price rises result in a substantial increase in the consumer price index (of 9.6 per cent) and in (indexed) nominal wages in non–agriculture. With the increase in agricultural and non–agricultural production, real GDP at factor cost increases significantly by 5.2 per cent. Distributionally, the agriculturalists benefit most from the inflation, triggered off by the policy change. The share of agricultural income in GDP at factor cost increases dramatically from 32.7 to 36.7 per cent. Non–agricultural wage earners are the main victims of the inflation, the share in GDP of their income declines from 37.2 per cent in the base run to only 34.8 per cent.

With the inflation, the share in GDP at market prices of gross domestic fixed investment declines considerably from 21.0 to 19.1 per cent. The decline can be attributed to the fall in private non–agricultural investment demand in real terms, caused by the fact that the increase in the rate of inflation is higher than the rate of growth of non–agricultural mark–up income. As such, the decline in real private investment demand in non–agriculture exerts a dampening influence on the inflation rate. Because of the rise in the share in GDP of aggregate stock changes, the decline in the share in GDP of gross domestic investment is much smaller, i.c. 0.2 percentage points. Still, savings have to adjust. With respect to the different sources of savings, the following observations can be made. First, net public savings increase following the policy change. Current revenue of the government increases due to higher mobilisation of direct and indirect taxes (in particular import

---

[10] It should be noted in interpreting the results that the system of public foodgrain procurement is maintained, while the PDS is abolished. The government can decide to dispose of the procured grains in the world market, although there are numerous difficulties involved in the export of foodgrains (see Section 1.5).

duties), and due to higher revenue from the procurement tax.[11] Simultaneously, current expenditure increases (although less than proportionate to current receipts) due to higher outlays on producers' subsidies and export subsidies.[12] Second, the share in GDP of foreign savings increases from 2.4 to 2.5 per cent. This rise is the net result of two opposite effects, *i.c.* a decrease in the share of foreign savings accompanying the increase in inflation, on the one hand, and an increase in the share of foreign savings on account of higher fertiliser imports and higher intermediate input imports, on the other. Third, with the inflation, the share in GDP of depreciation allowances declines. And finally, with the decline in the share in GDP of mark–up income, the share in GDP of net private savings declines.

Policy $F - 1.1$ is considerably inflationary in terms of the consumer price index. The inflationary impact on the economy is augmented by the rise in nominal wages, indexed to the consumer price index. The public revenue deficit declines – mainly due to the elimination of expenditure on food subsidies and the increase in revenue from the procurement tax.

Experiment $F - 1.2$:
Increase in the Rate of Fertiliser Subsidy up to 50 per cent and an Equivalent Reduction in the Level of Public Investment in Agriculture

While the government budget has come under severe pressure during the 1980s, even in years bringing good monsoons, the share of fertiliser subsidies in total public expenditure has been increasing. To neutralise the further increase in budgetary pressures arising from a rise in the subsidy rate on fertilisers, the government may reduce its investment outlays in agriculture. A simulation was performed in which the rate of fertiliser subsidy was raised from 27.3 to 50 per cent, while public agricultural investment was reduced by the same amount as by which the fertiliser subsidy burden rises.

The increase in the rate of fertiliser subsidy provides a stimulus to crop production which leads to downward pressure on crop prices. The prices of rice and wheat are kept at their minimum support levels by a substantial quantity increase in public procurement. Prices of other food crops and commercial crops decline, due to which the mark–up price of consumer goods (which are mainly produced in agro–based industries) also declines. Due to these price decreases, the amount of 'supernumerary' expenditure of both agricultural and non–agricultural consumers increases, implying an increase in consumer demand which, to some extent, mitigates the downward pressure on prices. Reducing investment expenditure proves to be effective in reducing the inflationary impact of an increase in the rate of fertiliser subsidy.

---

[11] The market prices of rice and wheat are substantially higher than their procurement prices. Consequently, farmers were taxed when selling their output of rice and wheat (at lower than market prices) to the government.

[12] The difference between domestic prices and world market prices increased. In the model, this difference is compensated by the government via variable export subsidies. Therefore, export subsidies increased.

Eventually, the impact of the policy change on the consumer price index is negative (−2.6 per cent). Hence, in contrast to in $F-1$, prices decline in experiment $F-1.2$ because of the simultaneous introduction of a demand management policy in which public agricultural investment is reduced by the same amount as by which the fertiliser subsidy burden rises. However, the fall in public investment in agriculture which leads to an immediate decline in the demand for capital (sector 7) goods, sets in motion a negative multiplier process, the result of which is a decline in real GDP at factor cost. With the deflation, the share in GDP at factor cost of non−agricultural wage income increases from 37.2 to 37.5 per cent, whereas the share in GDP of agricultural income declines from 32.7 to 32.3 per cent.

Following the reduction of public agricultural investment, the share in GDP at market prices of gross fixed investment declines from 21 to 20.6 per cent. Because the share in GDP of aggregate stock changes rises from 5 to 5.2 per cent, the share in GDP of gross domestic investment declines from 25.9 to 25.8 per cent. Savings adjust, mainly through a decline in net public savings. Government current expenditure increases more than current revenue, mainly on account of the higher fertiliser subsidy burden. The revenue deficit rises from 1.1 to 1.4 per cent of GDP. In sum, the immediate impact of a reduction in public investment is to reduce demand which, through the multiplier mechanism, leads to a considerable fall in real GDP. Its impact on the public revenue deficit is negative which stands in contrast to the outcomes of experiments $F-1$ and $F-1.1$. Finally, possible negative effects on GDP growth in the medium run which operate through a decline in irrigated area and cropping intensity, will be examined in Chapter 7.

Experiment $F-1.3$:
Increase in the Rate of Fertiliser Subsidy by 50 per cent and a Reduction in the Procurement Prices of Rice and Wheat by 15 per cent

One may try to curb the inflationary consequences of an increase in the rate of fertiliser subsidy (see $F-1$) by reducing the level of procurement/minimum support prices. To this end, a policy experiment was performed in which the level of the minimum support prices of rice and wheat was reduced by 15 per cent, while at the same time the rate of fertiliser subsidy was raised from 27.3 to 50 per cent.

The immediate impact of the policy change is deflationary which may be explained from the following three factors. First, the increase in the rate of fertiliser subsidy raises crop production which leads to downward pressure on crop prices. Second, the reduction of the procurement prices of rice and wheat enlarges the range within which market prices are allowed to balance supply and demand and, with the increase in crop supply, market prices decline. Third, because some of them are contractually obliged to deliver part of the produce to the Food Corporation, the reduction of the procurement prices leads to a loss of income for agriculturalists, reducing their demand which adds to the deflation. Following the policy change, all prices and wages decline, with the exception of the price of other agricultural products. Prices decline faster than (non–agricultural) wages.

The policy change has a mixed impact on non–agricultural production. On the one hand, with the fall in agricultural income, there is a decline in demand for non–agricultural products. On the other hand, demand increases due to the following factors. First, the increase in the rate of fertiliser subsidy raises fertiliser demand, stimulating fertiliser production. Second, the increase in crop output leads to a rise in agriculture's demand for non–agricultural intermediates. And finally, with the decline in crop prices, the amount of fixed consumer expenditure declines in money terms, which increases 'supernumerary' expenditure and, hence, consumer demand for non–agricultural (as well as agricultural) goods. In effect, the policy change raises both agricultural and non–agricultural production. Real GDP at factor cost increases by 1.4 per cent. The share in GDP at factor cost of agricultural income declines to 31.9 per cent; the share of non–agricultural wage income increases to 37.6 per cent.

With the deflation, the share in GDP at market prices of gross domestic investment rises from 25.9 per cent in the base run to 26.2 per cent. Investment–savings equality is re–established by the following adjustments. First, foreign savings rise, mainly due to higher complementary imports. Second, net public savings rise as a result of higher revenue from direct taxation, a decline in expenditure on export subsidies, and a rise in revenue from the procurement tax. Third, with the deflation, the share in GDP of depreciation allowances rises. And finally, net private savings increase, following the change in income distribution in favour of non–agricultural mark–up income.

Experiment F – 1.4
Increase in the Rate of Fertiliser Subsidy Financed by an Equivalent Increase in the Direct Tax Rate on Mark – up Income

To neutralise the negative budgetary impact of a rise in the subsidy rate on fertilisers, the government could raise additional revenue from direct taxation by increasing the direct tax rate on non–agricultural mark–up income. This is what is attempted in *F – 1.4* in which the direct tax rate on non–agricultural mark–up income increases from 13.1 to 17.1 per cent to finance the increase in expenditure on fertiliser subsidy. Note that this experiment implies a reallocation of resources *via* government channels from non–agriculture to agriculture.

Following the change in policy, crop production increases. With the increase in their supply, the prices of rice and wheat are kept at their minimum support levels through additional procurement operations. The increase in production and the rise in public procurement demand augment the income earned in the agricultural sectors. The increase in the farmers' demand for fertilisers raises the capacity utilisation in fertiliser production. Other non–agricultural sectors also benefit from the increase in crop supply and in agriculturalists' demand. Their capacity utilisation is, however, negatively affected by the fall in private non–agricultural demand, following the increase in the direct tax rate on non–agricultural mark–up income. In effect, real GDP at factor cost increases by 1.6 per cent. Distributionally, the impact of the policy experiment is to the benefit of the farmers. Their share in GDP increases from 32.7 to 33.1 per cent. The consumer price index increases by 0.5 per cent which suggests that the inflationary impact of the increase in the rate of fertiliser subsidy, which materialised under experiment F–1, can be contained at reasonable levels through an adequate fiscal policy response, $i.c.$ increasing the direct tax rate.

Due to the policy change, the government's budgetary position improves, the public revenue deficit declines from 1.1 to 0.9 per cent of GDP. The increase in net public savings mainly results from the rise in revenue from direct taxation and indirect taxation (following the increase in real GDP). The shares in GDP of the other savings sources are only slightly affected.

The outcome of this simulation experiment indicates that the financing of a higher rate of fertiliser subsidy by raising direct tax rates may be an economically feasible option to increase agricultural production, stimulate non–agricultural production, and raise the rate of growth of real GDP, while containing inflationary and budgetary pressures.

Experiment F – 2:
Removal of the Fertiliser Subsidy

Perhaps no other issue invokes so much debate as the one relating to the rising fertiliser subsidy burden. This is not surprising considering that the fertiliser subsidy alone amounted to Rs. 3651 crore in 1989–90 (BE) or 43 per cent of total subsidy outlays. Recently, the EAC (1989) expressed concern about the rising government expenditure, particularly pointing out the growing subsidy burden. Earlier, the Long Term Fiscal Policy document (Ministry of Finance, 1985a) explicitly singled out fertiliser subsidy as a major item of non–plan expenditure, saying that '... if subsidies continue to grow at the present rate, they will either be at the expense of developmental expenditures or they will lead to higher budget deficits ...'. In this context, it is important to search for options to reduce the fertiliser subsidy. Perhaps a beginning can be made by taking a look at the impact on the economy of the withdrawal of the fertiliser subsidy. The fertiliser subsidy can be removed by either raising prices charged to the farmers or by lowering the retention price paid to the fertiliser producers, or a combination of these policies. Here only the fertiliser subsidy removal through increasing the price charged to farmers is considered. The suppliers get the price they received before the policy change.

The immediate consequences of a removal of the fertiliser subsidy are twofold. First, farmers have to pay more for fertilisers – following the policy change, the fertiliser price increases by 30 per cent. Second, fertiliser use goes down and hence agricultural production declines, due to the reduction of per hectare fertiliser application and crop yields. Because crop supply declines more than demand, agricultural prices increase, particularly for rice and wheat, the production of which is relatively price–responsive. Since the consumption of food is price–inelastic to a relatively large degree, consumers spend more of their budgets on foodgrains, commensurately reducing their expenditure on other commodities. As a result, final demand for non–food commodities declines, particularly for 'other agricultural products', the price of which declines by 5.3 per cent.

With both intermediate and final demand declining, the capacity utilisation rates in non–agriculture decline. Because crop production also declines, the result of the policy change is a fall in real GDP at factor cost of 1.2 per cent. The inflationary pressure following the policy change is limited as is indicated by the increase in both the consumer price index and the GDP deflator of 0.1 per cent. Removal of the fertiliser subsidy has a positive impact on the public revenue deficit which declines from 1.1 to 0.9 per cent of GDP. The deficit on the nation's current account is only marginally affected by the policy change.

A few studies including Parikh and Suryanarayana (1989) and Bhide et al. (1986) have examined the impact of a reduction in the rate of fertiliser subsidy on agricultural production, income and prices. According to Parikh and Suryanarayana, withdrawal of the fertiliser subsidy by increasing the prices charged to farmers will lead to a 14 per cent reduction in fertiliser consumption and a decline of 3.4 per cent of foodgrains output in the short run, a larger decline than the one suggested by the outcome of $F-2$. The difference in outcomes can be explained for by the values of cropwise price elasticities of fertiliser demand, which Parikh and Suryanarayana assumed to be –1, but which (in absolute terms) are lower in the present model. In contrast to the outcome of $F-2$, according to their results, the growth rate of GDP measured at constant prices is not significantly affected by the withdrawal of the fertiliser subsidy. Their results further show that the withdrawal of the fertiliser subsidy makes the rural lower income groups worse off (not only in the short run, but even after a period of 10 years). Elimination of the fertiliser subsidy without any other associated policy is therefore not deemed desirable. Using an econometric model, Bhide et al. (1986) arrive at similar conclusions. They show that a 5 per cent increase in fertiliser prices (due to a reduction of the fertiliser subsidy rate) reduces both the growth rate of fertiliser consumption and of foodgrain production by half. They do not analyse the likely impact of this policy change on inflation nor do they deal with its impact on the government budget.

Experiment F – 2.1
Removal of the Fertiliser Subsidy while Maintaining the Base – run Ratio of the
Fertiliser Price relative to the Market Price of Rice and Wheat through
Appropriate Procurement Price Adjustment

The effect of the removal of the fertiliser subsidy on the level of crop production is negative. In an attempt to maintain cropwise output at its base–year level, while eliminating the fertiliser subsidy, the government may increase its procurement prices with the aim of keeping constant the base–year ratio of input (fertiliser) price to output (crop) price. Such a policy change implies a switch–over from input subsidies to output subsidies.

As can be seen from Table 6.8, the negative impact of this policy change on agricultural output is minimal. Crop outputs of rice and wheat remain unaffected, while the production of other food crops and commercial crops declines marginally. Cropwise yield levels and levels of fertiliser consumption also do not change much. To compensate farmers for the loss of input subsidy, procurement prices of rice and wheat are raised by 35 per cent and public procurement of rice is stepped up by 19.9 per cent and of wheat by 19.3 per cent. As a result of the policy change, market prices of rice and wheat increase by 35 per cent, of other food crops by 13.9 per cent, and of commercial crops by almost 13.7 per cent. Apart from the cost incurred on account of the extra procurement, the rise in market prices of foodgrains results in an almost doubling of public expenditure on food subsidies rom Rs. 1650 crore to Rs. 3223 crore, with the share of food subsidies in public expenditure increasing from 2.6 per cent in the base run to 4.8 per cent.

The policy change has several opposing effects on non–agricultural production. On the one hand, the rise in foodgrain prices leads to a rise in the consumer price index which, in turn, triggers off increases in non–agricultural wages and prices, which raises demand pressure. The consumer price index increases by 9.5 per cent. Demand is also augmented by the increase in agricultural income, resulting from the agricultural price increases. On the other hand, the rise in foodgrain prices substantially raises fixed consumer expenditure in money terms, since foodgrain consumption is to a relatively large extent 'committed' in nature, which, in turn, leads to a fall in 'supernumerary' expenditure and a decline in demand for non–agricultural goods – the demand of which is characterised by relatively large marginal budget shares. The net impact of both effects is a small increase in demand for non–agricultural products in real terms, which – apart from fertiliser output – leads to small increases in the levels of in non–agricultural production. Fertiliser production declines due to the fall in output of other food crops and commercial crops.

In the event, the policy change is contractionary. Real GDP at factor cost declines by 0.3 per cent, while its distribution changes in favour of the agricultural sector. The share of agricultural income in GDP increases from 32.7 to 36.0 per cent. Within the agricultural sector, the procurement subsidy most likely accrues to the surplus states. To the extent that the benefits from the fertiliser subsidy are more equally distributed across farm households of different size, the intra–sectoral distribution of agricultural income may have become more skewed. Moreover, the purchasing power of net–buyers of food is eroded by the sharp increases in foodgrain prices.

With the inflation, the share in GDP at market prices of gross domestic investment declines from 25.9 to 25.0 per cent (including an even larger decline in the share of gross domestic fixed investment). Restoration of the savings–investment balance requires the share in GDP of savings to decline. To this end, the shares in GDP of net public savings, foreign savings and depreciation allowance all decline. The shares of foreign savings and depreciation allowances decline with the inflation – as explained earlier. The share of net public savings falls due to the increase in government spending on food, fertiliser and export subsidies, wages, and items of final consumption, and the decline in revenue from public undertakings and from direct taxation (following the fall in the share in GDP of mark–up income).

The impact of the change–over from a regime of agricultural input subsidies to a regime of output price subsidisation is strongly inflationary. The policy change sets in motion a process of cost–push inflation which eventually results in inflation rates, almost reaching the two–digit level. Most likely, the policy change leads to a further rise in income inequality, both across regions and income groups.

Experiment P – 1:
Increase in the Procurement Prices of Rice and Wheat of 20 per cent

In the early 1980s, procurement price fixation started to take account of the changes in the terms of trade between the agricultural and the non–agricultural sectors – to guarantee some kind of parity between agricultural input costs and output prices. The arbitrariness in which the different elements have in practice entered procurement price fixation over the years has made it easy for those who argue for procurement price increases to invoke this or that principle of parity as the occassion demands (Krishnaji 1990). For example, if fertiliser prices are raised by the government, that alone is sufficient to ensure political mobilisation in favour of the demand for more remunerative procurement prices regardless of the total cost of production or market conditions. Upward adjustment in procurement prices may have considerable effects on the economy, however, as is shown by the outcome of the present policy experiment.

Aware of the higher procurement prices of rice and wheat, farmers start selling more of their produce at the procurement price to the Food Corporation which is obliged to buy. In effect, public procurement of rice and wheat is stepped up, which implies a reduction in the availability of rice and wheat in the market and, with unchanged demand, market prices of rice and wheat rise. The improvement in the prices of rice and wheat relative to the fertiliser price induces farmers to increase the per hectare input of fertiliser in the

Table 6.8
Results of the Fertiliser Policy Experiments

	Base-Run	F-1	F-1.1	F-1.2	F-1.3	F-1.4	F-2	F-2.1
		percentage change from initial base-run values						
x_1	1.884	2.7	10.6	0.1	1.9	2.8	-1.9	0.0
x_2	1.076	5.2	18.0	0.2	3.2	5.4	-3.1	0.0
x_3	0.941	0.9	2.2	-0.1	0.7	0.8	-0.8	-0.5
x_4	3.945	1.6	4.0	-0.3	1.4	1.5	-1.4	-1.0
x_6	0.413	12.0	35.2	-0.1	8.3	12.0	-7.7	-1.3
x_7	15.093	1.3	2.6	-2.6	0.8	0.9	-1.0	0.0
x_8	6.453	2.3	5.2	-1.6	0.7	1.5	-1.7	1.5
x_9	10.198	1.9	3.3	-1.7	1.0	1.2	-1.5	0.3
p_1	1.0	0.0	37.4	0.0	-8.9	0.0	5.8	35.0
p_2	1.0	0.0	37.4	0.0	-11.6	0.0	9.8	35.0
p_3	1.0	3.3	9.4	-5.4	-3.2	0.1	-0.1	13.9
p_4	1.0	0.9	0.6	-5.5	-4.5	-2.2	1.0	13.7
p_5	1.0	8.7	23.4	-6.8	1.6	5.1	-5.3	9.3
p_6	1.0	-23.2	-49.3	-1.2	-25.2	-24.4	30.0	35.0
p_7	1.0	0.9	3.5	-1.2	-0.7	0.2	-0.1	3.6
p_8	1.0	1.3	4.5	-2.3	-1.4	0.0	-0.1	6.1
p_9	1.0	1.0	4.3	-1.3	-0.9	0.3	-0.1	4.2
w_6	1.0	1.2	5.8	-1.6	-1.2	0.3	0.1	5.7
w_7	1.0	0.7	3.2	-0.9	-0.7	0.2	0.0	3.1
w_8	1.0	0.5	2.2	-0.6	-0.5	0.1	0.0	2.2
w_9	1.0	0.8	3.8	-1.1	-0.8	0.2	0.1	3.7
w_g	1.0	1.2	5.9	-1.6	-1.3	0.3	0.1	5.8
cpi	1.0	2.0	9.6	-2.6	-2.0	0.5	0.1	9.5
p	1.0	1.6	8.3	-2.4	-2.5	0.2	0.1	9.9
		in constant prices						
Y_a	7.654	4.2	17.9	-2.6	-1.0	2.8	-1.6	9.7
Y_w	8.699	0.7	-1.4	-0.2	2.5	0.9	-1.2	-5.3
Y_z	5.405	2.1	1.6	-2.1	2.6	1.6	-2.0	-3.5
Y_f	23.406	2.0	5.2	-1.3	1.4	1.6	-1.5	-0.3
Y_m	26.251	1.7	5.0	-1.5	1.1	1.2	-1.2	0.0
		share in GDP at factor cost						
Y_a	0.327	0.334	0.367	0.323	0.319	0.331	0.326	0.360
Y_w	0.372	0.367	0.348	0.375	0.376	0.369	0.373	0.353
Y_z	0.231	0.231	0.223	0.229	0.234	0.231	0.230	0.223
ΣN_{gi}	0.070	0.068	0.062	0.073	0.072	0.069	0.071	0.064

229

Table 6.8 *Continued*

	Base–Run	F–1	F–1.1	F–1.2	F–1.3	F–1.4	F–2	F–2.1
percentage of GDP at market prices								
S_p	14.62	14.68	14.53	14.60	14.65	14.58	14.55	14.59
S_g	−1.07	−1.18	−0.37	−1.38	−0.97	−0.88	−0.91	−1.34
H	2.37	2.39	2.46	2.35	2.45	2.41	2.33	2.18
$Q + Q_a$	9.99	9.77	9.12	10.23	10.02	9.86	10.08	9.53
I	20.95	20.60	19.10	20.60	21.23	20.79	21.02	19.64
Δst	4.95	5.05	6.63	5.21	4.93	5.18	5.03	5.33
share in gross domestic savings								
Y_a	0.133	0.139	0.153	0.132	0.129	0.135	0.132	0.155
Y_w	0.265	0.265	0.250	0.270	0.265	0.264	0.264	0.263
Y_z	0.166	0.168	0.162	0.165	0.166	0.162	0.163	0.162
H	0.092	0.093	0.096	0.091	0.094	0.093	0.090	0.088
S_g	−0.041	−0.046	−0.014	−0.053	−0.037	−0.034	−0.035	−0.054
$Q + Q_a$	0.386	0.381	0.354	0.397	0.383	0.380	0.387	0.382
share in net private savings								
Y_a	0.236	0.242	0.271	0.233	0.229	0.241	0.236	0.265
Y_w	0.470	0.464	0.443	0.477	0.474	0.470	0.472	0.449
Y_z	0.294	0.294	0.287	0.291	0.297	0.289	0.292	0.286
share in government expenditure								
$\Sigma_i p_i g_i$	0.190	0.187	0.189	0.191	0.190	0.187	0.194	0.186
$w_g l_g$	0.274	0.269	0.278	0.274	0.272	0.267	0.279	0.267
V	0.097	0.094	0.093	0.099	0.098	0.095	0.099	0.092
$\overline{V}$	0.121	0.118	0.116	0.123	0.122	0.119	0.123	0.114
$(1-\phi_z)Q$	0.181	0.178	0.180	0.182	0.181	0.178	0.185	0.177
Z	0.000	0.000	−0.031	0.000	−0.004	0.000	−0.006	0.000
U_1	0.101	0.118	0.154	0.100	0.116	0.117	0.086	0.087
U_2	0.026	0.026	0.000	0.027	0.019	0.026	0.032	0.048
U_3	0.009	0.011	0.019	0.003	0.005	0.008	0.009	0.023
share in government revenue								
R_1	0.616	0.621	0.632	0.609	0.615	0.608	0.614	0.628
R_2	0.109	0.111	0.112	0.108	0.110	0.125	0.108	0.110
ΣN_{gi}	0.275	0.268	0.256	0.283	0.275	0.267	0.278	0.262

Note: for a list of variables included in the table, see Table 6.1.

cultivation of these crops. As a result, rice production rises by 1.5 per cent, wheat output by 2.9 per cent. The increases in rice and wheat production negatively affect their market prices, which forces the government to buy up even more of their supplies. The market prices of rice and wheat increase up to their minimum support levels. With rising prices and crop supply, agricultural income considerably increases, raising agriculturalists' demand. Demand pressure in the economy is augmented by the increase in indexed nominal wage rates in non–agriculture, following the rise in the consumer price index, and in non–agricultural mark–up prices. The rate of demand–pull/cost–push inflation in terms of the GDP deflator is 6.9 per cent. Real GDP at factor cost increases by 0.9 per cent. Farmers gain most from the policy change, their share in GDP rises from 32.7 to 35.1 per cent.

With the inflation, the share in GDP at market prices of gross domestic investment declines from 25.9 per cent in the base run to 25.2 per cent. To re–establish the investment–savings equality, the share in GDP of savings declines in the following two ways. First, with the inflation, the shares in GDP of foreign savings and depreciation allowances decline. Second, net public savings decline mainly due to an increase in expenditure on food, fertiliser and export subsidies, a rise in wage payments, and an increase in consumption expenditure, on the one hand, and a decline in revenue from public enterprises, on the other hand. Although the share in GDP of net private savings does not change, with the redistribution of income following the inflation, its composition changes. In particular, the share in net private savings of savings from agricultural income increases from 23.6 per cent in the base run to 25.7 per cent.

The present results which suggest that raising procurement prices is an effective instrument to raise public procurement, however, have to be qualified in view of the econometric results by Gulati and Sharma (1990), which indicate that there exist important regional differences in the efficacy of procurement prices in raising the quantity procured. Their results show that, in surplus areas such as the Punjab and perhaps Haryana, procurement of foodgrains can be increased by raising procurement prices in relation to market prices. In other states, procurement prices are not an effective instrument to raise procurement.

Experiment P – 1.1:[13]
10% Increase in Procurement Prices for Rice, Wheat and Other Food Crops and Elimination of the Fertiliser Subsidy

In an attempt to compensate farmers for the rise in production costs following the elimination of the subsidy on fertilisers, the government might raise the

---

[13] Experiment $P-1.1$ differs from $F-2.1$ in that in $P-1.1$ no attempt is made to maintain the base–run ratio of the fertiliser price relative to the market price of rice and wheat. Accordingly, while in $F-2.1$ fertiliser use remains unaffected by the policy change, fertiliser use is reduced in $P-1.1$ following the increase in the fertiliser price relative to crop prices.

procurement prices for foodgrains. To assess the outcome of such a policy, an experiment was performed in which foodgrain procurement prices were raised by 10 per cent while fertiliser subsidisation was abolished.

The policy change has two effects. First, it raises the fertiliser price relative to the prices of crops which leads to a decline in crop output and an increase in foodgrain prices. Second, by raising the minimum support prices of rice and wheat, the government is obliged to commensurately step–up its procurement of these crops, raising foodgrain demand and foodgrain prices. As a result, market prices for rice and wheat increase. Because of the fact that a large part of the consumption demand for rice and wheat is 'committed' in nature, total 'committed' consumer expenditure rises in money terms following the foodgrain price increases. As a result, the amount of 'supernumerary' consumer expenditure declines, with consumer demand declining most for those commodities having the largest marginal budget shares, *i.c.* non–agricultural goods. Hence, following the hike in foodgrain prices, consumer demand falls for non–agricultural goods.

Three other factors contribute to a decline in aggregate demand for non–agricultural commodities. First, with the fertiliser price increasing relative to crop prices, farmers' demand for fertilisers declines. Second, the reduction in per hectare fertiliser use, in turn, leads to a decline in crop production, resulting in a fall in agriculture's demand for intermediate inputs from non–agriculture. Third, with the inflation, private investment demand in the consumer goods and services sectors declines. The fall in demand for non–agricultural goods is to some extent offset by the increase in agriculturalists' consumption demand, following the increase in (real) agri-cultural income. In effect, however, both agricultural and non–agricultural production declines. As a result, the policy change is contractionary, real GDP at market prices declines by 0.9 per cent. Mainly due to foodgrain price increases, the consumer price index increases. With nominal wages in non-agriculture rising less than the consumer price index, non–agricultural wage income in real terms falls. Its share in GDP at factor cost declines from 37.2 per cent in the base run to 36.9 per cent. Since real non–agricultural mark–up income also declines following the contraction, the increase in real GDP is entirely due to a rise in real agricultural income. The share in GDP of agricultural income rises to 33.3 per cent.

Because of the step–up in public foodgrain procurement, the share in GDP at market prices of aggregate stock changes slightly rises. With the inflation, the share in GDP of gross domestic fixed investment falls. The net effect of both changes is a decline in the share of gross domestic investment from 25.9 per cent in the base run to 25.8 per cent. The re–establishment of investment–saving balance involves a decline in the shares in GDP of foreign savings and net private savings. The decline in the share of foreign savings can be attributed to a decline in complementary intermediate imports on the one hand, and to the rise in the rate of domestic inflation, on the other. The decline in the share of net private savings is due to the redistribution of income in favour of agricultural income (which has the lowest propensity to save) and to the decline of non–agricultural income in real terms.

The outcome of $P-1.1$ suggests that, although raising foodgrain procurement prices may be an effective instrument to compensate farmers for the loss of the fertiliser subsidy, its impact is significantly stag-flationary. Following the policy change, output of all crops declines which reduces the availability of agricultural goods, raises the rate of inflation, and leads to a considerable redistribution of income in favour of agricultural income.

Experiment P-2:
20% Increase in the Quantity of Rice and Wheat Procured

Instead of increasing procurement *prices*, the government may increase the scope of its procurement scheme by enlarging the *quantities* of foodgrains to be procured by the Food Corporation. With unchanged public distribution of foodgrains, an increase in public foodgrain procurement implies a step–up in the accumulation of food stocks. Given agriculture's continuing sensitivity to adverse weather conditions, food stock accumulation may be important as it provides an insurance cover against a poor harvest, but, as can be inferred from the outcome of $P-2$, it also imposes a burden on the economy.

The immediate impact of the policy change is to raise market demand for rice and wheat, which leads to upward pressure on rice and wheat prices. These price increases, in turn, have a number of important effects. First, they lead to a rise in agricultural income, raising agriculturalists' demand and adding to demand pressure. Second, they lead to an increase in 'committed' consumption expenditure and a fall in demand for other, particularly non–agricultural, goods. Third, by raising the consumer price index, they trigger off increases in non–agricultural nominal wages and mark–up prices. Finally, due to the inflation, real private investment demand in non–agriculture declines. In the event, the policy change results in inflation, the consumer price index rises by 3.8 per cent.

With the rise in crop prices relative to the fertiliser price, crop supply increases. With rising prices and crop supply, agricultural income increases, augmenting aggregate demand for non–agricultural products. This increase in the demand for non–agricultural products is partly offset by the decline in investment demand in the consumer goods and services sectors. In effect, capacity utilisation in non–agriculture increases. The policy change is modestly expansionary as real GDP at factor cost increases by 0.4 per cent. With the inflation, the ensuing gains in non–agricultural wage income get eroded in real terms; real wage income in non–agriculture falls by 2.9 per cent. Agriculturalists gain most from the rise in procurement quantities, the share in GDP at factor cost of agricultural income increases from 32.7 per cent in the base run to 34.0 per cent.

With the inflation, the share in GDP at market prices of gross domestic investment declines to 25.7 per cent and, hence, the share of savings has to decline. The decline in the share of savings is the net effect of two opposing forces. On the one hand, the shares of foreign savings and depreciation allowances fall due to the inflation, while the share of net private savings falls following the income redistribution in favour of agriculturalists. On the other hand, the share of net public savings increases. The improvement in the government's budgetary position is mainly the result of a sharp increase in revenue from the procurement tax.

It can be seen that a stock management policy in which precedence is accorded to accumulation over depletion of food stocks may contribute in a substantial measure to inflation in grain prices. According to Krishnaji (1990), the Indian government pursued a similar stock management policy during the 1970s and 1980s, when good harvests were utilised more for stock-building than for improving the level of foodgrain availability. Although imports contributed to this stock-piling, it was almost wholly the internal procurement effort that enabled the government to accumulate these stocks. Stock levels which were about 3 million tonnes in the early 1970s grew close to 30 million tonnes in 1985 (the drought of 1987 has led to a depletion of these stocks).

Experiment P – 2.1
20% Increase in the Quantity Procured and Distributed of Rice, Wheat, and Other Food Crops.

If the range of price variation is to be limited so as to benefit both producers and consumers, it may be sensible to adopt a policy which assures both the depletion of stocks in adequate amounts when necessary as well as their accumulation to the desired extent. To evaluate the implications of such a policy, an experiment was performed in which both the quantities of foodgrains procured and the quantities of foodgrains publicly issued through the Fair–Price Shops were increased by 20 per cent.

The policy change has two immediate effects. On the one hand, the rise in the quantities procured raises foodgrain demand, which, with *initial* supply, leads to upward pressure on foodgrain prices. On the other hand, the rise in the quantities of foodgrains publicly distributed implies a rise in foodgrain supply, which, with *initial* demand, results in downward pressure on foodgrain prices. Because of the fact that the rise in public procurement demand is larger in absolute terms than the increase in public distribution, the net effect of the policy change is to raise foodgrain prices.

The increase in foodgrain prices relative to the fertiliser price, in turn, leads to a rise in crop output and an increase in agricultural income and demand, providing a stimulus to non–agricultural production. As a result, the policy change is modestly expansionary as real GDP at factor cost increases by 0.3 per cent. Agriculturalists gain most from the policy change, their share in GDP at factor cost rises from 32.7 to 33.2 per cent. Non–agricultural wage earners are the main losers. Due to the increase in the rate of inflation, their income share in GDP at market prices declines from 37.2 to 36.8 per cent.

The particular 20 per cent rise in the quantity of foodgrains publicly procured and distributed leads to an increase in public stock changes of foodgrains in real terms. As a result, the share in GDP at market prices of aggregate stock changes increases. The share in GDP of gross domestic fixed investment, however, declines, following the rise in inflation. In effect, the share in GDP of gross domestic investment declines and the share of savings has to fall. The decline in the share of savings can be attributed to a decrease in the shares of net public savings and depreciation allowances. The share in GDP of net public savings declines mainly due to increased expenditure on food subsidisation.

Although the increases in crop output are much smaller under policy package P–2.1 than the crop production increases in P–1 and P–2, its impact is less inflationary than the policies implemented either under P–1 or P–2, which suggests that public distribution of foodgrains is an effective way of regulating food price movements. The GDP deflator increases by only 2.6 per cent, the consumer price index rises by 1.6 per cent. Inflationary pressure is mainly the result of foodgrain price increases, which vary between 3.4 and 5.9 per cent. The outcome of this experiment shows that the availability of foodgrains, $i.e$ domestic production augmented by imports and by changes in stock, is more relevant to price movements than is domestic production. It is in this context that the government's stock management assumes a critical role in bringing about price stability.

Experiment P – 3:
Removal of the Public Procurement Scheme and the PDS

Given the limited coverage of government operations, with respect to crops on the one hand, and the quantities procured and distributed on the other, it would appear *prima facie* that the impact of these operations, for example on agricultural and non–agricultural prices, would also be limited. That this understanding of the present situation is questionable, because the markets for foodgrains are strongly integrated *via* demand, supply and price conditions with the markets for commercial crops, other agricultural products, and non–agricultural commodities, is carried out by the outcome of a policy experiment in which both the public procurement scheme and the PDS are completely removed.

The policy change has two immediate effects. First, the removal of the food subsidies under the PDS raises consumers' demand for foodgrains, which, with *initial* supply, leads to upward pressure on food prices. Second, the elimination of the public procurement scheme leads to a decline in foodgrain demand, due to which prices for foodgrains decline. Because government intervention is higher in terms of procurement than in terms of distribution, the net impact of the policy change is a sharp fall in foodgrain prices. In turn, the decline in foodgrain prices has a number of effects. First, it leads to a decline in agricultural income, due to which agriculturalists' demand declines. Second, with the decline in foodgrain prices relative to the fertiliser price, per hectare fertiliser input is reduced, yield levels decline, and crop output falls. Finally, through its impact on the consumer price index, the fall in foodgrain prices leads to a decline in nominal wage rates in non–agriculture. In effect, the policy change is both contractionary and deflationary. Real GDP at factor cost is reduced by 1.1 per cent and the consumer price index by 7.7 per cent. Distributionally, the share of agricultural income earners declines from 32.7 to 29.6 per cent of GDP at factor cost. Non–agricultural wage earners gain most from the deflation, created by the policy change, their share in national income rises from 37.2 to 39.0 per cent.

With the deflation, the share in GDP at market prices of gross domestic investment increases from 25.9 per cent in the base run to 26.8 per cent. To re–establish the investment–savings balance, the share of savings increases as the net result of the following changes. First, with the deflation, the shares in GDP of foreign savings and depreciation allowances rise. Second, net public savings increase; the net budgetary effect of the loss of revenue from the procurement tax and the gain from not having to subsidise non–agricultural foodgrain distribution is a decline in the public revenue deficit from 1.1 to 0.7 per cent of GDP at market prices. Third, in contrast to the other savings sources, the share in GDP of net private savings declines mainly on account of the contraction, caused by the policy change.

The outcome of the experiment indicates that the present procurement and distribution policy makes a net contribution to the revenue deficit and transfers income from non–agricultural to agricultural income earners. It adds to inflationary pressure in the economy, but also augments the nation's income in real terms.

Experiment P – 3.1:
Removal of the Public Procurement Scheme, the Public Distribution System and Fertiliser Subsidisation

To assess the economy–wide consequences of government involvement in the agricultural sector, the following simulation experiment was run in which the public procurement scheme, the PDS and the fertiliser subsidy scheme are eliminated all at one stroke. The radical policy change sets in motion a number of counteracting forces. Two factors lead to upward pressure on crop prices. First, removal of the fertiliser subsidy leads to a decline of crop prices relative to the fertiliser price, a reduction of fertiliser input, and a decline in crop output, which results in upward pressure on crop prices. Second, the withdrawal of food subsidies forces non–agricultural consumers to spend a larger proportion of their budgets on foodgrains, the consumption demand of which is to a relatively high proportion fixed, which leads to a reduction of their demand for non–agricultural commodities. The impact of both these forces is, however, more than offset by the deflationary effects following the elimination of public procurement. Removal of public procurement leads to a considerable fall in aggregate demand for rice, wheat, and other food crops, which leads to downward pressure on the prices of these crops. In effect, crop prices fall dramatically, contributing to a decline in the consumer price index.

With the fall in crop prices and the decline in crop production, the real income of farmers declines by more than 10 per cent. The fall in agriculture's intermediate demand (following the decline in production) and the fall in agriculturalists' final demand (following the decline in their real income) have a negative impact on capacity utilisation in non–agriculture. With the deflation, real non–agricultural income (both of wage earners and mark–up recipients) rises, despite the decline in capacity utilisation. Income distribution changes distinctly in favour of non–agriculture. The policy change is contractionary, real GDP at factor cost declines by 2.5 per cent. Again, the share in GDP at market prices of gross domestic investment rises in deflationary circumstances. The share of savings increases through the following adjustments. First, with the deflation, the shares in GDP of foreign savings and depreciation allowances rise. Second, net public savings rise; the increase is mainly due to the reduction of expenditure on food and fertiliser subsidies (following the policy change), export subsidies (because, with the deflation, the gap between domestic prices and world prices narrows), and producers' subsidies (following the contraction of real GDP). Finally, the above increases in savings were to some extent offset by the fall in net private savings which is mainly the result of the decline in real GDP.

A sudden and almost complete withdrawal of public price–intervention in agriculture will have a considerable negative effect on the level of gross domestic income as well as on the price level and the government budget, while at the same time altering the distribution of GDP in favour of non–agricultural wage earners. Its impact on agricultural production is negative and varies between –1.1 (other food crops) and –5.6 per cent (wheat), which is comparable to the impact of a major drought.

Experiment P – 3.2:
Removal of the Public Procurement Scheme and the Public Distribution System, while Simultaneously Increasing the Rate of Fertiliser Subsidy to 50%

In view of the low per capita availability of foodgrains, the outcome of experiment P-3.1, particularly the decline in crop output, may be regarded as undesirable. To compensate for a potential negative impact on foodgrain production, while reducing its involvement in procurement and distribution, the government may raise the rate of fertiliser subsidy instead of eliminating it alltogether. Hence, a final procurement policy experiment was performed

Table 6.9
Results of the Procurement Policy Experiments

	Base-Run	P-1	P-1.1	P-2	P-2.1	P-3	P-3.1	P-3.2
	percentage change from initial base-run values							
x_1	1.884	1.5	-1.6	0.5	1.4	-2.3	-4.1	-0.2
x_2	1.076	2.9	-2.9	0.5	2.3	-2.5	-5.6	1.0
x_3	0.941	0.2	-0.7	0.1	0.1	-0.4	-1.1	0.4
x_4	3.945	0.3	-1.3	0.1	0.1	-0.4	-1.9	1.1
x_6	0.413	5.8	-6.9	1.4	4.7	-6.6	-14.0	2.2
x_7	15.093	0.8	-0.8	0.2	0.2	-0.9	-1.9	0.2
x_8	6.453	2.3	-1.0	0.6	0.9	-2.9	-4.6	-1.2
x_9	10.198	1.3	-1.1	0.4	0.4	-1.7	-3.1	-0.2
p_1	1.0	20.0	10.0	5.9	17.0	-24.6	-21.5	-28.0
p_2	1.0	20.0	12.0	3.5	14.6	-15.7	-8.0	-22.9
p_3	1.0	10.3	2.1	3.4	4.3	-15.3	-16.2	-14.6
p_4	1.0	8.7	3.5	2.3	3.5	-10.1	-9.2	-11.1
p_5	1.0	10.8	-2.5	2.7	4.6	-12.2	-16.9	-7.1
p_6	1.0	2.7	30.9	0.7	1.5	-3.2	25.8	-26.9
p_7	1.0	2.6	0.6	0.7	1.4	-3.1	-3.2	-2.9
p_8	1.0	4.4	1.1	1.1	2.1	-5.1	-5.3	-4.9
p_9	1.0	3.0	0.7	0.8	1.7	-3.6	-3.7	-3.4
w_6	1.0	4.1	1.1	1.1	2.3	-4.8	-4.8	-4.7
w_7	1.0	2.2	0.6	0.6	1.3	-2.7	-2.7	-2.6
w_8	1.0	1.6	0.4	0.4	0.9	-1.9	-1.9	-1.9
w_9	1.0	2.7	0.7	0.7	1.5	-3.2	-3.2	-3.1
w_g	1.0	4.1	1.1	1.1	2.3	-4.8	-4.9	-4.7
cpi	1.0	6.8	1.7	1.7	3.8	-7.7	-7.7	-7.5
p	1.0	6.9	1.9	1.6	3.6	-7.9	-7.9	-8.1
	in constant prices							
Y_a	7.654	8.2	0.6	1.9	4.4	-10.4	-11.9	-8.7
Y_w	8.699	-2.9	-2.0	-1.7	-2.9	3.7	2.5	5.2
Y_z	5.405	-1.1	-2.2	-0.1	-0.9	1.3	-0.7	3.6
Y_f	23.406	0.9	-1.2	0.3	-0.4	-1.1	-2.5	0.6
Y_m	26.251	0.9	-0.9	0.1	-0.2	-1.0	-2.1	0.4
	share in GDP at factor cost							
Y_a	0.327	0.351	0.333	0.332	0.340	0.296	0.295	0.297
Y_w	0.372	0.358	0.369	0.368	0.364	0.390	0.391	0.389
Y_z	0.231	0.226	0.229	0.230	0.228	0.237	0.235	0.238
ΣN_{gi}	0.070	0.065	0.070	0.069	0.068	0.077	0.078	0.076

Table 6.9 Continued

	Base–Run	P–1	P–1.1	P–2	P–2.1	P–3	P–3.1	P–3.2
			percentage of GDP at market prices					
S_p	14.62	14.63	14.57	14.62	14.58	14.58	14.51	14.64
S_g	−1.07	−1.30	−1.07	−1.12	−0.96	−0.66	−0.52	−0.77
H	2.37	2.27	2.30	2.35	2.31	2.51	2.47	2.56
$Q + Q_a$	9.99	9.58	9.98	9.89	9.76	10.50	10.61	10.39
I	20.95	19.94	20.76	20.71	20.36	22.15	22.34	22.19
$\Delta\,st$	4.95	5.24	5.02	5.03	5.33	4.68	4.73	4.63
			share in gross domestic savings					
Y_a	0.133	0.149	0.136	0.137	0.141	0.114	0.112	0.115
Y_w	0.265	0.264	0.264	0.265	0.262	0.266	0.265	0.267
Y_z	0.166	0.168	0.164	0.166	0.165	0.162	0.159	0.164
H	0.092	0.090	0.089	0.091	0.090	0.093	0.091	0.095
S_g	−0.041	−0.052	−0.041	−0.043	−0.037	−0.024	−0.019	−0.029
$Q + Q_a$	0.386	0.381	0.387	0.384	0.380	0.390	0.392	0.387
			share in net private savings					
Y_a	0.236	0.257	0.241	0.241	0.248	0.210	0.209	0.210
Y_w	0.470	0.454	0.468	0.466	0.462	0.491	0.494	0.489
Y_z	0.294	0.289	0.291	0.293	0.291	0.299	0.297	0.301
			share in government expenditure					
$\Sigma_i p_i g_i$	0.190	0.186	0.192	0.189	0.190	0.197	0.201	0.194
$w_g l_g$	0.274	0.270	0.277	0.273	0.275	0.279	0.284	0.275
V	0.097	0.092	0.097	0.096	0.096	0.104	0.106	0.103
$\overline{V}$	0.121	0.115	0.121	0.120	0.119	0.130	0.132	0.128
$(1-\phi_z)Q$	0.181	0.177	0.183	0.180	0.181	0.188	0.192	0.185
Z	0.000	0.000	−0.001	−0.005	−0.016	0.000	0.000	0.000
U_1	0.101	0.103	0.085	0.102	0.104	0.099	0.084	0.114
U_2	0.026	0.038	0.034	0.034	0.037	0.006	0.007	0.006
U_3	0.009	0.019	0.012	0.011	0.014	−0.005	−0.005	−0.005
			share in government revenue					
R_1	0.616	0.626	0.617	0.619	0.621	0.603	0.601	0.606
R_2	0.109	0.111	0.110	0.110	0.110	0.109	0.108	0.109
$\Sigma\,N_{gi}$	0.275	0.263	0.275	0.272	0.269	0.289	0.292	0.285

Note: for a list of variables included in the table, see Table 6.1.

with the general equilibrium model to evaluate the effects of the elimination of public procurement and the removal of the PDS, while at the same time raising the rate of fertiliser subsidy from 27.3 to 50 per cent.

The policy change has the following effects. First, the increase in the rate of fertiliser subsidy leads to an increase in cropwise fertiliser input, and a rise in crop supply, which results in downward pressure on crop prices. Downward pressure on prices is augmented by the fall in demand resulting from the removal of public procurement. The withdrawal of food subsidies, on the other hand, leads to a rise in demand for agricultural commodities. In effect, crop prices fall dramatically, contributing to a decline in the consumer price index of 7.5 per cent. Because of the fact that the ratio of crop prices to the fertiliser price is more favourable for farmers in $P-3.2$ than in $P-3$ or $P-3.1$, policy package $P-3.2$ is expansionary instead of being contractionary. Real GDP at market prices rises by 0.4 per cent. Although the increase in the rate of fertiliser subsidy stimulates farmers to step up their crop production, it does not reward them in income–distributional terms. With the deflation, the share of agricultural income in GDP at factor cost declines to 29.7 per cent.

The results of experiments $P-3$, $P-3.1$, and $P-3.2$ reveal the major role in price and income formation which the government has assumed in the agricultural sector, following the adoption of the 'new agricultural strategy' in the mid–1960s. They further indicate that any radical change in the agricultural policy package, as it has evolved over the years, will lead to a significant redistribution of income from agriculturalists to non–agricultural income (particularly wage income) earners. In view of this, it is not surprising that the politically powerful 'farm lobby' which is believed to influence agricultural policy–making with a fair degree of success (Mitra, 1977; Kumar, 1988), has a vested interest in sustaining the present government interference in agricultural price formation.

Experiment S–1:
Elimination of Food Subsidies

Reviewers of the working of the public distribution system (PDS) suggest that while the PDS off–take for the country as a whole has increased substantially over the years, the PDS was expensive because, wherever it was introduced, no efforts were made for targetting, *i.e.* limiting it to lower–income groups. They also indicate that the food subsidy has cut into the resources meant for development expenditure, apart from increasing rural–urban inequity since the large majority of the rural population are denied access to the PDS. To evaluate the impact of the PDS on the economy, the present simulation experiment was run in which the system of urban food subsidisation is eliminated.

The elimination of food subsidies has two immediate effects. First, it raises market demand for foodgrains of non–agricultural consumers which, with *initial* levels of crop supply, leads to foodgrain price increases. Second, it forces non–agricultural consumers to spend a larger proportion of their budget on foodgrains, the consumption demand of which is fixed to a relatively high degree, and to reduce their effective demand for non–foodgrain commodities. The initial impact of the policy change therefore is a rise in foodgrain prices and a reduction in non–foodgrain demand. Its second and higher round effects include a rise in crop output (following the increase in crop prices relative to the fertiliser price), an increase in agricultural income (following the rise in crop output and in crop prices), and an increase in agriculturalists' final demand, adding to demand pressure. Inflationary pressure in the economy is augmented by nominal wage rate and mark–up price increases in non–agriculture. In the event, the GDP deflator rises by 10.6 per cent as compared to the base run.

For foodgrains, prices rise relative to the fertiliser price and, consequently, per hectare fertiliser use is raised, with foodgrain production increasing concomitantly. Notwithstanding the decline in the production of commercial crops (following the decline in the price of commercial crops relative to the fertiliser price), agricultural income increases, with both foodgrain output and prices on the rise. With the inflation, real wages in non–agriculture decline. Due to the fall in capacity utilisation in some of the non–agricultural sectors, non–agricultural mark–up income also declines in real terms. Hence, income distribution shifts in favour of agricultural income, the share in GDP at factor cost of which increases from 32.7 per cent to 37.1 per cent.

With the inflation, the share in GDP at market prices of gross domestic fixed investment declines from 21 per cent in the base run to only 19 per cent. This decline is more than offset by the increase in the share in GDP of aggregate stock changes, which rises following the removal of the PDS, so that the share in GDP of gross domestic investment eventually increases to 26 per cent. Due to the policy change, the composition of savings changes significantly. First, with the inflation, the shares in GDP of foreign savings and depreciation allowances decline. The decline in foreign savings is augmented by the fall in complementary intermediate imports which accompanies the decline in non–agricultural output. Second, following the redistribution of income in favour of agriculture, the share of net private savings also declines. The fall in the share in GDP of savings is, however, completely offset by a spectacular increase in net public savings which increase from –1.1 per cent of GDP in the base run to 0.3 per cent. Due to higher revenue from import duties and the procurement tax and due to the reduction of expenditure on food subsidies the government is able to operate a surplus on its current account, an increase in public wage payments notwithstanding.

The analysis of the macro–economic impact of the elimination of the PDS suggests its importance in maintaining price stability. In the short run, elimination of the PDS results in double–digit inflation. Mounting inflationary pressures are mainly due to steep price increases for rice and wheat, triggering off a process of nominal wage and price increases in non–agriculture. The impact of the elimination of the PDS on GDP is modestly expansionary, real GDP at factor cost increases by 0.4 per cent. This increase is mainly due to the rise in real agricultural income following the increase in rice and wheat output and prices. Income distribution changes sharply in favour of agricultural income. The drastic cut in food subsidy outlays has a beneficial effect both on the public budget and on the nation's current account. What is important from a medium–term perspective is that the policy change through its inflationary impact leads to an erosion of gross domestic fixed investment in real terms.

In experiment $F-1.1$, elimination of food subsidies to finance a rise in the rate of fertiliser subsidy turned out to be both inflationary and expansionary. The same conclusion holds for the removal of the PDS without any other supportive policy. The present findings correspond to the results obtained by De Janvry and Subbarao (1986) showing that, in the short run, eliminating the PDS, while reallocating the same budget expenditure to increased government spending on industrial investment, is inflationary.

Experiment $S-1.1$:
Elimination of Food Subsidies and Reallocation of Government Spending to Producers' Subsidies on Rice, Wheat and Other Food Crops

If, in contrast to the previous experiment, the budget saved on consumer food subsidies is used to lower farm prices by reallocating it to producer subsidies on rice, wheat and other food crops, the outcome is even more inflationary. This is because the rise in producers' subsidy for farmers considerably enhances their incomes, and, in turn, considerably augments their consumption demand both for agricultural and non–agricultural commodities. The increase in the domestic market for non–agricultural goods leads to a significant rise in the capacity utilisation rates in non–agriculture. Production of fertiliser industries increases by almost 21 per cent, following the decline in the fertiliser price relative to crop prices. As a result, non–agricultural GDP increases, which raises final demand from non–agricultural income earners and contributes to mounting demand pressures in the economy. The increase in demand for foodgrains by far outpaces the step–up in their supply (barring any public distribution of foodgrains), on account of which foodgrain prices increase dramatically. The consumer price index rises by 16.0 per cent and the GDP deflator by 16.4 per cent. Nominal wages increase by only 5.2 to 9.5 per cent, implying a real wage fall and a dampening of the cost–push pressure. The policy change is expansionary. Real GDP at factor cost rises by 1.3 per cent. Not surprisingly, agriculturalists gain most from the spiraling foodgrain prices. Their share in GDP at factor cost increases from 32.7 to 38.9 per cent. With the double–digit inflation, the income position of both non–agricultural wage earners and mark–up income recipients as well as of the public enterprises significantly deteriorates.

The share in GDP at market prices of gross domestic investment declines to 25.2 per cent. To restore the investment–savings balance, the corresponding share of savings has to fall. With the inflation, the shares of foreign savings and depreciation allowances automatically decline. The share of net private savings also declines, following the decrease in the share in GDP at factor cost of non–agricultural mark–up income. The decline in savings is partly offset by the increase in net public savings which is mainly due to higher revenue from the procurement tax and indirect taxation, and lower expenditure on food subsidisation.

The most important impact of S–1.1 is raising the general price level by more than 15 per cent, which hurts those groups in non–agriculture the income of which is not or imperfectly indexed to inflation. To the extent that they are net buyers of foodgrains, the inflation also erodes the gains in real income of agriculturalists (De Janvry and Subbarao, 1986). Lower–income groups most likely belong to either of the above mentioned categories.

Experiment S – 2:
10% Increase in the Quantity of Food Publicly Issued under Minimum Support Pricing

From the viewpoint of the consumer, the income transfer realised through the PDS is equal to the difference between the market price of the commodities and the issue prices, multiplied by the quantities of foodgrains supplied *via* the PDS. To assess the consequences of a rise in consumer food subsidies, the quantities of foodgrains supplied were raised by 10 per cent in experiment S–2.

Because of the increase in the quantities issued of particularly rice and wheat, which are available at subsidised prices, consumers have to spend less of their budgets on rice and wheat and can demand more of other commodities. As a result, prices increase for other agricultural products (the output of which is fixed in the short run), commercial crops and other food crops, which, in turn, leads to non–agricultural wage and price increases. In effect, the increase in food subsidies turns out to be slightly inflationary in terms of the consumer price index and the GDP deflator which both increase by 0.2 per cent. The main factor behind the inflationary impact of the increase in food subsidies is the public procurement policy for rice and wheat. As expected, through a decline in consumer demand, the increase in food subsidies puts downward pressure on the prices of rice and wheat, but the decline in private consumer demand is offset by a rise in public procurement at the announced procurement prices, the government being committed to procure whatever quantities are offered for sale. With slightly higher agricultural prices, agricultural income increases which leads to a rise in agriculturalists' final demand. As a result, non–agricultural production also slightly increases. Real GDP at factor cost increases by 0.1 per cent. Income distribution is only marginally affected by the policy change. Its impact on public, private and foreign savings is also limited.

Experiment S – 2.1:
10% Increase in the Quantity of Food Publicly Issued without Minimum Support Pricing

The importance of the public procurement scheme can be grasped by comparing the results of the policy experiment *S – 2* to the outcome of scenario *S – 2.1* in which food subsidies are also increased by 10 per cent, but in which the Food Corporation refuses to procure more than the exogenously given quantity.

Without a procurement/minimum support scheme, the impact of a rise in food subsidies is deflationary – witness the 1.0 per cent fall in the consumer price index under *S – 2.1*. As can be seen from comparing the fourth and fifth column of Table 6.10, the inflationary impact of public procurement of rice and wheat on the prices of the other three agricultural commodities is quite substantial. Further, in contrast to experiment *S – 2*, the increase in food subsidy has a small contractionary impact, real GDP at factor cost declining by 0.1 per cent, and income distribution is also differently affected – the share of agricultural income declines to 32.3 per cent and the share of non–agricultural wage income rises to 37.4 per cent.

The above results show that a rise in the quantity of foodgrains issued through Fair–Price Shops may be an effective instrument to contain short–run inflationary pressures. Its income distributional impact is rather modest, although there is a tendency for the income share of agriculturalists to decline at the expense of a rise in the income share of non–agricultural wage earners. The results further indicate that, in the short run, price–support programmes have considerable economy–wide effects, in particular through their positive impact on inflation.

Experiment S – 2.2:
20% Increase in the Quantity of Foodgrains Publicly Distributed and the Removal of the Fertiliser Subsidy

By increasing the quantity of foodgrains issued under the PDS the government may try to protect consumers from the foodgrain price increases, which are often believed to follow from the removal of the fertiliser subsidy scheme. To this end, the quantity of foodgrains publicly distributed was raised by 20 per cent and the fertiliser subsidy eliminated.

The impact of the policy package on foodgrains demand is twofold. First, the elimination of the fertiliser subsidy leads to a decline in per hectare fertiliser use and a fall in crop output, which, with *initial* demand, results in upward pressure on crop prices. Second, the increase in food subsidisation leads to a decline in foodgrain demand, which, with *initial* supply, causes food prices to decrease. The net impact is a downward pressure on foodgrain prices. To prevent the prices of rice and wheat from declining below their floor levels, their public procurement is considerably increased. Consequently, only the price of other food crops is allowed to decline.

Another effect of the removal of the fertiliser subsidy is to reduce the income of the agricultural sector, which leads to a decline in agriculturalists' final demand for non–agricultural goods. With the fall in crop output which follows from the reduction in fertiliser use, agriculture's demand for non–agricultural intermediate inputs also decreases. The decline in demand for non–agricultural goods – originating from agriculture – is partly offset by a rise in private effective consumption demand for non–agricultural products, which increases following the decline in private expenditure on foodgrains. The net impact of the policy change, however, is a fall in the level of non–agricultural production.

As a result, the policy change is contractionary. Real GDP at factor cost declines by 1.5 per cent. With foodgrain prices declining, the consumer price index also decreases. Due to the contraction, non–agricultural income declines. The real income fall is largest for agricultural income, which declines by 3.1 per cent in real terms because of the fall in crop output. As a result, the share in GDP at factor cost of agricultural income declines to 32.1 per cent.

With the deflation, the share in GDP at market prices of gross domestic investment rises. The share of savings increases as follows. First, with the deflation, the share in GDP of depreciation allowances increases. Second, the share of net public savings rises, mainly due to the reduction of expenditure on the fertiliser subsidy, export subsidies (with the deflation, the gap between domestic prices and world prices narrows), wages, and final consumption, and an increase in revenue from public enterprises (which are fixed in nominal terms). The policy change affects foreign savings in two opposing ways. On the one hand, the share of foreign savings rises due to the deflation. On the other hand, with the contraction, complementary intermediate imports are reduced, which leads to a decline in the share of foreign savings. In effect, the share in GDP of foreign savings does not change, with the two forces – in absolute terms – being of equal strength.

The outcome of experiment $F-2$ already indicated that the inflationary impact of the removal of the fertiliser subsidy is rather modest. Protecting consumers from the potential inflationary impact of the elimination of fertiliser subsidisation, by increasing the scope of the PDS, leads to considerable contraction – with both crop production as well as non–agricultural production declining.

Experiment $S-3$:
10% Reduction in Issue Prices of Foodgrains

Instead of raising the quantity of foodgrains issued at a subsidised price, food subsidies can also be increased by lowering the (subsidised) issue prices of foodgrains, while keeping the quantity publicly issued constant. The immediate impact of the reduction in the issue prices of foodgrains is to raise non–agricultural 'supernumerary' consumer expenditure which, in turn, leads to a rise in consumer demand, with the demand for the commodities having the largest marginal budget shares increasing most. Hence, consumer demand for non–agricultural goods increases, raising capacity utilisation rates and income in non–agriculture. Due to the rise in non–agricultural production and income, non–agricultural intermediate and final demand increases which, with relatively inelastic agricultural supply, leads to agricultural price increases. In effect, the GDP deflator increases by 0.9 per cent.

Given that nominal wage rate increases in non–agriculture are smaller than the rate of increase of the consumer price index, non–agricultural wage income declines in real terms (–0.2 per cent). Non–agricultural mark–up income increases, mainly on account of the rise in real non–agricultural output. With crop price increases being larger than the increase in the rate of inflation and with crop production on the rise, real agricultural income rises. Consequently, income distribution improves for agricultural income. The policy change is marginally expansionary, real GDP at factor cost increases by 0.2 per cent. With the inflation, the share in GDP at market prices of gross domestic investment declines. The required downward adjustment in the share of savings is brought about by a decline in the share of net public savings, which is mainly due to the rise in government expenditure on food subsidies.

De Janvry and Subbarao (1986) also studied the impact of a rise in food subsidies. Their results show that, with inelastic agricultural output, a doubling of food subsidies results in inflation due to which the non–indexed income earners (mainly belonging to the lower income groups) suffer a loss in real income. They conclude that a rise in food subsidy is regressive on the distribution of income, unless accompanied by price control or output increase. Because, in their model, food subsidies are treated as income transfers from the government to the (urban) households, a rise in food subsidisation *via* an increase in the quantity of foodgrains issued is equivalent in terms of its impact on the economy to a rise in food subsidies *via* an increase in the gap between the subsidised issue price and the market price. This is different in the present model, in which food subsidies are conceptualised as the difference between the market price of commodity i ($i = 1, 2, 3$) and its issue prices, multiplied by the quantity of foodgrain i supplied *via* the PDS, and in which they are incorporated in the linear expenditure system. As such, the effects on the economy of a rise in the quantity of foodgrains issued (experiment $S-2$) are significantly different from the effects of a reduction in issue prices (experiment $S-3$). The increase in food subsidies *via* a reduction of issue prices turns out to be more inflationary in terms of both the GDP deflator and the consumer price index than an increase in food subsidies *via* a rise in the quantity of foodgrains issued, both in the presence as well as in the absence of a price–support scheme. Its impact on real GDP at factor cost is, however, more expansionary than the impact of policy S–2.

Experiment S–3.1:
10% Reduction in Issue Prices of Foodgrains and Increase in the Rate of Fertiliser Subsidy upto 50%.

The final short–run experiment, the results of which are reported here, extends experiment S–3 to include an increase in the rate of fertiliser subsidy from 27.3 to 50 per cent; the increase in fertiliser subsidy can be seen as an attempt to curb the inflationary pressures arising from S–3.

The immediate impact of policy S–3.1 is to raise non–agricultural output through increases in both final and intermediate demand. First, with respect to final demand, the reduction in the issue prices of foodgrains leads to an increase in consumer demand for the non–food commodities. This leads, on the one hand, to a sharp increase in the market prices of commercial crops and other agricultural products, and, on the other hand, to an increase in the levels of non–agricultural production. Second, with respect to intermediate demand, the increase in the rate of fertiliser subsidy leads to a rise in fertiliser use and an increase in crop output. The increase in crop output leads to increased demand for intermediate inputs, both agricultural and non–agricultural. In particular, the sharp rise in fertiliser demand leads to a substantial increase in fertiliser production which in turn raises this sector's demand for intermediate inputs, mainly originating from non–agriculture. As a result, real non–agricultural production and income rise.

Crop output is positively affected by the increase in the fertiliser subsidy, in particular in the case of wheat and rice, the yield of which is relatively fertiliser–responsive. The increase in the supply of wheat and rice does, however, not result in a decline in their market prices, since these are kept at the minimum support levels by a significant quantity increase in public procurement. In effect, S–3.1 is inflationary (against its original intention!): the consumer price index rises by 2.5 per cent. Following the increase in crop output and the rise in some of the agricultural prices, real agricultural income increases (by 4.7 per cent). Given the increase in real agricultural and non–agricultural incomes, S–3.1 is expansionary: real GDP at market prices rises by 1.8 per cent. Distributionally, the farmers gain most. Their income share in GDP at factor cost increases from 32.7 per cent to 33.5 per cent. Non–agricultural wage earners are the main losers of the policy change, apart from the government, the budgetary position of which considerably deteriorates. This decline in net public savings is to be attributed to increased public expenditure on food and export subsidies (the latter rise because of the increase in the gap between domestic and world market prices) and the decline in revenue from public enterprises in nominal terms, which is only partly offset by increased revenue from indirect taxation (due to the rise in production and prices).

Table 6.10
Results of the Food Subsidisation Experiments

	Base-Run	S-1	S-1.1	S-2	S-2.1	S-2.2	S-3	S-3.1
		percentage change from initial base-run values						
x_1	1.884	4.8	5.3	0.0	-0.4	-2.3	0.1	2.7
x_2	1.076	9.6	10.3	0.0	-0.9	-4.7	0.2	5.2
x_3	0.941	0.1	0.3	0.0	0.0	-0.8	0.0	0.8
x_4	3.945	-0.1	0.3	0.0	0.0	-1.5	0.1	1.7
x_6	0.413	18.2	20.6	0.0	-1.5	-9.7	0.4	11.9
x_7	15.093	-0.6	0.4	0.1	0.0	-1.0	0.2	3.3
x_8	6.453	0.2	2.8	0.2	-0.2	-1.9	0.4	2.7
x_9	10.198	-1.3	0.2	0.1	-0.1	-1.4	0.3	2.2
p_1	1.0	66.8	78.7	0.0	-4.8	0.0	1.3	0.0
p_2	1.0	70.4	81.0	0.0	-5.0	0.0	1.2	0.0
p_3	1.0	6.8	17.8	0.4	-1.1	-2.0	1.7	4.5
p_4	1.0	1.8	11.0	0.5	-0.8	0.4	1.6	2.2
p_5	1.0	5.2	16.5	0.1	-0.8	-6.3	1.8	10.2
p_6	1.0	3.5	5.9	0.1	-0.4	29.4	0.4	-23.7
p_7	1.0	3.1	5.4	0.1	-0.4	-0.5	0.4	1.1
p_8	1.0	3.7	7.9	0.2	-0.5	-0.7	0.7	1.8
p_9	1.0	4.1	6.7	0.1	-0.4	-0.6	0.4	1.3
w_6	1.0	6.1	9.5	0.1	-0.6	-0.7	0.6	1.6
w_7	1.0	3.3	5.2	0.1	-0.3	-0.4	0.3	0.9
w_8	1.0	2.4	3.7	0.1	-0.2	-0.3	0.2	0.6
w_9	1.0	4.0	6.2	0.1	-0.4	-0.5	0.4	1.1
w_g	1.0	6.2	9.7	0.1	-0.6	-0.7	0.6	1.6
cpi	1.0	10.2	16.0	0.2	-1.0	-1.2	0.9	2.5
p	1.0	10.6	16.4	0.2	-1.0	-1.1	0.9	2.1
		in constant prices						
Y_a	7.654	13.1	20.6	0.2	-1.2	-3.1	1.0	4.7
Y_w	8.699	-6.5	-8.2	0.0	0.6	-0.4	-0.2	0.6
Y_z	5.405	-6.1	-6.0	0.1	0.4	-1.4	0.1	2.3
Y_f	23.406	-0.2	1.3	0.1	-0.1	-1.5	0.2	2.2
Y_m	26.251	0.4	1.3	0.0	-0.1	-1.3	0.1	1.8
		share in GDP at factor cost						
Y_a	0.327	0.371	0.389	0.328	0.323	0.321	0.329	0.335
Y_w	0.372	0.348	0.337	0.371	0.374	0.375	0.370	0.366
Y_z	0.231	0.217	0.214	0.231	0.232	0.231	0.231	0.231
ΣN_{gi}	0.070	0.064	0.060	0.070	0.071	0.072	0.070	0.068

Table 6.10   *Continued*

	Base − Run	S − 1	S − 1.1	S − 2	S − 2.1	S − 2.2	S − 3	S − 3.1
percentage of GDP at market prices								
S_p	14.62	14.30	14.37	14.63	14.63	14.57	14.63	14.69
S_g	−1.07	0.25	−0.23	−1.11	−1.12	−1.01	−1.15	−1.26
H	2.37	2.14	2.07	2.37	2.39	2.36	2.36	2.38
$Q + Q_a$	9.99	9.28	8.97	9.97	10.05	10.17	9.94	9.74
I	20.95	18.95	18.26	20.93	21.13	21.26	20.85	20.55
$\Delta \, st$	4.95	7.02	6.92	4.94	4.83	4.84	4.94	5.01
share in gross domestic savings								
Y_a	0.133	0.151	0.166	0.134	0.131	0.129	0.134	0.140
Y_w	0.265	0.245	0.246	0.266	0.266	0.266	0.264	0.266
Y_z	0.166	0.154	0.158	0.166	0.166	0.164	0.165	0.169
H	0.092	0.082	0.082	0.092	0.092	0.090	0.091	0.093
S_g	−0.041	0.009	−0.009	−0.043	−0.043	−0.039	−0.044	−0.049
$Q + Q_a$	0.386	0.357	0.356	0.386	0.387	0.390	0.382	0.381
share in net private savings								
Y_a	0.236	0.275	0.291	0.237	0.233	0.231	0.238	0.243
Y_w	0.470	0.446	0.432	0.470	0.473	0.475	0.468	0.462
Y_z	0.294	0.280	0.277	0.294	0.295	0.293	0.294	0.294
share in government expenditure								
$\Sigma_i p_i g_i$	0.190	0.200	0.193	0.190	0.190	0.193	0.189	0.186
$w_g l_g$	0.274	0.295	0.286	0.273	0.273	0.277	0.272	0.268
V	0.097	0.099	0.093	0.097	0.098	0.099	0.096	0.094
$\overline{V}$	0.121	0.123	0.116	0.121	0.122	0.124	0.120	0.117
$(1 - \phi_z)Q$	0.181	0.190	0.183	0.181	0.181	0.184	0.180	0.177
Z	0.000	−0.059	−0.065	0.000	0.004	0.000	−0.001	0.000
U_1	0.101	0.120	0.153	0.101	0.100	0.084	0.101	0.117
U_2	0.026	0.013	0.013	0.028	0.024	0.031	0.031	0.030
U_3	0.009	0.020	0.029	0.009	0.007	0.007	0.010	0.013
share in government revenue								
R_1	0.616	0.628	0.637	0.616	0.615	0.612	0.617	0.622
R_2	0.109	0.109	0.110	0.110	0.109	0.108	0.110	0.111
$\Sigma \, N_{gi}$	0.275	0.2263	0.253	0.274	0.276	0.279	0.273	0.267

Note: for a list of variables included in the table, see Table 6.1.

6.4   *Conclusions*

The results of the experiments of Section 6.2.1 underscore the importance of increasing the domestic availability of foodgrains for macro–economic policy–making. The experiments suggest that policies which concentrate on macro–economic variables such as the current account deficit or the government budgetary deficit, while neglecting measures to strengthen agricultural production, may lead to unexpected results. Specifically, it was found that, given relatively inelastic agricultural supply, policies involving a reduction in the direct tax rate on non–agricultural mark–up income, an increase in non–agricultural public investment, and a rise in public transfer payments to non–agricultural wage earners ultimately benefit farmers most. These results pointed out the importance of raising agricultural output and, particularly, increasing agriculture's short–run supply responsiveness.

The short–run economy–wide effects of changes in agricultural policy instruments which can be used to this end, were assessed in Section 6.3.2. The results of these agricultural policy experiments give a clear indication of the high degree of interdependence between the agricultural and the non–agricultural sectors in the Indian economy. They suggest that agricultural policy changes have a considerable impact not only on the performance of the agricultural sector itself, but also have important spillover effects on output and income in the other sectors of the economy, on the budgetary position of the government, the balance on the nation's current account, and the inflation rate.

Before drawing (policy) conclusions, the following general observations concerning the simulation results have to be made. First, results always critically depend on the assumptions made in the analysis. A crucial assumption on which the present outcomes depend, is the one regarding the investment–determinedness of savings (see Chapter 4). Due to this assumption, income distribution between agriculture and non–agriculture and, within non–agriculture, between wage income and mark–up income has to adjust to permit the supply of savings to equal investment demand. The justification for the particular specification, which may be labelled 'post–Keynesian', was provided in Chapter 3. Other assumptions important to the simulation outcome include the treatment of foreign trade, the specification of agricultural and non–agricultural production, and the treatment of consumer behaviour (see Chapter 4). Second, results always depend on the values of the model parameters (primarily elasticities). As far as possible, parameter values have been econometrically estimated, rather than prespecified by taking them from the relevant empirical literature. Comparison of the present estimation results to available empirical estimates, in Chapter 5, revealed that the parameter values included in the model generally fall within the (often large) range between upper and lower values of available empirical estimates.

Figure 6.1
Short-Run Experiments:
Inflation and Real GDP Growth

Percentage
change in the
GDP deflator

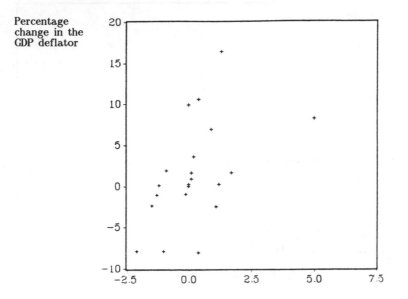

Figure 6.2
Short-Run Experiments:
The Share in GDP of Non-Agricultural Wage Income and Inflation

The share in GDP
at factor cost of
non-agricultural
wage Income

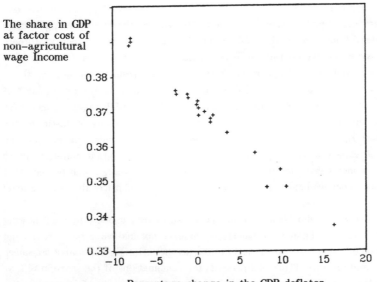

Percentage change in the GDP deflator

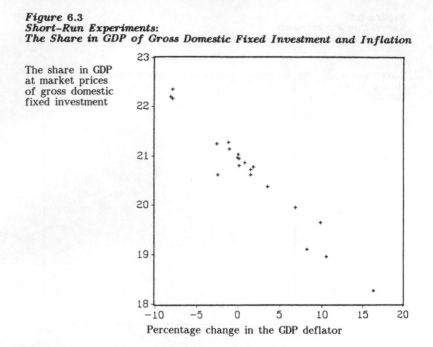

The share in GDP
at market prices
of gross domestic
fixed investment

Percentage change in the GDP deflator

A general result emerging from the simulation outcomes is that, in the short run, an increase in real GDP is accompanied by an increase in inflation. In Figure 6.1, the average rates of inflation recorded in the twenty–one agricultural policy experiments are plotted against the corresponding average rates of increase in real GDP. From the figure, it can be seen that there exists a positive co–relation between the growth rate of real GDP at market prices and the inflation rate. As the simulation results indicate, relatively low price–responsiveness of crop supply is the main factor explaining this result: an increase in the growth rate of real GDP raises demand for agricultural products, the supply of which is relatively inelastic in the short run, and, hence, agricultural prices increase, triggering off through their impact on mark–up prices and indexed nominal wages in non–agriculture an economy–wide inflationary process. From the figure, it can be seen that policy changes have a larger impact on the level of prices than on the level of (real) income.

However, short–run inflationary pressures are dampened by the following three factors. First, with imperfectly indexed nominal wage rates, real wage income in non–agriculture declines due to the inflation, containing consumer demand pressure. Figure 6.2 presents the combinations of the share in GDP at factor cost of non–agricultural wage income and the rate of increase in the GDP deflator. It can be seen that the two variables are negatively co–related, which implies a fall in real wage income when the rate of inflation increases. Second, when the rise in the rate of inflation exceeds the rate of increase in sectoral mark–up income, private fixed investment demand in the consumer goods sector and in services declines in real terms, containing pressure from investment demand. From Figure 6.3 in which the shares in GDP at market prices of gross domestic fixed investment are plotted against the increase in the GDP deflator, it can be seen that a rise in the rate of inflation is co–related with a decline in real fixed investment. Thirdly, inflationary pressures are dampened by the fall in real terms of public interest and transfers payments, revenue from public undertakings, and remittances from abroad – which are all fixed in nominal terms.

When the general equilibrium model is solved under variations in policy parameters or policy variables, it is useful – given its complexity – to think of its solution in terms of macro–economic adjustments that bring savings in line with investment (or, what amounts to the same, adjustments that lead to aggregate supply–demand balance). To discuss the macro–economic adjustment mechanisms in greater detail, consider the example of an increase in public investment. With relatively inelastic agricultural supply, the increase in aggregate demand raises prices, with agricultural prices generally increasing most. Due to the inflation, the share in GDP of gross domestic investment declines (despite the initial increase in public investment) – as can be seen from Figure 6.3. All this leads to the following adjustments on the savings side to re–establish the investment–savings equality. First, the share of foreign savings (denominated in domestic currency) in GDP at market prices tends to decline with a rise in domestic inflation (see Figure 6.4). This decline in foreign savings is partly offset by the increase in complementary intermediate imports following the increase in real GDP, which – with *exogenous* exports, final imports and exchange rate – leads to an increase in the country's current account deficit or (in other words) a rise in foreign savings. Second, the impact of the rise in inflation on the share in GDP of net public savings is complex and of uncertain sign. With the inflation, a number of items of public expenditure including interest and transfer payments decline, but so does revenue from public undertakings, while revenue from indirect taxation increases following the price increase. Third, the rise in inflation leads to a decline in the share in GDP of depreciation allowances as is illustrated by Figure 6.5. Depreciation allowances are related to sectoral capital stocks – the sizes of which are assumed fixed in the short run – which largely consist of capital goods (produced by sector 7). Because the price of sector 7 goods tends to rise less fast than the general price level (which increases mainly due to agricultural price increases), the share in GDP of depreciation allowances falls with inflation. Finally, with fixed average propensities to save by income category, the impact of the increase in the rate of inflation on the share in GDP of aggregate net private savings is of uncertain sign, depending on the redistribution of income which accompanies

Figure 6.4
Short-Run Experiments:
The Share in GDP of Foreign Savings and Inflation

The share in GDP
at market prices
of foreign savings

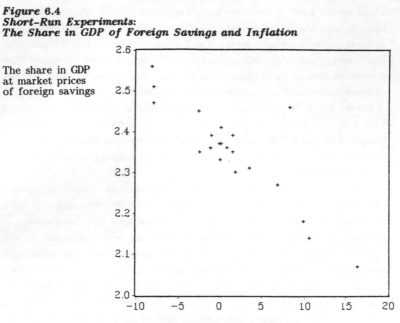

Percentage change in the GDP deflator

Figure 6.5
Short-Run Experiments:
The Share in GDP of Depreciation Allowances and Inflation

The share in GDP
at market prices
of depreciation
allowances

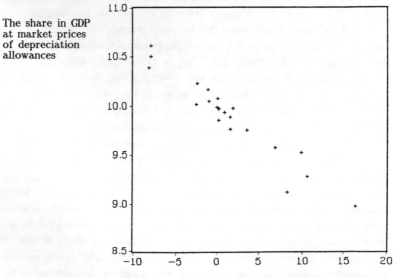

Percentage change in the GDP deflator

Figure 6.6
Short-Run Experiments:
The Share in GDP of Net Private Savings and Inflation

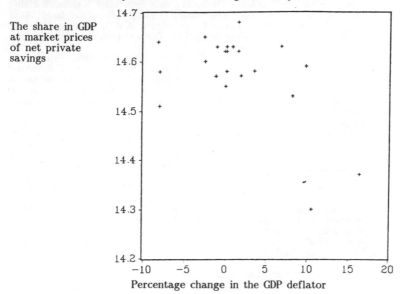

The share in GDP
at market prices
of net private
savings

Percentage change in the GDP deflator

the inflation. Due to the increases in agricultural prices, income distribution shifts in favour of agriculturalists whose (average) propensity to save is lower than the saving propensities out of non–agricultural income and, hence, one would expect the share of net private savings to decline. However, from Figure 6.6, it can be seen that the tendency of the share of net private savings to fall with a rise in inflation is not very pronounced.

In more detail, the following policy lessons can be drawn from the simulation results:

1. A rise in the rate of fertiliser subsidy has a modest, but positive impact on the level of real GDP. It augments inflationary pressures in the economy which can, however, be counteracted through adequate policies of demand management including raising direct tax rates or reducing public (investment) expenditure. Reallocating public expenditure on food subsidies to fertiliser subsidies turns out to be highly inflationary. Distributionally, a rise in the rate of fertiliser subsidy benefits agriculturalists.

2. Removal of fertiliser subsidisation does not lead the economy to the brink of disaster as is often argued by farmers' organisation, although its impact on real GDP is significantly negative. Other negative effects include a considerable decline in crop production and a marginal increase in the inflation rate. On the positive side, one must mention that the budgetary position of the government improves. Remarkably, the distribution of incomes is only marginally affected. On the other hand, a supportive policy to keep the cropwise fertiliser terms of trade unchanged through appropriate procurement price adjustment, after the removal of the fertiliser subsidy, results in almost two–digit inflation and a shift of income distribution in favour of agriculture.

3. Increasing the scope of public procurement – by increasing either the quantity to be procured or the procurement price – is expansionary. Expanding the public procurement scheme through increasing the quantities procured is less inflationary than expanding it through higher procurement prices. The inflationary impact of public food stock accumulation can be contained by combining it with an adequate stock depletion (or public distribution) policy. Farmers gain considerably from an expansion of public procurement.
4. The presence of a procurement/minimum support scheme restricts the range in which the market prices of rice and wheat – two of the major foodgrains – are allowed to balance supply and demand. The simulation results indicate that, unless a suitable procurement pricing policy is followed, the potential deflationary impact of a rise in agricultural input subsidisation may not materialise.
5. Elimination of the present system of food subsidies results in double-digit inflation, raising the share of agriculturalists in national income and erasing gross domestic fixed investment in real terms. Compensatory mesaures such as an increase in the rate of fertiliser subsidy or in the rate of producers' subsidies for foodgrains do not adequately contain inflationary pressures.
6. Extending the scope of the PDS through an increase in the quantities of foodgrains issued is less expansionary than extending it through a decrease in issue prices. The latter option, however, results in a larger increase in the rate of inflation than the former. In both cases, increasing food subsidies leads to a decline in the income share of non–agricultural wage earners, to whose benefit food subsidies were raised in the first place.

In addition, it was found that the total effect of a combination of two (or more) policy mesaures often differs from the sum of the results of changes in the individual instruments. In particular, it was found that, unless a suitable procurement price policy is followed, the deflationary impact of a rise in the rate of fertiliser subsidy or an increase in food subsidies will not materialise. These results underline the importance of finding a proper balance between the different elements of agricultural price policy.

To summarise, the general view I arrive at from the simulation results is that any attempt to raise agricultural production in the short run through the use of some of the major instruments of agricultural price policy turns out to have considerable economywide effects, particularly in terms of raising the rate of inflation and redistributing income in favour of agriculturalists, while its impact on agricultural production often is much more limited. On the other hand, attempts to reduce the subsidy rates of fertilisers and foodgrains generally have a negative impact on the objectives which these subsidies were meant to achieve, *viz.* promoting the use of fertilisers in the country, protecting (poorer) consumers from high foodgrain prices, and protecting producers from the consequences of volatile output prices and high input prices. This may explain the government's reluctance to reduce its subsidy outlays, even though – in the 1980s – they began to assume proportions which threatened the resource availability for plan expenditures.

CHAPTER SEVEN

MEDIUM-TERM SIMULATION EXPERIMENTS

7.1   *Introduction*

This chapter presents the results of a large number of medium-term or, as I will call them, dynamic simulation experiments. The distinction between short term and medium term is based on the presumption that some interval of time must elapse after investment decisions are made and expenditures undertaken, before the resulting investment goods are available for use. Specifically, it is assumed in the model that net investment in a particular year is equal to the addition to the sectoral stocks of capital goods available for use the next year.

The chapter is organised as follows. In Section 7.2, I give a brief account of the Seventh Plan strategy, before proceeding to the results of the reference run for the period 1985–90. In 7.3., I present the results of a number of dynamic experiments which were performed to assess the impact of agricultural performance on non-agricultural growth in the medium run; these experiments do not yet involve any change in agricultural policy instruments. In 7.4, the medium-run effects of a number of agricultural policy alternatives are examined. Most of these policy experiments amount to once-and-for-all changes in one or more of the agricultural policy parameters imposed on a system whose time path is set by a benchmark policy package or reference scenario. Section 7.5 concludes by drawing out the main (policy) implications arising from the results.

7.2   The Seventh Plan Period, 1985–1990

Section 7.2.1. gives a brief summary of the Seventh Five Year Plan (1985–90) document which provides the starting point for the analysis of the economy, because it includes all the details of the development strategy adopted by the government for the period 1985–90. In Section 7.2.2, the reference run is presented in some detail to give the reader some idea of the amount and type of information obtained from the simulation experiments.

7.2.1   The Seventh Plan Strategy

The Seventh Plan strategy which aims at a significant increase in productive employment in a context of self–reliance and improved efficiency is founded on two premises. The first premise is that control of inflation is essential for preventing the erosion of savings of the government and that, unless inflationary pressure is contained, the adequate mobilisation of private savings would also prove a difficult task. The importance of price stability was augmented by the increasing openness of the economy, the need to service external debt, and the importance of improving the competitiveness of non–traditional exports, which requires that the domestic price level does not rise unnecessarily, particularly in years in which India's major trading partners experience price stability. According to the second premise, the unsatisfactory rate of agricultural growth may act as a major constraint on industrial growth (Planning Commission, 1984:2). Presuming that the growth in (industrial) employment would be non–inflationary only if agricultural production was augmented significantly, the loosening of the agricultural constraint on industrial growth, which was expected to occur during the Seventh Plan period, was believed to be critical to the success of the strategy.

According to the Seventh Plan, given the planned growth rate of real GDP, maintaining price stability required an increase in the growth rate of agricultural production from 4 per cent per annum (achieved during the Sixth Plan) to 5 per cent per annum during 1985–90. Given the growing demographic pressure and the progressive decline in the size of agricultural holdings, this target could only be met if obstacles to increased productivity of small farms were removed. To this end, a programme of irrigation development with an emphasis on the economically backward regions and small and marginal farmers was considered required, along with greater emphasis on extension work to ensure that the average yields per hectare were raised to higher levels, adequate provision of credit, supply of inputs at stabilised prices, and appropriate price policies for the different competing crops. Irrigation support was provided through major and medium irrigation projects[1], command

---

[1] According to the revised classification (1978), irrigation projects having a

258

area development, tank irrigation and the use of ground water. Since minor irrigation schemes including ground water and surface water schemes, are quick maturing and labour intensive by nature, increasing emphasis was laid on the development of minor irrigation structures.[2]

In the expectation that it was possible to achieve the planned increase in the agricultural growth rate, in the Seventh Plan, attention could be directed towards the industrial sectors. With respect to these sectors, the aims of the Seventh Plan strategy are raising efficiency, increasing the rates of utilisation of existing capacity, and modernisation and upgradation of industrial technology. To achieve these ends, the following measures were taken: (*i*) the infrastructural constraints affecting the industrial sectors were tackled by giving the infrastructure sectors including energy and transport, investment priority, where necessary; (*ii*) emphasis shifted from administrative controls in achieving the objectives of industrialisation towards greater reliance on financial incentives in channelling investments in the desired areas; (*iii*) the limits for industrial investments not requiring a license were raised; and (*iv*) the trade policy regime was further 'liberalised' to facilitate access to raw materials, intermediates and capital goods needed for the maintenance and enhancement of domestic production, in the belief that increased (international) competition 'can enhance productivity, quality and growth, reduce costs and provide a basis for faster industrial growth.' (Planning Commission, 1984:19). As a complement to the above-mentioned measures, the income–tax rate was reduced in the Budget of 1985. With agricultural incomes remaining largely untaxed, the tax changes essentially concerned the non–agricultural sectors.

The fulfilment of the Seventh Plan objectives required a growth rate of real GDP of a little over 5 per cent. Over the five year period, aggregate investments were required of the order of Rs. 320,000 crores at 1984–85 prices of which public investment would make up about Rs. 150,000 crores. The rate of investment was projected to increase from 24.5 per cent of GDP in 1984–85 to 25.9 per cent in 1989–90. To finance the required investment outlays, the level of national savings was planned to increase. Adequate domestic mobilisation of savings was regarded as critical in view of the diminished inflow of concessional financial assistance from abroad, sizeable debt service obligations, and a global environment where real interest rates were expected to remain high with only limited possibilities of any significant increase in

---

culturable command area of more than 10 thousand hectares each are classified as major irrigation schemes, those having a culturable command area between 2 thousand and 10 thousand hectares as medium projects, and those having a culturable command area of 2 thousand or less hectares are classified as minor irrigation schemes.

[2] The Minor Irrigation Programme was essentially a farmers' programme which is implemented primarily through individual and cooperative efforts, with finance obtained from institutional and private sources. Public sector outlays, by and large, are only invested in medium and major irrigation projects.

the growth rate of export volume. In fact, the rate of domestic savings was projected to rise from 23.3 per cent of GDP in 1984–85 to 24.5 per cent in 1989–90. The public sector was expected to contribute about one quarter of aggregate savings in the plan period, arising entirely from the mobilisation of resources generated as surpluses of public enterprises.

The external financing of the Seventh Plan was expected to involve a current account deficit of no more than 1.6 per cent of GDP. To achieve this, the country's export performance had to be substantially improved and the growth of imports (of especially petroleum and petroleum products) to be curbed. The volume of exports was projected to rise by nearly 7 per cent per annum during 1985–90. Imports were projected to grow at an annual rate of only 5.8 per cent. No foodgrain imports were envisaged because of the high level of food stocks, the expected production growth in agriculture, and the reduced impact of possible droughts with the further extension of irrigation. The flow of remittances from Indians abroad was expected to remain more or less stable in nominal terms, implying a decline in real terms. On the whole, net invisible earnings were projected to offset somewhat less than half of the deficit on the merchandise account.

7.2.2 *The Reference Run*: 1985–86 *to* 1989–90

For each year of the period 1985–86 to 1989–90, the model was calibrated to reproduce as good as possible the actually observed course of the economy in terms of most of the major endogenous variables (see Section 5.5). The reference scenario thus obtained serves as a benchmark for comparison of the policy scenarios. Tables 7.1 to 7.4 present the results of the reference run in some detail. Even though the model is not a 'forecasting' model and the reference run is not meant to be subjected to evaluation procedures (determining whether the model reaches some acceptable standard of 'tracking' performance), in what follows I do compare some results with actual data for the period 1985–90 if only to show that the results obtained from the general equilibrium model are credible for India.

Beginning with macroeconomic data, the record of aggregate economic growth during the Seventh Plan period was strong as can be seen from Table 7.1 in which the actual growth rates of a number of selected variables are compared to corresponding growth rates taken from the reference run. Growth in GDP (at market prices) in base–year prices over the 1985–89 period turned out to be 5.8 per cent per annum in the reference run, comparable to about 6.1 per cent according to the NAS data. The largest deviations between actual and simulated growth rates are registered by aggregate exports and imports. The model's overoptimistic assessment of export and import growth partly stems from the fact that projections of exogenous exports and final imports include the so–called adjustment of merchandise exports/imports to the change of

Table 7.1
Average Annual Growth Rates of Selected Variables

	Reference Run 1985–86/ 1989–90	Reference Run 1985–86/ 1988–89	Actuals 1985–86/ 1989–90	Actuals 1985–86/ 1988–89
in real terms				
GDP at factor cost	5.2	5.6		6.1
GDP at market prices	5.4	5.8		6.1
Gross Domestic Investment	4.1	4.2		3.3
Public Final Consumption	8.2	8.8		8.7
Private Final Consumption	5.2	5.7		6.1
Exports	11.1	13.5		9.7
Imports	7.8	9.7		3.6
prices:				
Rice	9.0		7.4	
Wheat	9.6		5.6	
Other Food Crops	11.3		10.5	
Commercial Crops	12.4		8.0	
Other Agriculture	7.0		7.2	
Fertilisers	6.2		– 0.4	
Basic, Intermediate & Capital Goods	7.1		6.0	
Consumer Goods	6.7		8.8	
Services	5.4		7.2	
Consumer Price Index	7.9		8.3	
commoditywise output:				
Rice	1.4		3.8	
Wheat	2.6		1.4	
Other Food Crops	0.3		–1.5	
Commercial Crops	0.7		n.a.	
Other Agriculture	3.6		n.a.	
Fertilisers	3.7		11.9	
Basic, Intermediate & Capital Goods	6.8		9.1	
Consumer Goods	9.2		6.0	
Services	9.3		n.a.	

Note: n.a. = not available.
Sources: *CSO* (1990); Ministry of Finance (1991).

ownership basis reported in the NAS.[3] When this adjustment is taken into account, the actual growth rate of the import volume changes to 9.8 per cent per annum in the first four years of the Seventh Plan period (Ministry of Finance, 1991:158).

During the Seventh Plan period, including a major drought in 1987–88, the average rate of inflation as measured by the consumer price index was 8.3 per cent per year (Table 7.1), which is somewhat higher than the average rate of inflation recorded in the reference run. Inflationary pressures during the Seventh Plan period were largely due to the widening gap between demand and

---

[3] The adjustment of merchandise imports to the change in ownership basis accounts for the difference between the figures of merchandise exports/imports from the two sources, *viz.* the RBI and DGCI&S.

261

Table 7.2
Real Gross Domestic Product and Expenditure
(in milliards of Rupees at 1985–86 prices)

	1985–86 Actual	1985–86 RR	1986–87 Actual	1986–87 RR	1987–88 Actual	1987–88 RR	1988–89 Actual	1988–89 RR	1989–90 RR
Publ. Cons.	292	292	325	328	354	338	375	376	400
Priv. Cons.	1729	1729	1842	1812	1905	1870	2065	2044	2118
GFI	550	550	582	601	581	596	661	668	685
Stock Changes	130	130	87	70	75	76	89	101	115
Exports	156	156	155	184	175	189	206	228	235
Imports (−)	233	233	210	237	219	240	259	308	315
Expenditure	2625	2625	2781	2759	2872	2830	3137	3109	3240
NDP	2078	2078	2162	2179	2246	2235	2483	2437	2529
Deprec.	262	262	281	281	292	295	310	318	336
Indir. Taxes	370	370	400	383	431	394	456	430	453
Subsidies (−)	85	85	92	85	102	93	112	75	78
GDP	2625	2625	2751	2759	2867	2830	3137	3109	3240

in percentages of GDP

	1985–86 Actual	1985–86 RR	1986–87 Actual	1986–87 RR	1987–88 Actual	1987–88 RR	1988–89 Actual	1988–89 RR	1989–90 RR
Publ. Cons.	0.11	0.11	0.12	0.12	0.12	0.12	0.12	0.12	0.12
Priv. Cons.	0.66	0.66	0.66	0.66	0.66	0.66	0.66	0.66	0.66
GFI	0.21	0.21	0.21	0.22	0.20	0.21	0.21	0.22	0.21
Stock Changes	0.05	0.05	0.03	0.03	0.03	0.03	0.03	0.03	0.04
Exports	0.06	0.06	0.06	0.07	0.06	0.07	0.07	0.07	0.07
Imports (−)	0.09	0.09	0.08	0.09	0.08	0.09	0.08	0.10	0.10
Expenditure	1.00	1.00	1.00	1.00	1.00	1.00	1.00	1.00	1.00
NDP	0.79	0.79	0.79	0.79	0.78	0.79	0.79	0.78	0.78
Deprec.	0.10	0.10	0.10	0.10	0.10	0.10	0.10	0.10	0.11
Indir. Taxes	0.14	0.14	0.15	0.14	0.15	0.14	0.15	0.14	0.14
Subsidies (−)	0.03	0.03	0.03	0.03	0.04	0.03	0.04	0.02	0.02
GDP	1.00	1.00	1.00	1.00	1.00	1.00	1.00	1.00	1.00

Note: (1) NDP is Net Domestic Product at factor cost; (2) GDP is Gross Domestic Product at market prices; (3) GFI is gross fixed investment; and (4) RR is reference run.
Source: *CSO* (1990).

supply of other food crops (pulses) and commercial crops (in particular, edible oils) and to import price rises for petroleum and petroleum products (included in the basic, intermediate and capital goods sector).[4] With respect to the evolution of the commodity prices, the reference run reasonably reproduces the actual annual price increases during 1985–89. It is to be noted that, in the model, prices in non–agriculture are cost–determined and, hence, that their evolution over time has a considerable autonomous character as it is partly based on the annual changes in the prices of imported intermediate

---

[4] Stagnation in domestic oil production has increased the country's dependence on imported petroleum and petroleum. See EAC (1989).

inputs. The time path of agricultural prices is affected by the yearly changes in procurement prices determining the floor level below which agricultural prices do not fall. The simulated average annual price increase of fertilisers of 6.2 per cent differs considerably from the actual average price decline of 0.4 per cent per annum. This difference is due to the fact that in reality the level of nominal fertiliser prices was kept fixed for farmers during most of the 1980s in a situation of rising (imported) petroleum prices, implying a substantial increase in the rate of fertiliser subsidy. In the reference run, on the other hand, the rate of fertiliser subsidy was kept fixed at its 1985–86 level and (imported) input–cost increases are transmitted onto (domestic) fertiliser prices.

From a comparison of the simulated and actual growth rates of sectorwise production (Table 7.1), it can be seen that the performance of the model is not outstanding, particularly not in the case of crop production. The considerable differences between actual and simulated growth rates may be attributed to factors the influence of which on crop output is not accounted for in the agricultural production submodel. The most important of factors omitted from the model is, of course, rainfall. As such, the model is not particularly suited for describing the (short–term) fluctuations in output levels inherent to agricultural production. During the severe drought year 1987–88, for example, foodgrain production declined by 2.1 per cent, although the decline in agricultural production was only 0.8 per cent. In 1988–89, agricultural production increased by 21 per cent and in 1989–90 by 1.7 per cent.

Gross industrial production, which grew at a little over 6 per cent per annum during the Sixth Plan period, has accelerated to an average of 8.5 per cent during the Seventh Plan period. As Table 7.1 shows, the growth performance varied considerably across different sectors. The simulated growth rate of fertiliser production is 3.7 per cent per annum which is about one–third of the actual annual growth rate of 11.9 per cent. The difference between simulated and actual performance may be attributed to the fact that the rate of fertiliser subsidy is much lower in the reference run as compared to the actual rate prevailing during the Seventh Plan period.

Table 7.2 presents the actual and simulated real national accounts for the period 1985–86 to 1989–90. Although the simulated national accounts when expressed as percentages of GDP reproduce the actual national accounts quite closely, there are a few differences. First, the simulated levels of gross fixed investment in real terms exceed the actual levels. Second, for reasons explained earlier, simulated import demand (as a proportion of GDP) exceeds actual levels of import demand. Third, simulated subsidy expenditure falls short of actual subsidy expenditure which, of course, is largely due to the fact that the rate of fertiliser subsidy used in the simulation is lower than in reality.

The evolution of the economy during the Seventh Plan period in terms of

Table 7.3
Savings and Investment Balances, 1985-86 *to* 1989-90
(percentage of GDP at market prices)

	1985–86 Actual	RR[1]	1986–87 Actual	RR	1987–88 Actual	RR	1988–89 Actual	RR	1989 –90 RR
Publ. Saving[2]	−1.1	−1.1	−1.7	−2.0	−2.3	−2.8	−2.5	−2.7	−2.7
Foreign Saving	2.4	2.4	2.2	1.5	2.1	1.5	2.8	2.5	2.3
Private Sav.[2]	14.6	14.6	9.9	14.6	12.5	14.6	13.7	14.8	14.7
Publ. Depr.	4.3	4.3	4.3	4.5	4.5	4.6	4.4	4.6	4.6
Priv. Depr.	5.6	5.6	5.6	5.7	5.6	5.8	5.5	5.7	5.7
Aggr. Saving[3]	25.9	25.9	20.5	24.3	22.4	23.8	23.9	24.9	24.7
Publ. GFI	10.5	10.5	11.3	11.2	10.4	10.5	10.0	10.3	10.0
Priv. GFI	10.5	10.5	9.5	10.5	10.9	10.6	11.1	11.3	11.2
Stock Changes	5.0	5.0	2.0	2.5	1.4	2.7	2.8	3.3	3.5
Discrepancies[4]	–	–	−2.4	–	−0.3	–	–	–	–
Aggregate Inv.	25.9	25.9	20.5	24.3	22.4	23.8	23.9	24.9	24.7

Note: (1) RR = taken from reference run; (2) Refers to *net* savings; (3) Refers to *gross* aggregate savings; and (4) Discrepancies are due to errors and omissions in the National Accounts Statistics.
Source: *CSO* (1990).

savings–investment balances is depicted in Table 7.3. The table is based on the accounting identity that, in an open economy, the balance on the current account (foreign savings) equals the gap between private domestic investment demand and private savings supply, on the one hand, and public savings, on the other hand. Table 7.3 provides some perspective on the government's handling of its finances *via* the figures on the ratio of the public revenue deficit (or net public savings) to GDP at market prices. In absolute terms, this ratio has risen since 1985–86, from 1.1 per cent in 1985–86 to 2.5 per cent of GDP in 1988–89. The revenue deficit increased from 0.8 per cent of GDP on average per annum in the Sixth Plan to 1.9 per cent on average per annum during the first four years of the Seventh Plan. In the reference run, the share in GDP of net public savings amounts to −2.3 per cent on average per annum. The large revenue deficit means that a significant part of public revenue expenditure was financed by borrowed resources on which there are interest and repayment liabilities. While the growth target of the Seventh Plan has been more or less achieved, the pattern of financing has been different from what was anticipated, the magnitude of deficit financing significantly exceeding the level that was projected. The magnitude of the actual budget deficit, defined as the difference between all receipts and expenditures (both revenue and capital), during the Seventh Plan was of the order of Rs. 29,503 crores (at 1984–85 prices) which was more than double the estimate of Rs. 14,000 crores. In effect, interest payments (which are exogenous in the model) substantially increased from around 9.7 per cent of public current expenditure in 1985–86 to 13.1 per cent in 1989–90. As such, the large revenue deficit eroded the

Table 7.4
Reference Run: Income Distribution, 1985–86 to 1989–90

	Income shares:					Annual
	1985 –86	1986 –87	1987 –88	1988 –89	1989 –90	Growth Rate
Agricultural Income	0.327	0.320	0.332	0.309	0.309	3.9
Non–Agr. Wage Income	0.372	0.374	0.367	0.377	0.376	5.4
Non–Agr. Mark–up Inc.	0.231	0.230	0.224	0.236	0.234	5.5
Government Income	0.070	0.076	0.077	0.078	0.081	8.3
GDP at factor cost[1]	2340.6	2460.4	2529.3	2754.6	2864.7	5.2

Note: (1) In Rs. milliard at 1985–86 prices.
Source: Computed.

capacity to finance plan expenditure.

The ratio of the deficit on the nation's current account to GDP increased from 2.4 per cent in 1985–86 to 2.8 per cent in 1988–89. The current account deficit amounted to 2.2 per cent of GDP at market prices on average per annum (Ministry of Finance, 1991), comparable to an average of 2.0 per cent per annum in the reference run. This rise in the deficit on the current account was largely due to a shrinking of the surplus on the merchandise account. Following the wide array of export promoting measures taken in 1985–86, export performance improved during 1985–90 as compared to the Sixth Plan period. The annual growth rate of export volume increased from 3 per cent during 1980–85 to 9.7 per cent during 1985–89 (Table 7.1). Despite the improvement in export performance, the balance on the current account did not improve due to the continuing growth in import volume, the rise in world market prices of major import goods, the steep rise in debt service payments (associated with earlier borrowings), and the levelling off of workers' remittances from abroad (EAC, 1989:11). The more liberal trade regime is likely to have enabled a rise in imports of both consumer goods and capital goods, consequent on the rise in the domestic consumer demand following the tax reduction of 1985.

From Tables 7.1 to 7.3, the conclusion can be drawn that the reference run reasonably reproduces the evolution of most of the macro–economic variables over time, while the model's performance at the sectoral level, particularly for the cropping sectors, is not outstanding. Its poor performance at the sectoral (output as well as price) level is mainly the result of the fact that – due to the exclusion of variables such as rainfall – the model is not able to reproduce the weather–induced fluctuations in agricultural output which occur in reality (Rao et al., 1988). This was to be expected since the model is built on the assumption of a stable reference path which serves as a benchmark for the evaluation of (agricultural) policy changes.

Table 7.4 presents the time paths of the shares in real GDP at factor cost and the annual rates of real income growth of the different income categories.[5] It can be seen that the annual rates of real income growth vary considerably between the income categories. On the one extreme, real agricultural income increases by only 3.9 per cent per annum, on the other extreme, government income rises by 8.3 per cent per annum. As a result, the distribution of real GDP at factor cost changes substantially. In particular, the share of agricultural income declines from 32.7 per cent in 1985–86 to 30.9 per cent in 1989–90, although it rises to 33.2 per cent in 1987–88. The distributional shift in favour of agriculture in 1987–88 can be attributed to the sharp increases in agricultural prices following the drought. With less than perfectly indexed nominal wages, rising inflationary pressures following the drought of 1987–88 led to a fall in real wages, reducing the share of non–agricultural wage earners in GDP. In effect, the inflationary pressures were dampened considerably by these income redistributions, with the cost borne largely by the non–agricultural wage earners.

Table 7.5 gives details of the evolution of net sown area, net irrigated area, gross cropped area, and gross irrigated area over the reference run. The ultimate irrigation potential from major, medium and minor irrigation schemes is estimated at 113.5 million hectares (gross irrigated area) of which 58.5 million hectares stems from major and medium irrigation works and 55 million hectares from minor irrigation projects. At the beginning of the Seventh Plan period, out of this potential only 54.2 million hectares were actually brought under irrigation. During the Sixth Plan period, gross irrigated area increased by 4.2 million hectares (FAI, 1989–90). According to the reference scenario, gross irrigated area rises by 4.7 million hectares during the Seventh Plan period, accruing to rice (32 per cent), wheat (32 per cent), other food crops (13 per cent), and commercial crops (23 per cent).

In 1985–86, rice was the most important cereal crop, grown over an area of about 41 million hectares with an aggregate irrigation coverage of 43 per cent. In the reference run, gross cropped area under rice increases to 42.5 million hectares (or 23.2 per cent of total gross cropped area) in 1989–90, with an irrigation coverage of 45.2 per cent. Although it accounts for only 13 per cent of gross cropped area, wheat production plays an important role in stabilising foodgrains production in the country. The relative stability of the growth rate of wheat production is largely due to its high irrigation coverage (of more than 75 per cent). Other food crops including coarse cereals such as jowar, bajra, maize, barley and small millets, and pulses, are largely grown by small and marginal farmers under rainfed conditions. Other food crops production occupies about 36 per cent of gross cropped area and has an aggregate irrigation coverage of less than 10 per cent. According to the

---

[5] Except for in the base year, there were no data available concerning the distribution of income. Hence, it was not possible to evaluate the simulated evolution of income distribution.

Table 7.5
Acreage Statistics, 1985–86 to 1989–90
(in millions of hectares)

	1985–86 RR	1985–86 Actual	1986–87 RR	1986–87 Actual	1987–88 RR	1987–88 Actual	1988–89 RR	1989–90 RR
nsa	140.9	140.9	140.2	140.2	138.0	–	141.5	141.5
nia	42.8	42.8	43.3	43.1	43.5	–	44.5	46.5
gca:	178.8	178.8	178.4	176.9	176.7	–	181.0	183.1
Rice	41.1	41.1	41.2	41.2	40.7	38.9	41.4	42.5
Wheat	23.0	23.0	23.5	23.1	23.5	23.1	23.7	24.6
Oth. Food	63.9	63.9	63.2	62.9	62.0	57.7	63.2	64.3
Comm. Crops	50.8	50.8	50.6	49.7	50.4	–	52.8	51.7
gia	54.2	54.2	54.8	55.6	55.0	–	56.3	58.9
Rice	17.7	17.7	17.8	18.2	17.8	17.0	18.1	19.2
Wheat	17.5	17.5	17.9	17.7	18.1	17.9	18.2	19.1
Oth. Food	4.9	4.9	4.9	5.9	4.8	5.6	4.8	5.5
Comm. Crops	14.1	14.1	14.1	14.0	14.3	–	15.1	15.1

Note: RR = taken from reference run.
Source: Ministry of Finance (1991).

Economic Survey 1990–91, the main constraints to increasing the production of other food crops are (i) the low coverage of area under high yielding varieties, because of the non–availability of these seeds in sufficient quantities, and (ii) the reluctance of farmers to invest in inputs as these crops are sensitive to climatic conditions (farmers in rainfed areas which constitute 70 per cent of the gross cropped area, consume only about 20 per cent of the total amount of fertilisers consumed). The latter constraint can be overcome by increasing the irrigation coverage of other food crops production. Finally, during the Seventh Plan period, around 28 per cent of gross cropped area is used for the growing of commercial crop including edible oils, sugarcane, coffee, tea, jute and cotton. Only about 28 per cent of area under commercial crops is irrigated.

7.3   Agriculture–Industry Interaction: The Medium Term

In this section, the results are reported of four dynamic simulation experiments which were designed to highlight the major interrelationships between agriculture and non–agriculture, affecting the performance of the Indian economy. Specifically, the following questions were asked: (i) How would the economy have evolved had it not experienced a major drought in 1987–88? (experiment $DN–1$); (ii) What would have been the consequences of an even more favourable evolution of world market demand for Indian exports? (experiment $DN–2$); (iii) What would have been the impact of re–allocating public investment from agriculture towards non–agriculture? (experiment *DN* – 3); and (*iv*) What would have been the effects of pursuing an 'industry–first' investment policy financed by an increase in direct taxation of agricultural income? The simulation results are reported in Section 7.3.1. The conclusions are drawn in 7.3.2.

7.3.1 Simulation Results

Detailed results from each experiment are presented in the tables collected in Appendix 7.1. It should be noted that the results of the experiments are discussed in comparison to the reference run.[6]

Experiment DN – 1: 'No Drought' Scenario in which Net Sown Area in 1987 – 88 is Raised from 138 Million Hectares in the Reference Run to 141.5 Million Hectares.

This experiment was performed to assess the impact of the absence of the 1987–88 drought on the economy's performance during the Seventh Plan period. To this end, the level of net sown area in 1987–88 which was taken as a proxy for weather–related fluctuations, was raised from 138 million hectares in the reference run to 141 million hectares. This helps to bring out the impact of fluctuations in agricultural output on the time path of the economy.

During the first two years of the simulation period, the evolution of the economy is similar to the reference run. However, with the increase in net sown area in 1987–88, the economy starts taking a different course. The increase in net sown area leads to an increase in crop production which, with *given* demand, results in a decline in agricultural prices as compared to the reference run. The fall in crop prices has two immediate effects. First, it leads to a decline in 'committed' consumer expenditure on foodgrains and commercial crops and an increase in expenditure on other commodities, including non–agricultural goods. As a result, capacity utilisation rates in non–agriculture improve. Second, it reduces the consumer price index due to which nominal wage rates in non–agriculture decline. With the decline in consumer prices and nominal wages, the immediate impact of *DN* – 1 is deflationary.

Following the decline in the terms of trade for agriculture, private agricultural investment demand declines, leading to a fall in net irrigated area and aggregate cropping intensity in later years. The decline in cropping intensity is one of two factors mitigating the positive impact of increased net sown area in 1987–88 on the growth rates of crop output during 1988–89 to 1989–90. The other factor is the increase in the fertiliser price relative to crop prices due to which farmers reduce their fertiliser input. Because both

---

[6] This means, for example, that when the consequences of a simulation experiment are labeled 'contractionary', one should read 'contractionary as compared to the reference run'.

the price elasticity of fertiliser demand and the fertiliser–response of yield are highest for wheat, the fall in wheat production is relatively larger than the declines in the production levels of the other crops. In effect, the improvement in agricultural performance during 1987–88 leads to a deterioration in the performance of wheat during 1988–90, whereas the growth performance of the other crops improves (Table 7.A.3). With the relatively large decline in wheat output, the market price for wheat increases, partly offsetting the short–run deflationary impact of $DN-1$. In the event, $DN-1$ has a limited, but negative, impact on inflation. The average annual rate of inflation as measured by the consumer price index declines from 7.6 per cent in the reference run to 7.2 per cent.

The real income gains following from the increase in crop production (with the exception of wheat) are more than offset by the real income loss due to the decrease in agricultural prices and, as a result, real agricultural income declines as compared to the reference run. This reduces domestic final demand for non–agricultural products and, hence, negatively affects non–agricultural production and incomes. Consequently, the growth rates of real non–agricultural incomes decline (Table 7.A.3) and experiment $DN-1$ turns out to be slightly contractionary. The average annual growth rate of real GDP at factor cost declines from 5.2 per cent per annum in the reference run to 5.1 per cent per annum.

According to the simulation outcome, the economy's performance in terms of real GDP growth and inflation during the Seventh Plan period would not have improved substantially with an increase in net sown area in 1987–88. This results is primarily to be attributed to the decline in the final demand of farmers following the deterioration of the terms of trade for agriculture. These results underline the importance of domestic demand conditions for the process of economic growth.

Experiment DN–2: The Growth Rate of Real Exports of the Non–agricultural Sectors 7, 8, and 9 is Raised from 10 Per Cent Per Year in the Reference Run to 15 Per Cent Per Annum.

This experiment extends experiment $N-5$ in which the short–run effects of an increase in world demand for non–agricultural goods were examined, to the medium run. The medium–run effects on the domestic economy of an increase in world market demand for basic, intermediate, and capital goods, consumer goods, and services are basically similar to its short–run effects. Following the increase in world demand, non–agricultural production (which is demand-determined) and incomes increase, leading to a sharp increase in intermediate and final demand for agricultural goods. With relatively inelastic agricultural supply, agricultural prices increase, raising the consumer price index as well as non–agricultural wages and prices. Hence, $DN-2$ is inflationary (Table 7.A.2).

Indirectly, the increase in non–agricultural exports provides a stimulus to crop production. This has two causes. First, due to the increase in crop prices relative to the fertiliser price, fertiliser input is increased. Second, with the improvement in the terms of trade for agriculture, private agricultural investment increases which results in a rise of net irrigated area and aggregate cropping intensity in the medium run. Both the increase in fertiliser use and the increase in cropping intensity contribute to a rise in crop outputs as compared to the reference run (Table 7.A.3). Due to the increase in agricultural prices and the rise in the growth rates of crop production, the average annual growth rate of real agricultural income increases, i.c. from 3.9 per cent in the reference run to 5.6 per cent. In turn, the increase in agricultural production and income provides a 'second–round' stimulus to non–agricultural production, following the initial increase in world market demand. As a result, the growth rates of non–agricultural production and real incomes increase (Table 7.A.3). In effect, the impact of the increase in world market demand is expansionary, raising the average annual growth rate of real GDP at factor cost from 5.2 per cent in the reference run to 5.8 per cent.

Distributionally, the benefits of the non–agricultural export drive accrue mainly to agricultural income, the share of which in GDP at factor cost increases from 31.9 per cent on average per annum in the reference run to 32.7 per cent on average per annum (Table 7.A.7). The share in GDP of non–agricultural wage income declines from 37.3 per cent on average per annum to 36.9 per cent. Hence, also in the medium run, a non–agricultural export drive leads to a redistribution of income from non–agricultural wage earners towards agriculturalists.

In drawing conclusions from these simulations results it is important to keep in mind that, in the model, real export growth is not affected by the rate of domestic inflation relative to price changes in the world market. To the extent that real export growth would have been negatively affected by a relative increase in domestic inflation, the simulation results do not adequately capture the agricultural constraint on export–led growth.

Experiment DN – 3: Public Investment in Agriculture is Reduced by 20 Per Cent and Re – allocated to Public Investment in the Basic, Intermediate and Capital Goods Sector.

It is sometimes argued that India, at its current stage of development, should follow a long–term policy of 'industry–first', implicitly assuming that agriculture is no longer a constraint on industrial growth and, hence, can be treated as a 'bargain sector'[7]. Experiment DN – 3 looks at the medium–run consequences of a particular 'industry–first' strategy, i.c. one involving a substantial re-allocation of public investment from agriculture to non–agriculture.

---

[7] The meaning of 'bargain sector' has been explained in Chapter 3. For the origins of the concept, the reader may consult Chakravarty (1987:94).

In the medium run, the reduction of public agricultural investment (and, consequently, of private agricultural investment) leads to a fall in net irrigated area, a decline in aggregate cropping intensity, and a decrease in the levels of crop output (Table 7.A.3). The decline in crop outputs has two major effects. First, given the level of crop prices, it leads to a decline in agricultural income which, in turn, reduces domestic demand for non–agricultural goods and, hence, results in a decrease in non–agricultural production and income. The income decline in both agriculture and non–agriculture also reduces demand for agricultural goods, putting downward pressure on agricultural prices. Second, with *given* demand, the decline in crop outputs leads to increases in crop prices which raise the consumer price index and nominal non–agricultural wage rates; the increase in nominal wages, in turn, raises non–agricultural mark–up prices. The net effect on agricultural prices of these two opposite forces is positive: agricultural prices increase relative to the reference run.

The increase in agricultural prices forces consumers to spend more on agricultural goods, the consumption of which is fixed to a relatively large extent, and less on non–agricultural goods. Consequently, final demand for non–agricultural goods declines as compared to the reference run. The size of the home market for non–agricultural goods is further reduced by the decline in agriculture's intermediate demand for non–agricultural inputs, following the decrease in crop outputs. As a result, the growth rates of non–agricultural production decline, leading to a fall in the growth rates of real non–agricultural wage and mark–up income. The decline in non–agricultural income growth, in turn, mitigates the upward pressure on crop prices and, as a result, $DN-3$ turns out to be only marginally inflationary. The average rate of inflation as measured by the consumer price index increases from 7.6 per cent per annum in the reference run to 7.7 per cent per annum. With the decline in crop outputs and in non–agricultural production, policy $DN-3$ leads to contraction. The average annual growth rate of real GDP at market prices declines from 5.7 per cent in the reference run to 5.5 per cent.

These results suggest that, with a relatively inelastic agricultural supply, the dangers of stagflation are particularly acute. They further indicate that, in such circumstances, raising the 'agriculture–constrained' growth rate of real GDP hinges on the adequate extension of infrastructural facilities in agriculture, particularly related to irrigation and electricity. It is in this context that public agricultural investment aimed at increasing agriculture's production capacity assumes critical importance.

Experiment DN – 4: The Direct Tax Rate on Agricultural Income is Raised from Zero Per Cent in the Reference Run to 2.5 Per Cent. The Revenue from this Direct Tax Increase is Used to Raise Public Investment in the Basic, Intermediate and Capital Goods Sector.

Experiments $DN-4$ presents another clear–cut example of an 'industry–first' development strategy which aims at accelerating the pace of industrialisation by an increase in public investments in basic, intermediate and capital goods, financed by an outflow of resources (*via* direct taxation) from agriculture. In emphasizing agriculture's role as a contributor of food and raw materials and surplus savings, $DN-4$ echoes the policy lessons drawn from the classical approach articulated by Preobrazhensky and Lewis (see Chapter 2). What are the effects of pursuing such an 'industry–first' investment policy?

The immediate impact of $DN-4$ is twofold. First, the increase in direct taxation reduces disposable agricultural income, leading to a decline in agriculturalists' final demand. Second, the increase in public investment raises capacity utilisation and production in sector 7, resulting (through a multiplier process) in an increase in non–agricultural incomes. Hence, due to $DN-4$, income and, hence, effective demand are redistributed from agriculture to non–agriculture. Given the initial configuration of marginal budget shares (with marginal budget shares of agriculturalists being higher for agricultural than for non–agricultural goods and of non–agricultural consumers being higher for non–agricultural than for agricultural commodities), this redistribution of income leads to a decline in the demand for agricultural goods and an increase in the demand for non–agricultural products. As a result, agricultural prices decline and non–agricultural capacity utilisation rates increase.

In the medium run, the decline in agricultural prices leads to a fall in the growth rates of crop outputs because of the following two factors. First, due to the decrease in crop prices relative to the fertiliser price, fertiliser use is reduced, which leads to a decline in yield levels. Second, with the deterioration of the terms of trade for agriculture, private agricultural investment demand declines as compared to the reference run, due to which the growth rate of net irrigated area declines and the aggregate cropping intensity is reduced. As a result of the decline in the levels of crop production and the fall in crop prices, the growth rate of real agricultural income over the Seventh Plan period declines (Table 7.A.3). This decline in the growth rate of real agricultural income reduces the growth of the domestic market for non–agricultural goods, which negatively affects non–agricultural income growth. The decline in non–agricultural income growth is more than offset by the increase in public investment in basic, intermediate and capital goods production, which is further magnified by the multiplier mechanism. As a result, the average annual growth rates of non–agricultural production and real incomes improve as compared to the reference run. However, the net impact on real GDP at market prices of the decline in crop outputs and the increase in non–agricultural production (with the exception of fertiliser production) is only modest, but positive (Table 7.A.3).

Following the fall in agricultural prices, the consumer price index declines and, as a result, nominal wages in non–agriculture decline (Table 7.A.2). Consequently, policy $DN-4$ turns out to be deflationary. Hence, despite the considerable change in investment strategy, the medium–run effect on real GDP of $DN-4$ are marginal at best, while its impact on inflation is negative. Distributionally, $DN-4$ favours non–agricultural wage earners. Their share in GDP at factor cost increases from 37.3 per cent on average per annum in the reference run to 37.6 per cent (Table 7.A.7). In contrast, the share in GDP of agricultural income declines.

According to the simulation results, it is the decline in real agricultural income growth that is responsible for the limited impact of $DN-4$ on real GDP growth. The results thus indicate that, in a situation in which the opportunities for exporting industrial products are limited and the agricultural sector is large, the demand for non–agricultural goods emanating from agriculture is an important determinant of the size of the domestic market and – as such – a critical factor in affecting non–agricultural performance over time. Finally, these results should caution against treating agriculture as a 'passive' sector which merely needs to provide the required savings funds to industry.

7.3.2   *Conclusions*

The results of the four experiments presented in the Section 7.3 indicate that the performance of the non–agricultural sectors is harmed both by too high a level of agricultural prices as well as by too low a level of these prices. Too high a level of agricultural prices restricts the size of the home market for non–agricultural commodities because it leads consumers to spend more on agricultural goods and less on non–agricultural goods. It also leads to an increase in non–agricultural nominal wage rates, which, in combination with higher prices of agricultural raw materials, adds up to considerable cost–push inflation. Because of all this, too high a level of agricultural prices may result in stagflation – a point which was already stressed by Mitra (1977) and Nayyar (1978) in the context of the debate on the causes of the industrial slowdown in India during 1966–1979. Too low a level of agricultural prices, on the other hand, also restricts the size of the domestic market for non–agriculture as it results in a decline in agricultural production and income and, hence, in agriculture's (intermediate and final) demand for non–agricultural products. Bagchi (1970) and Raj (1976) based their arguments against an 'industry–first' development strategy on this negative impact on industrial performance of low levels of domestic demand by agriculturalists. Because of the fact that agriculture accounts for a substantial part of the domestic market of non–agricultural goods (both intermediates and final goods), an 'industry–first' investment strategy financed by a transfer of resources from agriculture to non–agriculture may not succeed in raising the growth rate of real GDP. More specifically, it was found that

> *Experiment DN–1*: In the medium run, increases in crop outputs due to improved weather conditions may – by reducing crop prices – result in a decline in agricultural income and a reduction in agriculturalists' final

273

demand, negatively affecting non–agricultural production and income.
Experiment DN–2: With relatively inelastic agricultural supply, a substantial increase in world market demand for non–agricultural goods leads to considerable domestic inflation. Distributionally, the step–up in non–agricultural exports benefits the farmers.
Experiment DN–3: A reduction in public agricultural investment which is used to finance an increase in public non–agricultural investment, leads to both inflation as well as contraction.
Experiment DN–4: A redistribution of income from agriculture towards non–agriculture results in a decline in the demand for agricultural goods, a fall in agricultural prices, and a decrease in crop outputs. The ensuing decline in agricultural income restricts the size of the home market for non–agricultural goods and acts as a constraint on non–agricultural production and income growth.

This razor's edge character of agriculture as a constraining sector – to borrow a phrase from Alagh (1991:50) – arises because there is an asymmetry of adjustments in the demand for and the supply of agricultural goods. Given the particular structure of demand, an increase in non–agricultural production immediately leads to an increase in intermediate and final demand for agricultural goods, whereas supply–side adjustments involving a reallocation of resources and net investment for capacity expansion take much longer to effect. As is illustrated by the outcomes of *DN–3* and *DN–4*, policy interventions in which the asymmetrical speeds of adjustment of agricultural demand and supply are not taken into account, will not yield the desired results. It is in this context that policies aimed at raising the speed of adjustment of agricultural supply assume critical importance. These policies are the subject of the next section.

7.4   *Agricultural Policy Simulation: Medium–Run Results*

Now we turn to the analysis of the dynamic agricultural policy experiments. Sixteen dynamic experiments are reported here, eight out which involve a change in public agricultural investment. Table 7.6 (below) gives an overview of these experiments. It includes five 'pure' experiments in which only one policy variable was changed at the time, and eleven 'mixed' experiments in which combinations of changes in policy variables (or policy packages) were introduced simultaneously. In general, the policy packages were designed as a combination of a change in a policy parameter involving an increase in public expenditure and changes in one or more instruments aimed at financing this additional expenditure. The total amount of simulation results was reduced to a handful of tables, appearing as Appendix 7.2. Before proceeding to the discussion of the simulation results, it is worth making two observations. First, the agricultural policy experiments reported here involve once–and–for–all changes in one or more policy instruments. Second, in the discussion, the results of the experiments are compared to the reference run. For example, when the impact of a policy experiment is termed 'deflationary', this means 'deflationary as compared to the reference run'.

Table 7.6
Catalogue of Medium–Term Agricultural Policy Experiments

Designations	Description
$D-1$	j_{ga} is raised by 20%.
$D-1.1$	j_{ga} is raised by 20%; $\sigma_6 = 0$.
$D-1.2$	j_{ga} is raised by 20%; j_{g3} is reduced by the same amount.
$D-1.3$	j_{ga} is raised by 20%; j_{g3} is reduced by the same amount; $\sigma_6 = 0$.
$D-2$	$\sigma_6 = 0$.
$D-3$	$\sigma_6 = -0.5$.
$D-3.1$	$\sigma_6 = -0.5$; j_{ga} is raised by 20%.
$D-3.2$	$\sigma_6 = -0.5$; j_{ga} is raised by 20%; j_{g3} is reduced by the same amount.
$D-3.3$	$\sigma_6 = -0.5$; j_{ga} is reduced proportionately.
$D-4$	f_{ni} are raised by 20% for $i = 1, 2, 3$.
$D-4.1$	f_{ni} are raised by 20% for $i = 1, 2, 3$; $\sigma_6 = -0.5$
$D-4.2$	f_{ni} are raised by 20% for $i = 1, 2, 3$; j_{ga} is raised by 40%.
$D-5$	p_i^* are raised by 10% for $i = 1, 2$.
$D-5.1$	p_i^* are raised by 10% for $i = 1, 2.|$ f_{ni} are raised by 10% for $i = 1, 2, 3$.
$D-5.2$	$z_i = 0$, for $i = 1, .., 3$; $f_{ni} = 0$, for $i = 1, .., 3$.
$D-5.3$	j_{ga} is raised by 50%; $\sigma_6 = -0.5$; $p_i^* = p_6$.

Note: j_{ga} is real public agricultural investment; j_{g3} is real public investment in the basic, intermediate and capital goods sector; σ_6 is the rate of producers' subsidy for fertiliser production; f_{ni} is the quantity of foodgrains issued from the Fair Price Shops; p_i^* is the procurement price of good i; $\bar{z}_i$ is the quantity of public procurement of good i; and p_6 is the market price for fertilisers. The initial value of σ_6 is –0.27.

Experiment D – 1: Public Investment in Agriculture is Raised by 20 Per Cent in Each Year of the Seventh Plan Period.

According to Chakravarty (1987:75–76), public investment in agriculture plays a leading role in the provision of adequate infrastructure required for a step–up in the agricultural growth rate. To evaluate the impact on agricultural growth of an increase in public agricultural investment, experiment $D-1$ was performed. Two effects of increased public agricultural investment over time can be distinguished. First, in the short run, it raises aggregate demand which, with relatively inelastic agricultural supply, leads to inflationary pressures in the economy. Through nominal wage indexation in non–agriculture, this short–run inflation is carried over into the medium run.[8] Second, over time, it contributes to a dampening of inflationary pressures as it increases crop production by raising agriculture's cropping intensity. The rise in cropping intensity is due to the increase in net irrigated area, resulting from increased agricultural investment, both public and private. Private agricultural investment increases following the rise in public investment and the improvement of the terms of trade for agriculture. The annual increase in net irrigated area in D–1 amounts to an additional one million hectares (or 2.2 per cent) of net irrigated area in 1989–90 as compared to the reference run.

Following the policy change, the average annual rates of production growth increase for all crops (Table 7.B.4), raising agricultural income and agriculturalists' (intermediate and final) demand both for agricultural and non–agricultural commodities. As a result, the rates of non–agricultural production growth increase, augmenting national income growth and demand pressure. With relatively inelastic agricultural supply, the policy change is inflationary, raising the average annual rate of inflation as measured by the consumer price index from 7.6 per cent in the reference run to 8.4 per cent in the $D-1$ run (Table 7.B.3). Price increases are particularly large for other food crops, the production of which is relatively price–inelastic, and other agricultural products, the output of which is completely price–inelastic. These price increases have three effects. First, agricultural price increases lead to a decrease in consumer demand for non–agricultural goods. Second, due to the inflation, real private investment demand declines in the consumer goods sector and in services. Finally, private investment in agriculture increases following the increase in public agricultural investment and the improvement in the terms of trade for agriculture.

With the rise in crop production and the increase in agricultural prices, the average annual growth rate of real agricultural income increases – from 3.9 per cent in the reference run to 4.4 per cent in the $D-1$ run (Table 7.B.5). Due to the particular specification of nominal wage indexation, real

---

[8] Note that nominal wage rates in period t are used to update the beginning–of–the–period nominal wage rates in period $t+1$. See Chapter 4.

wages do not fall over the medium run – in contrast to what happened in the short period. The annual average growth rate of real non–agricultural wage income increases from 5.4 per cent in the reference scenario to 5.7 per cent. With the increase in inflation, the growth rate of revenue from public enterprises which is fixed in nominal terms, falls in real terms. The growth rate of real non–agricultural mark–up income rises following the increase in non–agricultural production and the fall in real revenue from public undertakings. The average annual growth rate of real GDP at market prices increases from 5.7 per cent in the reference run to 6.1 per cent. Income distribution shifts from non–agricultural wage earners and public enterprises to agriculturalists and non–agricultural mark–up recipients (Table 7.B.9).

The share in GDP at market prices of aggregate gross domestic investment is affected by two mutually offsetting forces. On the one hand, the increase in public agricultural investment and the improvement in the terms of trade for agriculture in period t raise private agricultural investment in period $t+1$, which leads to a rise in gross domestic investment. On the other hand, with the inflation, private investment demand in consumer goods production and services falls in real terms, which contributes to a decline in gross domestic investment. The composition of aggregate savings required to finance gross domestic investment changes in the following ways (Table 7.B.7). First, with the rise in inflation, the share in GDP of depreciation allowances declines for reasons explained earlier. Second, the share in GDP of foreign savings is affected by two offsetting forces. On the one hand, with the rise in real GDP, complementary intermediate imports increase, which leads to a rise in foreign savings; on the other hand, the share in GDP of foreign savings declines with the inflation. Third, the share in GDP of net public savings increases from –2.3 per cent on average per annum in the reference run to –2.1 per cent on average per annum in $D-1$. The improvement in net public savings is the result of a combination of factors, the most important of which are on the revenue side: a substantial rise in revenue from indirect taxation (concomitant with price and production increases), an increase in direct tax mobilisation (following the increase in non–agricultural mark–up income), and a relatively large resource inflow on account of the procurement tax[9]. On the expenditure side, expenditure on a number of items including interest payments and current transfers which are fixed in nominal terms, declines. Expenditure on items such as producers' subsidies, export subsidies, and consumer (food) subsidies increases with the rise in real GDP and in the rate of inflation.

In view of the above, there is much to be said for a rise in public investment in agriculture. It leads to a rise in the growth rate of real

[9] In a situation in which procurement prices are lower than market prices, public procurement of foodgrains which did take place at procurement prices, has to be valued against market prices on the government account, the difference in price (times the quantity procured) being accounted for as revenue from the procurement tax.

aggregate GDP, an increase in the income growth rates of all private income categories, and an improvement in the public revenue account. A drawback of the policy change is its positive impact on the inflation rate, which erodes part of the ensuing income gains.

Experiment D – 1.1: Public Investment in Agriculture is Increased by 20 Per Cent and the Fertiliser Subsidy Rate is Eliminated.

Experiment $D-1.1$ was run, extending $D-1$ by adding to it the elimination of the fertiliser subsidy. The short–run impact of $D-1.1$ is inflationary on account of the following two factors. First, the increase in public agricultural investment raises aggregate demand, which – with *initial* agricultural supply – results in agricultural price increases. Second, the removal of the fertiliser subsidy raises the market price of fertilisers relative to the market prices of crops which – by inducing farmers to reduce the level of per hectare fertiliser input – immediately leads to a drop in the growth rates of crop production; as a result, crop supply falls and, given *initial* demand, crop prices rise. Hence, the policy change results in a rise in demand for agricultural products and a fall in their supply.

The fall in supply is largest for wheat and rice, the production of which is relatively price–responsive. Because private consumption of rice and wheat is 'committed' to a relatively high degree, the increase in the prices for rice and wheat leads to a fall in 'supernumerary' consumer expenditure, implying large declines in the consumption demand for those commodities, the marginal budget shares of which are large. In particular, consumption demand for other agricultural products declines which, with fixed supply, leads to a decline in their price. The fall in consumer demand for other agricultural products is but one of four factors which lead to a dampening of inflationary pressures in the short run. The other three factors were already mentioned in Section 6.4, *viz.* a real wage fall in non–agriculture, a fall in real private investment demand in the consumer goods and services sectors, and a decline in real terms in (public) payments which are nominally fixed.

In the medium run, however, inflationary pressures increase, mainly because of the fact that increases in crop supply lag behind increases in demand. Demand for crops increases, because, given the particular specification of nominal wage indexation, at the beginning of each year, there is an autonomous rise in nominal wage rates in non–agriculture which, on the one hand, adds to demand pressure in the economy and, on the other hand, leads to a rise in the (mark–up) price of fertiliser. Further, at the beginning of each year, the fertiliser price rises due to an (exogenous) increase in imported intermediate input costs, which, with *initial* crop prices, leads to less fertiliser use, a decline in per hectare yield levels, and a fall in crop supply. With the increase in aggregate demand and the rise in the fertiliser price relative to crop prices, the macro–economic effect of the policy change is inflationary. The average annual rate of inflation during the Seventh Plan period as measured by the consumer price index is 9.7 per cent. Nominal wage rate increases in non–agriculture vary between 12.1 per cent per annum (for workers in the basic, capital, and intermediate goods sector) and 8.7 per cent per annum (for workers in the consumer goods sector).

Figure 7.1 presents the time–path of the fertiliser price relative to each one of the four crop prices. It can be seen that, following the removal of the fertiliser subsidy, it takes almost the whole of the Seventh Plan period for the ratios of the fertiliser price to the crop price to return to a level of parity. This implies that cropwise per hectare fertiliser use only gradually increases beyond the base–year levels and, hence, that the crop output growth recorded under $D-1.1$ is to be attributed wholly to the rise in cropping intensity – from 129.4 in 1989–90 in the reference run to 130.9 in $D-1.1$. The increase in cropping intensity, in turn, is due to the rise in public as well as private agricultural investment. Private agricultural investment increases following the rise in public investment and due to the shift in the agricultural–non–agricultural terms of trade in favour of agriculture. With the crop prices increasing, the growth rates of crop production rise substantially, raising the average annual growth rate of agricultural income to 4.5 per cent (Table 7.B.5). The increase in agricultural income augments the size of the domestic market for non–agricultural commodities, the production of which increases. Hence, the policy change is strongly expansionary. The average annual growth rate of real GDP at market prices increases to 6.0 per cent. With imperfectly indexed nominal wage rates, non–agricultural wage earners lose ground. Their average annual share in GDP at factor cost declines to 37.0 per cent in $D-1.1$ (Table 7.B.9).

With the inflation, the share in GDP at market prices of gross domestic investment declines (Table 7.B.7). The required reduction in the share in GDP of savings is the outcome of the following, partly offsetting, adjustments. On the one hand, following the policy change, the share in GDP of net public savings rises which is mainly due to increased tax revenues. With output growth and a rise in the rate of inflation, revenue from indirect taxation increases as its price times quantity base increases. Revenue from direct taxation also rises following the increase in the average annual rate of growth of real non–agricultural mark–up income from 5.5 per cent in the reference scenario to 6.2 per cent. On the other hand, with the increase in inflation, the shares in GDP of foreign savings and depreciation allowances decline.

Experiment $D-1.2$: Public Investment in Agriculture is Raised by 20 Per Cent and Public Investment in Basic, Intermediate and Capital Goods is Reduced by the Same Amount in Each Year of the Seventh Plan Period.

To contain both inflationary as well as budgetary pressures, the government may implement policy package $D-1.2$ in which the level of aggregate public investment is kept unchanged as compared to the reference scenario, but in

Figure 7.1
Dynamic Experiments:
The Ratio of the Fertiliser Price to Crop Prices, 1985-89

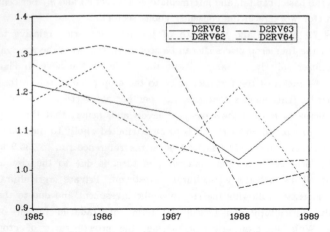

Note: RV61 refers to the fertiliser price relative to the price of rice; RV62 refers to the fertiliser price relative to the price of wheat; RV63 refers to the fertiliser price relative to the price of other food crops; and RV64 refers to the fertiliser price relative to the price of commercial crops.

which its composition is changed in favour of the agricultural sector. As compared to the reference run, the impact of the policy change is slightly deflationary. With an unchanged level of aggregate autonomous expenditure, the deflation is entirely due to the increase in the growth rates of crop production, which, in turn, results from a rise in net irrigated area. Net irrigated area is larger in 1989-90 by 1.9 million hectares than in the reference run (Table 7.B.6). The smaller impact on net irrigated area of experiment $D-1.2$ as compared to $D-1$ is to be attributed to a lower growth rate of private agricultural investment in scenario $D-1.2$ as compared to scenario $D-1$ which, in turn, is due to the smaller increase in the agricultural–non-agricultural terms of trade in $D-1.2$ *vis-à-vis* scenario $D-1$. The growth rates of crop production are higher than the ones recorded in the reference run, but are lower than those realised in scenario $D-1$. Consequently, the positive impact of the present policy change on agricultural income, agriculturalists' demand, non–agricultural income, and non–agriculturalists' demand turns out to be less than in $D-1$. Real GDP at market prices records an average annual increase of 6.0 per cent which constitutes an improvement over the growth rate of 5.7 per cent per annum realised in the reference run. With the growth rates of real income of the income groups included in the model all improving as compared to the reference run (Table 7.B.4), the impact of $D-1.2$ on income distribution is negligible. According to these results, the adoption of an 'agriculture–first' policy in terms of public investment allocation is to the equal benefit of both agricultural and non–agricultural income groups.

Following the introduction of policy $D-1.2$, the share in GDP at market prices of gross domestic investment rises (Table 7.B.7). This increase is the result of two factors. On the one hand, with the decrease in inflation, real private investment demand in the consumer goods and services sectors rises. On the other hand, agricultural investment increases, since the rise in public agricultural investment in year t leads to a rise in private agricultural investment in year $t+1$. To finance the increase in investment, savings increase, with the burden of the adjustment borne by net public savings, the share in GDP of which rises from –2.3 per cent per year in the reference run to –2.1 per cent per annum. The increase in net public savings is due to a combination of factors, including a rise in revenue from direct and indirect taxation (following the increase in real GDP), a decline in expenditure on export subsidies (following the deflation), and a rise in revenue from public enterprises (which are nominally fixed and, hence, increase with deflation).

Experiment $D-1.3$: Public Investment in Agriculture is Increased by 20 Per Cent, Public Investment in Basic, Intermediate and Capital Goods Production is Reduced by the Same Amount, and the Fertiliser Subsidy Rate is Eliminated.

Experiment $D-1.3$ extends $D-1.2$ by adding to it the elimination of the fertiliser subsidy. It aims at raising the agricultural growth rate (through increased investment in irrigation), while reducing the public revenue deficit (by cutting fertiliser subsidies). $D-1.3$ has two effects. First, the immediate impact of the removal of the fertiliser subsidy is to raise the ratio of the fertiliser price to the crop price (for all crops). In turn, this leads to a fall in crop output and, given demand, to a rise in crop prices. Through the indexation of nominal wage rates in non–agriculture, the short–run rise in crop prices is carried over into the medium run, triggering off nominal wage increases which considerably augment demand pressure in the economy. At the same time, the fertiliser price rises on account of an (exogenous) increase in imported intermediate input costs, leading to a further decline in crop output and a further increase in crop prices. Second, in the medium run, the increase in agricultural investment – both public and private – raises the average annual growth rate of net irrigated area, contributing to a rise in aggregate cropping intensity and enhancing the growth rates of crop production. With given demand, the rise in the growth rates of crop production leads to downward pressure on crop prices. However, given the particular parameter specification of the model, the policy change is inflationary (Table 7.B.3).

With the crop prices increasing, the average annual growth rate of agricultural income increases from 3.9 per cent in the reference run to 4.2 per cent. The increase in agricultural income augments the size of the domestic market for non–agricultural commodities (apart from fertilisers), leading to a rise in their production levels. The growth rates of real

281

non-agricultural wage and mark-up income also increase as compared to the reference run. Hence, the policy change is slightly expansionary. The average annual growth rate of real GDP at market prices increases to 5.8 per cent. Distributionally, the farmers benefit most from policy package $D-1.3$, their income share in GDP at factor cost increases from 31.9 per cent on average per annum in the reference run to 32.2 per cent. The share in GDP of agricultural income increases at the expense of the shares of income from public enterprises and non-agricultural wage income (Table 7.B.9).

The impact of $D-1.3$ on the share in GDP at market prices of gross domestic investment is twofold. With the improvement in the terms of trade for agriculture, real private agricultural investment rises, but this rise is offset by the decline in real private investment in the consumer goods sector and in services following the rise in inflation. Although the share in GDP of aggregate savings is not affected by the policy change, its composition is (Table 7.B.7). First, the share in GDP of net public savings increases mainly due to increased revenue from direct taxation (following the increase in real mark-up income), indirect taxation (with the rise in real GDP growth and the rise in the rate of inflation), and the procurement tax, and due to a decline in expenditure on fertiliser subsidies; the decline in the public revenue deficit is, however, partly offset by a rise in expenditure on food and export subsidies (following the increase in inflation), on wages and items of final consumption , and a fall in revenue from public enterprises. Second, with the inflation, the share in GDP of foreign savings declines; this decline is, however, partly offset by a rise in complementary intermediate imports, accompanying the rise in real GDP. Third, the share of depreciation allowances declines following the increase in the rate of inflation. Finally, the share in GDP of net private savings is only marginally affected, although the composition of net private savings changes considerably; with the income redistribution in favour of agriculture, the share in aggregate savings of savings from agricultural income rises, while the share of savings from non-agricultural wage income declines (Table 7.B.7).

Experiment $D-2$: The Fertiliser Subsidy is Eliminated.

The immediate effect of a removal of the fertiliser subsidy is an increase in crop prices which, in turn, results in a rise in 'committed' consumption expenditure on these goods and a concomitant decline in consumer demand – backed by 'supernumerary' expenditure – for other goods. This decline in consumer demand which leads to a decline in the market price of other agricultural products, is one of the more important factors dampening short-run inflationary tendencies. Due to this dampening, the increase in crop prices falls short off the increase in the market price for fertilisers, initiated by the removal of the fertiliser subsidy. As a result, in the short run, the ratio of the fertiliser price to the crop price rises considerably for all crops, leading to a decline in fertiliser use and a decline in crop output. In effect, the short–run effects of $D-2$ include a contraction in real GDP and a modest increase in the inflation rate.

In the medium run, crop output is affected by a number of, partly offsetting, forces. On the one hand, the tendency for crop output to decline is strengthened by a further increase in the fertiliser price, which follows from a rise in fertiliser production costs. The increase in production costs is due to a rise in the nominal wage rate earned in that sector – caused by the rise in consumer price inflation – and to an exogenous rise in the costs of imported intermediates. On the other hand, the decline in crop output is partly offset by two other factors. First, with the autonomous increase in nominal wage rates in non–agriculture, demand for agricultural products increases which, with falling supply, leads to considerable increases in crop prices. Consequently, the ratio of the fertiliser price to crop prices declines, leading to an increase in fertiliser use and an increase in crop yields. Second, with the inflation, the terms of trade improve for agri- culture, leading to a rise in (real) private agricultural investment, which raises the growth rate of net irrigated area and increases the aggregate cropping intensity. In effect, the net impact of the policy change is a fall in the average annual rates of growth of crop output (Table 7.B.5). The gain in income due to the rise in agricultural prices more than offsets the loss of income resulting from the lower crop output growth and, consequently, the average annual growth rate of real agricultural income increases as compared to the reference run. $D-2$ proves inflationary (Table 7.B.3). The rise in the inflation is mainly the result of agricultural price increases, witness the average annual increase in the wheat price of as much as 15 per cent.

With the decline in agriculture's demand for fertilisers, the growth rate of fertiliser production declines. The growth rate of basic, capital and intermediate goods production is affected by the following two factors. On the one hand, the increase in inflation leads to a decline of real private investment demand in the consumer goods and services sectors which implies a fall in the demand for basic, capital and intermediate goods. On the other hand, with the shift in the terms of trade in favour of agriculture, real private investment in agriculture rises which leads to a rise in demand for sector 7 goods. Demand for non–agricultural goods further increases due to the rise in real agricultural income. As a result, the average annual growth rates of consumer goods and services production slightly improve as compared to the reference run. Despite these improvements, following the decline in crop output and the fall in fertiliser production, the eventual impact of the policy change is marginally contractionary, leading to a decline in the average annual rate of growth of real GDP at market prices from 5.7 per cent in the reference run to 5.6 per cent in $D-2$. The agricultural sector benefits most from the elimination of the fertiliser subsidy. With rising agricultural prices, the average annual rate of growth of agricultural income increases from 3.9 per cent in the reference run to 4.2 per cent (Table 7.B.5).

Following the change in policy, the share in GDP at market prices of gross domestic investment declines (Table 7.B.7). Savings–investment balance is re–established in the following way. First, the share in GDP of net private savings declines following the redistribution of income in favour of agriculturalists, who have the lowest propensity to save. Second, the share in GDP of foreign savings declines due to the increase in inflation, on the one hand, and due to the decline in complementary intermediate imports (following the contraction), on the other hand. Third, with the inflation, the share of depreciation allowances declines. Although the removal of the fertiliser subsidy leads to a decline in public expenditure, this is offset by an increase in expenditure on export subsidies (following the increase in the gap between domestic prices and world prices) and on food subsidies (following the rise in foodgrain prices). As a result, the share in GDP of net public savings is only marginally affected by the introduction of policy $D-2$.

Experiment $D-3$: The Rate of Fertiliser Subsidy is Raised from 27.3 to 50.0 Per Cent Throughout the Seventh Plan Period.

In the short run, the rise in the rate of fertiliser subsidy is both inflationary and expansionary (see experiment $F-1$). The main source of real GDP expansion is the rise in crop output, resulting from the policy change. The short–run inflationary impact of the policy change can be attributed to, on the one hand, the downward rigidity in rice and wheat prices, due to which the rise in rice and wheat output does not lead to a decline in their prices, and, on the other hand, the fact that the supply of other agricultural products is inelastic. With the decline in the prices of other food crops and commercial crops, consumer demand for other agricultural goods rises, which, with their supply being fixed, leads to a rise in their price.

The short–run effects of the policy change further include an improvement in the terms of trade for agriculture, which has two important medium–run effects. First, it leads to an increase in private investment in agriculture, which, by raising its cropping intensity, enhances crop production growth. Second, it leads to a decline in the minimum support prices for rice and wheat which, with the rise in crop output, allows the market prices of rice and wheat to fall relatively to the levels recorded in the reference run. As a result of both these factors, all crop prices decline as compared to the reference run and the short–run rise in inflationary pressures tapers off in the medium run – as is illustrated by Figure 7.2, the consumer price index in $D-3$ is higher than in the reference run only in the first two years of the Seventh Plan period. Of course, with the decline in crop prices over the medium run, the terms of trade deteriorate for agriculture, but it can be seen from Figure 7.2 that this occurs only after 1987–88. In the event, in 1989–90, both net irrigated area and aggregate cropping intensity are higher in $D-3$ than in the reference run, despite the deterioration of the terms of trade for agriculture in the last two years of the Seventh Plan period (Table 7.B.6).

Figure 7.2
Dynamic Experiments:
The Evolution of the Consumer Price Index, 1985–89

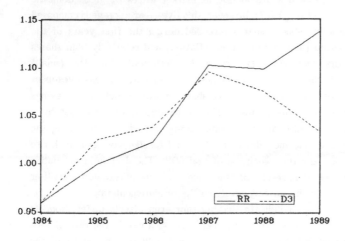

Note: RR refers to the reference run.

The fall in crop prices leads to a rise in consumer demand for other agricultural goods as well as for non–agricultural goods. While in the case of other agricultural goods, it leads to a rise in their price, it leads to a rise in production levels in the case of non–agricultural goods, as a result of which non–agricultural income rises. Because it leads to a decline in non–agricultural prices and wages, the fall in crop prices has an economy–wide deflationary impact, despite the rise in the price of other agricultural goods. The annual rate of increase of the consumer price index declines to 7.0 per cent as compared with an annual increase of 7.6 per cent in the reference run. With the deflation, private investment demand in the consumer goods and services sectors rises, augmenting the expansionary impact of $D-3$.

With the increase in the growth rates of crop output, the average annual growth rate of agricultural income increases, despite the decline in the growth rates of crop prices. Non–agricultural production and real income increase because of the following factors. First, the increase in crop output and in agricultural income lead to a rise in agriculture's intermediate and final demand. Second, the relative decline in crop prices results in an increase in consumer demand for other (in particular, non–agricultural) goods. Finally, with the deflation, real private investment demand in non–agriculture rises. As a result, the growth rates of real wage and mark–up income in non–agriculture increase. In effect, policy experiment $D-3$ registers a growth rate of real GDP at market prices of 6.0 per cent per annum. Distributionally, the share in GDP at factor cost of mark–up income rises from 23.1 per cent per annum in the reference run to 23.3 per cent (Table 7.B.9).

The average annual share in GDP at market prices of gross domestic investment declines (Table 7.B.7). However, this five–year average is composed of relatively low investment shares recorded during the first years of the Seventh Plan period (due to the rise in inflation) and relatively high shares registered in the later years (following the deflation). With the (small) average decline in the share of gross domestic investment, savings–investment balance is restored by a decrease in the shares in GDP of net public savings and depreciation allowances. This decline in savings is partly offset by a rise in the shares in GDP of net private savings (which rise following the increase in mark–up income relative to GDP) and foreign savings (which rise with the deflation and the expansion of real GDP). The decline in net public savings is mainly the result of the rise in expenditure on fertiliser subsidies and the decline in revenue from the procurement tax.

The results of $D-3$ indicate that its short–run effects differ from its medium–run effects. From a short–run perspective, a rise in the rate of fertiliser subsidy proves both inflationary and is mainly to the benefit of the agriculturalists. In the medium run, however, $D-3$ is deflationary and the policy–induced expansion of real GDP benefits the non–agricultural mark–up income recipients.

Experiment $D-3.1$: The Rate of Fertiliser Subsidy is Raised from 27.3 to 50 Per Cent and Public Agricultural Investment is Raised by 20 Per Cent.

The outcome of $D-3$ indicates that, in the medium run, a rise in the rate of fertiliser subsidy is deflationary and expansionary. As such, a rise in the rate of fertiliser subsidy provides policymakers with some scope to pursue an expansionary policy, including a rise in public agricultural investment, without augmenting inflationary pressures. This is what $D-3.1$ attempts.

In the short run, the rise in the rate of fertiliser subsidy leads to downward pressure on crop prices (although the prices of rice and wheat do not fall below their minimum support levels due to additional public procurement). Due to the decline in some of the crop prices, consumer demand increases most for other goods. As a result, demand rises considerably for other agricultural products, the supply of which is fixed, and, hence, their price increases. The price increase for other agricultural products is an important source of economy–wide cost–push inflation. First, because other agricultural products are major inputs into consumer goods production, the increase in their price leads to a rise in the price of consumer goods and, hence, to a rise in the consumer price index. Second, because they are important items of final consumption, the increase in their price raises the consumer price index directly as well, which, through nominal wage indexation, further augments cost–push pressures. Inflationary pressures are augmented further by the increase in public agricultural investment, which immediately raises the capacity utilisation rate in the basic, capital and intermediate goods sector and (through a multiplier process) augments domestic income and demand. The short–run impact of $D-3.1$ is both inflationary as well as expansionary.

In the medium run, however, inflationary pressures are considerably dampened by the following factors. On the one hand, the growth rates of crop output increase following the increase in net irrigated area and in aggregate cropping intensity – resulting from the increase in public agricultural investment – and following the rise in per hectare yield levels – resulting from higher fertiliser use. Yield levels rise substantially in rice, wheat and commercial crop cultivation, which is characterised by relatively high price elasticities of fertiliser demand (in absolute terms) and high yield responses to fertiliser use. On the other hand, over time, with the terms of trade improving for agriculture, the level of minimum support prices for rice and wheat gradually declines relative to their market prices, raising the scope for these prices to decline as a response to increases in their supply. As a result, the average annual rates of increase of the prices of rice, wheat and commercial crops decline as compared to the reference run.

With the prices of rice, wheat and commercial crops declining, the demand for other commodities rises, leading to price increases in the case of other food products (the production of which is relatively price–inelastic) and other agricultural products (the production of which is assumed completely price–inelastic). In the case of non–agricultural goods, it leads to increases in production levels. With the increase in some agricultural prices and the decrease in others, the impact on the consumer price index is of uncertain sign. In the event, the policy change leads to a small increase in the rate of inflation as measured by the consumer price index, indicating that most of the short–run inflationary pressures are levelled–off in the medium run.

The policy change raises the average annual growth rates of production of all crops. The real income gain due to the increase in crop output growth is larger (in absolute terms) than the income loss following from the decline in some of the crop prices. Hence, the average annual growth rate of real agricultural income increases which, *via* increased demand, leads to an improvement in non–agricultural capacity utilisation rates. The growth rate of non–agricultural (both wage and mark–up) income also improves as compared to the reference run. As a result, the average annual growth rate of real GDP at market prices increases to 6.3 per cent (Table 7.B.5). Income distribution changes in favour of agricultural income and non–agricultural mark–up income (Table 7.B.9).

The share in GDP at market prices of gross domestic investment is affected by two mutually offsetting forces. On the one hand, there is the increase in public agricultural investment, which is, on the other hand, offset by the decline in real private investment in non–agriculture following the increase in inflation. On the savings–side, the following adjustments occur. The share in GDP of net public savings rises, mainly due to the fact that the increase in expenditure on fertiliser subsidisation is more than offset by the increase in revenue from direct and indirect taxation. With the inflation, the share of depreciation allowances declines. Further, the decline in foreign savings, caused by the increase in inflation, is more than compensated for by the rise in foreign savings due to the increase in complementary intermediate imports. Finally, the share of net private savings rises as a result of the income redistribution in favour of mark–up income.

Experiment D – 3.2: Public Investment in Agriculture is Raised by 20 Per Cent, Public Investment in Basic, Intermediate and Capital Goods is Reduced by the Same Amount, and the Rate of Fertiliser Subsidy is Raised from 27.3 to 50.0 Per Cent.

Experiment $D-3.2$ extends $D-1.2$ by adding to the reallocation of public investment expenditure a considerable increase in the rate of fertiliser subsidy from 27.3 to 50.0 per cent. Both the increase in irrigated area and the reduction in the market price for fertilisers are expected to induce farmers to raise their levels of fertiliser use, thereby increasing the level of crop production and relaxing the agricultural constraint on industrial growth. Compared to the previous experiment, $D-3.2$ attempts to realise a similar rate of real GDP growth, while containing inflationary pressures.

The short–run consequences of $D-3.2$ are almost similar to the ones of $D-3.1$. The rise in the rate of fertiliser subsidy raises crop production which, with *initial* demand, leads to downward pressure on crop prices (with the prices of rice and wheat remaining at their minimum support levels because of additional public procurement). Due to the decline in some of the crop prices, consumer demand increases for other goods, in particular for other agricultural products. Again, the price increase for other agricultural products is an important source of economy–wide cost–push inflation, but – this time – inflationary pressures are not augmented by an increase in public investment. Hence, in the short run, the inflationary impact of $D-3.2$ is smaller than that of $D-3.1$.

In the medium run, the crop outputs increase following the increase in aggregate cropping intensity – resulting from the increase in public agricultural investment – and following the rise in per hectare yield levels – resulting from higher fertiliser use. Yield levels rise substantially in rice, wheat and commercial crop cultivation. With the improvement in the terms of trade for agriculture, the level of minimum support prices for rice and wheat gradually declines over time relative to their market prices, allowing these prices to decline as a response to the increases in supply. As a result, the average annual rates of increase of the prices of rice, wheat and commercial crops decline as compared to the reference run. With an unchanged level of aggregate public investment, these crop price declines contribute to overall deflation, the average annual rate of increase in the consumer price index declines from 7.6 per cent in the reference run to 7 per cent in $D-3.2$.

288

With the increase in the growth rates of crop output, real agricultural income increases as compared to the reference run. The rise in crop production raises agriculture's demand for non–agricultural intermediate inputs, while the increase in agricultural income leads to an increase in agriculturalists' final demand for non–agricultural goods. Consequently, the average annual growth rates of non–agricultural production and income (both wage and mark–up income) increase. The average annual rate of growth of real GDP at factor cost of 5.7 per cent constitutes an improvement over the growth rate of 5.2 per cent registered during the reference run. Distributionally, the policy change mainly benefits non–agricultural mark–up income.

Although its impact on gross domestic investment is small, $D-3.2$ has considerable repercussions on the savings–side of the investment–savings balance (Table 7.B.7). First, the share in GDP at market prices of foreign savings rises, both because of the deflation and the increase in complementary intermediate imports. Second, the share of net public savings rises mainly through the increase in revenue from direct taxes, which results from the income redistribution in favour of mark–up income. The change in income distribution further leads to an increase in the share in GDP of net private savings. Finally, because the reallocation of public investment towards agriculture leads to a decline in real private investment demand in the basic, intermediate and capital goods sector, the capital stock of the latter declines as compared to the reference run, due to which depreciation allowances decline in this sector. As a result, the share in GDP of aggregate depreciation declines.

Experiment $D-3.3$: The Rate of Fertiliser Subsidy is Raised from 27.3 to 50.0 Per Cent and Public Agricultural Investment is Reduced Proportionately.

In the short run, raising the rate of fertiliser subsidy while reducing the level of public agricultural investment concomitantly, turned out to be deflationary as well as contractionary (see Section 6.3.2). Experiment $D-3.3$ examines the medium–run effects of this policy package. The various effects resulting from the policy change over time, must be separated.

In the short run, $D-3.3$ is deflationary. There is downward pressure on crop prices, since the increase in the rate of fertiliser subsidy leads to an increase in crop output levels. Market prices for rice and wheat, however, do not decline due to additional public procurement. The tendency for prices to decline is strengthened by the reduction in public agricultural investment, which reduces aggregate demand, while it is partly offset by a rise in the price of other agricultural products. This price increases because, with the decrease in the prices for other food crops and commercial crops and the concomitant increase in 'supernumerary' consumer demand, demand for other agricultural products increases, while their supply is fixed.

In the medium run, $D-3.3$ has two important effects on crop production. On the one hand, the decline in public agricultural investment leads to a reduction in private agricultural investment, a fall in the growth rate of net irrigated area, and a decline in the growth rate of gross cropped area as compared to the reference scenario. With given yield levels, the reduction in gross cropped area implies a decline in the level of crop production, leading to upward pressure on crop prices. On the other hand, the effect of the rise in the rate of fertiliser subsidy is to increase the instability of crop production. The rise in the rate of fertiliser subsidy raises the output of wheat, the production of which is relatively price responsive, more than the output levels of the other crops and, as a result, leads to a decline in the wheat price relative to the prices of the other three crops. This, in year $t+1$, leads to a reallocation of a part of gross cropped area from wheat to the other three crops, with the result that the level of wheat output declines and the wheat price rises as compared to the other crop prices. As a result, in year $t+2$, area is again reallocated to wheat, wheat output increases and wheat prices decline, leading to a decline in area under wheat in year $t+3$. In effect, the amplitude of the fluctuations in the share of gross cropped area under wheat in total gross cropped area (as measured by its standard deviation) increases as compared to the reference scenario, which contributes to the decline in the average annual growth rate of wheat ouput and to the rise in the average annual rate of price increase for wheat.

Hence, the short–run deflationary impact of $D-3.3$ is partly offset in the medium run. The result is a decrease in the rate of inflation (as measured by the consumer price index) from 7.6 per cent per annum in the reference run to 7.4 per cent in $D-3.3$. With the decline in the growth rate of wheat output and the fall in the market prices of the other three crops, the average annual growth rate of real agricultural income declines. The decline in agricultural income contributes to a fall in domestic demand – both for agricultural and non–agricultural goods – by which non–agricultural production is negatively affected. Hence, the growth rate of non–agricultural (wage and mark–up) income declines. The policy change proves slightly contractionary, the average annual growth rate of real GDP at factor cost declines to 5.0 per cent.

Mainly due to the fall in agricultural investment, the share in GDP at market prices of gross domestic investment declines. Investment–savings balance is re–established by a decline in the share in GDP of net public savings. This decline is primarily the result of a fall in revenue from direct and indirect taxation (following the contraction and deflation) and the rise in expenditure on fertiliser subsidisation. Part of the decline is offset by a rise in the share in GDP of depreciation allowances which increases with the deflation.

As can be judged from the simulation outcome, the medium–run effects of policy package $D-3.3$ including a decline in real GDP and a decrease in the rate of inflation, are not very different from its short–run effects.

Experiment D-4: The Quantity of Foodgrains Publicly Distributed is Raised by 20 Per Cent throughout the Seventh Plan Period.

According to the results of experiment *S-2*, in the short–run, a rise in the quantity of foodgrains publicly distributed leads to a small rise in the rate of inflation, while its impact on real GDP is negligible. In the medium run, however, an increase in the quantity of foodgrains publicly distributed is significantly deflationary as well as contractionary. The average annual rate of inflation as measured by the GDP deflator declines from 7.9 per cent in the reference run to 6.2 per cent in *D-4*; the average annual growth rate of real GDP at market prices declines from 5.7 to 5.6 per cent. How can these medium–run results be explained ?

The policy change has two opposing effects. First, consumers have to spend less in money terms on the purchase of foodgrains, which enables them to raise their demand for other products. Second, with foodgrain demand declining, foodgrain prices fall, leading to a fall in crop production and a decrease in agriculturalists' income. As a result, both agriculture's inter- mediate as well as final demand for non–agricultural goods declines. In effect, the decline in demand from agriculture is larger (in absolute terms) than the increase in demand following from the decline in food prices. With the decline in the size of the domestic market, the result is deflation, with in particular the average annual rates of increase in agricultural prices being considerably below the corresponding rates recorded in the reference run.

With the decline in foodgrain prices relative to non–agricultural prices, the terms of trade deteriorate for agriculture, leading to a fall in private agricultural investment, which, in turn, has two opposing effects. First and foremost, it leads to a decline in the aggregate cropping intensity. Second, it leads to a decline in the demand for capital goods, due to which non– agricultural production and income decline and the deflation is augmented. Crop production growth is negatively affected, but not to the extent of falling short off the growth in demand for agricultural commodities. Hence, agricultural prices continue to increase less rapidly in *D-4* as compared to the reference scenario. The ultimate impact of the policy experiment is contractionary, the average annual growth rate of real GDP at factor cost falls to 5.0 per cent. The deterioration in growth performance is largely concentrated in the agricultural sectors. The average annual rate of growth of real income of agriculturalists declines to 3.1 per cent. The average annual growth rate of non–agricultural mark–up income declines from 5.5 per cent in the reference run to 5.1 per cent in *D-4*. Non–agricultural wage earners are the main beneficiaries of the deflation, their share in GDP at factor cost increases to 37.7 per cent.

With the deflation, real private investment demand in the consumer goods and services sectors rises. As a result, the share in GDP at market prices of gross domestic investment increases. To restore savings–investment equality, the share of savings increases as follows. First, the share in GDP of net public savings increases, mainly due to the decline in expenditure on export subsidies (since, with the deflation, domestic prices come more in line with world market prices) and the rise in revenue from public enterprises. Second, the share of foreign savings increases as a result of the deflation and due to the decline in complementary intermediate imports. Finally, with the deflation, the share in GDP of depreciation allowances rises.

Experiment D − 4.1: Public Distribution of Foodgrains is Raised by 20 Per Cent and the Rate of Fertiliser Subsidy is Raised from 27.3 to 50.0 Per Cent throughout the Seventh Plan Period.

To compensate farmers for the fall in output prices due to the increase in the size of the PDS, $D-4$ may be extended to include a substantial increase in the rate of fertiliser subsidy. With increased public distribution, the increase in the rate of fertiliser subsidy aims at improving the parity between agricultural input costs and output prices by reducing input costs.

The short−run impact of $D-4.1$ on agricultural prices is mixed. On the one hand, there are two factors leading to upward pressure on (some of the) agricultural prices. First, the rise in the rate of fertiliser subsidy leads to a reduction in the price of fertilisers which, at *initial* levels of crop output and fertiliser use results in a reduction in agricultural production costs and a rise in agricultural income; the increase in agricultural income leads to a rise in aggregate demand, which, with *initial* agricultural supply, leads to upward pressure on *all* agricultural prices. Second, due to the increase in the rate of food subsidy, consumers have to spend less in money terms on the purchase of foodgrains, which enables them to raise their demand for non−foodgrains. This leads to price increases for commercial crops and other agricultural products. On the other hand, the policy change results in downward pressure on agricultural prices. The increase in the rate of fertiliser subsidy leads to a rise in crop output, which, with *initial* demand, results in downward pressure on crop prices. The output increase is particularly large for rice and wheat, the production of which is relatively price−responsive. For foodgrains, the downward pressure on prices is augmented by the decline in consumer demand, following the increase in the rate of food subsidy.

For rice and wheat, the increase in supply is larger than the rise in demand, but through a step−up in public procurement their prices are kept at minimum support levels. The increase in public procurement further raises agricultural income, which, in turn, enhances demand pressure in the economy. With the other agricultural prices increasing, the short−run impact of $D-4.1$ is inflationary, notwithstanding considerable increases in crop output. By raising the intersectoral terms of trade for agriculture, it, however, sets in motion forces which lead to a dampening of inflationary pressures in the medium run.

The improvement in the terms of trade for agriculture leads to a rise in private agricultural investment, on the one hand, and a relative decline in foodgrain procurement prices, on the other. While, by increasing the cropping intensity, the increase in agricultural investment raises crop output, the decline in procurement prices allows the increases in rice and wheat output to result in medium–run price decreases. As a result, all crop prices decline which, in turn, has a number of important effects. First, it leads to a decline in intermediate input costs and, hence, to a decline in mark–up prices and nominal wage rates in non–agriculture. It is important to note that, due to increases in exogenous cost items, non–agricultural prices and wages do not decline to the same extent as crop prices, implying a deterioration of the intersectoral terms of trade for agriculture in the medium run. Second, it leads to a further decline in 'committed' consumer expenditure, which results in a rise in consumer demand mainly for non–agricultural goods (the marginal budget shares of which are relatively large). Hence, the decline in agricultural prices leads to a reallocation of consumer demand from agricultural towards non–agricultural goods. Finally, the decline in crop prices leads to a decline in real agricultural income which is, however, partly offset by the rise in crop output. The decline in agricultural income results in a decline in aggregate domestic demand for agricultural as well as non–agricultural goods.

On balance, the impact of $D-4.1$ is to raise the demand for non–agricultural goods $vis-à-vis$ their supply and to raise the supply of crops as compared to the demand for crops. As a result, levels of production rise in non–agriculture and prices decline in agriculture as compared to the reference run. In effect, the impact of policy $D-4.1$ is deflationary (mainly due to agricultural price decreases) and expansionary (following the increase in non–agricultural income). With the decline in agricultural prices, the average annual growth rate of real agricultural income falls as compared to the reference run – despite the substantial increases in the growth rates of crop output. The growth rates of real non–agricultural incomes improve, particularly for wage income. With the deflation and the increase in non–agricultural production, the share in GDP at factor of non–agricultural wage income increases to 37.5 per cent on average per annum.

The share in GDP at market prices of gross domestic investment rises following the policy change (Table 7.B.7). This increase can be attributed to the rise in real private investment demand in the consumer goods and services sectors, following the increase in real sectoral mark–up income. The increase is partly offset by the decline in private agricultural investment, resulting from the deterioration of the terms of trade for agriculture. The increase in the share of gross domestic investment leads to the following adjustments in savings. First, following the redistribution of income in favour of non–agricultural mark–up income, the share in GDP of net private savings rises. Second, with the deflation and the increase in real GDP, the share of foreign savings increases. Finally, also due to the deflation, the share of depreciation allowances rises. These increases in the share of savings are, however, partly offset by the decline in the share of net public savings. Net public savings decline mainly due to the increase in expenditure on food and fertiliser subsidies and the decline in revenue from the procurement tax.

Experiment D – 4.2: The Quantity of Foodgrains Publicly Distributed is Raised by 20 Per Cent and Public Agricultural Investment is Increased by 40 Per Cent throughout the Seventh Plan Period.

While $D-4$ in which the quantity of foodgrains publicly distributed was raised, was both deflationary and contractionary, policy $D-1$ in which public agricultural investment was raised, was inflationary as well as expansionary. In an attempt to attain the best of both worlds (*i.e.* to realise a higher rate of real GDP growth and a lower rate of inflation), experiment $D-4.2$ combines $D-1$ and $D-4$. The particular combination turns out to be significantly expansionary and deflationary as compared to the reference run. This outcome can be explained as follows.

In the short run, the increase in public agricultural investment has the following two effects. On the one hand, because it directly adds to income (mainly of non–agriculturalists), $D-4.2$ raises demand and, with relatively inelastic supply, leads to increases in agricultural prices. On the other hand, due to the rise in the quantity of foodgrains publicly distributed, consumption demand declines for foodgrains, which, with *initial* supply, leads to downward pressure on foodgrain prices and upward pressure on the prices of commercial crops and other agricultural products, the demand for which increases. With the prices of rice and wheat kept at their minimum support levels, the net result is a rise in the GDP deflator.

In the medium run, $D-4.2$ augments the rate of growth of net irrigated area, both directly and indirectly by stimulating (with a lag) private agricultural investment. The average rate of growth of net irrigated area rises from 2.1 per cent in the reference run to 4.0 per cent. In 1989–90, about 35.4 per cent of net sown area has been brought under irrigation as compared to 32.9 per cent in the reference scenario (Table 7.B.6). As a result, the growth rates of crop production improve. With the decline over time of the minimum support prices of rice and wheat (following the shift in the terms of trade in favour of agriculture in the short run), the rise in crop output leads to a decrease in crop prices (relative to the reference run). Because of the decline in crop prices relative to the fertiliser price, the impetus to agricultural growth is not provided by a rise in yield levels due to increased fertiliser use, but by the extension of cropwise irrigation coverage. Following the relative decline in crop prices, the average annual rate of growth of fertiliser production even declines as compared to the reference run.

With the increase in crop output, the average annual rates of increase of agricultural prices decline as compared to the reference scenario, contributing to a decline in the overall rate of inflation as measured by the consumer price index from 7.6 per cent on average per annum in the reference run to 7.0 per cent on average per annum. The decline in agricultural price increases leads to a fall in the average annual growth rate of real agricultural income, notwithstanding the substantial increase in crop output growth. These higher growth rates of crop production do contribute to higher growth rates of non–agricultural production, mainly by demanding more non–agricultural intermediate inputs. As a result, the growth rates of real non–agricultural wage and mark–up incomes substantially improve. The average annual growth rate of real GDP at market prices increases from 5.7 per cent in the reference scenario to 6.2 per cent in $D-4.1$. Distributionally, the farmers are the main losers and non–agricultural mark–up income recipients the main gainers (see Table 7.B.9).

The share in GDP at market prices of gross domestic investment rises considerably due to the increase in public and private agricultural investment and the rise in the real private investment in the consumer goods and services sectors. Investment–savings equality is re–established through a substantial increase in the share in GDP of net public savings and a rise in the share of foreign savings (concomittant with deflation and real GDP growth). Net public savings rise due to the increase in revenue from direct taxation and from public enterprises and the decline in expenditure on export subsidies, wages and final consumption.

Experiment $D-5$: Procurement Prices of Rice and Wheat are Raised by 10 Per Cent throughout the Seventh Plan Period.

The aim of the public procurement/minimum support price policy is to provide incentives to farmers to increase their production either through increased use of modern inputs or through investment in cost–reducing technology. The effectiveness of procurement policy in raising crop output has been a matter of debate and controversy in India (Krishna and Raychaudhuri, 1980; Gulati, 1987), as are its effects on variables such as food consumption, wage rates, industrial cost structures, the rate of inflation, and so on (Gulati and Sharma, 1990). Experiment $D-5$ in which procurement prices of rice and wheat are raised by 10 per cent, examines some of these effects with the help of the general equilibrium model.

In the short run, $D-5$ implies a step–up in public procurement of rice and wheat, raising their market prices to their new minimum support levels. The increase in the market prices of rice and wheat relative to the fertiliser price leads to a rise in per hectare fertiliser use and an increase in rice and wheat output. By raising the prices of rice and wheat directly and the prices of other food crops, commercial crops and other agricultural products indirectly (*via* the increase in agriculturalists' income), the immediate impact of the policy change is inflationary. The consumer price index increases by 1.7 per cent in 1985–86. The indexation of nominal wage rates in non–agriculture carries this inflation over into the medium run.

With the change in the terms of trade in favour of agriculture, private agricultural investment increases. Consequently, net irrigated area and agriculture's cropping intensity increase, providing a stimulus to crop production. Because of more favourable crop prices relative to the fertiliser price, cropwise fertiliser use is higher in $D-5$ than in the reference run. As a result, the growth rates of crop output improve as compared to the reference run. The initial increase in the prices of rice and wheat leads to a reallocation of gross cropped area from other food crops and commercial crops towards rice and wheat in the next year, which – with given levels of yield – results in a decline in output of other food crops and commercial crops. This, in the third year, leads to increases in the prices of other food crops and commercial crops which, in turn, results in a reallocation of area to these crops, a decline in rice and wheat output, a rise in rice and wheat prices, and – again – a change in the aggregate cropping pattern in the fourth year. As a result, the introduction of $D-5$ leads to an increase in the rate as well as a rise in the instability of crop output growth.

With the increase in crop output and in crop prices, agricultural income increases. Following the increase in crop output and the rise in agricultural income, domestic demand for non–agricultural products rises, which leads to an increase in non–agricultural production. Although this increase is partly offset by the decline in consumption demand for non–agricultural goods, following the sharp increase in agricultural prices, the impact of $D-5$ on real agricultural (wage and mark–up) income is positive. Following the policy change, the average annual growth rate of real GDP at market prices increases to 5.9 per cent. Distributionally, agriculturalists benefit most. The share in GDP at factor cost increases from 31.9 per cent on average per annum in the reference run to 32.9 per cent on average per annum.

The share in GDP at market prices of gross domestic investment declines following the introduction of $D-5$. This decline is due to the fall in private investment in non–agriculture, accompanying the rise in inflation, which is, however, partly offset by the increase in private agricultural investment, resulting from the improvement in the terms of trade for agriculture. Investment–savings equality is restored mainly through the following two adjustments (Table 7.B.7). First, the share in GDP of net public savings declines. This decline is primarily to be attributed to the increase in expenditure on food subsidies (following the agricultural price rises), export subsidies (following the rise in the gap between domestic prices and world prices), government wages and final consumption, and a decline in the revenue from public enterprises. Second, with the increase in the rate of inflation, the shares in GDP of depreciation allowances and foreign savings decline.

Experiment D–5.1: Procurement Prices of Rice and Wheat are Raised by 10 Per Cent and the Quantity of Foodgrains Publicly Distributed is Increased by 10 Per Cent.

It follows from the previous experiment that raising procurement prices is effective in stimulating crop production, but is also inflationary. To contain inflationary pressures arising, experiment $D–5.1$ extends $D–5$ by simultaneously increasing the quantity of foodgrains publicly distributed.

In the short run, aggregate demand increases because of the following reasons. First, following the rise in procurement prices, public procurement of rice and wheat is increased. Second, the increase in rice and wheat procurement prices and quantities leads to a rise in agricultural income which results in an increase in final demand. Third, the increase in the quantities of foodgrains publicly distributed at subsidised prices leads to a fall in 'committed' expenditure on foodgrains and, hence, to a rise in consumption demand for non–foodgrains. These increases in demand are partly offset by the decline in demand for commodities other than rice and wheat, following the increase in their market prices. But the net effect of $D–5.1$ is an increase in the demand for non–foodgrains which leads to a rise in the prices of commercial crops and other agricultural products and an increase in capacity utilisation in non–agriculture. Consequently, in the short run, the impact of $D–5.1$ is even more inflationary than that of $D–5$.

In the medium run, however, the impact of the policy change is less inflationary than in $D–5$, particularly due to the fact that the average price increases of agricultural products turn out to be lower in $D–5.1$ than in $D–5$. With the market prices of rice and wheat rising above their minimum support levels, but keeping below the levels recorded in $D–5$ (due to the increase in food subsidies), agricultural prices increase less in $D–5.1$ than in $D–5$. Consequently, the levels of crop production do not increase as fast as in $D–5$ and the average annual growth rate of real agricultural income declines from 4.6 per cent in $D–5$ to 4.2 per cent in $D–5.1$ (which still constitutes an improvement over the reference run). Following the decline in agriculture's intermediate and final demand, the growth rates of non–agricultural production and (wage and mark–up) income also fall relative to $D–5$. As a result, the average annual growth rate of real GDP at market prices turns out at 5.8 per cent. With the agriculture–induced inflation, the share in GDP at factor cost of agricultural income increases to 32.6 per cent.

Following the introduction of $D–5.1$, the share in GDP at market prices of gross domestic investment declines from 24.7 per cent on average per annum in the reference run to 24.2 per cent on average per annum. Investment–savings equality is restored by the following two adjustments. First, with the inflation, the shares in GDP of foreign savings and depreciation allowances decline. Second, the share of net public savings declines due to the increase in expenditure on food and export subsidies and the decline in revenue from public undertakings.

Experiment D – 5.2: The Public Distribution System and the Public Procurement Scheme are Both Eliminated.

The government is sometimes urged to eliminate its Public Distribution System (PDS) and public procurement scheme in an attempt to 'get the prices right' domestically. In the short run, because of the government's much larger involvement in procuring than in distributing foodgrains, the complete withdrawal of public intervention in the foodgrains markets is strongly deflationary as well as contractionary (experiment *P* – 3). Experiment *D* – 5.2 evaluates the medium–run effects of this particular policy change.

With the removal of public procurement, foodgrain demand falls and, with the *initial* level of foodgrain supply, food prices decline. With the lower food prices, agricultural income and demand falls and non–agricultural capacity utilisation rates go down. Consequently, non–agricultural income and demand decline, contributing to the deflation. The deflationary tendencies are partly offset by the decline in crop supply, resulting from the reduction in fertiliser input in response to the decline in crop prices, and by the increase in non–agricultural consumers' demand for foodgrains following the removal of the PDS.

In effect, the policy change leads to a fall in the growth rate of real GDP at market prices from 5.7 per cent per annum in the reference run to 5.5 per cent per annum in *D* – 5.2. Distributionally, the average annual shares in GDP at factor cost of agricultural income and non–agricultural mark–up income decline. Income distribution changes in favour of non–agricultural wage earners whose income share rises to 37.8 per cent. With the deflation, the share in GDP of revenue from public undertakings increases from 7.6 per cent in the reference run to 8.4 per cent (Table 7.B.9).

With the deflation, the share in GDP at market prices of gross domestic investment rises to 25.5 per cent on average per annum. The required increase in the share of savings is brought about by increases in the shares of net public savings, foreign savings and depreciation allowances. The increase in net public savings is due to the decline in expenditure on food subsidies (following the elimination of the PDS), export subsidies (following the deflation), and producers' subsidies (following the contraction) and a rise in revenue from public enterprises. The increase in foreign savings is the net result of a rise in foreign savings due to the deflation and a decline, following the reduction in complementary intermediate imports. With the shift in income distribution towards non–agricultural wage income, the share in GDP of net private savings declines.

Experiment D – 5.3: The Rate of Fertiliser Subsidy is Raised from 27.3 to 50.0 Per Cent, Public Investment in Agriculture is Increased by 50 Per Cent, and Procurement Prices are Kept at the Level of the Market Price for Fertilisers.

In experiment *D* – 5.3, it is attempted to raise the growth rate of real GDP by increasing public agricultural investment and raising the rate of fertiliser subsidy, while reducing the rate of inflation by reducing the procurement prices for foodgrains to the level of the market price of fertilisers.

In the short run, $D-5.3$ is deflationary on two accounts. First, the rise in the rate of fertiliser subsidy raises crop supply, which, with *initial* demand, leads to downward pressure on crop prices. Second, following the decline in the market price for fertilisers, the procurement prices for foodgrains are reduced. With the decline in procurement prices, the rise in the supply of rice and wheat results in a decline in their market price. The deflationary impact is, however, partly offset by the increase in aggregate demand, resulting from the rise in public agricultural investment, and by the increase in the price of other agricultural products. The price of other agricultural goods increases as a result of the rise in their consumption demand which, in turn, results from the fall in foodgrain prices.

In the medium run, the ratio of the fertiliser price to the crop prices remains more favourable to farmers than in the reference run and, hence, $D-5.3$ registers higher levels of per hectare fertiliser use than the reference run. Over time, the substantial step–up in public agricultural investment results in an increase in the annual average rate of growth of net irrigated area to 4.4 per cent per annum. In 1989–90, net irrigated area amounts to 51 million hectares which is 4.5 million hectares more than in the reference run (Table 7.B.6). During 1985–90, the irrigation coverage increases to 36 per cent of net sown area. Both the rise in irrigation coverage and the increase in fertiliser use raise the growth rates of crop production as compared to the reference run.

With unchanged demand, the increase in the growth rates of crop supply puts downward pressure on agricultural prices which, in the presence of lower floor prices, is permitted to materialise in lower crop prices. The fall in crop prices leads to a decline in agricultural income which is, however, more than offset by additional revenue from increased crop production. The net effect is a rise in the annual average growth rate of real agricultural income from 3.9 per cent in the reference run to 4.4 per cent in $D-5.3$. Through their impact on non–agricultural mark–up prices and wage indexation, lower crop prices contribute to a lower rate of overall inflation. The average annual rate of increase of the consumer price index declines from 7.6 per cent in the reference run to 7.2 per cent in $D-5.3$.

The following factors lead to a considerable increase in non–agricultural production. First, with the increase in crop output (which raises agriculture's intermediate demand for non–agricultural inputs) and the rise in real agricultural income (which leads to a rise in agriculturalists' final demand for non–agricultural goods), non–agricultural production and income rise. Second, the rise in public investment in agriculture leads to a direct improvement in the performance of the basic, intermediate and capital goods sector. Third, with the deflation, private investment demand in the consumer goods and services sectors rises, leading to a further increase in non-agricultural production. In the event, the average annual growth rates of real wage and mark–up income considerably improve as compared to the reference run. With both real agricultural and non–agricultural income increasing, the average annual growth rate of real GDP at market prices rises to 6.6 per cent. Distributionally, mark–up income recipients benefit most. The share in GDP at factor cost of non–agricultural mark–up income rises from 23.1 per cent per year in the reference run to 23.7 per cent per annum.

With the increase in public agricultural investment and the rise in private investment in the consumer goods and services sectors, the share in GDP at market prices of gross domestic investment increases. Investment–savings equality is re–established through a rise in the shares in GDP of net public savings and foreign savings. The share of net public savings rises mainly due to the decline in expenditure on export subsidies and the rise in revenue from direct taxation, the procurement tax, and public enterprises. The share in GDP of foreign savings increases both due to the deflation and to the increase in real GDP.

7.5   *Concluding Observations*

To learn about the medium–run economywide effects of agricultural policies, a large number of dynamic policy experiments were performed in which a number of policy packages were tried. All the experiments amounted to changes imposed on a system, the time path of which is set by a reference scenario. By extrapolating the exogenous variables, short–term cyclical variations (or exogenous shocks) were purposely suppressed – with the exception of the agricultural shortfall of 1987–88.

The simulation results of Section 7.4 provide a longer–term perspective within which to formulate agricultural policies so as to raise real GDP growth while containing inflationary pressures at some tolerable level. The general view that I arrive at from the simulation outcomes is that there are relatively few parameters to which the major experimental results are sensitive. On the demand side, there are three important parameter specifications: (*i*) income elasticities of demand are high for agricultural products (in particular, foodgrains); (*ii*) agricultural households spend a larger share of their incomes on agricultural products than non–agricultural households; and (*iii*) the price responsiveness of demand for agricultural products tends to be fairly low and is less important in determining demand than changes in (real) income. On the supply side, there are also three significant specifications: (*i*) the responsiveness of per hectare crop yields to per hectare fertiliser input is rather low, particularly in unirrigated agriculture; (*ii*) the price responsiveness of fertiliser demand is relatively low, in particular for other food crops and commercial crops; and (*iii*) non–agricultural production is determined by demand subject to a capacity constraint. These features of the model economy are, in my opinion, valid for the Indian economy. The two supply specifications for agriculture, taken together, imply that the agricultural sectors are limited in their supply response to variations in price. The short–run effects of policy changes are transformed into consequences for the growth path of the economy by the following four medium–term adjustment mechanisms: (*i*) the price and wage–income adjustments related to nominal wage indexation in non–agriculture; (*ii*) the capacity–creating and aggregate demand effects of endogenous private investment demand; (*iii*) adjustments over time in the allocation of gross cropped area – both irrigated and non–irrigated – across crops; and (*iv*) the price and income effects of endogenous procurement price formation for foodgrains.

One general result emerging from the simulation results is worth mentioning before proceeding to the discussion of their policy implications. The results of Section 7.4. show that, while the shifts in income distribution accompanying the restoration of the investment–savings equality can be quite substantial in the short run (see Figure 6.2), the distribution of income over time exhibits a remarkable stability. Most of the policy experiments resulted in only small changes in the average annual shares in GDP at factor cost of the income categories included in the model.[10] The stability of income distribution in the medium run is to be attributed mainly to the fact that the real wage fall in non–agriculture which is built into the model, is less pronounced in the medium run than in the short run. This is because, at the beginning of each year, non–agricultural workers are able to negotiate for nominal wage increases, compensating for previous year's fall in real wages. Figure 7.3 in which the average annual share in GDP at factor cost of non–agricultural wage income is plotted against the average annual rate of inflation, gives an impression of the extent to which real wage income falls in the medium run (due to inflation).

A second general result emerging from the agricultural policy experiments is that the short–run trade–off between growth and inflation vanishes in the medium run – as can be seen from Figure 7.4 in which the average annual rates of inflation recorded in the sixteen agricultural policy experiments are plotted against the corresponding annual rates of real GDP growth. With the increase in agriculture's output and price–responsiveness, following the rise in irrigation coverage, inflationary pressures originating from agriculture decline and there is more room for expansionary policies. As a result of the improvement in agricultural performance *over time*, it is possible to raise the growth rate of real GDP over the Five–Year Plan period, while containing (or even reducing) inflation. Hence, the simulation outcomes suggest that it is possible to remove the agricultural constraint on non–agricultural growth by

---

[10] Similar medium–run results were obtained by Adelman and Robinson (1978) for South Korea, by Taylor *et al.* (1980) for Brazil, and by Narayana *et al.* (1987) for India.

Figure 7.3
Dynamic Experiments:
Share in GDP of Real Wage Income and Inflation

Average Annual
Share in GDP at
Factor Cost of
Real Wage Income
in Non–Agricul-
ture

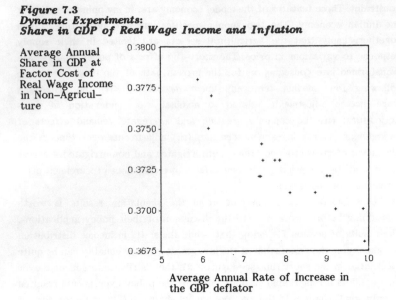

Average Annual Rate of Increase in
the GDP deflator

Figure 7.4
Dynamic Experiments:
Growth and Inflation

Average Annual
Rate of Change
in GDP deflator

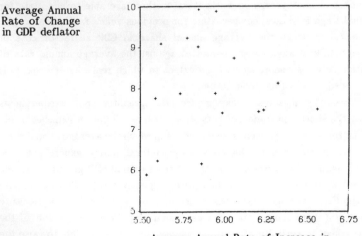

Average Annual Rate of Increase in
Real GDP at Factor Cost

deliberate government intervention aimed at raising the responsiveness of agricultural supply. The simulation results indicate that a policy of increased public investment in irrigation is of particular importance in this respect. In more detail, the following policy conclusions can be drawn from the medium–term simulations:

> *Experiments D–1 to D–1.3*: An increase in public agricultural investment is both significantly expansionary and inflationary. It leads to a redistribution of income in favour of agriculturalists and a reduction in the government's revenue deficit. Attempts to contain inflationary presssures by financing public investment at the cost of the fertiliser subsidy will be futile, because the increase in crop supply due to the rise in cropping intensity does not outweigh the fall in supply following the increase in the relative price of fertilisers. In contrast, a reallocation of public investments towards agriculture reduces the inflation rate, while raising the growth rate of real GDP. It also leads to a considerable improvement in the government's budgetary position. *Experiments D–2, D–3 and D–3.3*: Elimination of the fertiliser subsidy scheme leads to inflation and a redistribution of income in favour of agriculture. It does not result in an improvement of the government's budgetary position. On the other hand, an increase in the rate of fertiliser subsidy raises the growth rate of real GDP and reduces the rate of inflation. It leads to a decline in net public savings and redistributes income towards non–agricultural wage earners. When the increase in the rate of fertiliser subsidy is financed at the cost of public agricultural investment, the macro–economic effects include a modest decline in the growth rate of real GDP, a fall in the rate of inflation, and a decrease in net public savings. In view of the above results, farmers' agitations for a rise in the rate of fertiliser subsidy may be regarded as being based on short–sightedness. *Experiment D–3.1 and D–3.2*: A policy of public – investment – *cum*–ferti- liser–subsidy raises the growth rate of real GDP, while at the same time containing inflationary pressures. It leads to an improvement in the government's budgetary position and a redistribution of income in favour of agriculturalists and non–agricultural mark–up income recipients. *Experiment D–4 to D–4.2*: An increase in the quantity of foodgrains publicly distributed is both deflationary and contractionary. The contraction is mainly concentrated in the agricultural sectors. With the reduction in inflationary pressures originating from agriculture, an increase in food subsidisation provides room for complementary policy measures which are more expansionary. Combined with either a rise in the rate of fertiliser subsidy or an increase in public agricultural investment, an increase in food subsidisation turns out deflationary (mainly due to agricultural price decreases) as well as expansionary (mainly due to increases in non–agricultural production). *Experiments D–5 to D–5.2*: An increase in the procurement prices of rice and wheat leads to a sharp rise in the rate of inflation and a shift in income distribution towards agriculturalists. It raises the growth rate of real GDP and results in a decline in net public savings. The rise in inflation following an increase in procurement prices can be contained at tolerable levels by an increase in the quantity of foodgrains publicly distributed. This will, however, also reduce its expansionary impact. The removal of the PDS and the public procurement scheme is deflationary and contractionary. In view of these results, it is not surprising that the 'farmers' lobby' has a vested interest in sustaining these types of government interference in agricultural price formation. *Experiment D–5.3*: A policy of reducing agricultural production costs by raising the rate of fertiliser subsidy and of increasing agriculture's productivity by enhancing its cropping intensity, while simultaneously reducing the market prices of agricultural goods through a decrease in their procurement prices leads to a considerable increase in the growth rate of real GDP and a decline in the rate of inflation. It further results in an increase in net public savings and a redistribution of income in favour of non–agricultural mark–up income.

303

To put into perspective the magnitudes of the responses of the general equilibrium model to policy changes, the effects of a number of selected simulations are expressed in terms of marginal returns per Rupee of public expenditure – both in the short and medium run – in Table 7.7. The simulation experiments considered are the following, 'pure', experiments: public agricultural investment $(D-1)$, fertiliser subsidisation $(D-3)$, food subsidisation $(D-4)$, and public procurement $(D-5)$. According to the results, an additional Rupee allocated to public agricultural investment would have generated extra real GDP at factor cost worth Rs. 5.1 on average each year during the period 1985–89. Greater emphasis on public investment in agriculture (and particularly in irrigation) thus does seem to be an attractive policy, although – not surprisingly –, in the short run, its marginal returns turn out to be much smaller. It can be seen that – although an extra Rupee spent on fertiliser subsidisation does have the highest aggregate benefit–cost ratio in the short run – the marginal returns to increased fertiliser subsidisation (expressed in terms of additional real GDP) decline in the medium run. The marginal returns to a policy of increased food subsidisation also decline over time and – expressed as an annual average – even turn out negative in the medium run. From a medium–run perspective and in terms of additional domestic income created per Rupee of public expenditure, a policy of public agricultural investment is to be preferred to policies of fertiliser and food subsidisation as well as procurement pricing. Table 7.7 shows that the medium–run effects of a particular policy change may be opposite to its initial impact, the impact on real GDP of an increase in food subsidies being a case in point.[11]

In Table 7.7, the income–distributional implications of each of the four policy alternatives are also considered. It can be seen that the marginal returns to an extra Rupee allocated to public procurement largely accrue to agriculturalists, while its marginal returns are negative for non–agricultural wage earners and public enterprises – both in the short and the medium run. Higher non–agricultural prices thus hurt those income groups in non–agriculture the income of which is less than perfectly indexed. At least in the medium run, an increase in food subsidisation (through its deflationary impact) is beneficial to non–agricultural wage earners, although its aggregate marginal returns (in terms of real GDP at factor cost) are negative. This is mainly due to the fact that, in the medium run, the benefit–cost ratio of a rise in food subsidies is negative for farmers.

In the short run, for all crops, the marginal returns to an increase in fertiliser subsidisation are considerably larger than those to the other items of public expenditure considered in Table 7.7. Marginal returns to an increase in the fertiliser subsidy are particularly large in the production of wheat

---

[11] Other instances in which the short–run effects do not reflect the medium impact of a policy intervention, include experiments $D-3$ and $D-4.2$.

Table 7.7
Dynamic Experiments:
Annual Marginal Returns per Rupee Public Expenditure (in Rs.)

	Increase in Income due to one extra Rupee of public expenditure:			
	$D-1$	$D-3$	$D-4$	$D-5$
Short – Run				
GDP at factor cost	1.54	2.59	0.56	1.18
Agricultural Income	1.55	1.78	0.64	3.54
Non–Agr. Wage Income	−0.17	0.33	−0.11	−1.43
Non–Agr. Mark–up Income	0.46	0.62	0.16	−0.33
Revenue Public Enterprises	−0.30	−0.14	−0.13	−0.60
Rice production	0.03	0.28	−0.01	0.16
Wheat production	0.03	0.31	−0.01	0.18
Other Food Production	0.01	0.04	0.00	0.01
Commercial Crop Production	0.06	0.36	0.03	0.07
Medium – Run				
GDP at factor cost	5.05	2.47	−1.21	4.05
Agricultural Income	2.96	0.85	−3.15	6.02
Non–Agr. Wage Income	0.97	0.83	1.00	−0.88
Non–Agr. Mark–up Income	2.14	0.77	−0.21	1.42
Revenue Public Enterprises	−1.02	0.03	1.15	−2.52
Rice production	0.31	0.25	−0.26	0.23
Wheat production	0.21	0.20	−0.24	0.33
Other Food Production	0.17	0.05	−0.01	0.02
Commercial Crop Production	0.51	0.44	0.15	0.19

Note: Marginal returns are expressed in constant prices,
with base–year 1985–86.

and commercial crops. In the medium run, the marginal returns to increased public investment are largest in the cultivation of rice, other food crops and commercial crops. Only in the production of wheat – the most price–responsive crop –, the marginal returns to a rise in public procurement are largest.

Table 7.7 also gives a clear indication of the differential impact across crops – both in the short and medium run – of agricultural policies. Two particular examples stand out. First, it can be seen that, in the medium run, – for the agricultural policies considered – the marginal returns are lowest in the production of other food crops. This finding is not surprising in view of the sector's relatively low price–responsiveness and low irrigation coverage. In this sector, marginal returns to public investment in irrigation are larger than those to other agricultural policy measures – a finding which is consistent with the analysis included in the Economic Survey 1990 91. Second, in the medium run, the marginal returns to a rise in food subsidisation are found to be positive in the production of commercial crops, whereas they are negative in the production of the other crops. This result can be explained as follows. With the increase in food subsidies, market prices of foodgrains decline relative to the market price of commercial crops which – over time – leads to a rise in area allocated to commercial crop production and an increase in their growth rate. This result indicates that an increase in output of a particular crop may be at the cost of some decrease in the output of other crops. As such, it illustrates the often observed fact that the price–responsiveness of aggregate agricultural supply is lower – both in the short run and in the medium run – than are individual crop responses. The difference is due to the fact that farmers can shift land, labour, fertilisers, and irrigation water from one crop to another without raising their aggregate level of crop production.[12] Summarising, the results of the policy experiments considered in Table 7.7 suggest that in stimulating agricultural growth, the development of irrigation (through public investment) plays a more important role than some of the price policy measures – including output pricing and input subsidisation – which are often recommended. This finding is supported by the outcomes of the other policy experiments discussed in Section 7.4.

Table 7.8 gives a summary of the macro–economic consequences of the four agricultural policy alternatives considered in Table 7.7. It can be seen that, over the medium term, out of the four policy measures considered, only an increase in public agricultural investment $(D-1)$ has a beneficial impact on the government budget (or net public savings), even though the increase in public investment expenditure is not accompanied by a reduction in other items of public expenditure. The table further shows that both an increase in the rate of fertiliser subsidy $(D-3)$ and a rise in food subsidisation $(D-4)$ lead to a deterioration of the country's current account. The medium–run impact of an increase in food subsidisation is contractionary as was also clear from Table 7.7, while the other three policy experiments are expansionary. Finally, it can be seen that both an increase in public agricultural investment and an increase in procurement prices $(D-5)$ are inflationary. However, when the increase in public agricultural investment is financed by a reduction in public investment in non–agriculture, the result is both expansionary and deflationary (experiment $D-1.2$).

The results of the experiments underscore the macro–economic significance of agricultural policy–making in India, particularly in terms of inflation. Furthermore, it was found that the growth rates of real GDP from the different scenarios fall within a relatively small range. This shows how difficult it is to accelerate the growth rate of the economy once the various consistencies are ensured and the feedbacks are accounted for. Only when changes in different policy instruments were introduced simultaneously – amounting for all practical purposes to a drastic change in agricultural

---

[12] This implies that aggregate agricultural production is more likely to increase if more resources are devoted to agriculture or if technical change is introduced *via* price policy. See Binswanger (1991).

Table 7.8
Dynamic Experiments:
Macro–Economic Effects of Agricultural Policy Changes

	$D-1$	$D-3$	$D-4$	$D-5$
Net public savings	+	−	−	−
Foreign savings	*neg.*	−	−	+
Net private savings	+	+	−	+
Gross domestic investment	+	−	+	−
Real GDP growth	+	+	−	+
Inflation	+	−	−	+

Note: *neg.* = negligible.

policy – were deviations large from the reference run.[4] The general picture emerging from the simulation results is that the scenarios that record the highest rates of growth include those in which public agricultural (irrigation) investment is increased. Hence, the simulation results suggest that the country's macro–economic performance can be improved by changing the *structural* conditions for agricultural growth. This is because an 'adequate' rate of agricultural production growth is necessary to realise an increase in real GDP with an acceptable rate of inflation. As such, the agricultural constraint, in Sen's (1981) terminology, was still binding during the Seventh Plan period.

The degree of structural change which can be brought about in a five–year period by public agricultural investment, is illustrated by Figures 7.5 and 7.6 which depict the evolution of the short–run price elasticity of rice and wheat output during the reference run, during experiment $D-1$, and during an experiment in which public agricultural investment was raised by 40 per cent.[5] It can be seen that the price–responsiveness of rice and wheat production increase (in absolute terms) following an increase in public agricultural investment. Given that the price responsiveness is higher in irrigated agriculture than in unirrigated agriculture, this increase is the result of the rise in irrigation coverage of rice and wheat cultivation, brought about by increased public investment.

In my view, the most important lesson to be drawn from the simulation results is that there exists a fundamental asymmetry of adjustments on the agricultural demand and supply sides, with the speed of adjustment being much slower on the supply than on the demand side. Given this structural feature of the Indian economy, there is only little scope for raising the growth rate of real GDP in a non–inflationary way without increasing the rate of agricultural

---

[4] This conclusion is supported by the results of a longer–term modelling study by Narayana *et al.* (1987).

[5] The results of the experiment in which public agricultural investment was raised by 40 per cent, are not reported in Section 7.4.

***Figure* 7.5**
***Dynamic Experiments*:**
The *Evolution of the Short–Run Price Elasticity of Rice Output*

Short–Run
Elasticity of
Rice Output
with respect to
Relative Price
of Fertilisers
to Rice

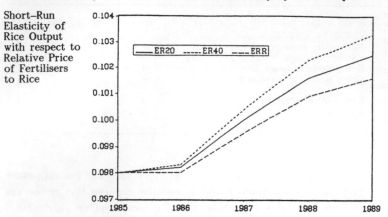

Note: ERR refers to the evolution of the price elasticity of rice output
during the reference run; ER20 refers to the evolution of the
price elasticity of rice output when public agricultural
investment is raised by 20 per cent; and ER40 refers to the
evolution of the price elasticity of rice output when public
agricultural investment is raised by 40 per cent.

***Figure* 7.6**
***Dynamic Experiments*:**
The *Evolution of the Short–Run Price Elasticity of Wheat Output*

Short–Run
Elasticity of
Wheat Output
with respect to
Relative Price
of Fertilisers
to Wheat

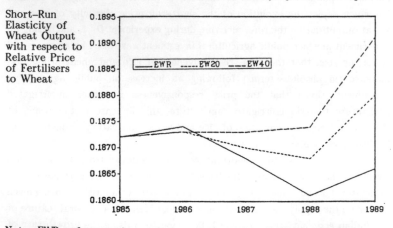

Note: EWR refers to the evolution of the price elasticity of wheat
output during the reference run; EW20 refers to the evolution of
the price elasticity of wheat output when public agricultural
investment is raised by 20 per cent; and EW40 refers to the
evolution of the price elasticity of wheat output when public
agricultural investment is raised by 40 per cent.

growth. It is in this context that chosing an agricultural policy mix which is effective in raising agriculture's (short–run as well as well medium–run) supply response, is critical to the success of non–agricultural policy initiatives. The simulation results of Section 7.3 indicate that the success of an 'industry–first' investment strategy will be frustrated by an inadequate expansion of the agricultural sector. The simulation results of Section 7.4 suggest that, in achieving adequate agricultural growth, public investment in irrigation is more effective than the major instruments of price policy considered in the analysis. They further show that those agricultural policies which are successful in enhancing the growth rate of agricultural production, also have a significant impact on the performance of the non–agricultural sectors and the country's macro–economy.

Below I describe the major features of the 'dynamic' experiments discussed in Section 7.3. The related tables follow. Columns in the table may not add to the given totals due to rounding.

Experiment DN – 1: Net sown area in 1987–88 is raised from 138 million hectares in the reference run to 141.5 million hectares.

Experiment DN – 2: The growth rate of exports of non–agricultural sectors 7, 8 and 9 in real terms is raised from 10 per cent in the reference run to 15 per cent.

Experiment DN – 3: Public investment in agriculture is reduced is by 20 per cent and re–allocated to public investment in the basic, intermediate and capital goods sector.

Experiment DN – 4: The direct tax rate on agricultural income is raised from zero per cent to 2.5 per cent. The revenue from this direct tax increase is used to raise public investment in basic, intermediate and capital goods production.

Table **7.A.1**
Dynamic Policy Experiments:
Nominal National Accounts, **1989–90** (Rs. milliard)

At Current Prices

	Base Run	DN–1	DN–2	DN–3	DN–4
Private Consumption	2901.0	2843.7	3382.5	2881.0	2740.0
Public Consumption	548.2	537.9	608.4	546.8	524.5
Gross Domestic Inv.	1096.2	1081.4	1189.8	1074.5	1096.7
Exports	322.4	322.4	375.2	322.4	322.4
Imports (−)	430.8	430.3	440.3	427.7	432.7
GDP market prices	4437.0	4355.0	5115.5	4396.9	4251.0
Current Account Deficit	103.4	102.9	60.1	100.4	105.3
Public Revenue Surplus	−119.8	−115.4	−123.6	−129.4	−82.9
Private Savings	652.8	640.1	756.6	646.5	620.4
Depreciation	459.9	453.8	496.6	457.0	453.9
Gross Domestic Inv.	1096.2	1081.4	1189.8	1074.5	1096.7
Agricultural Income	1210.5	1182.9	1472.8	1211.2	1130.4
Non–agr. wage Income	1475.9	1448.7	1670.1	1459.3	1420.4
Non–agr. Mark–up Inc.	919.4	898.4	1089.4	903.5	878.9
Government Income	317.6	317.6	317.6	317.6	317.6
GDP factor cost	3923.4	3847.5	4549.9	3891.5	3747.1

Real National Accounts at Constant 1985 – 86 *Prices*

	Base Run	DN–1	DN–2	DN–3	DN–4
Private Consumption	2150.7	2147.1	2204.2	2127.3	2132.6
Public Consumption	396.3	396.3	396.3	396.3	396.3
Gross Domestic Inv.	845.2	844.4	855.6	830.5	870.7
Exports	249.3	254.4	253.6	249.2	261.5
Imports (−)	386.9	389.7	375.8	384.2	396.2
GDP market prices	3254.6	3252.4	3333.8	3218.9	3264.9
Agricultural Income	883.9	879.6	955.7	883.1	864.4
Non–agr. wage Income	1077.6	1077.3	1083.8	1063.9	1086.1
Non–agr. Mark–up Inc.	671.3	668.1	706.9	658.7	672.0
Government Income	231.9	236.2	206.1	231.5	242.8
GDP factor cost	2864.7	2861.2	2952.6	2837.2	2865.3

Table 7.A.2
Dynamic Policy Experiments:
Average Annual Price and Wage Changes, **1984–85** *to* **1989–90**
(in percentage change)

Price Changes

	Base Run	DN – 1	DN – 2	DN – 3	DN – 4
Rice	8.0	7.3	11.2	9.1	6.8
Wheat	9.2	10.2	12.6	10.2	8.2
Other Food Crops	10.0	9.2	14.1	9.7	8.6
Commercial Crops	10.4	9.7	11.4	10.7	9.0
Other Agriculture	7.0	6.5	5.3	6.3	5.6
Fertilisers	5.2	4.9	6.8	5.2	4.6
Basic, Intermediate & Capital Goods	7.7	7.4	9.3	7.7	7.1
Consumer Goods	6.0	5.7	8.4	6.1	5.2
Services	5.5	5.2	7.4	5.5	4.8
Consumer Price Index	7.6	7.2	10.5	7.7	6.5
GDP Deflator	7.9	7.5	10.4	7.9	6.9
A–NA Terms of Trade	3.5	3.3	5.3	3.7	3.3

Nominal Wage Changes

	Base Run	DN – 1	DN – 2	DN – 3	DN – 4
Fertilisers	7.5	7.1	10.0	7.5	6.5
Basic, Intermediate & Capital Goods	10.4	10.0	12.1	10.3	9.6
Consumer Goods	7.3	7.1	8.6	7.3	6.7
Services	8.1	7.8	10.0	8.1	7.3
Government	9.4	8.9	12.2	9.4	8.3

Table 7.A.3
Dynamic Policy Experiments:
Average Annual Rate of Growth of Production and Income,
1984-85 to 1989-90
(in percentage change)

	Base Run	DN-1	DN-2	DN-3	DN-4
Production					
Rice	1.9	1.9	2.1	1.5	1.8
Wheat	2.3	1.9	2.5	1.9	2.1
Other Food Crops	0.5	0.6	0.5	0.4	0.4
Commercial Crops	1.4	1.6	1.6	1.1	1.4
Other Agriculture	3.6	3.6	3.6	3.6	3.6
Fertilisers	4.4	4.4	5.2	4.3	4.2
Basic, Intermediate & Capital Goods	7.7	7.6	8.5	7.4	7.9
Consumer Goods	8.2	8.2	9.3	8.0	8.0
Services	8.3	8.2	9.3	8.2	8.2
Income at 1985-86 prices:					
Agricultural Income	3.9	3.8	5.6	3.9	3.4
Non-agr. Wage Income	5.4	5.4	5.5	5.1	5.6
Non-agr. Mark-up Income	5.5	5.4	6.6	5.1	5.5
GDP at Factor Cost	5.2	5.1	5.8	5.0	5.2
GDP at Market Prices	5.7	5.7	6.2	5.5	5.8

Table 7.A.4
Dynamic Policy Experiments: Land Statistics, 1989-90
(million hectares)

	Base Run	DN-1	DN-2	DN-3	DN-4
Net Irrigated Area	46.5	46.4	46.8	44.7	46.4
Net Irrigated Area/ Net Sown Area (%)	32.9	32.8	32.3	31.6	32.8
Aggr. Cropping Intensity	129.4	129.3	129.6	128.1	129.3
Gross Irrigated Area	58.9	58.7	59.2	56.5	58.6
under Rice	19.2	19.4	19.3	18.4	19.1
under Wheat	19.1	18.5	19.0	18.5	18.9
under Other Food Crops	5.5	5.6	5.6	5.2	5.4
under Commercial Crops	15.1	15.3	15.3	14.4	15.1
Gross Cropped Area	183.1	183.0	183.4	181.2	182.9
under Rice	42.5	42.7	42.6	41.9	42.5
under Wheat	24.6	23.9	24.5	24.1	24.5
under Other Food Crops	64.3	64.6	64.4	64.3	64.3
under Commercial Crops	51.6	51.8	51.9	50.9	51.7

Table 7.A.5
Dynamic Policy Experiments:
Savings and Investment Balances, 1985–1990
(Average annual proportion of GDP at market prices)

Scenario	Sources of Savings:				Gross Domestic Investment
	Public Revenue Deficit	Current Account Deficit	Net Private Savings	Deprec.	
RR	−2.26	2.05	14.67	10.24	24.69
DN−1	−2.22	2.07	14.67	10.30	24.79
DN−2	−2.12	1.50	14.70	10.39	24.03
DN−3	−2.39	2.03	14.66	10.21	24.59
DN−4	−1.49	2.15	14.58	10.40	25.63

Table 7.A.6
Dynamic Policy Experiments:
Distribution of Savings, 1985–1990
(Average annual proportion of Gross Domestic Saving)

	Savings from:					
	Agric. Income	Non–Agr. Wage Income	Non–Agr. Mark–up Income	Foreign Savings	Public Savings	Deprec.
RR	13.65	28.06	17.75	8.27	−9.23	41.51
DN−1	13.51	28.01	17.68	8.32	−9.00	41.48
DN−2	14.46	28.42	18.42	6.21	−8.91	41.40
DN−3	13.71	28.23	17.73	8.22	−9.83	41.93
DN−4	12.54	27.22	17.15	8.35	−5.88	40.63

Table 7.A.7
Dynamic Policy Experiments:
Income Distribution, 1985–1990
(average annual proportion of GDP at factor cost)

	Agric. Income	Non–Agr. Wage Income	Non–Agr. Mark–up Income	Govt. Income
RR	0.319	0.373	0.231	0.076
DN−1	0.318	0.374	0.231	0.077
DN−2	0.327	0.369	0.233	0.072
DN−3	0.319	0.374	0.231	0.077
DN−4	0.313	0.376	0.232	0.078

Appendix 7.2

Results of the 'Dynamic' Experiments of Section 7.4

Below I describe the major features of the 'dynamic' agricultural policy experiments discussed in Section 7.4. The related tables follow. Columns in the table may not add to the given totals due to rounding.

Experiment D–1: Public investment in agriculture is raised by 20 per cent.

Experiment D–1.1: Public investment in agriculture is raised by 20 per cent and the fertiliser subsidy is eliminated.

Experiment D–1.2: Public investment in agriculture is increased by 20 per cent and public investment in basic, intermediate and capital goods production is reduced by the same amount.

Experiment D–1.3: Public investment in agriculture is increased by 20 per cent, public investment in basic, intermediate and capital goods production is reduced by the same amount, and the fertiliser subsidy rate is eliminated.

Experiment D–2: The fertiliser subsidy is eliminated.

Experiment D–3: The rate of fertiliser subsidy is raised from 27.3 to 50.0 per cent.

Experiment D–3.1: The rate of fertiliser subsidy is raised from 27.3 to 50.0 per cent and public agricultural investment is raised by 20 per cent.

Experiment D–3.2: Public investment in agriculture is increased by 20 per cent, public investment in basic, intermediate and capital goods production is reduced by the same amount, and the fertiliser subsidy rate is raised from 27.3 to 50.0 per cent.

Experiment D–3.3: The rate of fertiliser subsidy is raised from 27.3 to 50.0 per cent and public agricultural investment is reduced proportionately.

Experiment D–4: The quantities of foodgrains publicly distributed are raised by 20 per cent.

Experiment D–4.1: The quantities of foodgrains publicly distributed are raised by 20 per cent and the rate of fertiliser subsidy is raised from 27.3 to 50.0 per cent.

Experiment D–4.2: The quantity of foodgrains publicly distributed is raised by 20 per cent and public agricultural investment is increased by 40 per cent.

Experiment D–5: Procurement prices of rice and wheat are raised by 10 per cent.

Experiment D–5.1: Procurement prices of rice and wheat are raised by 10 per cent and the quantities of foodgrains publicly distributed are increased by 10 per cent.

Experiment D–5.2: The Public Distribution System and the public procurement scheme are both eliminated.

Experiment D–5.3: The rate of fertiliser subsidy is raised from 27.3 to 50.0 per cent, public investment in agriculture is increased by 50 per cent, and procurement prices are kept at the level of market price for fertilisers.

Table 7.B.1
Dynamic Policy Experiments:
Nominal National Accounts, **1989-90** (Rs. milliard at current prices)

	Base Run	D-1	D-1.1	D-1.2	D-1.3
Private Consumption	2901.0	3068.5	3229.6	2925.3	3078.5
Public Consumption	548.2	572.2	603.5	550.4	580.3
Gross Domestic Inv.	1096.2	1161.5	1208.8	1118.0	1163.0
Exports	322.4	322.4	322.4	322.4	322.4
Imports (−)	430.8	436.4	436.4	433.6	433.6
GDP market prices	4437.0	4688.2	4927.9	4482.4	4710.6
Current Account Deficit	103.4	109.0	109.0	106.2	106.2
Public Revenue Surplus	−119.8	−117.7	−122.1	−111.2	−115.4
Private Savings	652.8	691.2	726.2	659.8	693.1
Depreciation	459.9	479.0	495.7	463.1	479.1
Gross Domestic Inv.	1096.2	1161.5	1208.8	1118.0	1163.0
Agricultural Income	1210.5	1284.8	1366.0	1213.0	1290.0
Non-agr. wage Income	1475.9	1559.0	1635.9	1494.0	1567.4
Non-agr. Mark-up Inc.	919.4	988.9	1042.7	936.2	987.4
Government Income	317.6	317.6	317.6	317.6	317.6
GDP factor cost	3923.4	4150.3	4362.1	3960.7	4162.3

	Base Run	D-2	D-3	D-3.1	D-3.2
Private Consumption	2901.0	3064.2	2878.6	3025.5	2906.6
Public Consumption	548.2	580.2	540.1	560.0	542.8
Gross Domestic Inv.	1096.2	1142.4	1090.6	1150.2	1112.9
Exports	322.4	322.4	322.4	322.4	322.4
Imports (−)	430.8	430.7	433.3	438.9	436.3
GDP market prices	4437.0	4678.4	4398.3	4619.2	4448.5
Current Account Deficit	103.4	103.3	105.9	111.5	108.9
Public Revenue Surplus	−119.8	−126.0	−121.0	−117.4	−112.8
Private Savings	652.8	688.1	649.1	683.0	656.9
Depreciation	459.9	476.9	456.5	473.1	460.0
Gross Domestic Inv.	1096.2	1142.4	1090.6	1150.2	1112.9
Agricultural Income	1210.5	1293.4	1189.3	1253.7	1194.0
Non-agr. wage Income	1475.9	1553.5	1471.1	1544.2	11490.6
Non-agr. Mark-up Inc.	919.4	973.5	917.4	979.2	935.2
Government Income	317.6	317.6	317.6	317.6	317.6
GDP factor cost	3923.4	4137.9	3895.4	4094.7	3937.4

Continued overleaf.

Table 7.B.1
Concluded

	Base Run	$D-3.3$	$D-4$	$D-4.1$	$D-4.2$
Private Consumption	2901.0	2869.0	2651.3	2684.9	2895.5
Public Consumption	548.2	550.0	509.8	511.8	542.3
Gross Domestic Inv.	1096.2	1073.0	1030.7	1039.8	1135.5
Exports	322.4	322.4	322.4	322.4	322.4
Imports (−)	430.8	427.5	427.6	430.6	438.1
GDP market prices	4437.0	3881.0	4086.6	4128.2	4457.4
Current Account Deficit	103.4	100.1	100.2	103.2	110.7
Public Revenue Surplus	−119.8	−130.8	−106.7	−111.7	−97.3
Private Savings	652.8	645.9	599.4	607.9	656.1
Depreciation	459.9	457.7	437.8	440.4	466.0
Gross Domestic Inv.	1096.2	1073.0	1030.7	1039.8	1135.5
Agricultural Income	1210.5	1187.4	1074.2	1081.3	1179.2
Non–agr. wage Income	1475.9	1471.1	1369.7	1390.7	1492.7
Non–agr. Mark–up Inc.	919.4	904.9	836.7	854.3	941.3
Government Income	317.6	317.6	317.6	317.6	317.6
GDP factor cost	3923.4	3881.0	3598.1	3643.8	3930.6

	Base Run	$D-5$	$D-5.1$	$D-5.2$	$D-5.3$
Private Consumption	2901.0	3231.4	3110.7	2588.5	2925.7
Public Consumption	548.2	604.5	586.3	496.7	543.1
Gross Domestic Inv.	1096.2	1178.1	1146.1	1017.2	1161.9
Exports	322.4	322.4	322.4	322.4	322.4
Imports (−)	430.8	433.9	432.4	426.2	443.0
GDP market prices	4437.0	4902.5	4733.0	3998.7	4537.0
Current Account Deficit	103.4	106.5	105.0	98.8	115.6
Public Revenue Surplus	−119.8	−147.3	−142.2	−92.4	−91.9
Private Savings	652.8	725.4	699.7	582.8	668.6
Depreciation	459.9	493.5	483.5	428.0	469.6
Gross Domestic Inv.	1096.2	1178.1	1146.1	1017.2	1161.9
Agricultural Income	1210.5	1372.4	1305.3	1069.1	1213.3
Non–agr. wage Income	1475.9	1632.2	1581.7	1320.0	1510.4
Non–agr. Mark–up Inc.	919.4	1037.4	998.3	802.5	964.9
Government Income	317.6	317.6	317.6	317.6	317.6
GDP factor cost	3923.4	4359.5	4202.8	3509.2	4006.1

Table 7.B.2
Dynamic Policy Experiments:
Real National Accounts, 1989–90 (*at* 1985–86 *prices*)
(Rs. milliard)

	Base Run	D–1	D–1.1	D–1.2	D–1.3
Private Consumption	2150.7	2187.5	2175.4	2173.1	2161.5
Public Consumption	396.3	396.3	396.3	396.3	396.3
Gross Domestic Inv.	845.2	869.1	870.5	858.9	860.3
Exports	249.3	238.1	224.4	249.0	235.8
Imports (−)	386.9	385.3	377.7	389.2	381.9
GDP market prices	3254.6	3305.6	3288.8	3288.0	3272.0
Agricultural Income	883.9	901.3	908.8	885.4	893.1
Non–agr. wage Income	1077.6	1093.6	1088.3	1090.5	1085.2
Non–agr. Mark–up Inc.	671.3	693.7	693.7	683.3	683.6
Government Income	231.9	227.8	211.3	231.8	219.9
GDP factor cost	2864.7	2911.5	2902.0	2891.0	2881.8

	Base Run	D–2	D–3	D–3.1	D–3.2
Private Consumption	2150.7	2138.6	2186.5	2223.6	2209.6
Public Consumption	396.3	396.3	396.3	396.3	396.3
Gross Domestic Inv.	845.2	845.9	849.4	873.4	863.2
Exports	249.3	235.1	254.7	245.6	254.2
Imports (−)	386.9	378.9	392.4	392.1	394.6
GDP market prices	3254.6	3236.9	3294.5	3346.8	3328.6
Agricultural Income	883.9	892.5	887.8	904.9	890.1
Non–agr. wage Income	1077.6	1071.9	1098.2	1114.6	1111.3
Non–agr. Mark–up Inc.	671.3	671.7	684.9	706.7	697.2
Government Income	231.9	219.1	237.1	229.2	236.7
GDP factor cost	2864.7	2855.2	2907.9	2955.4	2935.4

Continued overleaf.

Note: Figures in the table are taken from Table 7.B.1 and are deflated by the GDP defator.

Table 7.B.2
Concluded

	Base Run	D-3.3	D-4	D-4.1	D-4.2
Private Consumption	2150.7	2143.8	2123.2	2170.5	2201.3
Public Consumption	396.3	396.3	396.3	396.3	396.3
Gross Domestic Inv.	845.2	825.6	832.1	837.5	878.0
Exports	249.3	251.7	268.2	268.4	253.6
Imports (−)	386.9	385.5	395.0	397.8	396.0
GDP market prices	3254.6	3231.8	3233.8	3274.9	3333.2
Agricultural Income	883.9	871.4	847.0	855.5	700.7
Non−agr. wage Income	1077.6	1079.5	1080.0	1100.3	1111.1
Non−agr. Mark−up Inc.	671.3	664.0	659.7	675.9	700.7
Government Income	231.9	233.0	250.4	251.2	236.4
GDP factor cost	2864.7	2848.0	2837.1	2882.9	2925.8

	Base Run	D-5	D-5.1	D-5.2	D-5.3
Private Consumption	2150.7	2179.1	2170.1	2110.2	2234.2
Public Consumption	396.3	396.3	396.3	396.3	396.3
Gross Domestic Inv.	845.2	848.6	841.3	841.0	901.4
Exports	249.3	222.9	231.4	272.3	251.8
Imports (−)	386.9	374.0	377.6	396.0	399.2
GDP market prices	3254.6	3272.8	3261.5	3223.7	3384.4
Agricultural Income	883.9	911.3	894.9	856.4	902.1
Non−agr. wage Income	1077.6	1083.8	1084.4	1057.5	1122.9
Non−agr. Mark−up Inc.	671.3	688.8	684.4	642.9	717.4
Government Income	231.9	210.9	217.7	254.4	236.1
GDP factor cost	2864.7	2894.8	2881.4	2811.1	2978.5

Table 7.B.3
Dynamic Policy Experiments:
Average Annual Price Changes, 1984–85 to 1989–90
(in percentage change)

	Base Run	D–1	D–1.1	D–1.2	D–1.3
Rice	8.0	8.0	9.4	7.0	8.4
Wheat	9.2	9.2	14.9	8.4	14.1
Other Food Crops	10.0	11.5	13.3	10.3	12.1
Commercial Crops	10.4	11.2	12.1	10.1	10.9
Other Agriculture	7.0	8.9	9.8	7.6	8.5
Fertilisers	5.2	5.9	12.4	5.3	11.8
Basic, Intermediate & Capital Goods	7.7	8.3	9.1	7.8	8.5
Consumer Goods	6.0	6.8	7.7	6.1	6.9
Services	5.5	6.3	7.2	5.6	6.5
Consumer Price Index	7.6	8.4	9.7	7.5	8.8
GDP Deflator	7.9	8.7	9.9	7.8	9.0
A–NA Terms of Trade	3.5	3.7	4.3	3.2	3.8

	Base Run	D–2	D–3	D–3.1	D–3.2
Rice	8.0	9.4	6.3	6.0	5.4
Wheat	9.2	15.0	7.8	8.3	7.2
Other Food Crops	10.0	11.8	9.5	10.9	9.9
Commercial Crops	10.4	11.4	9.1	9.6	8.7
Other Agriculture	7.0	7.9	7.4	9.2	8.1
Fertilisers	5.2	11.8	−0.7	−0.2	−0.7
Basic, Intermediate & Capital Goods	7.7	8.5	7.5	8.1	7.6
Consumer Goods	6.0	6.9	5.6	6.3	5.7
Services	5.5	6.5	5.3	6.0	5.4
Consumer Price Index	7.6	9.0	7.0	7.8	7.0
GDP Deflator	7.9	9.1	7.4	8.1	7.4
A–NA Terms of Trade	3.5	4.1	1.5	3.2	2.8

Continued overleaf.

Table 7.B.3
Concluded

	Base Run	$D-3.3$	$D-4$	$D-4.1$	$D-4.2$
Rice	8.0	7.5	5.4	4.3	4.8
Wheat	9.2	11.7	6.2	4.8	6.9
Other Food Crops	10.0	9.8	7.7	7.6	10.1
Commercial Crops	10.4	9.2	8.5	7.8	9.2
Other Agriculture	7.0	6.5	4.8	5.6	8.0
Fertilisers	5.2	5.2	4.2	-1.5	5.1
Basic, Intermediate & Capital Goods	7.7	7.7	6.7	6.7	7.6
Consumer Goods	6.0	5.8	4.7	4.7	5.8
Services	5.5	5.8	4.3	4.4	5.4
Consumer Price Index	7.6	7.4	5.8	5.7	7.0
GDP Deflator	7.9	7.7	6.2	6.1	7.4
A–NA Terms of Trade	3.5	3.1	2.5	2.2	2.8

	Base Run	$D-5$	$D-5.1$	$D-5.2$	$D-5.3$
Rice	8.0	10.2	9.1	7.7	4.9
Wheat	9.2	10.9	9.3	2.7	4.0
Other Food Crops	10.0	12.8	11.7	7.1	10.2
Commercial Crops	10.4	12.8	12.1	9.2	9.7
Other Agriculture	7.0	9.8	8.8	3.7	9.1
Fertilisers	5.2	6.7	6.3	3.8	-0.6
Basic, Intermediate & Capital Goods	7.7	9.2	8.7	6.2	7.6
Consumer Goods	6.0	7.9	7.3	4.5	5.9
Services	5.5	7.3	6.8	3.8	5.4
Consumer Price Index	7.6	9.7	8.9	5.6	7.2
GDP Deflator	7.9	9.9	9.2	5.9	7.5
A–NA Terms of Trade	3.5	4.2	3.4	3.0	3.1

Table 7.B.4
Dynamic Policy Experiments:
Average Annual Nominal Wage Changes, 1984–85 *to* 1989–90
(in percentage change)

	Base Run	$D-1$	$D-1.1$	$D-1.2$	$D-1.3$
Fertilisers	7.5	8.5	9.8	7.6	8.9
Basic, Intermediate & Capital Goods	10.4	11.1	12.1	10.5	11.4
Consumer Goods	7.3	7.9	8.7	7.4	8.1
Services	8.1	9.0	10.0	8.2	9.2
Government	9.4	10.6	12.0	9.5	11.0
	Base Run	$D-2$	$D-3$	$D-3.1$	$D-3.2$
Fertilisers	7.5	8.9	7.1	7.9	7.2
Basic, Intermediate & Capital Goods	10.4	11.4	10.2	10.8	10.3
Consumer Goods	7.3	8.1	7.2	7.7	7.3
Services	8.1	9.2	7.9	8.6	8.0
Government	9.4	11.0	9.0	10.0	9.2
	Base Run	$D-3.3$	$D-4$	$D-4.1$	$D-4.2$
Fertilisers	7.5	7.6	5.8	5.8	7.2
Basic, Intermediate & Capital Goods	10.4	10.5	9.1	9.3	10.2
Consumer Goods	7.3	7.4	6.4	6.5	7.3
Services	8.1	8.2	6.8	6.9	8.0
Government	9.4	9.6	7.5	7.6	9.1
	Base Run	$D-5$	$D-5.1$	$D-5.2$	$D-5.3$
Fertilisers	7.5	9.8	9.0	5.3	7.2
Basic, Intermediate & Capital Goods	10.4	12.2	11.7	8.5	10.2
Consumer Goods	7.3	8.8	8.4	5.8	7.2
Services	8.1	10.0	9.5	6.2	8.0
Government	9.4	12.1	11.2	6.8	9.1

Table 7.B.5
Dynamic Policy Experiments:
Average Annual Rate of Growth of Production and Income,
1984-85 *to* 1989-90
(in percentage change)

	Base Run	$D-1$	$D-1.1$	$D-1.2$	$D-1.3$
Production					
Rice	1.9	2.3	2.2	2.2	2.1
Wheat	2.3	2.7	1.5	2.6	1.4
Other Food Crops	0.5	0.5	0.4	0.5	0.3
Commercial Crops	1.4	1.7	1.8	1.7	1.7
Other Agriculture	3.6	3.6	3.6	3.6	3.6
Fertilisers	4.4	4.7	3.3	4.5	3.1
Basic, Intermediate &					
Capital Goods	7.7	8.2	8.3	7.9	8.0
Consumer Goods	8.2	8.6	8.7	8.4	8.5
Services	8.3	8.7	8.7	8.5	8.5
Income at 1985-86 *prices:*					
Agricultural Income	3.9	4.4	4.5	4.0	4.2
Non-agr. Wage Income	5.4	5.7	5.6	5.6	5.5
Non-agr. Mark-up Income	5.5	6.2	6.2	5.8	5.8
GDP at Factor Cost	5.2	5.5	5.4	5.4	5.3
GDP at Market Prices	5.7	6.1	6.0	6.0	5.8

	Base Run	$D-2$	$D-3$	$D-3.1$	$D-3.2$
Production					
Rice	1.9	1.8	2.3	2.6	2.7
Wheat	2.3	1.1	2.7	2.9	3.0
Other Food Crops	0.5	0.3	0.7	0.7	0.7
Commercial Crops	1.4	1.4	1.9	2.1	2.2
Other Agriculture	3.6	3.6	3.6	3.6	3.6
Fertilisers	4.3	3.1	6.3	6.5	6.4
Basic, Intermediate &					
Capital Goods	7.7	7.7	7.8	8.1	8.1
Consumer Goods	8.2	8.3	8.5	8.7	8.7
Services	8.3	8.3	8.5	8.7	8.7
Income at 1985-86 *prices:*					
Agricultural Income	3.9	4.2	4.0	4.4	4.1
Non-agr. Wage Income	5.4	5.3	5.8	6.1	6.0
Non-agr. Mark-up Income	5.5	5.5	5.9	6.6	6.3
GDP at Factor Cost	5.2	5.1	5.5	5.8	5.7
GDP at Market Prices	5.7	5.6	6.0	6.3	6.2

Continued overleaf.

Table 7.B.5
Concluded

	Base Run	D−3.3	D−4	D−4.1	D−4.2
Production					
Rice	1.9	1.9	1.5	2.0	2.4
Wheat	2.3	1.5	2.0	2.7	2.6
Other Food Crops	0.5	0.4	0.5	0.7	0.6
Commercial Crops	1.4	1.6	1.3	1.7	2.0
Other Agriculture	3.6	3.6	3.6	3.6	3.6
Fertilisers	4.4	4.4	3.8	5.7	4.3
Basic, Intermediate & Capital Goods	7.7	7.3	7.4	7.6	8.4
Consumer Goods	8.2	8.2	7.8	8.2	8.6
Services	8.3	8.1	8.0	8.3	8.7
Income at 1985−86 *prices:*					
Agricultural Income	3.9	3.6	3.1	3.3	3.8
Non−agr. Wage Income	5.4	5.4	5.4	5.8	6.0
Non−agr. Mark−up Income	5.5	5.2	5.1	5.6	6.4
GDP at Factor Cost	5.2	5.0	5.0	5.4	5.6
GDP at Market Prices	5.7	5.6	5.6	5.9	6.2

	Base Run	D−5	D−5.1	D−5.2	D−5.3
Production					
Rice	1.9	2.0	1.8	1.3	3.0
Wheat	2.3	2.5	2.5	3.3	4.3
Other Food Crops	0.5	0.5	0.5	0.4	0.8
Commercial Crops	1.4	1.6	1.5	0.7	2.1
Other Agriculture	3.6	3.6	3.6	3.6	3.6
Fertilisers	4.4	4.8	4.5	3.9	6.6
Basic, Intermediate & Capital Goods	7.7	7.9	7.8	7.3	8.8
Consumer Goods	8.2	8.6	8.4	7.5	8.9
Services	8.3	8.6	8.5	7.8	9.1
Income at 1985−86 *prices:*					
Agricultural Income	3.9	4.6	4.2	3.3	4.4
Non−agr. Wage Income	5.4	5.5	5.5	5.0	6.3
Non−agr. Mark−up Income	5.5	6.0	5.9	4.6	6.9
GDP at Factor Cost	5.2	5.4	5.3	4.8	6.0
GDP at Market Prices	5.7	5.9	5.8	5.5	6.6

Table 7.B.6
Dynamic Policy Experiments: Land Statistics, 1989-90
(million hectares)

	Base Run	D-1	D-1.1	D-1.2	D-1.3
Net Irrigated Area	46.5	48.6	48.7	48.4	48.5
Net Irrigated Area/ Net Sown Area (%)	32.9	34.3	34.4	34.2	34.3
Aggr. Cropping Intensity	129.4	130.8	130.9	130.7	130.8
Gross Irrigated Area	58.9	61.4	61.6	61.2	61.4
under Rice	19.2	20.1	20.6	20.0	20.5
under Wheat	19.1	19.7	18.7	19.6	18.6
under Other Food Crops	5.5	5.8	5.8	5.8	5.8
under Commercial Crops	15.1	15.9	16.5	15.8	16.5
Gross Cropped Area	183.1	185.1	185.3	184.9	185.1
under Rice	42.5	43.2	43.8	43.1	43.8
under Wheat	24.6	25.1	23.9	25.1	23.8
under Other Food Crops	64.3	64.4	64.3	64.4	64.3
under Commercial Crops	51.6	52.4	53.3	52.3	53.3

	Base Run	D-2	D-3	D-3.1	D-3.2
Net Irrigated Area	46.5	46.7	46.6	48.6	48.5
Net Irrigated Area/ Net Sown Area (%)	32.9	33.0	32.9	34.3	34.2
Aggr. Cropping Intensity	129.4	129.5	129.5	130.9	130.8
Gross Irrigated Area	58.9	59.1	59.0	61.5	61.3
under Rice	19.2	19.7	19.3	20.3	20.1
under Wheat	19.1	18.1	18.7	19.0	19.1
under Other Food Crops	5.5	5.5	5.6	5.9	5.9
under Commercial Crops	15.1	15.7	15.4	16.3	16.2
Gross Cropped Area	183.1	183.2	183.2	185.2	185.0
under Rice	42.5	43.2	42.5	43.2	43.1
under Wheat	24.6	23.4	24.0	24.3	24.5
under Other Food Crops	64.3	64.2	64.4	64.5	64.5
under Commercial Crops	51.6	52.5	52.2	53.1	53.0

Continued overleaf.

Table 7.B.6
Concluded

	Base Run	D − 3.3	D − 4	D − 4.1	D − 4.2
Net Irrigated Area	46.5	45.9	46.3	46.5	50.1
Net Irrigated Area/ Net Sown Area (%)	32.9	32.5	32.7	32.8	35.4
Aggr. Cropping Intensity	129.4	129.0	129.2	129.4	131.9
Gross Irrigated Area	58.9	58.1	58.6	58.8	63.4
under Rice	19.2	19.3	19.0	19.1	20.7
under Wheat	19.1	18.0	19.2	19.0	19.9
under Other Food Crops	5.5	5.4	5.5	5.6	6.1
under Commercial Crops	15.1	15.4	15.0	15.1	16.6
Gross Cropped Area	183.1	182.5	182.9	183.0	186.7
under Rice	42.5	42.7	42.2	42.1	43.5
under Wheat	24.6	23.3	24.7	24.5	25.2
under Other Food Crops	64.3	64.2	64.5	64.6	64.7
under Commercial Crops	51.6	52.4	51.5	51.8	53.3

	Base Run	D − 5	D − 5.1	D − 5.2	D − 5.3
Net Irrigated Area	46.5	47.1	47.0	46.0	51.0
Net Irrigated Area/ Net Sown Area (%)	32.9	33.3	33.2	32.5	36.0
Aggr. Cropping Intensity	129.4	129.8	129.7	129.0	132.5
Gross Irrigated Area	58.9	59.6	59.5	58.2	64.5
under Rice	19.2	19.4	19.2	18.2	20.8
under Wheat	19.1	19.3	19.5	20.9	21.1
under Other Food Crops	5.5	5.6	5.6	5.1	6.2
under Commercial Crops	15.1	15.3	15.2	14.0	16.4
Gross Cropped Area	183.1	183.6	183.6	182.6	187.5
under Rice	42.5	42.6	42.4	41.5	43.5
under Wheat	24.6	24.8	25.1	27.1	26.6
under Other Food Crops	64.3	64.3	64.4	64.2	64.7
under Commercial Crops	51.7	51.9	51.7	49.9	52.7

Table 7.B.7
Dynamic Policy Experiments:
Savings and Investment Balances, 1985–1990
(Average annual proportion of GDP at market prices)

	Sources of Savings:				
Scenario	Public Revenue Deficit	Current Account Deficit	Net Private Savings	Deprec.	Gross Domestic Investment
RR	−2.26	2.05	14.67	10.24	24.69
D−1	−2.11	2.05	14.69	10.08	24.71
D−1.1	−2.08	1.95	14.65	10.06	24.60
D−1.2	−2.14	2.07	14.68	10.18	24.78
D−1.3	−2.11	1.98	14.64	10.16	24.67
D−2	−2.24	1.96	14.63	10.21	24.57
D−3	−2.34	2.10	14.73	10.14	24.63
D−3.1	−2.17	2.11	14.74	10.00	24.68
D−3.2	−2.21	2.12	14.73	10.08	24.72
D−3.3	−2.41	2.02	14.67	10.42	24.52
D−4	−2.25	2.11	14.66	10.27	24.94
D−4.1	−2.34	2.14	14.73	11.90	24.79
D−4.2	−1.92	2.14	14.69	10.16	25.08
D−5	−2.52	1.96	14.73	9.95	24.11
D−5.1	−2.54	1.98	14.73	10.02	24.19
D−5.2	−1.80	2.15	14.55	10.59	25.51
D−5.3	−1.63	2.22	14.70	10.08	25.19

Table 7.B.8
Dynamic Policy Experiments:
Distribution of Savings, 1985–1990
(Average annual proportion of Gross Domestic Saving)

	Savings from:					
	Agric. Income	Non–Agr. Wage Income	Non–Agr. Mark–up Income	Foreign Savings	Public Savings	Deprec.
RR	13.65	28.06	17.75	8.27	−9.23	41.51
D−1	13.80	27.82	17.89	8.29	−8.61	40.82
D−1.1	13.97	27.80	17.85	7.99	−8.53	40.93
D−1.2	13.60	27.90	17.77	8.32	−8.70	41.12
D−1.3	13.77	27.88	17.74	8.01	−8.62	41.22
D−2	13.84	28.05	17.73	7.96	−9.21	41.62
D−3	13.77	28.11	17.97	8.49	−9.54	41.20
D−3.1	13.85	27.86	18.07	8.53	−8.84	40.55
D−3.2	13.71	27.95	17.99	8.54	−9.00	40.82
D−3.3	13.82	28.26	17.79	8.22	−9.90	41.81
D−4	13.14	28.09	17.60	8.41	−9.05	41.81
D−4.1	13.38	28.17	17.88	8.60	−9.48	41.45
D−4.2	13.25	27.60	17.77	8.51	−7.68	40.55
D−5	14.57	28.31	18.27	8.09	−10.54	41.31
D−5.1	14.37	28.36	18.24	8.15	−10.58	41.47
D−5.2	12.65	27.55	16.93	8.40	−7.15	41.61
D−5.3	13.08	27.21	17.67	8.71	−6.47	39.79

Table 7.B.9
Dynamic Policy Experiments:
Income Distribution, 1985–1990
(average annual proportion of GDP at factor cost)

	Agric. Income	Non–Agr. Wage Income	Non–Agr. Mark–up Income	Govt. Income
RR	0.319	0.373	0.231	0.076
D – 1	0.322	0.371	0.233	0.073
D – 1.1	0.325	0.370	0.233	0.072
D – 1.2	0.319	0.373	0.232	0.076
D – 1.3	0.322	0.372	0.232	0.074
D – 2	0.322	0.372	0.231	0.075
D – 3	0.320	0.372	0.233	0.075
D – 3.1	0.322	0.371	0.235	0.073
D – 3.2	0.320	0.372	0.234	0.074
D – 3.3	0.320	0.373	0.230	0.077
D – 4	0.312	0.377	0.231	0.080
D – 4.1	0.314	0.375	0.233	0.077
D – 4.2	0.316	0.374	0.235	0.075
D – 5	0.329	0.368	0.232	0.070
D – 5.1	0.326	0.370	0.232	0.072
D – 5.2	0.309	0.378	0.228	0.084
D – 5.3	0.315	0.373	0.237	0.075

MACRO-ECONOMIC CONSIDERATIONS
IN THE CHOICE OF AN AGRICULTURAL POLICY:
CONCLUSIONS

8.1   *Introduction*

The time has come now for a summing up of what has been done in the preceding
chapters, why it has been done and what can be learnt from it. In so doing, I
review in Section 8.2 what I regard as the crucial assumptions made in the
analysis. In Section 8.3, I present the main conclusions following from the
research, with reference to the different theoretical approaches discussed in
Chapter 2. In Section 8.4, the major policy implications of the simulation
results are discussed against the background of the debate on the Seventh Plan
development strategy and of the evolution of the Indian economy during the
1980s, discussed in Chapter 3. Section 8.5 reviews what I perceive as the
major shortcomings of the present general equilibrium model. Section 8.6
compares the present model and the conclusions drawn from it with other
modelling projects addressing similar policy problems. Finally, in Section
8.7, I shall make some further comments on the critical policy issues
highlighted by my findings.

8.2   *Approach and Assumptions*

The purpose of the research was, firstly, to assess whether and, if so, *via*
which channels and to what extent, in India, the rest of the economy is
affected by the performance of the agricultural sectors, and, secondly, in
case the relationships between agriculture and the rest of the economy proved

to be important, to identify those (agricultural) policy measures that are successful in improving both agricultural and non–agricultural performance. To answer these questions I constructed a computable general equilibrium model of India's mixed and open economy and used it to generate a large number of scenarios reflecting certain policy changes. The focus on agriculture–non–agriculture relationships, of course, conditioned the model specification. In fact, the following linkages between agriculture and non–agriculture were included in the model:

(a) final demand linkages relating to agriculturalists' final demand for non–agricultural goods and to non–agriculturalists' final demand for agricultural goods;
(b) intermediate demand linkages including the demand of agricultural producers for non–agricultural inputs and *vice versa*;
(c) wage goods linkages, whereby changes in agricultural prices affect – through nominal wage indexation – non–agricultural wages, production costs, and (mark–up) prices;
(d) savings and investment linkages;
(e) fiscal linkages involving public expenditure allocated to the agricultural sectors as well as public revenue from agriculture; and finally
(f) balance of payments linkages operating through agricultural exports and agriculture's direct and indirect import requirements.

The model was used to track the Seventh Plan period (1985–1990), the simulated values of the endogenous variables describing the reference run. By comparing the outcomes of the policy experiments with the reference scenario which describes the economy's evolution over time with 'unchanged' policy, I could assess the economy–wide effects of agricultural as well as non–agricultural policy changes and obtain insight into the functioning of the Indian economy. The following agricultural policy instruments were considered in the analysis:

(1) procurement/minimum support prices and procurement quantities;
(2) the rate of fertiliser subsidy;
(3) food subsidisation under the Public Distribution System (which takes the form of subsidised prices as well as quantities of foodgrains issued); and
(4) public investment in irrigation.

Because the macro–economic outcome of a change in one or a combination of these policy instruments is largely determined by the interplay of the reactions of the private sector, the model tries to capture these responses and their first and higher round effects on the country's macro–economy. The results of the simulation experiments underscore the importance of these higher round effects and show that there is a strong interdependence between the various sectors and groups in the economy.

Results always depend critically on the assumptions, frequently implicit, made in the analysis. Therefore, before proceeding to the discussion of the simulations results, I will briefly review a limited number of assumptions which (in my view) are critical to the simulation outcomes. Some of the assumptions are controversial, while other assumptions are likely to arouse only little disagreement. First, in the model, agricultural production is treated as being relatively price–inelastic, both in the short and medium term, which implies that agricultural production is largely supply–determined.[1] Further, agricultural prices are determined by the prevailing demand and supply conditions and the prices of rice and wheat are not allowed to fall below their minimum support levels. Second, in the model, consumers spend a considerable share of their budgets on agricultural goods, with the average budget share of agricultural goods being higher for agricultural than for non–agricultural consumers. The price responsiveness of private consumption demand for agricultural goods is relatively low, both for agricultural and non–agricultural consumers. The specification of both agricultural production and consumer demand is in accordance with known empirical 'facts', discussed in Chapter 3.

Third, exports and final imports are assumed exogenous in real terms, while complementary intermediate imports are endogenous, *i.c.* dependent on sectoral production levels.[2] What this implies is that there is no scope for increasing exports or reducing imports through exchange rate or relative price adjustment. Given that India's international trade in foodgrains is the monopoly of the Food Corporation, which decides on exports and imports of foodgrains on grounds other than merely relative prices, this specification seems appropriate for the foodgrain sectors. With respect to the imports of manufactured goods, there is evidence that the income (or production) elasticity of import demand is considerably larger than the corresponding (relative) price elasticities, suggesting that manufactured imports are to a large extent complementary to domestic output (Pandit, 1985). Finally, there is empirical evidence which indicates that Indian exports are determined by world demand and domestic supply conditions rather than by relative prices (Ghosh, 1990).

Fourth, with respect to the non–agricultural sectors, it is assumed that production is perfectly elastic and is determined by (intermediate and final) demand, a substantial part of which originates from agriculture.[3] Non–

---

[1] The treatment of agricultural output as being supply–determined is a common feature of most computable general equilibrium as well as econometric models of the Indian economy (see Krishna *et al.*, 1991).

[2] This specification is common to many general equilibrium models developed for the Indian economy (Taylor, 1983; De Janvry and Subbarao, 1986; Rattsø, 1989; and Narayana *et al.*, 1991).

[3] Krishna *et al.* (1991:47) observe that, although supply inflexibility arising from such factors as inadequate infrastructure, shortage of imported inputs and capital goods, and poor harvests due to adverse weather conditions cannot be assumed away, it should not be exaggerated as has often been done. However, so far, no common understanding has arisen about the treatment of the non–agricultural sectors. This is exemplified by the fact that non–agricultural production is determined by demand in three out of the seven macro–econometric models considered by Krishna *et al.* (1991), while, in the other four it

agricultural prices are 'administered' prices in the sense of being determined by the producers as a mark–up over variable costs.[4] Nominal wage rates in non–agriculture are indexed to the consumer price index, which is for a significant part made up of agricultural prices. In my view, there are at least three facts to suggest that, during the Seventh Plan period, the production growth of the non–agricultural sectors was not constrained by supply–side bottlenecks. First, although the industrial sectors were able to realise high growth rates during the Seventh Plan period, industrial capacity utilisation did not increase substantially, as is shown by figures provided by the World Bank (1989). Second, given the liberalisation of imports and in view of the large increase in import volume (unhindered by a foreign exchange shortage) during the Seventh Plan period, it seems unlikely that the availability of imported inputs and capital goods was a binding supply constraint on non–agricultural production growth. Finally, the performance during the Seventh Plan period of key infrastructure sectors such as energy and transportation also appears not to have been hindered by any supply constraints; according to the Economic Advisory Council (1989), the high growth rates of these infrastructure sectors mainly reflect higher utilisation of existing capacities, which suggests a fairly elastic supply of energy and transportation.

Fifth and finally, in the model, investment demand is independent of savings supply in the sense that the interest rate is not able to bring investment demand into equality with savings supply nor are all savings automatically ploughed back into the circular flow of income as investments. Consequently, in the model, investment and saving are brought in $ex-post$ equality through adjustments in the level of income and/or shifts in income distribution. This specification is based on historical evidence (discussed in Chapter 3) suggesting that at least part of the increase in savings during the post–green revolution period was financed through changes in income distribution, while indicating that private investment demand in India does not respond regularly and predictably to changes in real interest rates. Further evidence on the lack of correlation between real private investment

---

is determined by supply conditions.

[4] The assumption of 'administered prices' is controversial because it is based on the view that the non–agricultural sectors are predominantly oligopolistic in nature, with prices being controlled by the producers. An indication of the oligopolistic nature of Indian industry is provided by data on industrial concentration in terms of both market shares and capital stock. These data are reported by Katrak (1980) and Chandra (1981). Evidence provided by Siddhartan (1980) has already been summarised in Table 3.10. Empirical support for mark–up pricing in India's major registered industrial sectors including the sugar, textiles, iron and steel, chemicals, and general engineering sectors, which account for approximately 70 per cent of total industrial output, can be found in Chatterji (1989). Her results show that cost and price changes are very closely associated and that, in a majority of cases, price responds almost fully to cost.

demand and the real interest rate is given by Bhattacharya (1984) and Pandit (1985).[5] With respect to the relationship between private savings and the real interest rate, there is mostly indirect evidence, because, in most of the existing econometric studies, the usual practice is to explain private disposable income and private consumption expenditure so that the volume of savings is obtained as a residual. For example, Bhattacharya (1984) found the relationship between real private consumption and the real interest rate to be insignificant (and taking the wrong sign).

To conclude this section, I feel that the above assumptions which are important to the simulation results, are not unreasonable for the Indian economy at the time of the Seventh Plan period. Taken together, they constitute a 'stylised', but in my opinion valid, representation of the Indian economy.

8.3   *Demand Constraints versus Supply Constraints*

The main conclusion drawn from the simulation experiments is that the agricultural sector may constrain non–agricultural performance both from the demand and the supply side. On the one hand, I find that, if inflation is to be kept within reasonable bounds, the economy's growth performance is likely to be constrained by inadequate (agricultural) *demand*. This conclusion is based, *inter alia*, on the outcome of experiment $D-4$ (Chapter 7) in which the quantities of foodgrains publicly distributed were raised by 20 per cent. The increase in public food distribution leads to a decline in agricultural prices and, hence, a fall in agricultural output. Taken together, these two effects imply a decrease in agricultural income which, in turn, imposes a demand–side constraint on the economy's medium–run growth. The demand–side constraint is further magnified by the multiplier mechanism to generate a low level of aggregate domestic demand. In turn, if this low level of aggregate demand leads to a decline in agricultural prices, there is no incentive for farmers to increase production by applying more fertilisers or step–up their investments and, hence, agricultural income remains low, restricting the domestic market for non–agricultural goods even further. As was pointed out by Rosenstein–Rodan (1943) and Nurkse (1953), it is due to such circumstances that the economy may remain caught in a 'low–level equilibrium'.

On the other hand, the results show that, with relatively inelastic agricultural *supply*, if sectoral imbalances become too large, agricultural

---

[5] According to the latter's results, when included in the equations explaining real household investment and real fixed investment by the corporate sector, the real interest rate proves not sigificant; only in the equation for real inventory investment by the corporate sector is the real rate of interest statistically significant and has the expected sign.

prices increase and – *via* increases in indexed nominal wages and mark–up prices in non–agriculture – these price rises are transmitted to the rest of the economy. The increase in agricultural prices forces consumers to spend more on agricultural goods and to reduce their expenditure on non–agricultural goods, which, in turn, limits domestic demand for non–agricultural commodities and reduces non–agricultural production and income. The importance for Indian industrialisation of domestic demand (a significant part of which originates in agriculture) is underscored by the outcomes of experiments $DN-3$ and $DN-4$ (Chapter 7). The results from these experiments suggest that, in a situation in which the opportunities for exporting industrial goods are limited and in which the supply of the agricultural sectors is relatively inelastic, there is a real danger of stagflation. This conclusion is a confirmation of Kalecki's (1960) assertion that the problem of financing Indian economic growth was essentially a problem of increasing the availability of agricultural supplies. It is also in agreement with Sen (1981) who, too, has identified inadequate aggregate demand as an integral part of the agricultural supply constraint. Hence, the conclusion that it is the basic inflexibility in demand associated with structural supply problems in the agricultural sectors which is the root cause of agriculture's macro–economic significance, is not particularly original.

However, I think that the approach adopted here does help to clarify both the origins and consequences of the agriculture–non–agriculture imbalances and to show the limitations of alternative approaches. Further, I believe that the significance of the results is in their implications for policies which aim to ease the agricultural constraint. Specifically, the results indicate that raising the 'agriculture–constrained' growth rate of real GDP hinges on the adequate extension of infrastructural facilities in agriculture, particularly related to irrigation, and that this, in turn, critically depends on a policy of public agricultural investment (given that the profitability of private agricultural investment depends on past public investments). In other words, it is only by changing the structural conditions for agricultural growth, through the extension of agriculture's irrigation coverage, that the country's macro–economic performance over time can be improved.

The simulation results have important implications for policies which try to ease the agricultural constraint by the provision of adequate (*i.e.* increased) price incentives. In fact, this is the main policy recommendation of neoclassical economists (*e.g.* Timmer, 1986) who tend to see public investment as a less critical determinant of agricultural growth than the incentives for private investment. In this context, they place particular emphasis on the agricultural–non–agricultural terms of trade. In their view, a terms–of–trade improvement for agriculture has two effects. First, in the short run, it will raise agricultural supply *via* increased use of intermediate inputs. Second, in the medium run, it will lead to a reallocation of private investment from non–agriculture to agriculture which enhances agriculture's productive capacity. The simulation results cast doubt on the efficacy of the terms of trade mechanism in a mixed economy with little government control over industrial pricing. For example, a policy of increased price incentives for farmers, brought about by an increase in foodgrain procurement prices (as in experiment $D-5$), also raises non–agricultural mark–up prices, through its impact on intermediate input costs and wage costs in non–agriculture. In the short run, these non–agricultural price increases, particularly for fertilisers, mitigate the relative price movements in favour of agriculture, restricting agriculture's short run price response (which was already relatively low). In the medium run, the non–agricultural price increases restrict the shift in the intersectoral terms of trade in favour of agriculture and, hence, limit the increase in private agricultural investment. This reduces agriculture's medium–term supply response. It is due to these two factors that an increase in foodgrain procurement prices turns out to be relatively inflationary, both in the short and medium term. In view of the fact that this inflation leads to the erosion of the real incomes of those who are net buyers of food and those whose incomes are not indexed to the inflation rate, a policy of increased agricultural price–incentives can be said to offer, at best, high growth at the cost of increased poverty. Moreover, this process of fast growth can only be sustained as long as public investment in real terms is not eroded by or cut down in response to the inflation. Accordingly, the simulation results suggest that more is needed than providing supply incentives to farmers through higher agricultural prices. The need for adequate public intervention must be recognised, especially for restructuring the agricultural sector. As is clear from the simulation results, this often calls for an expanded programme of public agricultural investment, particularly in agricultural infrastructure.

The results also have important implications for the policies proposed by classical economists such as Preobrazhensky and Lewis, according to whom industrial growth is supply–constrained by the limited capacity of the domestic capital goods sector to expand. Assuming that all savings are used for investment, because the savings and investment decisions are taken by the same (group of) individuals, the industrial rate of growth can be raised by increasing the amount of savings available to finance industrial investment. According to classical economists, to achieve this rise in savings, governments should try to transfer resources from agriculture to industry, in terms of either surplus labour or financial savings, through manipulating the intersectoral terms of trade. This can be brought about by administratively holding down agricultural prices or by imposing heavy indirect commodity taxes on essential industrial consumer goods bought by the farmers. However, according to the simulation results of Chapters 6 and 7, by depressing agricultural prices and income and, hence, restricting the home market for domestically manufactured non–agricultural commodities, such 'classical' attempts at industrialisation may be frustrated, particularly in a situation in which profitable opportunities for exporting industrial goods are limited. Specifically, I find that, due to its negative impact on agricultural income and demand, a policy aimed at accelerating the pace of industrialisation *via* a substantial increase in public non–agricultural investment, financed by direct tax revenue from agricultural income, has only a limited impact on the growth rate of real GDP (experiment $DN-4$). When the increase in public non–agricultural investment is financed by a reduction in public agricultural investment, the result is stagflation (experiment $DN-3$). These findings should caution against treating agriculture as a 'passive' sector which merely provides the required savings for industrialisation. This point will be taken up in more detail in the next section.

8.4   Implications for Policy: 'Agriculture-First' versus 'Industry-First' ?

During the 1980s, the process of modification of economic policy which originated in response to the foodgrain crisis of the mid–sixties, gained further momentum, particularly after the changes towards greater internal and external competition to promote efficiency and modernisation were confirmed by the Planning Commission (1984) in the report on the Seventh Five–Year Plan (see Chapter 3). This 'new' economic policy was explicitly based on the belief that liberalisation of domestic markets and imports would lead to 'efficient' and faster growth of industry and overall GDP, based on the demands generated by growing middle class incomes and on an increase in exports (Ahluwalia, 1985). Implicitly, it was assumed that agriculture is no longer a constraint on economic growth and hence, it was argued, should be subjected to 'benign neglect' (Singh and Tabatabai, 1992). At this point, it is important to note that, by underemphasizing the demand–generating role of domestic agriculture, the new economic policy was forced to rely on demand from the 'foreign' as opposed to the 'home' market. Policy–makers felt convinced in their arguments, when, following the 1987–88 drought, the economy's growth performance was significantly better than in earlier drought and post–drought years and the inflation rate, as measured by the consumer price index, was significantly lower than in most earlier episodes of drought. According to official statements, these facts demonstrated certain basic strengths in the economy: 'The first is the resilience of the economy in the face of severe weather stress and the second is the sustained growth performance in the sphere of industry and infrastructure.' (Ministry of Finance, 1989:1). Consequently, it is argued that India, at its present stage of development, should follow essentially a long term policy of export–led industrialisation.

336

It is this view that has to be contrasted with an alternative, 'agriculture–first' long–term strategy, proposed by Sukhamoy Chakravarty in his Radhakrishna Lectures at Oxford University (Chakravarty, 1987). Based on profound scepticism about the desirability as well as the feasibility of an export–led strategy in a slow–growing world economy, he suggested that long–term growth in India must primarily be based on the expansion of internal rather than external demand. This, he argued, was best achieved by a large–scale programme of public investment in irrigation and other agriculture–related infrastructure which would enable the green revolution technologies to spread from Punjab and Haryana to other parts of the country. He expected such an investment strategy to lead to an acceleration in the rate of growth of agricultural productivity, a rise in farm incomes, a reduction in rural poverty and hence an expansion of demand for non–agricultural goods (Singh and Tabatabai, 1992).

In drawing out the implications of the present simulation results for this debate about the future development strategy for India after four decades of planning, it is useful to reframe the debate in terms of Bhaduri's (1992) characterisation of development strategies. In Bhaduri's view, the debate over the 'priority' of agriculture *vis–à–vis* industry in a development strategy reduces essentially to the question of whether or not the performance of one of the two sectors is constrained by the performance of the other sector. This implies that the 'agriculture–first' strategy proposed by Chakravarty can be justified if its performance is not constrained by the performance of industry or, in other words, if industrial performance adjusts endogenously to agricultural performance. Similarly, but the other way round, the industrialisation–led development strategy adopted by the government assumes, explicitly or implicitly, that the agricultural sector adjusts more or less endogenously to the requirements of industrialisation. If it fails to adjust, however, the process of industrialisation will run into difficulties. Viewed from this perspective, the appropriateness of an industrialisation–led development strategy for India depends on the viability of the assumption that the agricultural sector will adjust endogenously in response to industrialisation.

It will be clear from the simulation results of Chapters 6 and 7 that, in India, the scope for an 'industry–led' investment strategy is limited, the growth of the non–agricultural sectors being constrained by agricultural performance. The simulation experiments show that policy recommendations favouring industrial growth in which the interdependence between agriculture and the non–agricultural sectors is not taken into account, turn out to be self–defeating, mainly because they fail to acknowledge the impact of agricultural price changes on demand. Specifically, the short–run experiments of Chapter 6 show that, with a relatively inelastic agricultural supply, short–term management of demand using trade and fiscal policies (including a devaluation and a reduction in the direct tax rate on non–agricultural income) may not yield the expected results. If exports and final imports are insensitive to changes in the exchange rate, then a devaluation of the Rupee *vis – à – vis* other currencies will merely have domestic price and income effects, leading to contraction as well as deflation (experiment $N-3$). Distributionally, one would have expected non–agricultural mark–up income recipients to benefit most from the reduction in the direct tax rate, but (according to the outcome of experiment $N-4$) the agriculturalists are its main beneficiaries. According to the results of medium–run experiment $DN-3$ (Chapter 7), an increase in public non–agricultural investment at the cost of public agricultural investment leads to an increase in the level of agricultural prices (and the general price level) which in turn results in stagnation, because it reduces consumption demand for non–agricultural goods, restricting non–agricultural production. Too low a level of agricultural prices which may be believed to be beneficial to industrial growth, may also lead to contraction because of its negative impact on agricultural income and demand (experiment $D-4$). In view of the above findings it seems reasonable to conclude that the pace of industrialisation is forced to adjust (downwards) to be compatible with the availability of agricultural goods.

The results of the simulation experiments show that not merely as a provider of agricultural commodities, but also as a demander of industrial goods, the agricultural sector is able to affect the pace of industrialisation. Of course, one may argue that the demand–generating role of agriculture can be substituted for by a major export thrust, but (as is indicated by the results of experiment $DN-2$) such a policy of export–led industrialisation may run into trouble due to an inadequate agricultural support base. With relatively inelastic agricultural supply, increases in (non–agricultural) exports result in a considerable increase in domestic inflation, which may erode the country's competitiveness over time and may constrain the scope for export–led growth. This is not to deny the importance of stepping–up exports, but only to stress that, if it is to contribute to a non–inflationary acceleration of real GDP growth, non–agricultural export growth needs to be supplemented by adequate domestic policies aimed at raising agriculture's relatively sluggish supply response. But the results suggest that the Indian economy does not have to be so dependent on exports in its development strategy, because there is available an alternative to increased reliance on foreign demand, namely policies aimed at expanding the Indian home market. Policy–makers should look more to the home market, because what hinders the growth of domestic industrial production is the relatively low level of home demand for manufactured goods, which is caused by either too low or too high a level of agricultural prices. I find that those policies which are successful in raising agricultural production as well as agricultural real income, through enhancing the size of the home market, also lead to a significant improvement in non–agricultural performance. Hence, the most important item on the policy agenda is to transform the agricultural sector in the sense of making it less sensitive to adverse weather conditions and less inelastic *vis – à – vis* short–term demand increases, to increase its land productivity, raising its income, and to create agricultural surpluses to be absorbed by non–agricultural intermediate and final demand. Thus, the domestic demand is created which is required for the expansion of domestic manufacturing and services.

The results of the agricultural policy experiments suggest that the required transformation of the agricultural sector cannot be brought about by a mere reliance on the price–mechanism. Given the relatively small price elasticities of fertiliser demand and the relatively limited response of yield levels to changes in fertiliser input, higher agricultural prices (due to, for example, an increase in minimum support prices) tend to have a larger effect on demand (*via* increased agricultural income) than on crop outputs and, hence, result in considerable economy–wide inflation. To be successful, any attempt at transforming the agricultural sector should aim at raising the sector's short–term as well as medium–term price–responsiveness. This requires, as the outcomes of the simulation experiments indicate, an increase in public investment in agricultural infrastructure and particularly in irrigation, because agricultural price policy performs only reasonably well *provided* a certain minimum infrastructure is available to farmers. This is underscored by the simulation results which show that, when combined with an increase in public agricultural investment, the positive impact on agricultural performance of an increase in the rate of fertiliser subsidy is considerably enhanced. Hence, the role for price policy that emerges from my study is basically a *supportive* one, which aims at supplementing the extension of irrigation.[6]

Policies which are successful in raising agricultural production and real agricultural income are found to have a considerable positive impact on non–agricultural performance. Although this is not surprising since both the supply of agricultural surplus as well as a large part of the demand for industrial goods depends on the agricultural sector, the fact that agriculture can provide an important home market during industrialisation is often neglected by policy–makers. This neglect may lead to insufficient expansion of the home market, forcing the non–agricultural sectors to rely on world market conditions. The simulation results suggest that any development strategy for India should take into account agriculture's dominant influence in shaping the course of industrialisation. The implication of recognising agriculture's

---

[6] Higher prices may not provide adequate supply incentives to all agricultural producers if minimum irrigation, drainage, land consolidation and improvement, *etc.* are not ensured beforehand as several econometric studies have shown (Krishna, 1963; Narain, 1965; Gulati, 1987; and Gulati and Sharma, 1990).

importance to industrial growth is that it is besides the point to counterpose industry against agriculture, because what is needed is a 'balanced' pattern of growth of industry and agriculture. Hence, the question to ask is not whether agriculture should receive priority over industry or *vice versa*, but what kind of agricultural–industrial policy mix is most effective in improving both agricultural as well as non–agricultural performance.

To answer the latter question, a large number of short–term and medium-term agricultural policy experiments were performed with the general equilibrium model discussed in Chapter 4. On the basis of the simulation results, I find that a policy of increased public agricultural investment is most effective in raising agriculture's short–run responsiveness as well as in stimulating non–agricultural growth. In fact, in the medium run, due to both demand and supply effects, it generates larger marginal returns in terms of income than any of the price policy measures considered in the analysis. Furthermore, out of four 'pure' policy measures, only an increase in public agricultural investment results in an increase in government savings. A drawback of this policy its positive impact on inflation. However, its inflationary impact can be contained, while preserving its expansionary effects, by financing it through a reallocation of public investment from industry towards agriculture.

With respect to the price policy measures considered, an increase in procurement prices turns out to be highly inflationary and redistributing income from non–agriculture to agriculture, in spite of the substantial increases in crop outputs which it brings about. The marginal returns to increases in procurement prices are negative for non–agricultural wage earners, both in the short and medium run. Obviously, this result underlines the important distributional consequences of higher procurement prices. An increase in the rate of fertiliser subsidy is found to be both deflationary as well as expansionary, whereas the income benefits generated by it are distributed relatively equally. Its impact on the budgetary position of the government and the country's balance of payments position is negative. In the medium run, however, the marginal returns to an increase in the rate of fertiliser subsidy are modest as compared to the marginal returns to increased public agricultural investment. Finally, I find that the marginal returns to increased food subsidisation are negative in the medium run, mainly because it unduly depresses agricultural prices and, hence, agricultural output and real income. Its impact on public as well as foreign savings is negative. In view of the above, it is not unreasonable to conclude that the agricultural–industrial policy mix that is most effective in improving both agricultural and non–agricultural performance should at least contain a policy of increased public agricultural investment, in combination with one or more deflationary policy measures such as an increase in the rate of fertiliser subsidy, an increase in food subsidisation, or a decrease in public investment in industry.

In the discussion of the model's structure in Chapter 4, the model's data base in Chapter 5 and the simulation results in Chapters 6 and 7, a number of shortcomings of the model have already been identified. It shares some of these shortcomings, *e.g.* the approximate nature of the model's data base, with other modelling projects. Apart from such basic limitations inherent in the modelling approach which were discussed in Chapter 1, the present approach suffers from a number of more specific shortcomings which one should keep in mind in interpreting the model results. This section is to remind the reader of the following remaining limitations:

(a)   *Registered versus Unregistered Production*

In the simulation results, the degree of wage indexation in non–agriculture is overestimated because the sector classification underlying the model does not include a distinction between registered and unregistered non–agricultural production. Unregistered production activities are particularly important in the consumer goods sector and in services, although they also make up a non–negligible part of the basic, intermediate and capital goods sector. The important point is that the system of nominal wage indexation is (almost) absent in unregistered non–agricultural production, whereas it is an important element in registered non–agricultural production. Because – in the model – nominal wages are indexed in all non–agricultural sectors (although to a lesser extent in the consumer goods sector and services than in the other non–agricultural sectors, including the public sector), the simulation results underestimate the fall in real wages due to agriculture–induced inflation of a considerable proportion of the labour force, *i.c.* those employed in unregistered non–agricultural production. Concommittantly, the model exaggerates the short–run inflationary impact of agricultural shortfalls.

(b)   *Income Distribution (in Agriculture)*

Although the model was not meant to address the consequences of public policy for income distribution within agriculture, but was constructed to trace the effects of policy changes on the distribution of incomes between agriculture and non–agriculture, it is obvious that agricultural policy changes will have a considerable impact on the intra–agricultural distribution of incomes, both between various categories of agricultural households as well as between regions.

With respect to the inter–households distribution of income, it is important to note that farmers producing a marketable surplus are differently affected by price policy changes than subsistence farmers, producing for own consumption. Although there is no direct relationship between the size of operational holdings and the extent to which farmers engage in production for

341

the market, there is some evidence that the percentage of output marketed increases with farm size (Patnaik, 1975). This is because the distribution of operational holdings is highly unequal, with 80 per cent of the cultivating population having to subsist on holdings smaller than 10 hectares. The data collected from the National Sample Surveys (N.S.S.) by Haque (1987) show that in 1981 large and medium operational holdings above four hectare formed 10 per cent of all holdings, operating 48 per cent of total area, while marginal holdings below one hectare constituted 56 per cent of all operational holdings, but operated only on 11 per cent of total area.[7] The implication of this is that higher agricultural prices are a *cost* to the rural landless and the marginal and small farmers, the majority of whom are net buyers of food, because higher agricultural prices result in lower real incomes, while they are a source of *benefit* for the surplus–producing medium and large farmers (De Janvry and Subbarao, 1986).

With respect to the inter–regional differences, it may be noted that the regional distribution of the benefits from minimum support prices mainly depends on (*a*) the extent to which support prices exceed regional production costs, and (*b*) the share of different regions (or states) in aggregate procurement. Not only are there important differences in statewise production costs (Kahlon and Tyagi, 1983), but also the statewise shares in public procurement vary enormously (see Table 6.5). Hence, income benefits of mini–mum support prices accrued largely to only a few states, *i.c.* Punjab and Haryana. Evidence gathered by Subbarao (1985) suggests that the same is true for the benefits from other agricultural policies including fertiliser subsidies and subsidised credit.[8]

(c) Debt and Interest Payments

The simulation results show that changes in agricultural policy may considerably affect net public savings or, since net public savings are negative throughout the reference run, the government's revenue deficit. Because an increase in the public revenue deficit implies a rise in the proportion of revenue expenditure financed by borrowed resources, a change in agricultural policy (through its impact on the revenue deficit) affects the government's borrowing requirements. Given the level of interest rates, any agricultural policy change which leads to an increase in government borrowing,

---

[7] The ownership distribution of land is even more unequal. Large and medium holdings above four hectares which constituted only 8 per cent of all ownership holdings, owned 48 per cent of total area. Marginal ownership holdings smaller than one hectare amounted to 67 per cent of all holdings, owning only 12 per cent of total area. The N.S.S. data further show that the proportion of landless households to total rural households amounted to 11.3 per cent for the country as a whole.

[8] See also Table 6.15 for the regional distribution of fertiliser consumption in 1985–86.

will also lead to an increase in public interest payments over time, resulting in additional pressure on the government budget from the expenditure side. Because the model does not include debt–variables and treats public interest payments as exogenous, the simulation results capture only the partial impact of an agricultural policy change on the public revenue deficit, ignoring its impact on public interest payments.

8.6 *Comparison with Results from Other Studies*

In this section, I review a number of earlier applications of general equilibrium models addressing similar policy questions as the ones addressed in the present analysis and compare them to the present application.[9] The emphasis of the comparison is on the economic structure and the policy simulations of the models, and not on the econometrics and the solution algorithms that were used. In particular, the survey focuses on: (*i*) the institutional background of the modelling project; (*ii*) its main purpose; (*iii*) technical characteristics; (*iv*) sectoral disaggregation; (*v*) model agents; (*vi*) main assumptions; and (*vii*) main findings. Use is made of a synoptical table (see Appendix 8.1). The text is reduced as far possible, avoiding duplication of information already contained in the table. Note that the first three models in the table are static, one–period models, while the latter three are dynamic, multi–period models.

The following generalisations can be made on the basis of Table 8.1. First, one feature common to all the models considered is the distinction between agricultural (rural) and non–agricultural (urban) production and consumption, although the models differ in level of sectoral desaggregation and in degree of income distributional detail. In all the models, agricultural production is supply–determined,[10] either by assuming it exogenously fixed (De Janvry and Subbarao, 1986; Sarkar and Subbarao, 1981; Taylor, 1983; Taylor, Sarkar and Rattsø, 1984; and Sarkar and Panda, 1991) or by deriving it from a production function (Rattsø, 1989; Narayana *et al.*, 1987; and Mitra and Tendulkar, 1986), while (with the only exception of Mitra and Tendulkar) output in non–agriculture is determined by (expected) demand, subject to a capacity constraint. Hence, most models allow for underutilisation of

---

[9] India is one of the first countries in which (forerunners of) computable general equilibrium (CGE) models were developed. Already in the early 1970s, a model with many CGE characteristics was developed by Sukhamoy Chakravarty, under the auspices of the Planning Commission (1973) for India's Fifth Five Year Plan. Since then, a number of CGE models have been developed and used for policy analysis. For a survey of general equilibrium models applied to India see McMahon (1989) and Narayana *et al.* (1991).

[10] This is also a feature common to most macro–econometric models of the Indian economy. See Krishna *et al.* (1991) for a review of the major macro–econometric models of the Indian economy.

non–agricultural production capacity, which is an empirically important phenomenom in manufacturing (see Chapter 3). Second, with respect to price adjustments, in all models, agricultural prices are determined by the market clearing conditions. In a number of models, non–agricultural prices are determined by cost factors and a mark–up pricing rule, but in Narayana *et al.* and Mitra and Tendulkar non–agricultural prices also follow from the market clearing conditions. Finally, India being a large and relatively closed economy, foreign trade is largely assumed exogenous in the majority of the models considered, as was done in the present analysis. Only Mitra and Tendulkar (1986) and Sarkar and Panda (1991) include export and import demand functions. In most of the other models only complementary imports are endogenously determined, with competitive imports and all exports being exogenous.

The first model in the table – the one by De Janvry and Subbarao (1986) – represents an ambitious attempt to quantify the interrelationships between the government's agricultural (pricing) policies and income distribution. De Janvry and Subbarao's model differs in a number of important respects from my general equilibrium model. First, in their model, short–run agricultural supply response is absent, since the outputs of the agricultural sectors are fixed exogenously. This leads one to expect that the inflationary impact of expansionary policy changes will be larger in their model than in my model. Second, their model does not include public procurement of foodgrains nor guaranteed minimum support prices for rice and wheat, which – in my view – constitutes an important omission in any description of the economy–wide impact of the performance of India's foodgrain economy. Third, income distribution – both in agriculture and non–agriculture – is far more disaggregated (according to fixed rules) in De Janvry and Subbarao's model than in my model. They distinguish up to seven categories of income earners which they label 'social classes'. Finally, sectoral investment demand is treated as an exogenous variable, *i.e.* it is assumed to remain unaffected by changes in factors such as aggregate demand and the terms of trade between agriculture and non–agriculture. Unfortunately, De Janvry and Subbarao's model suffers from a number of technical drawbacks. First, although the consumers pay trade margins, these do not accrue to anyone in the economy as income, with the result that the income generated by production and trade does not add up to income earned. As a result, the national accounts are not balanced nor is the balance between investment and savings ensured. In addition, as pointed out by Narayana *et al.* (1987), the physical flows do not balance, since both changes in stocks and net exports are determined as residuals. Consequently, the model may have many solutions because any linear combination of stock changes and net exports of a solution also is a solution of the model. Despite these shortcomings, the interrelationship the model accounts for satisfactorily is the effect of agricultural price changes on incomes and consumption (assuming that the problem concerning the trade margins does not differentially affect the scenarios compared).

According to De Janvry and Subbarao, their results show that all social classes can only be made to gain by raising agricultural production, while keeping agricultural prices fixed. An agricultural output increase with flexible (*i.e.* declining) agricultural prices has a highly progressive effect on the distribution of income, benefitting small farmers and urban low–income groups and negatively affecting large farmers. They further claim that future shifts in the supply of agricultural products will be larger following a policy of public investments in infrastructure and technology than following a policy of increased reliance on price incentives. These results are consistent with my findings (see Table 7.7). However, a problem with their results is that they do not fully follow their analysis. One is left wondering how agricultural output is to be increased with fixed or declining foodgrain prices. Government policy required to keep prices fixed may have costs which will have repercussions on the growth rate of the economy. Also would farmers increase their production levels when foodgrain prices remain fixed or even decline? In my view, De Janvry and Subbarao's model in which agricultural supply response behaviour is not included, but only assumed, is not able to address these and related questions fully.

Table 8.1 includes several versions and applications of the general equilibrium model constructed at the National Council of Applied Economic Research (NCAER) including Sarkar and Subbarao (1981), Taylor (1983), Taylor, Sarkar and Rattsø (1984), and Sarkar and Panda (1991).[11] These models (which may be labeled 'NCAER models') vary in sectoral detail and economic structure, the most elaborate version being Taylor (1983). Although, in a number of important respects, my model can be regarded as belonging to the NCAER tradition, there are some basic differences between the NCAER models and my model. The major difference relates to the treatment of agricultural production, both in terms of degree of sectoral detail as well as in terms of economic structure. In general, the treatment of agricultural production in the NCAER models is rather rudimentary. While NCAER models generally distinguish only between food and non–food agriculture, they do not include any distinction between irrigated and unirrigated cultivation, between crop agriculture and other agriculture, and, within cereal crops, between rice and wheat, on the one hand, and other food crops, on the other hand, while these distinctions are important in determining agriculture's (short–run) supply response. In the NCAER models, agriculture's short–run supply response is assumed to be zero, which is not realistic as follows from the results of numerous studies dealing with the subject (*e.g.* Sirohi, 1984; Bhide *et al.*,

---

[11] Other versions include Sarkar and Kadekodi (1988) dealing with energy pricing policies and Sarkar and Panda (1987) which addresses the issue of resource mobilisation through administered prices.

1986; Gulati, 1987; Gulati and Sharma, 1990). Further, the NCAER models include only one aspect of the public procurement/minimum price support scheme for foodgrains, *i.c.* the income and demand effects of changes in the quantities of foodgrains procured. Since in these models the minimum support pricing scheme is completely ignored, their results have to be considered as partial effects: as is clear from the results of the short–run experiments of Section 6.2.3, the economy–wide effects of minimum support pricing often are too large to be ignored. Hence, to appreciate the (short–run) implications of agricultural policy–making, its effects need to be considered in a framework which takes account of the existence of floor levels of market prices for important cereals such as rice and wheat.[12] A second difference is that, with the exception of Sarkar and Panda (1991), the NCAER models do not include endogenous private investment demand functions. As a result, the $ex-post$ investment–savings balance is established by adjustments only on the (income and) savings side. Private investment demand is neither affected by changes in aggregate demand nor by changes in the rate of inflation. Despite these differences, the main findings of the NCAER modelling project are broadly consistent with my results which is not surprising in view of the basic similarities between the two approaches. The NCAER finding that, in the short run, an increase in non–agricultural investment is inflationary and benefits the farmers relative to the other income groups, corresponds to the results of experiment $N-7$ (Section 6.2.1). However, the outcomes of the devaluation experiments differ in an important aspect. According to the results from the NCAER models, a nominal devaluation tends to be inflationary (as well as contractionary), whereas I find a devaluation to be deflationary and contractionary (see experiment $N-3$). The difference in results is due to a difference in assumptions about agricultural income formation and in particular about whether farmers are able to obtain income compensation for cost increases of imported intermediate inputs. In my model, agricultural income is determined as the difference between the value of agricultural output and the value of intermediate costs, which implies that, with *given* agricultural prices, a devaluation through raising intermediate input costs leads to a decline in agricultural income. In other words, farmers are not able to immediately transmit input cost increases onto other agents in the economy. With the increase in non–agricultural prices following the devaluation, the decline in agricultural income leads to a fall in aggregate demand, a decline in production and a decrease in the general price level. The NCAER models, on the other hand, assume that all imported intermediate inputs

---

[12] It is to be noted that Sarkar and Panda (1991) treat both agricultural supplies and prices as exogenously fixed, with the level of foodstocks adjusting to balance agricultural supply and demand. Hence, with their model, there is no possibility of analysing the effects of agriculture–induced inflation.

into agricultural production are fertilisers[13] and that any difference between the price of imported fertilisers and their domestic (subsidised) price is absorbed as a subsidy by the government. Hence, following the devaluation, the fall in agricultural income is smaller in the NCAER model than in the present model, because the increase in imported intermediate input costs is paid for by the government. Taken together with the increase in non–agricultural prices and the ensuing rise in non–agricultural income and demand, this results in inflation.

In contrast to the other models included in the table, the model by Narayana *et al.* (1991) is of an *applied* (as compared to a computable) general equilibrium genre.[14] Further, unlike most other models, many of the behavioural functions relating to demand and supply were econometrically estimated on the basis of time series data. The model essentially is a neoclassical general equilibrium model in which an equilibrium price vector is computed for each year in succession. Great simplification was achieved by imposing a one–year lag between production and market sale. As a result, domestic supplies are given in the exchange process and equilibrium is achieved if a price vector (as well as a net import vector and an inventory change vector) can be found that matches aggregate demand with the sum of predetermined domestic supplies from production and stocks and imports. The only constraints on the search for the equilibrium price vector are an overall trade balance constraint and sector specific constraints on exports, imports and inventory changes. In effect, the model represents a *pure exchange* economy.

Given its specification, the Narayana *et al.* model is not particularly suited to deal with the (short–run) inflationary impact of changes in agricultural policies. This is because any aggregate excess demand (or, what amounts to the same, any excess of investment over savings) will be removed by an increase in taxation of private non–agricultural income (implying an increase in public savings) – without affecting the general price level.[15] Hence, despite the claim of the authors that their model is designed to trace the important effects of agricultural policy alternatives, it is not able to adequately analyse the (short–run) inflationary impact of agricultural

---

[13] It is to be noted that, in rice and wheat production, a non–negligible part of imported intermediate inputs is not related to fertilisers or pesticides. For instance, according to projections for 1984–85, around 70 per cent of imported intermediate inputs in wheat production is related to fertilisers, while the corresponding percentage for rice production was around 78 per cent. See Planning Commission (1981:178–179).

[14] Applied general equilibrium (AGE) models have their origins in activity analysis (see Fischer *et al.*, 1988). Computable general equilibrium models, on the other hand, are derived from input–output multisector models (see Dervis *et al.*, 1982).

[15] However, in a multisectoral context, an increase in the non–agricultural tax rate will affect the composition of demand which leads to a change in relative prices and, hence, in sectoral levels of production (Rattsø, 1982).

policies, which (as can be judged from the present simulation results) also has important medium–run consequences. The reliance on changes in the non–agricultural income tax rate as a mechanism to bring about investment–savings balance is unrealistic as it overstates the scope for the government to raise direct taxes. According to the Narayana *et al.* reference scenario, the aggregate average tax rate on non–agricultural incomes rises from 2.3 per cent in 1980 to 9.8 per cent in 2000. This upward adjustment in the tax rate on non–agricultural incomes seems overly optimistic in view of the historical evolution of the system of direct taxation. Recent years witnessed considerable reductions in direct tax rates on incomes earned in the registered sectors, while incomes earned in the non–registered sectors largely remained untaxed (Chakravarty, 1987:76–77). Hence, adequate mobilisation of direct taxes may prove a difficult task.

Narayana *et al.* stress the fact that their model is designed to represent a mixed economy in which a significant part of the relevant decisions are taken by private agents, *i.c.* producers, consumers and traders. Because they believe that in a mixed economy the outcome of public policy largely depends on the reactions of those private decision–makers, great effort has been put in modelling private agents' responses to changes in public policy. In view of the above, it is a pity that their model does not include private investment demand functions, by which the level of private investment demand is determined, since it is all too clear that, in so–called mixed economies, private investment decisions have a large bearing on the economy's aggregate performance.[16] The medium–run simulation results of Chapter 7 indicate that the fact that the level of private investment demand – both in agriculture and non–agriculture – is differently affected by the various agricultural policy changes, may have important consequences for medium–run growth. Nevertheless, despite the obvious differences, the policy conclusions drawn by Narayana *et al.* are not very different from my findings. They too find that an increase in public agricultural investment is more effective in raising agricultural growth and overall growth than an increase in fertiliser subsidies.

Rattsø (1989) presents a five–sector, dynamic version of the NCAER–type of models which is used to investigate the medium–run adjustment of the economy, during the Sixth Plan period, to base–year changes in policy instruments or to base–year exogenous shocks. The main intertemporal adjustment mechanisms included in his model are related to (private) investment demand and creation of productive capacity in all sectors and nominal wage indexation in non–agriculture. In my model, intertemporal adjustment of non–agricultural production capacity and wage rates is based on

---

[16] Instead, they assume aggregate investment (both private and public) to be an exogenous proportion of GDP.

similar adjustment mechanisms, but I have included different and – in my view – more appropriate adjustment mechanisms in agriculture, *i.c.* the expansion of irrigated area through investment, the re–allocation of gross cropped area across crops on the basis of the (expected) relative revenue of a crop compared with that of its competing crops, and the annual adjustment of the procurement prices for foodgrains. Further, in contrast to the present analysis in which the economy–wide effects of once–and–for–all changes in one (or more) of the policy instruments were assessed, Rattsø focuses on medium–run adjustment processes affecting the country's macro–economic performance over time that are initiated by disturbances or policy changes in the first year of the five–year planning period.

Rattsø's main conclusion is that strong growth in agriculture is necessary to realise sustained real GDP growth with an acceptable rate of inflation. The model's results indicate that agricultural price increases are a driving force in overall inflation. These results, as far as they go, are consistent with my results. However, Rattsø's model does not allow for any short–run agricultural supply response nor does it incorporate any medium–run re–allocations of acreage between crops. Hence, on the one hand, his model results may overestimate the short–run inflationary impact of an agricultural supply shortfall, while, on the other hand, the de–stabilising effects of inter–crop acreage adjustments in the medium run are under–estimated. Further, Rattsø does not treat the procurement price as a guarantee price, at which the government is committed to make purchases. In his model, market prices are allowed to fall below the level of procurement/minimum support prices, which is a phenomenom not supported by price data (Krishnaji, 1990).

The final modelling project included in Appendix 8.1 is the one by Mitra and Tendulkar (1986). In their model, all agricultural production is lumped into one single sector, the production of which is represented by a nested CES production function. Only one out of five counter–factual simulations conducted over the reference period 1973–74 to 1983–84 deals with agriculture, assessing the impact of a drought on income distribution. One of their comparative statics experiments also deals with the effects of an agricultural failure. They find that a decline of around 12 per cent in agricultural output leads to a fall in real GDP of 6 per cent; real agricultural income declines by only 0.8 per cent. This is consistent with my results. However, their results differ from mine in the following two respects. In their model, because the consumer price deflator, in which foodgrains have a large weight, increases more than the GDP deflator, household savings decline even more than GDP declines and, hence, investments (since they are savings–determined) decline. Furthermore, the increase in inflation reduces the competitiveness of Indian exports and, because foreign savings are assumed fixed, imports also have to decline. Finally, it should be noted that Mitra and Tendulkar do not take account of the existence of minimum support pricing in agriculture.

8.7   To Conclude

My findings point to the overriding importance for Indian industrialisation of building a domestic (consumption) market by improving the productivity of agriculture and letting those employed in agriculture share in the benefits from increased productivity. They suggest that, with the possibility of extensive agricultural growth through area expansion essentially exhausted since the mid–1960s and with the process of land reforms held at a standstill, this can be achieved only by further intensification of agricultural production, *i.e.* by spreading the use of higher yielding seed varieties and of 'modern' inputs across the country, which in turn requires improving agriculture's infrastructure and in particular increasing its irrigation coverage. It is in this context that *public* investment in irrigation and other agricultural infrastructure acquires critical importance, given that most farmers, particularly those operating marginal and small holdings, are unable to provide the resources to finance the required infrastructural facilities themselves, either individually or through co–operative efforts. In view of the fact that the marginal returns to increased public agricultural investment are higher in those regions which are relatively less endowed with irrigation facilities, than in the better–endowed regions (De Janvry and Subbarao, 1986) and given the present unequal regional distribution of irrigation facilities, it seems reasonable to conclude that the increase in public investment resources should be directed to the lesser endowed regions to be most effective. Such a shift in the regional allocation of public investment will enhance the regional diversification in crop output growth, raising the stability of agricultural growth at the national level (because of compensatory movements in output growth between different regions), and contribute to a reduction in the inequality in the interregional distribution of incomes.

The results further indicate that, to be successful, attempts at increasing agricultural production and productivity require appropriate price and income incentives, since farmers can only be expected to increase (per hectare) production if they experience improvements in their real incomes. Otherwise, they will neither be able or willing to step–up their production nor will they be able to increase their effective demand for (domestic) non–agricultural goods, required for raising the pace of industrialisation. The findings show that the appropriate price and income incentives will not materialise if a (relative) decline in agricultural prices is allowed to negate the income benefits arising out of the increase in crop outputs. This implies that, in the absence of a price support scheme, which slows down the fall in price relative to the fall in production cost, the adverse movement in prices may well dampen farmers' inclination to intensify farming under irrigated conditions. Therefore, what is required as *complementary* to a productivity–improving investment policy is a 'terms–of–trade' policy which allows farmers to increase their real incomes while raising output. The results suggest that, with little government control over non–agricultural prices, this 'terms–of–trade' policy may be implemented either through agricultural input–price subsidies, *i.c.* fertiliser subsidies, or through a policy of procurement pricing for the agricultural sectors.

Ultimately, what is underlined by the results of this study is that any attempt at raising the rate of agricultural growth and improving non–agricultural performance cannot rely blindly on the market mechanism alone. The need for public intervention must be recognised, especially with respect to the development of agricultural infrastructure and maintaining price incentives for farmers.

Appendix 8.1
***A Tabular Survey of Six Computable General Equilibrium
Modelling Projects for India***

1. *Model*	De Janvry and Subbarao (1986)
2. *Base Year*	1977–78
3. *Background*	University research funded by the Ford Foundation, the Institute of Economic Growth (New Delhi), and the University of California (Berkeley, USA).
4. *Purpose*	Analysis of income distribution and sectoral growth effects of alternative agricultural policies.
5. *System*	Static, one–period SAM–based CGE model.
6. *Sectors*	(i) Rice; (ii) Wheat; (iii) Other food; (iv) Milk and animal products; (v) Other agriculture; (vi) Industry; and (vii) Services.
7. *Actors*	7.1. Seven social classes: (i) Landless agricultural workers; (ii) Small farmers (< 3.8 hectares); (iii) Medium–size farmers (between 3.8 and 6.9 hectares); (iv) Large farmers (> 6.9 hectares); (v) Urban workers; (vi) Urban marginals (poorest 82% self–employed); and (vii) Urban capitalists (richest 18% self–employed). 7.2. Government. 7.3. Traders. 7.4. Foreign Sector.
8. *Assumptions*	8.1. In principle, the five agricultural sectors have flexible prices; their outputs are exogenously specified; their prices are determined by the model. 8.2. The two non–agricultural sectors have mark–up prices and their outputs are demand–determined. 8.3. Incomes of the different social classes are related to sectoral production (and value added) through fixed coefficients and pre–determined transfers from the government. The nominal rural wage rate is assumed constant. 8.4. Fixed class specific savings rates are used to determine consumer expenditure and class specific linear expenditure systems characterise sectorwise demands. 8.5. Savings are determined by investment. 8.6. Exports and competitive imports are exogenous. The nominal exchange rate is exogenous. Complementary imports are endogenous.
9. *Findings*	9.1. Measures to increase wages by taxing higher incomes and transfering the tax intake to the lower income groups, and measures to increase food subsidies are all inflationary with constant agricultural output. 9.2. Price–support schemes are found to be highly regressive on the distribution of real incomes. High food prices hurt the lower–income groups which are net buyers of food. 9.3. Increasing agricultural output through techno–logical change and irrigation implies significant real income gains for all social classes and raises the growth of the non–agricultural sectors. The largest increases in income for the lower income groups are obtained in case food prices are flexible as compared to the situation in which they are fixed.

1. *Model*   Sarkar and Subbarao (1981); Taylor (1983); Taylor, Sarkar, and Rattsø (1984)
2. *Base Year*   1980–81
3. *Background*   Joint project of the National Council of Applied Economic Research (NCAER), New Delhi, and the Massachusetts Institute of Technology (MIT), Cambridge, Mass., USA.

4. *Purpose*   Analysis of the macro–economic effects of different short–term policy instruments, *viz.* the exchange rate and public investment.

5. *System*   A short–run, one–period SAM–based CGE model (including a money market in Taylor, 1983).

6. *Sectors*   (i) Food agriculture; (ii) Other agriculture; (iii) Manufacturing industries; (iv) Intermediate production (energy and transportation); and (v) Services.

7. *Actors*   7.1. Three income groups: Agricultural income earners; non–agricultural wage income earners; and non–agricultural mark–up income earners.
7.2. Government. 7.3. Foreign sector.

8. *Assumptions* 8.1. Agricultural outputs are assumed exogenous; agricultural prices are flexible, respond to demand, and clear the market.
8.2. In all non–agricultural sectors, output is demand determined; non–agricultural prices are determined by a mark–up pricing rule.
8.3. Different consumption demand elasticities are assumed for incomes generated in the agricultural and non–agricultural sectors. Different savings behaviour is assumed for agriculturalists, industrial capitalists and wage earners.
8.4. Savings are determined by investment.
8.5. Exports and competitive imports are exogenous. The nominal exchange rate is exogenous. Complementary imports are endogenous.

9. *Findings*:   9.1. The inflationary impact of an increase in non–agricultural investments may be considerable in case agricultural supply is fixed. Allowing for short–run agricultural supply responses moderates the inflationary impact.
9.2. In case the elasticity of export volumes from all sectors with respect to the exchange rate is zero, the result of a devaluation is contraction. When exports respond to the exchange rate, the contractionary effects on non–agricultural production and demand vanish. Even with a low elasticity (0.5), contractionary effects of the devaluation are offset.
9.3. Under the parametric specification of the model, a reduction in money supply is found to lead to a rise in prices of all sectors and output decreases in non–agriculture.

1. *Model*	Sarkar and Panda (1991)
2. *Base Year*	1985–86.
3. *Background*	Modelling project sponsored by the National Council of Applied Economic Research (NCAER), New Delhi.
4. *Purpose*	4.1. Analysis of the effects of changes in foodgrain bufferstocks and foodgrain prices, and of exchange rate changes. 4.2. Short–term forecasting of the macro–economic situation (for the Ministry of Finance).
5. *System*	A short–run, one–period SAM–based CGE model, including a monetary sector.
6. *Sectors*	(i) Food agriculture; (ii) Other crop agriculture; (iii) Livestock, forestry and fishing and other allied activities; (iv) Consumer goods industries; (v) Intermediate goods industries; (vi) Capital goods industries; (vii) Infrastructure (railways; mining; electricity); and (viii) Services.
7. *Actors*	7.1. Three income groups: Agricultural income earners; non–agricultural wage income earners; and non–agricultural mark–up income earners. 7.2. Government. 7.3. Foreign sector.
8. *Assumptions*	8.1. Agricultural outputs are assumed exogenous; agricultural prices are fixed. Agricultural markets are cleared by changes in stock. 8.2. In non–agriculture, output is determined by demand; non–agricultural prices are either administered by the government or based on a mark–up pricing rule. Excess capacity is postulated in all the non–agricultural sectors. 8.3. Different consumption demand elasticities are assumed for incomes generated in the agricultural and non–agricultural sectors. Different savings behaviour is assumed for agriculturalists, industrial capitalists and wage earners. 8.4. Savings are determined by investment. 8.5. Exports and competitive imports are exogenous. The nominal exchange rate is exogenous. Complementary imports are endogenous.
9. *Findings*:	9.1. If the elasticity of exports with respect to the exchange rate is zero, the effect of a devaluation is stagflationary; if the elasticity is around 0.8, the contractionary impact of the devaluation vanishes. 9.2. A 1% reduction of the foodgrain price requires an additional release of Rs. 90 crores (1985–86 prices) of food stocks to meet the additional demand – assuming zero agricultural supply response. This result implies an average 'general equilibrium' price elasticity of consumption demand for food of –0.3.

1. *Model*	Narayana, Parikh, and Srinivasan (1991)
2. *Base Year*	1980.
3. *Background*	Part of the Food and Agriculture Programme of the International Institute of Applied Systems Analysis (IIASA), Laxenburg, Austria, supported by the Indira Gandhi Institute of Development Research, Bombay, and the Indian Statistical Institute, Bangalore.
4. *Purpose*	Analysis of the economy–wide effects of agricultural policy alternatives during 1980–2000.
5. *System*	A dynamic, sequential, applied general equilibrium model.
6. *Sectors*	(i) Wheat; (ii) Rice; (iii) Coarse grains; (iv) Bovine and ovine meats; (v) Dairy products; (vi) Other animal products; (vii) Protein feeds; (viii) Other food; (ix) Non–food agriculture; and (x) Non–agriculture.
7. *Actors*	7.1. Consumers: 5 rural and 5 urban expenditure classes. 7.2. Producers: agricultural and non–agricultural producers. 7.3. Traders. 7.4. Government.
8. *Assumptions*	8.1. Agricultural production is based on (*a*) the land allocation decisions of farmers which are based on expected relative revenue of a crop compared to that of its competing crops, (*b*) irrigation, and (*c*) rainfall. Yield levels are functions of irrigation, fertiliser, rainfall, time or prescribed rates of adoption of HYVs. 8.2. Non–agricultural production is a function of expected demand and capacity constraints. Capacity expansion is the result of investments and/or imports which are considered partial substitutes. 8.3. The proportion of GDP that is allocated every year to fixed capital formation (both public and private) is stipulated exogenously, reflecting the investment targets in the respective Five Year plans. From this total investment target at current prices household savings are subtracted so that the difference represents the financing of investment through public savings and foreign capital inflow. With the inflow of foreign capital assumed exogenous, government savings adjust to establish the investment–savings equality. Government is treated as a residual saver who through direct taxes has to generate the needed savings to supplement private savings – a procedure often called the 'Johansen closure'.

| 1. *Model* | Narayana, Parikh, and Srinivasan (1987) |

8. *Assumptions* 8.4. Domestic supplies are assumed given in the exchange process and equilibrium is achieved if a price vector (as well as a net import vector and an inventory change vector) can be found that matches aggregate demand with the sum of predetermined domestic supplies from production and stocks and imports. In effect, the model represents a *pure exchange* economy for the purposes of computing equilibrium prices.
8.5. Producers, consumers, traders, and government all behave on the basis of *target* prices. Targetted supply and demand meet in the market (exchange model) which is cleared by price adjustments.
8.6. The trade deficit is specified as a fixed percentage (1.5 %) of GDP. Government decides on the level of imports and exports, and stocks of all commodities. There is only one non–agricultural sector, producing a single, tradable commodity.

9. *Findings* 9.1. An increase in fertiliser subsidisation leads to an increase in agricultural output, but when it is financed at the cost of agricultural investment it results in a decline of real GDP growth in the long run.
9.2. Greater emphasis on irrigation investment raises the growth rates of agricultural production and of real GDP. Its distributional impact – though not dramatic – is to improve equality.
9.3. Agricultural trade liberalisation is not conducive to agricultural growth.

1. *Model*   Rattsø (1989)
2. *Base Year*   1980–81
3. *Background*   University research, Department of Economics,
                   University of Trondheim, Norway.
4. *Purpose*   Analysis of the potential stabilisation problems
                   related to the implementation of the Sixth Five Year
                   Plan (1980–85), with particular emphasis on the
                   dynamic interplay between foodgrain prices,
                   manufacturing profitability and investment, and
                   wage indexation.

5. *System*   A five–sector time–recursive dynamic CGE model.

6. *Sectors*   (i) Cereal agriculture; (ii) Non–cereal agriculture;
                   (iii) Manufacturing industries; (iv) Intermediate
                   production (energy and transportation); and (v)
                   Services.

7. *Actors*   7.1. Three income classes: (i) Agricultural income
                   earners; (ii) Non–agricultural wage earners; and
                   (iii) Non–agricultural mark–up income recipients.
                   7.2. Government. 7.3. Foreign sector.

8. *Assumptions*   8.1. Fixed short–term supply of agricultural goods;
                   price–clearing markets in agriculture. In the
                   medium run, the supply of agricultural products is
                   determined by the development of agricultural
                   production capacity.
                   8.2. Excess capacity is postulated in all the
                   non–agricultural sectors, and their outputs are
                   demand–determined; non–agricultural prices are
                   either administered by the government or based
                   on a mark–up pricing rule.
                   8.3. Different consumption demand elasticities are
                   assumed for incomes generated in the agricultural
                   and non–agricultural sectors. Different savings
                   behaviour is assumed for agriculturalists,
                   industrial capitalists and wage earners.
                   8.4. Dynamic adjustment mechanisms include capital
                   accumulation and wage indexation. Different
                   investment demand functions are assumed for
                   agriculture and non–agriculture. The accumulation
                   of capital stock in agriculture determines the
                   annual level of production. In non–agriculture,
                   production capacity is increased even when the
                   capacity utilisation is low.
                   8.5. Savings are determined by investments.
                   8.6. Exports and competitive imports are exogenous.
                   The nominal exchange rate is exogenous. Complemen-
                   tary imports are endogenous.

9. *Findings*   9.1. In the medium run, the conditions for macro-
                   economic stability (in terms of inflation and
                   growth) are improved by according a higher priority
                   to agricultural growth.
                   9.2. There exist trade–offs between growth and the
                   balance of payments position and between growth
                   and income distribution.

1. *Model*	Mitra and Tendulkar (1986)
2. *Base Year*	1973–74
3. *Background*	Project of the International Bank for Reconstruction and Development, Washington D.C., U.S.A.
4. *Purpose*	Analysis of the adjustment of the economy to the twin exogenous shocks of oil price increases and and harvest failure during the period 1973–74 to 1983–84.
5. *System*	Six–sector, time–recursive dynamic CGE model.
6. *Sectors*	(i) Agriculture; (ii) Manufacturing of consumer goods; (iii) Manufacturing of capital goods; (iv) Manufacturing of intermediates; (v) Public Sector Infrastructure; and (vi) Services.
7. *Actors*	7.1. Fifteen (asset owning) classes each in rural and urban areas who derive their incomes from production and from interest receipts, transfers, and net factor income from abroad, according to fixed rules. 7.2. Government. 7.3. Foreign sector.
8. *Assumptions*	8.1. Agricultural production is represented by a nested CES production function, encompassing a wide range of substitution possibilities at every level. 8.2. Per capita income and expenditure are assumed to be jointly lognormally distributed. 8.3. Imports and exports are price–responsive. 8.4. All commodity–markets are price–clearing. Non–agricultural nominal wage rates are determined through wage–indexation rules, leading to rationing of jobs. Those unable to obtain employment become self–employed. The returns to self–employment adjust to clear the market. In agriculture, wages of hired labour are fixed, but returns to self–employment are flexible to clear the market. 8.5. Investments are determined by savings in the 'savings–driven' version; alternatively, in the 'investment–driven' version, investment is exogenously specified and foreign savings adjust to satisfy the investment–savings equality. 8.6. Foreign trade is endogenous.
9. *Findings*	9.1. The cumulative effects of weather–related agricultural peaks dominated those of the troughs over the reference period, resulting in greater availability of wage goods and higher savings, investments and terminal capital stock. 9.2. Workers' remittances, borrowing from oil facilities and concessional aid more than offset the adverse impact of terms of trade losses due to the two oil shocks, making possible higher con–sumption and investment and leading to higher external debt.

Acharya, S. (1988), 'India's fiscal policy', in Lucas, R.E.B. and Papanek, G.F. (eds.), *The Indian Economy. Recent Development and Future Prospects*, Delhi: Oxford University Press.

Adelman, I. (1984), 'Beyond export–led growth', *World Development*, 12 (9): 937–949.

Adelman, I. and Robinson, S. (1978), *Income Distribution in Developing Countries: A Case Study of Korea*, London: Oxford University Press.
–– (1988), 'Macroeconomic adjustment and income distribution: Alternative models applied to two economies', *Journal of Development Economics*, 29 (1): 23–44.
–– (1988a), 'Income distribution and development', in Chenery, H.B. and Srinivasan, T.N. (eds.), 949–1004.

Adelman, I. and Thorbecke, E. (eds.) (1966), *The Theory and Design of Economic Development*, Baltimore: The Johns Hopkins Press.

Ahluwalia, I.J. (1979), 'An analysis of price and output behavior in the Indian economy: 1951–1973', *Journal of Development Economics*, 6 (3): 363–390.
–– (1985), *Industrial Growth in India: Stagnation since the Mid–sixties*, Delhi: Oxford University Press.

Alagh, Y. (1991), *Indian Development Planning and Policy*, WIDER Studies in Development Economics, Delhi: Vikas Publishing House.

Ali, M. Shaukat (1985), 'Household consumption and saving behaviour in Pakistan: An application of the extended linear expenditure system', *Pakistan Development Review*, 24 (1): 23–37.

Arida, P. and Taylor, L. (1988), 'Short–run macroeconomics' in Chenery, H.B. and Srinivasan, T.N. (eds.), 856–885.

Arrow, K. and Hahn, F.H. (1971), *General Competitive Analysis*, San Francisco: Holden–Day.

Asimakopulos, A. (1980–81), 'Themes in a post Keynesian theory of income distribution', *Journal of Post Keynesian Economics*, 3 (2): 158–169.

Bagchi, A. (1970), 'Long–term constraints on India's industrial growth', in Robinson, E.A.G. and Kidron, M. (eds.), *Economic Development in South Asia*, London: Macmillan.

Bagchi, A.K. and Banerjee, N. (eds.) (1981), *Change and Choice in Indian Industry*, Calcutta: K.P. Bagchi & Co.

Balakrishnan, P. (1991), *Pricing and Inflation in India*, Delhi: Oxford University Press.

Barro, R.J. and Grossman, H.I. (1971), 'A general disequilibrium model of income and employment', *American Economic Review*, 61 (1): 82–93.

Basu, K. (1984), *The Less Developed Economy*, Oxford: Basil Blackwell.

Behrman, J. (1968), *Supply–Response in Underdeveloped Agriculture: A Case Study of Four Major Annual Crops in Thailand*: 1937–1963, Amsterdam: North–Holland.
Bhaduri, A. (1992), 'Alternative development strategies and the rural sector', in Singh, A. and Tabatabai, H. (eds.).

Bhagwati, J. and Chakravarty, S. (1969), 'Contributions to Indian economic analysis: A survey', *American Economic Review*, 59, supplement, 2–73.

Bhagwati, J. and Srinivasan, T.N. (1975), *Foreign Trade Regimes and Economic Development: India*, New York: National Bureau of Economic Research, Calcutta: Oxford & IBH Publishing Company.

Bhalla, G.S. (1991), 'Food security in South and South East Asian countries', paper prepared for the South Commission.
— and Tyagi, D.S. (1989), *Patterns in Indian Agricultural Development. A District Level Study*, Government of India, Planning Commission.

Bharadwaj, K. (1987), 'Analytics of agriculture–industry relation', *Economic and Political Weekly*, 17 (19–21): AN–15–AN–20.
— (1989), 'Agricultural prices policy for growth: Emerging contradictions', paper presented at the conference on The State and Development Planning in India, COAS/SOAS, London.

Bhattacharya, B. (1984), *Public Expenditure, Inflation and Growth: A Macroeconomic Analysis of India*, Delhi: Oxford University Press.

Bhide, S., Subba Rao, S.V. and Siddiqui, K.A. (1986), 'Growth of fertilizer and food subsidies', New Delhi: *NCAER Working Paper* No. 7, National Council of Applied Economic Research.
— (1989), 'Output performance and demand in Indian agriculture: The role of supply prices', *NCAER Occasional Paper* No. 26, New Delhi: National Council of Applied Economic Research.

Binswanger, H. (1991), 'The policy response of agriculture', *Proceedings of the World Bank Annual Conference on Development Economics* 1989, 231–258.

Borges, M.A. (1986), 'Applied general equilibrium models: An assessment of their usefulness for policy analysis', *OECD Economic Studies*, 7: 8–43.

Bulmer–Thomas, V. (1982), *Input–Output Analysis in Developing Countries*, New York: Wiley & Sons.

Canning, D. (1988), 'Increasing returns in industry and the role of agriculture in growth', *Oxford Economic Papers*, 40 (3): 463–476.

Capros, P., Karadeloglou, P., and Mentzas, G., (1990), 'An empirical assessment of macroeconometric and CGE approaches in policy modeling', *Journal of Policy Modeling*, 12 (3): 557–585.

Cardoso, E.A. (1981), 'Food supply and inflation', *Journal of Development Economics*, 8 (3): 269–284.

Carlton, D.W. (1989), 'The theory and the facts of how markets clear: Is industrial organization valuable for understanding macroeconomics ?', in Schmalensee, R. and Willig, D.W. (eds.), *Handbook of Industrial Organization*, vol. I., Amsterdam: North–Holland, 910–946.

Chakravarty, S. (1974), 'Reflections on the growth process in the Indian economy', Lecture for the Administrative Staff College of India, Hyderabad.
–– (1976), 'Economic theory and Indian planning', unpublished, Centre for Development Planning, Erasmus University Rotterdam.
–– (1979), 'On the question of the home market and prospects for Indian growth', *Economic and Political Weekly*, 14: 1229–1243.
–– (1979a), 'Keynes, classics and developing economies', in Rao, C.H.H. and Joshi, P.C. (eds.), *Reflections on Economic Development and Social Change*, Delhi: Allied Publishers.
–– (1983), 'Paul Rosenstein–Rodan: An Appreciation', *World Development*, 11 (1): 73–75.
–– (1984), 'Aspects of India's development strategy for the 1980s', *Economic and Political Weekly*, 19 (26): 845–852.
–– (1984a), 'Power structure and agricultural productivity', in Desai, M., Rudolph, S.H. and Rudra, A. (eds.), *Agrarian Power and Agricultural Productivity in South Asia*, New Delhi: Oxford University Press, 345–373.
–– (1987), *Development Planning: The Indian Experience*, Oxford: Clarendon Press.
–– (1987a), 'Marxist economics and contemporary developing economies', *Cambridge Journal of Economics*, 11 (1): 3–22.
–– (1987b), 'The state of development economics', *The Manchester School of Economic and Social Studies*, 55 (2): 125–143.
–– (1987c), 'Post–Keynesian theorists and the theory of economic development', Working Paper no. 23, World Institute for Development Economics Research of the United Nations University (WIDER).

Challen, D.W. and Hagger, A.J. (1983), *Macroeconometric Systems. Construction, Validation and Applications*, London: Macmillan.

Chandra, N.K. (1981), 'Monopoly capital, private corporate sector, and the Indian economy: A study in relative growth, 1931–1976', in Bagchi, A.K. and Banerjee, N. (eds.),

Chandrasekhar, C.P. (1988), 'Aspects of growth and structural change in Indian industry', *Economic and Political Weekly*, 23: 2359–2370.

Chatterji, R. (1989), *Industrial Prices in India*, Delhi: Oxford University Press.

Chenery, H.B. and Srinivasan, T.N. (eds.), *Handbook of Development Economics*, Amsterdam: North–Holland.

Chichilnisky, G. and Taylor, L. (1980), 'Agriculture and the rest of the economy: Macroconnections and policy restraints', *American Journal of Agricultural Economics*, 62 (2): 303–309.

Cowling, K. (1981), 'Oligopoly, distribution and the rate of profit', *European Economic Review*, 15 (2): 195–224.

Dantwala, M.L. (ed.) (1986), *Indian Agricultural Development since Independence: A Collection of Essays*, New Delhi: Oxford and IBH.

Dasgupta, A.K. (1987), 'Keynesian economics and under-developed countries again', *Economic and Political Weekly*, 22: 1601–1606.

Datta–Chaudhuri, M. (1990), 'The background to the current debate on economic reform: Oil–shocks, recession in world trade and adjustment problems for the Indian economy', in Guha, S. (ed.), 9–37.

Davidson, P. (1978), *Money and the Real World*, second edition, London: Macmillan.
–– (1991), 'Is probability theory relevant for uncertainty ? A Post Keynesian perspective', *Journal of Economic Perspectives*, 5 (1): 129–143.

Day, R.B. (1975), 'Preobrazhensky and the theory of the transition period', *Soviet Studies*, 27 (2): 196–219.

Deaton, A. and Muellbauer, J. (1980), *Economics and Consumer Behavior*, Cambridge: Cambridge University Press.

Decaluwé, B. and Martens, A. (1988), 'Developing countries and general equilibrium models: A review of the empirical literature', *Journal of Policy Modeling*, 10 (4): 529–568.

Decaluwé, B., Martens, A. and Monette, M. (1988), 'Macroclosures in open economy CGE models: A numerical appraisal', *International Journal of Development Planning Literature*, 3 (2): 69–91.

De Janvry, A. and Sadoulet, E. (1987), 'Agricultural price policy in general equilibrium models: Results and comparisons', *American Journal of Agricultural Economics*, 69 (2): 230–246.

De Janvry, A. and Subbarao, K. (1986), *Agricultural Price Policy and Income Distribution in India*, Delhi: Oxford University Press.
–– (1987), 'On the relevance of economic modelling for analysis of food price policy', *Economic and Political weekly*, 22 (25): 1001–1006.

Dervis, K., De Melo, J. and Robinson, S. (1982), *General Equilibrium Models for Development Policy*, Cambridge: Cambridge University Press.

Dhawan, B.D. (1988), *Irrigation in India's Agricultural Development. Productivity, Stability, Equity*, New Delhi: Sage.

Dixit, A. (1973), 'Models of dual economies', in Mirrlees, J.A. and Stern, N.H. (eds.), *Essays in the Theory of Economic Growth*, New York: Wiley.

Dow, S.C. (1985), *Macroeconomic Thought: A Methodological Approach*, Oxford: Basil Blackwell.

Dutt, A.K. (1984), 'Rent, income distribution and growth in an underdeveloped agrarian economy', *Journal of Development Economics*, 15 (1, 2 & 3): 185–211.
–– (1988), 'Sectoral balance: A survey', *Working Paper*, WIDER, Helsinki.

Dutta, J. (1988), 'The wage–goods constraint on a developing economy. Theory and evidence', *Journal of Development Economics*, 28 (3): 341–363.

Eichner, A.S. and Kregel, J.A. (1975), 'An essay on post–Keynesian theory: a new paradigm in economics', *Journal of Economic Literature*, 13 (4): 1293–1314.

Ellman, M. (1975), 'Did the agricultural surplus provide the resources for the increase in investment in the USSR during the First Five Year Plan?', *The Economic Journal*, 85 (340): 844–864.

Ewijk, C. van (1989), *On the Dynamics of Growth and Debt. A Post–Keynesian*

Analysis, Ph.D. thesis, Katholieke Universiteit Brabant, Tilburg.

Fei, J.C.H. and Ranis, G. (1964), *Development of the Labour Surplus Economy, Theory and Policy*, Homewood, Illinois: Yale University Press.
— (1966), 'Agrarianism, dualism, and economic development', in Adelman, I. and Thorbecke, E. (eds.), 3–43.

Fischer, G., Frohberg, K., Keyzer, M.A., and Parikh, K.S. (1988), *Linked National Models: A Tool for International Food Policy Analysis*, Dordrecht: Kluwer Academic Publishers.

Ghatak, S. and Ingersent, K. (1984), *Agriculture and Economic Development*, Brighton: The Harvester Press.

Ghose, A. (1974), 'Investment behaviour of monopoly houses: I. Structure of fixed investment decisions', *Economic and Political Weekly*, 9 (43): 1813–24.
— (1974a) 'Investment behaviour of monopoly houses: II. Economics of pre–emption', *Economic and Political Weekly*, 9 (44): 1868–1876.
— (1974b) 'Investment behaviour of monopoly houses: III. Time profile of fixed investment and other implications', *Economic and Political Weekly*, 9 (45): 1911–1915.

Ghosh, J. (1990), 'Exchange rates and trade balance. Some aspects of recent Indian experience', *Economic and Political Weekly* 25 (9): 441–446.

Gordon, R.J. (1990), 'What is New–Keynesian economics?', *Journal of Economic Literature*, 28 (3): 1115–1171.

Gruver, G.W. (1986), 'Computable general equilibrium models: an overview of applications to development', *International Journal of Development Planning Literature*, 1 (1): 85–104.

Guha, S. (ed.), *Economic Liberalization, Industrial Structure and Growth in India*, Delhi: Oxford University Press.

Gujarati, D. (1979), *Basic Econometrics*, New Delhi: McGraw–Hill.

Gulati, A. (1987), *Agricultural Price Policy in India. An Econometric Approach*, New Delhi: Concept Publishing Company.

Gulati, A. and Sharma, P.K. (1990), 'Prices, procurement and production. An analysis of wheat and rice', *Economic and Political Weekly* 25: A–36–A–47.
— (1990a), 'Fertiliser pricing and subsidy in India: An alternative perspective', paper presented at the National Workshop on *Agricultural Input Marketing*, held at IIM, Ahmedabad, February 15–16.

Gupta, S.P. (1989), *Planning and Development in India: A Critique*, New Delhi: Allied Publishers.

Hansen, B. (1970), *A Survey of General Equilibrium Systems*, New York: McGraw–Hill Book Company.

Haque, T. (1987), 'Temporal and regional variations in the agrarian structure in India', *Indian Journal of Agricultural Economics*, 42 (3): 313–318.

Harcourt, G. (1985), 'Post–Keynesianism: Quite wrong and/or nothing new', in Arestis, P. and Skouras, T. (1985), *Post Keynesian Economic Theory. A Challenge to Neo Classical Economics*, Sussex: Wheatsheaf Books, 125–145.

Hayami, Y. and Ruttan, V. (1985), *Agricultural Development: An International Perspective*, Baltimore: The Johns Hopkins University Press.

Hazari, R.K. (1967), *The Structure of the Private Corporate Sector: A Study of Concentration, Ownership and Control*, Bombay: Asia Publishing House.

Head, J. G. (1974), *Public Goods and Public Welfare*, Durham: Duke University Press.

Hornby, J.M. (1968), 'Investment and trade policy in the dual economy', *The Economic Journal*, 78 (317): 96–107.

Ishikawa, S. (1967), *Economic Development in Asian Perspective*, Tokyo: Kinokuniya Bookstore.

Johansen, L. (1960), *A Multi–Sector Study of Economic Growth*, Amsterdam: North–Holland.

Johnston, B.F. and Mellor, J.W. (1961), 'The role of agriculture in economic development', *American Economic Review*, 51 (4): 566–593.

Jonung, L. and Laidler, D. (1988), 'Are perceptions of inflation rational? Some evidence from Sweden', *American Economic Review*, 78 (4): 1080–1087.

Jorgenson, D.W. (1961), 'The development of a dual economy', *The Economic Journal*, 71 (2): 309–34.
–– (1966), 'Testing alternative theories of the development of a dual economy', in Adelman, I. and Thorbecke, E. (eds.), 45–60.
–– (1967), 'Surplus agricultural labour and the development of a dual economy', *Oxford Economic Papers*, 19: 288–312.
–– (1984), 'Econometric models for general equilibrium analysis', in Scarf, H. and Shoven, J.B. (eds.), *Applied General Equilibrium Analysis*, Cambridge: Cambridge University Press.

Kahlon, A.S. and Tyagi, D.S. (1980), 'Intersectoral terms of trade', *Economic and Political Weekly*, 15 (52): A–173–A–184.
–– (1983), *Agricultural Price Policy in India*, New Delhi: Allied Publishers.

Kahn, R. (1972), *Essays in the Theory of Growth*, Cambridge: Cambridge University Press.

Kaldor, N. (1956), 'Alternative theories of distribution', *Review of Economic Studies*, 23 (2): 83–100.
–– (1966), 'Marginal productivity and macro–economic theories of distribution', *Review of Economic Studies* 33 (4): 619–638.
–– (1967), *Strategic Factors in Economic Development*, Ithaca: Cornell University Press.
–– (1972), 'The irrelevance of equilibrium economics', *The Economic Journal* 82 (328), 1237–1255.
–– (1976), 'Inflation and recession in the world economy', *Economic Journal*, 86 (4): 703–714.
–– (1982), *The Scourge of Monetarism*, Oxford: Oxford University Press.
–– (1985), *Economics Without Equilibrium*, Cardiff: University College Cardiff Press.
–– (1986), 'Limits on growth', *Oxford Economic Papers*, 38 (2): 187–198.
–– (1989), *Further Essays on Economic Theory and Policy*, edited by F. Targetti and A.P. Thirlwall, London: Duckworth.
–– (1989a), *The Essential Kaldor*, edited by F. Targetti and A.P. Thirlwall, London: Duckworth.

Kaldor, N. and Mirrlees, J.A. (1962), 'A new model of economic growth', *Review of Economic Studies* 29: 174–192.

Kalecki, M. (1933), *Próba teorii Koniunktury* (Warszawa: Instytut Badan Koniunktur Gospodarczych i Cen), reprinted as 'A theory of the business cycle', *Review of Economic Studies* 4 (1): 77–97.
–– (1938), 'Distribution of national income', *Econometrica*, 6, reprinted in Kalecki, M. (1971), 62–77.
–– (1942), 'The determinants of profits', *The Economic Journal*, 52, reprinted in Kalecki, M. (1971), 110–123.

-- (1943), 'Costs and Prices', in reprinted Kalecki, M. (1971).
-- (1955), 'The problem of financing economic development', *Indian Economic Review*, 2 (1): 1–22, reprinted in Kalecki, M. (1976).
-- (1960), 'Financial problems of the third plan: some observations', *Economic Weekly* 28, reprinted in Kalecki, M. (1976).
-- (1970), 'The problem of financing economic development in a mixed economy', reprinted in Kalecki, M. (1976).
-- (1971), *Selected Essays on the Dynamics of the Capitalist Economy, 1933–1970*, Cambridge: Cambridge University Press.
-- (1976), *Essays on Developing Economies*, Hassocks: The Harvester Press.

Karshenas, M. (1989), 'Intersectoral resource flows and development: Lessons of past experience', working paper WEP 10–6/WP99, World Employment Programme Research, also published in Singh, A. and Tabatabai, H. (1992).

Katrak, H. (1980), 'Industry structure, foreign trade and price cost margins in Indian manufacturing industries', *Journal of Development Studies*, 17 (1): 62–79.

Kelley, A.C., Williamson, J.G. and Cheetham, R.J. (1972), *Dualistic Economic Development: Theory and History*, Chicago: university of Chicago Press.

Keuning, S. and Ruijter, W. de (1988), 'Guidelines to the construction of a social accounting matrix', *Review of Income and Wealth*, 34 (1): 71–91.

Keynes, J.M. (1936), *The General Theory of Employment, Interest and Money*, London: Macmillan, reprinted as Volume VII, *Collected Writings*, edited by Donald Moggridge, London: Macmillan for the Royal Economic Society.

Khan, M.S. and Montiel, P. (1989), 'Growth–oriented adjustment programs: a conceptual framework', *IMF Staff Papers*, 36 (2): 279–306.

Killick, T. (1985), 'Economic environment and agricultural development: the importance of macroeconomic policy', *Food Policy*, 10 (1): 29–40.

Koutsoyiannis, A. (1981), *Modern Microeconomics*, Second Edition, London: Macmillan.

Krishna, K.L., Krishnamurty, K., Pandit, V.N. and Sharma, P.D. (1991), 'Macro-econometric modelling in India: a selective review of recent research', *Development Papers No.9*, 28–43, Economic and Social Commission for Asia and the Pacific (ESCAP), Bangkok: United Nations Publications.

Krishna, R. (1963), 'Farm supply response in India and Pakistan: A case study of the Punjab regions', *The Economic Journal*, 73 (291): 477–487.
-- (1967), 'Agricultural price policy and economic development' in Southworth, H. and Johnston, B.F. (eds.), *Agricultural Development and Economic Growth*, Ithaca: Cornell University Press.
-- (1983), 'Some aspects of agricultural growth, price policy and equity in developing countries', *Food Research Institute Studies* 18 (3): 239–261.

Krishna, R. and Chhibber, A. (1983), 'Policy modeling of a dual grain market: The case of wheat in India', *Research Report* 38, International Food Policy Research Institute.

Krishna, R. and Raychaudhuri, G.S. (1979), 'Some aspects of wheat price policy in India', *Indian Economic Review*, 14 (2): 101–125.
-- (1980), 'Some aspects of wheat and rice price policy in India', *World Bank Staff Working Paper no.* 381, Washington D.C.: International Bank for Reconstruction and Development.

Krishnaji, N. (1988), 'Foodgrain stocks and prices', in A.K. Bagchi (ed.), *Economy, society and polity*, New Delhi: Oxford University Press.
-- (1990), 'Agricultural price policy: A survey with reference to the Indian foodgrain economy', *Economic and Political Weekly*, 25: A–54–A–63.

Krishnamurty, K. (1985), 'Inflation and growth: A model for India', in K. Krishnamurty and Pandit, V. (eds.), 16–111.

Krishnamurty, K. and Pandit, V. (eds.) (1985), *Macroeconometric Modelling of the Indian Economy. Studies on Inflation and Growth*, Delhi: Hindustan Publishing Corporation.

Krishnamurty, K. and Saibaba, P. (1981), 'Determinants of saving rate in India', *Indian Economic Review*, 16 (4): 225–249.

Krueger, A.O., Schiff, M. and Valdés, A. (1988), 'Agricultural incentives in devloping countries: measuring the effect of sectoral and economywide policies', *The World Bank Economic Review*, 2 (3): 255–271.

Kumar, G. (1988), 'On prices and economic power: Explaining recent changes in intersectoral relations in the Indian economy', *Journal of Development Studies*, 25 (1): 25–42.
—— (1990), 'Consumption disparities, food surpluses and effective demand failures. Reflections on macroeconomics of drought vulnerability', *Economic and Political Weekly*, 25 (10): 499–508.

Kumar,J., Katyal, R.P. and Sharma, S.P. (1987), 'Estimates of fixed capital stock and consumption of fixed capital in India', *Economic and Political weekly*, 22: 2003–2010.

Lahiri, A.K., Madhur, S., Purkayastha, D. and Roy, P. (1984), 'The industrial sector in India: a quantitative analysis', *Economic and Political Weekly*, 19: 1285–1306.

Lau, L.J. (1984), 'Comments' in Scarf, H.E. and Shoven, J.B. (eds.), *Applied General Equilibrium Analysis*, New York: Cambridge University Press.

Lawson, T. (1987), 'The relative/absolute nature of knowledge and economic analysis', *The Economic Journal* 97 (388): 951–970.
—— (1989), 'Abstraction, tendencies and stylised facts: a realist approach to economic analysis', *Cambridge Journal of Economics*, 13 (1): 59–78.

Lee, T.H. (1971), *Inter–sectoral Capital Flows in the Economic Development of Taiwan*, 1895–1960, Ithaca: Cornell University Press.

Leijonhufvud, A. (1968), *On Keynesian Economics and the Economics of Keynes*, Oxford: Oxford University Press.

Lewis, W.A. (1954), 'Economic development with unlimited supplies of labour', *Manchester School of Economic and Social Studies*, 22 (2): 139–191.

Lipton, M. (1977), *Why Poor People Stay Poor: A Study of Urban Bias in World Development*, London: Temple Smith.

Lluch, C. Powell, A.A., and Williams, R.A. (1977), *Patterns in Household Demand and Saving*, Oxford: Oxford University Press.

Mahalanobis, P.C. (1955), 'Draft plan–frame for the Second Five Year Plan of India, 1956–57 to 1960–61', *Sankhya* 16, (1): 63–90.

Malinvaud, E. (1977), *The Theory of Unemployment Reconsidered*, Oxford: Basil Blackwell.

Mansur, A. and Whalley, J. (1984), 'Numerical specification of applied general equilibrium models: Estimation, calibration, and data', in Scarf, H.E. and Shoven, J.B. (eds.), *Applied General Equilibrium Analysis*, New York: Cambridge University Press, 69–127.

Marglin , S.A. (1966), 'Comment on D.W. Jorgenson', in Adelman, I. and Thorbecke, E. (eds.), 60 – 66.

McMohan, G. (1989), 'Computable general equilibrium modeling: A survey with reference to India', *The Indian Economic Journal*, 37 (1): 1–14.

Mellor, J.W. (1973), 'Accelerated growth in agricultural production and the intersectoral transfer of resources', *Economic Development and Cultural Change*, 22 (1): 1–26.

Mensbrugghe, D. van der, Martin, J.P., and Burniaux, J–M. (1990), 'How robust are WALRAS results?', *OECD Economic Studies*, No. 13, Winter 1989–1990, Paris: Organisation for Economic Co-operation and Development.

Mitra, A. (1977), *Terms of Trade and Class Relations. An Essay in Political Economy*, London: Frank Cass.

Mitra, P. and Tendulkar, S. (1986), 'Coping with internal and external exogenous shocks: India, 1974–84', World Bank CPD, *Discussion Paper* no. 1986–21.

Molana, H. and Vines, D. (1989), 'North–South growth and the terms of trade: A model on Kaldorian lines', *The Economic Journal*, 99 (396): 443–453.

Morrison, C. and Thorbecke, E. (1990), 'The concept of the agricultural surplus', *World Development*, 18 (8): 1081–1095.

Mundle, S. (1975), 'Intersectoral flow of consumer goods. Some preliminary results', *Economic and Political Weekly*, 10: 165–174.
—— (1981), *Surplus Flows and Growth Imbalances*, New Delhi: Allied Publishers.
—— (1985), 'The agrarian barrier to industrial growth', *Journal of Development Studies*, 22 (1): 49–80.

Mundle, S. and Ohkawa, K. (1979), 'Agricultural surplus in Japan: 1888–1937', *The Developing Economies*, 17 (3): 247–265.

Murphy, K.M., Shleifer, A. and Vishny, R. (1989a), 'Income distribution, market size and industrialisation', *Quarterly Journal of Economics*, 106 (3): 537–564.
—— (1989b), 'Industrialisation and the big push', *Journal of Political Economy*, 97 (5): 1003–1026.

Myint, H. (1975), 'Agriculture and economic development in the open economy', in Reynolds, L.G. (ed.), *Agriculture in Development Theory*, New Haven: Yale University Press, 327–354.

Nadkarni, V.M. (1988), 'Crisis of increasing costs in agriculture: Is there a way out?', *Economic and Political Weekly*, 23: A-114–A-119.

Narain, D. (1961), 'Distribution of the marketed surplus of agricultural produce by size–level of holding in India, 1950–51', Occasional papers no.2, Institute of Economic Growth, Delhi, reprinted in Raj, K.N., Sen, A.K. and Rao, C.H.H. (eds.) (1988), *Studies on Indian Agriculture. Dharm Narain*, Delhi: Oxford University Press.
—— (1965), *Impact of Price Movements on Areas under Selected Crops in India 1900 – 1939*, Cambridge: Cambridge University Press.

Narain, D. and Roy, S.S. (1980), 'Impact of irrigation and labour availability on multiple cropping: A case study of India', *Research Report 20*, International Food Policy Research institute.

Narayana, N.S.S. and Parikh, K.S. (1987), 'Estimation of yield functions for major cereals in India', *Journal of Quantitative Economics*, 3 (2): 287–312.

Narayana, N.S.S., Parikh, K.S. and Srinivasan, T.N. (1987), *Policies and Impacts: Analysis with a GEM for India*, discussion paper no.3–1987, Indira Gandhi Institute of Development Research, Bombay.
—— (1987a), 'Indian agricultural policy: An applied general equilibrium model', *Journal of Policy Modeling*, 9 (4): 527–558.
—— (1991), *Agriculture, Growth and Redistribution of Income. Policy Analysis with an Applied General Equilibrium Model*, Contributions to Economic Analysis 190, Amsterdam: North–Holland.

National Council of Applied Economic Research (1980), *Household Income and Its Disposition*, New Delhi.
—— (1981), *A Computable General Equilibrium Model of the Indian Economy: Structure and Sensitivities*, New Delhi.

Nayyar, D. (1978), 'Industrial development in India: Some reflections on growth and stagnation', *Economic and Political Weekly*, 13 (31–33): 1265–1278.

Nerlove, M. (1958), *The Dynamics of Supply. Estimation of Farmers' Response to Price*, Baltimore: The Johns Hopkins University Press.

Nicholls, (1963), 'An agricultural surplus as a factor in economic development', *Journal of Political Economy*, 71 (1): 1–29.

Nurkse, R. (1953), *Problems of Capital Formation in Underdeveloped Countries*, Oxford: Basil Blackwell.
—— (1959), *Patterns of Trade and Development*, Wicksell Lectures 1959, Stockholm: Almqvist & Wiksells Boktryckeri.
—— (1961), *Equilibrium and Growth in the World Economy, Economic Essays by Ragnar Nurkse*, edited by G. Haberler and R.M. Stern, Cambridge, Mass.: Harvard University Press.

Okun, A. M. (1975), 'Inflation: Its mechanics and welfare costs', *Brookings Papers on Economic Activity*, 2, The Brookings Institution.
—— (1981), *Prices and Quantities. A Macroeconomic Analysis*, Oxford: Basil Blackwell.

Paldam, M. (1989), 'Comment on M. Bruno', *Scandinavian Journal of Economics*, 91 (2): 339–345.

Panchamukhi, V.R. (1975), 'Linkages in industrialisation: A study of selected developing countries in Asia', *Journal of Development Planning*, 8, 121–165.
—— (1986), *Capital Formation and Output in the Third World*, New Delhi: Radiant Publishers.

Panda, M. and Sarkar, H. (1987), 'Resource mobilisation through administered prices: Results from a CGE model for India', *NCAER Working Paper* no.11, New Delhi, also published in Taylor, L. (ed.) (1991), 147–176.

Pandit, V. (1985), 'Macroeconomic adjustments in a developing economy: A medium term model of output and prices in India', in Krishnamurty, K. and Pandit, V. (eds.), 112–156.

Parikh, K.S. and Srinivasan, T.N. (1974), *Optimum Requirements of Fertiliser for the Fifth Plan Period*, New Delhi: Indian Statistical Institute and Fertiliser Association.

Parikh, K.S. and Suryanarayana, M.H. (1989), 'Food and agricultural subsidies: incidence and welfare under alternative schemes', *Discussion Paper* no. 14, Indira Gandhi Institute of Development Research, Bombay.

Pasinetti, L.L. (1962), 'Rate of profit and income distribution in relation to the rate of economic growth', *Review of Economic Studies*, 29: 267–279.

Patnaik, P. (1972), 'Disproportionality crisis and cyclical growth', *Economic and Political Weekly*, 7: 329–336.
–– (1981), 'An explanatory hypothesis on the Indian industrial stagnation', in Bagchi, A.K. and Banerjee, N. (eds.), 65–89.

Patnaik, U. (1975), 'Contributions to the output and marketable surplus of agricultural products by cultivating groups in India, 1960–61', *Economic and Political Weekly*, 10: A-90–A-100.

Powell, A. (1981), 'The major streams in economy–wide modelling: Is rapprochement possible ?', in Kmenta, J. and Ramsey , J. (eds.), *Large – Scale Macro – Econometric Models: Theory and Practice*, Amsterdam: North–Holland, 219–264.

Preobrazhensky, E. (1965), *The New Economics*, London: Oxford University Press (first published in 1926).

Radhakrishna, R. (1978), 'Demand functions and their development implications in a dual economy: India', *The Developing Economies*, 16 (2): 199–210.

Radhakrishna, R. and Murty, K.N. (1980), 'Models of complete expenditure systems for India', Working Paper WP–80–98, IIASA, Laxenburg.
Raj, K.N. (1976), 'Growth and stagnation in industrial development', *Economic and Political Weekly*, 11: 223–236.

Rakshit, M. (1982), *The Labour Surplus Economy. A Neo – Keynesian Approach*, Delhi: Macmillan.
–– (1988), 'Uses and abuses of instruments for resource mobilisation: The Indian experience', in Lucas, R.E.B. and Papanek, G.F. (eds.), *The Indian Economy. Recent Development and Future Prospects*, Delhi: Oxford University Press.
–– (1989), (ed.) *Studies in the Macroeconomics of Developing Countries*, Delhi: Oxford University Press.

Rangarajan, C. (1982), 'Agricultural growth and industrial performance in India', *Research Report* 33, International Food Policy Research Institute.

Ranis, G. (1988), 'Analytics of development: Dualism', in Chenery, H.B. and Srinivasan, T.N. (eds.), 74–92.

Ranis, G. and Fei, J.C.H. (1961), 'A theory of economic development', *American Economic Review*, 51 (4), 535–565.

Rao, C.H. H. (1975), *Technological Change and Distribution of Gains in Indian Agriculture*, Delhi: Macmillan.

Rao, C.H.H, Ray, S.K. and Subbarao, K. (1988), *Unstable Agriculture and Droughts*, New Delhi: Vikas Publishing House.

Rao, M.J. (1986), 'Agriculture in recent development theory', *Journal of Development Economics*, 22 (1): 41–86.
–– and Caballero, J.M. (1990), 'Agricultural performance and development strategy: Retrospect and prospect', *World Development*, 18 (6): 899–913.

Rao, V.K.R.V. (1952), 'Investment, income and the multiplier in an underdeveloped economy', *Indian Economic Review*, 1 (1), 55–67.
–– (1983), *India's National Income*, 1950–1980, New Delhi: Sage Publications.

Rattsø, J. (1982), 'Different macroclosures of the original Johansen model and their impact on policy evaluation', *Journal of Policy Modeling* 4 (1): 85–97.
–– (1986), 'The macroeconomics of India's 6th Five Year Plan', *Economic Modelling*, 3: 269–282.
–– (1988), 'Macrodynamic adjustments in a dual economy under policy controlled domestic terms of trade', *Indian Economic Review*, 23 (1): 45–59.
–– (1988a), 'Macrodynamic adjustment mechanisms in India', *World Development*,

16 (8): 959–973.
–– (1989), *Macrodynamic Adjustment Mechanisms in India. A model analysis based on the 6th. Five Year Plan*, Memorandum No. 1–1989, Department of Economics, University of Trondheim.
–– (1990), 'Conflicting claims and dynamic inflationary mechanisms in India', in Taylor, L. (ed.), 241–268.

Robinson, J. (1977), 'Michal Kalecki on the economics of capitalism', *Oxford Bulletin of Economics and Statistics*, 39 (1): 7–17.

Robinson, S. (1988), 'Multisector models of developing countries: A survey', in H.B. Chenery and T.N. Srinivasan (eds.), 886–947.

Rosenstein–Rodan, P. (1943), 'Problems of industrialisation in Eastern and South–Eastern Europe', *The Economic Journal*, 53 (217): 202–211.

Roy, P. and Subramanian, A. (1983), 'Forecasting agricultural output: A model for winter crops in India', unpublished paper, quoted in Gulati (1987).

Sah, R.K. and Stiglitz, J. (1984), 'The economics of price scissors', *American Economic Review*, 74 (1): 125–138.

Saith, A. (1985), 'Primitive accumulation, agrarian reform and socialist transitions: An argument', *Journal of Development Studies*, 22 (1): 1–48.

Samuelson, P.A. (1947), *Foundations of Economic Analysis* (enlarged edition, 1983), Cambridge, Mass.: Harvard University Press.
–– (1954), 'The pure theory of public expenditure', *Review of Economics and Statistics*, 36: 387–89.

Sarkar, H. and Kadekodi, G.K. (1988), *Energy Pricing in India. Perspective, Issues and Options*, New Delhi, RAS/84/001, ILO.
–– and Panda, M. (1991), 'A short term structural macro economic model for India: Applications to policy analyses', *Development Papers No.9*, pp. 177–207, Economic and Social Commission for Asia and the Pacific (ESCAP), Bangkok: United Nations Publication.
–– and Subbarao, S.V. (1981), 'A short term macro forecasting model for India – structure and uses', *Indian Economic Review*, 16 (1 & 2): 55–80.

Sawhney, P.K. and Sawhney, B.L. (1974),'Capacity utilisation, concentration and price–cost margins: results for Indian industry', *Journal of Industrial Economics*, 22: 145–153.

Sawyer, M.C. (1985), *The Economics of Michał Kalecki*, London: Macmillan.

Scandizzo, P. and Bruce, C. (1980), 'Methodologies for measuring agricultural price policy intervention effects', *World Bank Staff Working Paper no.394*, Washington, D.C.: International Bank for Reconstruction and Development.

Schultz, T.W. (1964), *Transforming Traditional Agriculture*, New Haven: Yale University Press.
–– (1978), *Distortions of Agricultural Incentives*, Bloomington: Indiana University Press.

Scitovsky, T. (1954), 'Two concepts of external economies', *Journal of Political Economy*, 62 (1): 143–151.

Sen, A. (1981), *The Agrarian Constraint to Economic Development: The Case of India*, unpublished Ph.D. thesis, University of Cambridge.
–– (1986), 'Shocks and instabilities in an agriculture–constrained economy: India, 1964–1985', paper presented at the International Workshop on Rural Transformation in Asia, New Delhi, October 2–4, 1986.
–– (1988), 'Union budget 1988–89: on management of drought and of public opinion', *Economic and Political Weekly*, 23: 733–738.

—— (1988a), 'A note on unemployment and living standards in the unorganised sector', *Social Scientist*, 177.
—— (1990), 'Trade restrictions and growth constraints', in Guha, S. (ed.), 74–91.

Sen, A.K. (1963), 'Neo–classical and Neo–Keynesian theories of distribution', *Economic Record*, 39: 53–64.

Sen, P. (1986), 'The 1966 devaluation in India: A reappraisal', *Economic and Political Weekly*, 21 (30), 1322–1329.
—— (1987), 'Indian experiences with orthodox stabilization', Helsinki: WIDER.

Sharpley, J.G. (1976), *Intersectoral Capital Flows and Economic Development: Evidence from Kenya*, Ph.D. dissertation, Northwestern University, Evanston, Illinois, U.S.A.

Shetty, S.L. (1978), 'Structural retrogression in the Indian economy since the mid–sixties', *Economic and Political Weekly*, 13: 185–244.
—— (1990), 'Investment in agriculture. Brief review of recent trends', *Economic and Political Weekly*, 25: 17–24.

Shoven, J.B. and Whalley, J. (1984), 'Applied general equilibrium models of taxation and international trade: An introduction and survey', *Journal of Economic Literature*, 22 (3): 1007–1051.

Sidhu, J.S. and Sidhu, D.S. (1985), 'Price–support versus fertiliser subsidy', *Economic and Political Weekly*, 20 (13): A-17–A-22.

Singh, A. and Tabatabai, H. (1992) (eds.), *The World Economic Crisis and Agriculture in the Third World in the 1980s: The Changing Role of Agriculture in Economic Development*, Geneva: International Labour Organisation (forthcoming).

Singh, B. (1989), 'Money Supply–Prices: Causality Revisited', *Economic and Political Weekly*, 24: 2613–2615.

Sirohi, A.S. (1984), 'Impact of agricultural subsidies and procurement prices on production and income distribution in India', *Indian Journal of Agricultural Economics*, 38 (4): 563–585.

Srinivasan, T.N. and Narayana, N.S.S. (1977), 'Economic performance since the Third Plan and its implications for policy', *Economic and Political Weekly*, 12 (6–8): 225–239.

Srivastava, D.V. (1981), 'Policy simulation with a macro–economic model of the Indian economy', *Journal of Policy Modeling*, 3 (3): 337–360.

Stern, N.H. (1989), 'The economics of development: A survey', *The Economic Journal*, 99 (397): 597–685.

Stone, R.H. (1954), 'Linear expenditure system and demand analysis: An application to the pattern of British demand', *The Economic Journal*, 64 (264): 511–527.

Subbarao, K. (1985), 'State policies and regional disparity in Indian agriculture', *Development and Change*, 16 (4): 523–546.

Subramanian, K.N. (1977), *Wages in India*, New Delhi: Tata McGraw–Hill.

Targetti, F. (1985), 'Growth and the terms of trade: A Kaldorian two–sector model', *Metroeconomica*, 37 (1): 79–96.

Taylor, L. (1979), *Macromodels for Developing Countries*, New York: McGraw–Hill.
—— (1982), 'Food price inflation, terms of trade and growth', in Gersovitz,

M., Diaz–Alejandro, C.F., Ranis, G., and Rosenzweig, M.R. (eds.), *The Theories and Experience of Economic Development. Essays in Honour of Sir W. Arthur Lewis*, London: George Allen & Unwin, 60–77.
— (1983), *Structuralist Macroeconomics*, New York: Basic Books.
— (1985), 'A stagnationist model of economic growth', *Cambridge Journal of Economics*, 9 (4): 383–403.
— (1988), 'Macro constraints on India's economic growth', *Indian Economic Review*, 23 (2): 145–165.
— (1988a), 'Planners' progress', *Economic and Political Weekly*, 23: 2163–2165.
— (1990) (ed.), *Socially Relevant Policy Analysis: Structuralist Computable General Equilibrium Models for the Developing World*, Cambridge, Massachusetts: The MIT Press.

Taylor, L. and Arida, P. (1988), 'Long–run income distribution and growth', in Chenery, H.B. and Srinivasan, T.N. (eds.), 162–194.

Taylor, L., Bacha, E.L., Cardoso, E.A., and Lysy, F.J. (1980), *Models of Growth and Distribution for Brazil*, Oxford: Oxford University Press.

Taylor, L. and Lysy, F. (1979), 'Vanishing income distribution: Keynesian clues about model–surprises in the short–run', *Journal of Development Economics*, 6 (1): 11–29.

Taylor, L., Sarkar, H. and Rattsø, J. (1984), 'Macroeconomic adjustment in a computable general equilibrium model for India', in Syrquin, M. *et al.* (eds.), *Economic Structure and Performance*, New York: Academic Press.

Thamarajakshi, R. (1969), 'Intersectoral terms of trade and marketed surplus of agricultural produce 1951–52 to 1965–66', *Economic and Political Weekly*, 4 (26): A-91–A-102.
— (1977), 'Role of price incentives in stimulating agricultural production in a developing economy', in D. Ensminger (ed.), *Food Enough or Starvation for Millions*, New Delhi: FAO, 376–390.

Thirlwall, A.P. (1986), 'A general model of growth and development on Kaldorian lines' *Oxford Economic Papers*, 38 (2): 199–219.

Timmer, C.P. (1986), *Getting Prices Right: The Scope and Limits of Agricultural Price Policy*, Ithaca: Cornell University Press.
— (1988), 'The agricultural transformation', in Chenery, H.B. and Srinivasan, T.N. (eds.), 276–331.

Tobin, J. (1983), 'Macroeconomics under debate', *Cowles Foundation Discussion Paper No.* 669, Cowles Foundation for Research in Economics, New Haven: Yale University.

Tyagi, D.S. (1979), 'Farm prices and class bias in India', *Economic and Political Weekly*, 14: A111–A124.
— (1987), 'Domestic terms of trade and their effect on supply and demand of agricultural sector', *Economic and Political Weekly*, 22 (13), A–30–A–36.
— (1990), *Managing India's Food Economy: Problems and Alternatives*, New Delhi: Sage Publications.
— (1990a), 'Increasing access to food through interaction of price and technology policies – the Indian experience', in Tyagi, D.S. and Vyas, V.S. (eds), *Increasing Access to Food: The Asian Experience*, New Delhi: Sage Publications.

Vakil, C.N. and Brahmananda, P.R. (1956), *Planning for an Expanding Economy*, Bombay.

Vittal, N. (1986), 'Intersectoral terms of trade in India: A study of concept and method', *Discussion Paper no.188*, Norwich: University of East Anglia.

Weitzman, M.L. (1982), 'Increasing returns and the foundations of unemployment theory', *The Economic Journal*, 92 (376): 787–804.

World Bank, (1989), *India: Poverty, employment and social services* (two volumes), Report no.7617–IN, Resident Mission in India.

Young, A (1928), 'Increasing returns and economic progress', *The Economic Journal*, December, 38 (160): 527–42.

Official Publications

Central Statistical Organisation (1988), *Estimates of Capital Stock of Indian Economy as on 31 March*, 1981, New Delhi: Ministry of Planning.
––– (1989), *National Accounts Statistics (New Series)* 1950–51 – 1979–80, New Delhi: Ministry of Planning.
––– (1989a), *National Accounts Statistics* 1980–81 – 1986–87, New Delhi: Ministry of Planning.
––– (1989b), *Input–Output Transactions Table* 1978–79, New Delhi: Ministry of Planning.
––– (1989c), *Annual Survey of Industries* 1985–86 – *Summary Results for Factory Sector*, New Delhi: Ministry of Planning.
––– (1989d), *National Accounts Statistics: Sources and Methods*, New Delhi: Ministry of Planning.
––– (1990), *National Accounts Statistics*, New Delhi: Ministry of Planning.

Economic Advisory Council (1989), 'Report on the Current Economic Situation and Priority Areas for Action', New Delhi, December.
–– (1990), 'Towards Evolving an Employment Oriented Strategy for Development in the 1990s', Interim Report, New Delhi, March.

Fertiliser Association of India (1990), *Fertiliser Statistics* 1989–90, New Delhi.

Ministry of Agriculture (1985), *Indian Agriculture in Brief, 20th Edition*, New Delhi: Directorate of Economics & Statistics, Department of Agriculture & Cooperation.
––– (1986), *Bulletin on Food Statistics* 1985, New Delhi: Directorate of Economics & Statistics, Department of Agriculture & Cooperation.
––– (1986a), *Area and Production of Principal Crops in India* 1984–85, New Delhi: Directorate of Economics & Statistics, Department of Agriculture & Cooperation.
––– (1986b), *Indian Agriculture in Brief, 21st Edition*, New Delhi: Directorate of Economics & Statistics, Department of Agriculture & Cooperation.
––– (1987), *Area and Production of Principal Crops in India* 1985–86, New Delhi: Directorate of Economics & Statistics, Department of Agriculture & Cooperation.
––– (1988), *Bulletin on Food Statistics* 1986, New Delhi: Directorate of Economics & Statistics, Department of Agriculture & Cooperation.
––– (1988a), *Indian Agriculture in Brief, 22nd Edition*, New Delhi: Directorate of Economics & Statistics, Department of Agriculture & Cooperation.
––– (1989), *Area and Production of Principal Crops in India* 1986–88, New Delhi: Directorate of Economics & Statistics, Department of Agriculture & Cooperation.

Ministry of Finance (1976), *Economic Survey* 1975–76, Delhi: The Controller of Publications.
––– (1982), *Economic Survey* 1981–82, Delhi: The Controller of Publications.
––– (1985), *Economic Survey* 1984–85, Delhi: The Controller of Publications.
––– (1985a), *Long Term Fiscal Policy*, New Delhi.
––– (1986), *Economic Survey* 1985–86, Delhi: The Controller of Publications.
––– (1987), *Economic Survey* 1986–87, Delhi: The Controller of Publications.
––– (1988), *Economic Survey* 1987–88, Delhi: The Controller of Publications.
––– (1989), *Economic Survey* 1988–89, Delhi: The Controller of Publications.
––– (1990), *Economic Survey* 1989–90, Delhi: The Controller of Publications.

—— (1991), *Economic Survey* 1990–91, Delhi: The Controller of Publications.

National Sample Survey Organisation (1988), *Report on Consumer Expenditure*, *42nd Round, July 1986 – June 1987*, New Delhi.

Planning Commission (1951), *First Five Year Plan*, 1951 – 56, New Delhi.
—— (1956), *Second Five Year Plan: Draft Outline*, New Delhi.
—— (1973), *The Approach to the Fifth Five Year Plan* 1974 – 79, New Delhi.
—— (1973), *A Technical Note on the Approach to the Fifth Five Year Plan of India* (1973 – 74 to 1978 – 79), New Delhi.
—— (1979), *Report of the Task Force on Projections of Minimum Needs and Effective Consumption Demand*, New Delhi.
— – – (1981a), *A Technical Note on the Sixth Plan of India* (1980 – 85), New Delhi.
—— (1984), *The Approach to the Seventh Five Year Plan* 1985 – 90, New Delhi.
—— (1985), *The Seventh Five Year Plan* 1985 – 90, *volume I. Perspective, Objectives, Strategy, Macro – Dimensions and Resources*, New Delhi.
—— (1985a), *The Seventh Five Year Plan* 1985 – 90, *volume II. Sectoral Programmes of Development*, New Delhi.

Reserve Bank of India (1985), *Report of the Committee to Review the Working of the Monetary System*, Bombay: Reserve Bank of India.

374

Weitzman, M.L., 41
Whalley, J., 98*fn*, 99, 102
Wicksell, K., 19
Williamson, J.G., 7, 43, 45–47

Young, A., 41

341–342; regional, 342; remedying income inequality, 204–205
income distributional consequences of policy experiments, 304–305, 340
increasing returns to scale, 35, 37, 41, 51, 56
indicators for comparison of scenarios, 115
indivisibilities, 19, 35, 37, 147
industrial growth: 74; during 1950–65, 59;
'industry–first' strategy, 10, 20, 270, 273–274, 336, 337
input price subsidies, 64, 67
instability of agricultural production, 68–69
Intensive Agricultural District Programme (IADP), 62
interest elasticity of private investment demand: 12, 75, 91, 332; of private savings, 333
intermediate demand: structure of, 88
intertemporal adjustment model, 13–14, 112–113, 125–126
investors' expectations, 34–36, 44, 75, 91–92, 103–104
irrigation, 18–19, 63, 68–70, 93, 113, 116–117, 183–184, 258–259
irrigation coverage, 9, 68–70, 85, 266–267

Jacobian matrix, 151–153

Kaldorian distributional effects, 12, 42, 51, 92
Koyck transformation, 138

landlords: Ricardo's, 23–25; role of 32
land reforms: 40, 60–1; the practice of, 61–62;
'law of one price', 112
Leontief model, 97
Lerner's mark–up rule, 143
Lewis model, 2, 28–30, 57
Lewis turning point, 29
linear expenditure system (LES): 122, 146–150, 164–165; 'estimation' of, 180–182; restrictiveness of, 149–150
linkages between agriculture and non–agriculture, 126, 330
low–level equilibrium trap, 37, 46, 330

macroeconomic closure, 99–101
macroeconometric approach, 96–99
Mahalanobis model, 54, 56–57
manufacturing: the structure of, 88–90;
marginal returns to increased public expenditure on: fertiliser subsidisation, 21, 304–305, 340; foodgrain distribution, 21, 304–305, 340; public investment, 21, 304–305, 340; public procurement, 21, 304–305, 340
market failures, 19fn, 52
market mechanism: 42, 43, 45; allocative efficiency of, 43;
mark–up pricing, 38, 42, 51, 93, 111, 121, 141–143, 332
Marshall's excess price hypothesis, 108
Marx's reserve army, 28
Marx's two–departmental scheme, 57
minimum support pricing, 11, 65, 93, 111, 123, 199–200, 214–216, 346, 349
mixed economy, 13, 55–58, 92, 348
money supply process: the causality in, 112
money illusion, 149
multiplier principle, 34, 51, 74, 205, 223, 333

National Council of Applied Economic Research (NCAER): household income survey, 163; models, 345–346
National Sample Survey (NSS), 16, 157, 163
Nehru–Mahalanobis strategy, 55–64, 90
neoclassical approach, 6–8, 43–47, 54, 100–105
neoclassical welfare economics, 19fn, 101–102
Nerlovian partial adjustment model: 113, 117–118, 138–140, 167–168, 184–185; inadequacies of, 140
net finance contribution of agriculture: 30, 32, 37, 48; empirical estimates of, 32–33
net irrigated area, 117